LADIES OF THE CANYONS

LADIES OF THE CANYONS

A League of Extraordinary Women and Their
Adventures in the American Southwest

LESLEY POLING-KEMPES

THE UNIVERSITY OF
ARIZONA PRESS

TUCSON

The University of Arizona Press
www.uapress.arizona.edu

Printed in the United States of America

22 21 20 19 18 17   9 8 7 6 5 4

ISBN-13: 978-0-8165-2494-5 (paper)

Cover designed by Leigh McDonald
Cover photos: (*top*) Carol and Jack at Canyon de Chelly, Carol Stanley collection;
(*bottom left*) Natalie Curtis Burlin, Santa Fe, 1917, Natalie Curtis Burlin Archives;
(*bottom right*) Mary Cabot Wheelwright, Collection of the Wheelwright Museum
of the American Indian.

Library of Congress Cataloging-in-Publication Data
Poling-Kempes, Lesley, author.
  Ladies of the canyons : a league of extraordinary women and their adventures in
the American Southwest / Lesley Poling-Kempes.
      pages cm
  Includes bibliographical references and index.
  ISBN 978-0-8165-2494-5 (pbk. : alk. paper)
    1. Southwest, New—History—19th century. 2. Southwest, New—Social
conditions—19th century. 3. Women—Southwest, New—History. 4. Women—
Southwest, New—Biography. I. Title.
  F786.P85 2015
  979'.03109252—dc23

                              2015001524

♾ This paper meets the requirements of ANSI/NISO Z39.48-1992 (Permanence
of Paper).

This book is for Jim
and his inexhaustible joy and contagious
enthusiasm
for every adventure.

Women, when they are old enough to have done
with the business of being women,
and can let loose their strength, must be the most
powerful creatures in the world.

—*Isak Dinesen*

CONTENTS

LADIES OF THE CANYONS

PROLOGUE

Ladies of the Canyons

I BEGAN THE QUEST for the ladies of the canyons more than a decade ago. At the time, I was looking for a woman who had gone missing in history. Her name was Carol Bishop Stanley, and although she was the founder of Ghost Ranch, the place that would achieve celebrity status as the faraway nearby home of the American artist Georgia O'Keeffe, there was little to nothing written about Carol in the Ghost Ranch story. From oral histories and a handful of written accounts and letters, I learned that in 1931 Carol, a middle-aged divorcee from Boston, moved all that she owned to el Rancho de los Brujos, the Ranch of the Witches, the place she called Ghost Ranch, and with limited financial resources set about creating a home on the high desert of northern New Mexico. But how and why this woman had come to live in this austere, remote, and wildly beautiful landscape was lost to living memory.

O'Keeffe never acknowledged Carol's role in the creation of Ghost Ranch. But that was in character, since O'Keeffe rarely acknowledged that anyone, male or female, held a prior claim to Ghost Ranch, although she herself never legally owned more than ten of the ranch's nearly thirty thousand acres. Arthur Pack, the millionaire who bought the ranch from Carol in 1935, did mention Carol Pfäffle (her married name) in his memoir *We Called It Ghost Ranch*, and in doing so provided some of the only recorded glimpses of her life: "Close-in under the sheltering protection of magnificent buttes and sheer sandstone cliffs huddled a single low adobe building whose every door and window staggered crookedly. From it appeared a woman who spoke in cultured tones unmistakably Bostonian. . . . This homestead, which her ex-husband was said to have won in a

3

poker game, was all that Carol Pfäffle had left in the world except for a beautiful grand piano."[1]

Pack likely knew more about Carol's life than he shared in his memoir—like how a cultured woman from Boston came to be living alone (with a grand piano) in a decrepit homestead on the edge of the Colorado Plateau in the first years of the Depression. But Pack, like most chroniclers of his era, did not consider the immigration story of an ordinary woman worthy of more than a passing reference that gave context to his own story. "When you go looking for missing persons, you may not find them," the historian Virginia Scharff wrote, "but you are bound to find out a lot of other things."[2]

I did find Carol Stanley. I also found a lot of other people and things I did not even know to go looking for. While searching archives and public records for Ghost Ranch's founding mother, I discovered a narrative that connected Carol to an informal alliance of remarkable women. Women who, like Carol, had left the security and comfort of conventional society in the first decades of the twentieth century and journeyed to Indian Country in search of a wider, deeper view of themselves and the world. Natalie Curtis Burlin, Alice Ellen Klauber, Mary Cabot Wheelwright, and Carol Bishop Stanley were members of an intrepid group of ladies whose lives became entwined with and altered by the people and landscape of the Southwest outback. Their ranks included Louisa Wade Wetherill, Alice Corbin Henderson, Elsie Clews Parsons, the sisters Amelia Elizabeth and Martha Root White, Mabel Dodge Luhan, Margretta Dietrich, Mary Austin, Elsie Shepley Sergeant, and Willa Cather.

Unearthing Carol Stanley's half-century-long journey from her grandfather's beach house on Nahant Island, Massachusetts, to the ramshackle outpost built in Yeso Canyon, New Mexico, by infamous cattle rustlers meant following a road through the Southwest blazed by plucky and resourceful women. Within this landscape they imagined and created a new home territory, a new society, and a new identity for themselves and for all the women who would follow them.

The saga that emerged was far greater than Carol Stanley and Ghost Ranch. The story of the lady of the canyon became the stories of the ladies of the canyons and included Boston Brahmins and the Greenwich Village avant-garde, New York's Armory Show and the birth of modern art, a president and Indian music, the Snake Dance at Walpi and the Ute battle at Cottonwood Gulch, San Diego's Balboa Park and Santa Fe's Museum of Art, Florence before World War I and Paris in the Roaring Twenties. It was the story of New Women stepping bravely into the New World, of Anglo America waking up to Native America, of inconspicuous success and ambitious failure. "My thoughts now are the thoughts of a stone," Alice Corbin wrote after her move to New Mexico in 1916. "My substance now is the substance of life itself."[3]

Herein is the story of the ladies of the canyons, nearly buried by negligence and the inevitable avalanche of the decades that quietly claim the details and narratives of even remarkable lives. The ladies' trail remains true and shows the way into the vast territory of stone and sky and untold history.

1

IMPERFECTLY INDEPENDENT

No one can predict at the outset where the life stream will lead,
but those moments of fissure, rupture, diversion, and frustration
require choice and can even become springboards to opportunity.

—*Virginia Scharff*

ON A SPRING MORNING IN 1903, Natalie and George Curtis walked together down a dusty street in the border town of Yuma, Arizona, as far south and west as one could wander in the continental United States. Dressed in expedition khaki and wide-brimmed hats to shade their pale faces, their leather boots colored by the fine sand of the Sonoran Desert, Natalie and George talked and laughed with the comfortable ease of good friends, or sister and brother. They were both.

George DeClyver Curtis was tall and lanky, with an amiable, welcoming manner. His younger sister, Natalie, was blonde and petite, with intense blue eyes, and an easy, contagious smile. The Curtis siblings were newcomers to Yuma, gringos off the train. Their appearance certainly gave them away, as did their accents—upper-class Eastern Seaboard with the diction of the Greenwich Village–Washington Square blue blood laced with the soft *r* acquired in Harvard Yard and the parlors of the Boston Brahmins. How had these two aristocratic Anglo-Americans come to be renting rooms in a flea-bitten, cactus-and-snake-infested railway settlement on the farthest uncivilized edge of the great American desert?

Although the Colorado River irrigated a narrow corridor along the town's edge, Yuma was derided as the hottest, driest hellhole in the desert Southwest. It was not a particularly attractive or remarkable landscape—not like the iconic Indian Country of chiseled spires and carved canyons to the north—and there was no culture or industry here beyond the railroad yard and the fenced fortress of the state penitentiary. The community's population comprised Spanish Americans who lived on the Arizona side of the Colorado River and the thousand or so Quechan Indians who lived on their reservation on the California side.

Natalie Curtis was twenty-seven in the spring of 1903, on her inaugural journey into the vast, wild territory of the American Southwest. Her brother, George DeClyver Curtis, was thirty-two. George had come alone to Arizona in the winter of 1900 looking for reprieve from debilitating asthma. George found his good health and a lifestyle that suited him on an Arizona ranch, and was a renewed man when he returned for a visit to the Curtis home in Greenwich Village a year later. Natalie, herself in poor physical and emotional condition, saw the remarkable changes in her older brother and decided she, too, needed to experience the healing air and light of southern Arizona.

Natalie, George, and their siblings Constance, Bridgham, and Marian (an older sister, Julia, died as a child) enjoyed every advantage available to those born into Victorian New York City's upper class. In the family brownstone at 27 Washington Place, the Curtis children were surrounded by New York City's cultural and intellectual elite. Their father, Edward Curtis, called Bogey by Natalie, was a distinguished doctor on the faculty of the College of Physicians and Surgeons and had served on the staff of the army surgeon general during the Civil War. Mother Augusta, known as Mimsey, oversaw a household where everyone in the family circle excelled at *something*. Overachievers were the norm at the informal and animated family suppers at the Washington Place dining table. Boldness and self-confidence were encouraged in the Curtis household, even among the women, and success in a chosen endeavor a given, at least among the men.

George and Bridgham were Harvard educated, an option not available to Natalie, her sisters Connie and Marian, or any other woman in Victorian America. Until she climbed aboard the train that would take her to the desert in 1902, Natalie had lived most of her life within the warm, comfortable, but confining rooms of

the Washington Place house where she was born in 1875. She did
travel abroad with her family, and attended the Brearley School, a
private day school for privileged girls. Music was considered a female-
appropriate educational pursuit, and was also an important social
grace for upper-class Victorian women. Natalie's education included
piano lessons when she was a very young child. "There was always
music in the home," Natalie's brother Bridgham remarked years later.
Music and music teachers. Soon music was all Natalie cared and
talked about. A visit with little Natalie Curtis meant an afternoon of
piano duets and song.[1]

   Natalie's young voice was trained in Anton Seidl's festival chorus,
which accompanied the New York Philharmonic, and she was a featured soloist with the National Conservatory Chorus. She took piano
classes with the great Antonín Dvořák at the Conservatory of Music,
and studied privately with the German composer Arthur Friedham
and the Italian composer Ferruccio Busoni, both of whom had studied in Europe with Franz Liszt. By her teen years, Dr. Curtis's daughter Natalie was recognized as one of the most talented and serious
young pianists, male or female, in New York City.

   Although her father was not the Wagnerian enthusiast that Natalie
was, Bogey and Natalie were in the audience for every one of Wagner's operas performed at the Metropolitan Opera House. Bogey
often regretted taking Natalie to the Met, however, because she
became so emotionally involved and musically stimulated. At the
end of one Wagner opera, when the audience broke into applause
Natalie zealously pounded the opera house floor with a crutch (she
had a lame leg at the time) until Bogey reached over and snatched
the wood stick from her hands.[2] "Papa says that music is a bad habit
with me," she wrote a girlfriend, "and that I am nothing more nor
less than a musical drunkard."[3]

   While her contemporaries had crushes on stage actors, Natalie's
infatuations involved opera singers, pianists, and conductors. At seventeen, she was smitten by Walter Damrosch, a handsome, enigmatic,
married, and very popular-among-the-women Wagnerian conductor.
Damrosch, who Natalie nicknamed "It" and described as Adonis-like
in her letters to her friend Bessie, was ten years Natalie's senior. Even
so, Natalie managed to attract the celebrity conductor's eye, and in the
early 1890s the two began a friendship that would last several decades.

By her eighteenth birthday, Natalie was a musical tour de force whose entire life was organized around music. Four to six hours of piano practice was the norm, with choral classes, voice, and harmony lessons fitted in around schoolwork several times each week. A rigorous daily practice schedule, devised and enforced by Natalie, so wore down the patience and frayed the nerves of the Curtis family that a toneless practice clavier was placed on Natalie's keyboard to mute the sound, and eventually she was given a techniphone keyboard that made only soft clicks.[4]

Natalie's punishing schedule never stopped, even during holidays at the Curtis summer home, Wave Crest, in Far Rockaway, Long Island. While George and her other siblings went swimming and boating, rode horses, and sunned on the beach, Natalie commuted into the humid, hot city for her piano lessons. She practiced six to seven hours daily at Wave Crest, and when she wasn't practicing, Natalie was consuming the works of Goethe, Tennyson, Keats, and Schopenhauer.

Natalie's zealous commitment to her music, and her inability to moderate that commitment, would be responsible for her greatest achievements and most devastating disappointments. "Halfhearted" was not in her psyche or her vocabulary. The relentless routine she maintained at Wave Crest threatened her health, and exhaustion spawned depression and doubt. Still, she persisted with her routine, even using brandy and strong coffee to get through her lessons. Finally, Mimsey and Bogey said enough, and Natalie was sent to the Berkshire Hills in Massachusetts for rest and recovery.[5]

At eighteen, Natalie was the age when women were expected to marry, not begin careers as concert pianists. Natalie's parents understood that their daughter's talent was worthy of the professional stage. They understood, too, that a woman, a proper woman, did not choose the stage over marriage and a family. But the world was about to undergo a cultural revolution, and educated, talented, ambitious young women like Natalie Curtis would find themselves among the vanguard who would, almost in spite of themselves, untie the stays and dismantle the walls that defined Victorian American women. Natalie, just sixteen, wrote a friend: "I don't know myself, but I want to have a kind of profession just as a man would, so that I could be perfectly independent. Don't you think that it would be awful to feel as some girls do that they *must* marry? Just as though they were so many cows!"[6]

But for all her bravado and progressivism, Natalie *was* conflicted about the implications of a career: if she were a concert pianist she would have to leave home. And unless she was married, a woman, even a gifted one, did not leave home to pursue a profession in the 1890s. "I feel very well that my place is at home, in my family," Natalie wrote Bessie in 1893. "I know that Papa would feel my absence tremendously and I owe him *so much* that I can never pay him that the least I can do is to stay with him if my presence give him any pleasure." Leaving Mimsey and Bogey to go out into the world, Natalie confided to her girlfriend, would make her feel like an "ungrateful hog."[7]

George graduated from Harvard that year and, not burdened by his younger sister's sense of debt or duty to Mimsey and Bogey, began a career as a librarian at the Astor Library in New Haven, Connecticut.

The Curtis home "breathed of liberal reform, practical idealism, moral courage and love of the fine arts." Located two blocks from Washington Square, Natalie's world was the invigorating, upscale, fashionable, semibohemian community of Greenwich Village. Henry James was born a few doors down at 21 Washington Place, and the Vanderbilts lived in the next block at number 10. The Curtis brownstone had been the family home since Natalie's grandfather bought it in 1839. Natalie's father and his four brothers spent their childhoods in the quiet, gracious neighborhood. The older Curtis boys married or went off to the Civil War, and Bogey, the youngest, inherited the house on Washington Place, where he settled with his wife, Augusta, and raised Natalie and her siblings.[8]

The impetus for Natalie and George's unconventional journey into the rugged outback of the American West could be at least partly attributed to the example set by their father's half-brother, George William Curtis. The influence of Uncle George on the character and imagination of Natalie in particular cannot be overstated. George Curtis was a remarkable individual, and his life would serve as a template for his niece, who shared his spirited sense of adventure, sharp intellect, welcoming manner, and tactful but resolute temperament.

George Curtis, twenty years Bogey's senior, was more of a grandfather than an uncle to the Curtis children. Although he never attended college, by the 1880s George Curtis held honorary degrees from Harvard, Brown, and Columbia, and was the chancellor of the University of the State of New York. He was a self-taught scholar, an insatiable seeker, and a prolific writer who for twenty years was a popular and influential political editor at *Harper's Weekly*.

Although George Curtis had homes near Boston and on Staten Island, he was an experienced outdoorsman who encouraged Natalie and George to learn about the simple joys found in a life lived close to the land. As a young man, he was introduced to the gifts of nature at Brook Farm, where he was schooled in transcendentalism by Ralph Waldo Emerson, Henry David Thoreau, and their league of New England poet-farmers and philosophers.

George Curtis's friends came to include the literary elite and politically powerful of his time. Fluent in four languages (he taught himself Italian, French, and German), he traveled the world in his twenties before returning to the United States and settling into a career as a political writer. Although George Curtis was always comfortable in the company of writers—his closest acquaintances were Irving, Bryant, Lowell, Thackeray, and Longfellow—by the Civil War he had become a respected and high-profile American statesman, and had twice served as a delegate at Republican national conventions. In 1869 he was offered (but turned down) the nomination to be secretary of state under President Grant.

A fervent supporter and promoter of Abraham Lincoln, George Curtis was devastated by the president's assassination. Both George Curtis and Natalie's father gazed upon the slain body of President Lincoln—George Curtis as a colleague and devotee at the memorial service, Bogey as a member of the surgeon general's team at the autopsy.

Like many of their neighbors in Greenwich Village, the Curtises lost several family members in the Civil War, including Bogey's brother and George Curtis's stepbrother Joe, a lieutenant colonel who fell in the Battle of Fredericksburg. George Curtis's brother-in-law, Robert Shaw, was just twenty-seven when he died at the head of his regiment, the famous Massachusetts 54th, the first all-Negro regiment in the Civil War. Colonel Shaw and his troops stormed Fort Wagner in South Carolina on July 18, 1863. One-fourth of the regiment fell that day. Shaw was among the first killed, and the victorious Confederates stripped, robbed, and buried his body in a mass grave with his Negro comrades. When Uncle George's wife, Anna Shaw, and her family learned of Robert's dishonorable burial in South Carolina, the army offered to disinter his body and return it to Boston for a proper burial with full honors. Shaw's father, Frank, responded: "We can imagine no holier place than that in which he lies, among his brave and devoted followers, nor wish for him better company."[9]

A confirmed Independent by the 1880s, George Curtis's weekly political column in *Harper's* reached tens of thousands of devoted readers. With the spoken and written word his platform of choice, the gentle, even-tempered George Curtis had a "big manner," Walt Whitman wrote of his friend, "and without being offish his personality had a large swing, as if it had plenty of time and space in which to live."[10]

Fireside chats in the Curtis parlor in Greenwich Village were attended by the progressive individuals who were reshaping American principles, politics, and aesthetics in the second half of the nineteenth century. Natalie's civic and cultural education, and her moral conscience, were supplemented and influenced by the conversations and activities of her Uncle George and his famous peers, who debated political theory and social and educational reform around the Curtis dinner table.

For the precocious and gifted Natalie, George William Curtis exemplified a life devoted to intellectual exploration, creative expression, social reform, and the unrestrained pursuit of one's passion. Natalie adored him, and as she grew into maturity as a musician and a woman, and struggled to find her place—and to leave home to find that place—in the new world of the twentieth century, Uncle George's spoken and written wisdom guided her choices and bolstered her resolve.

Mainstream Protestantism was undergoing challenge from unconventional and esoteric religious movements in the 1890s. Natalie and Mimsey attended meetings of the Theosophical Society that introduced Buddhism, Sufism, and Hinduism to New York's upper class. Theosophy encouraged the study of comparative religion, philosophy, and science, and also endorsed the concepts of karma and reincarnation. Life was not haphazard, but part of a grand scheme. Theosophy affirmed teenage Natalie's intuition that her art and her life were one, and that music was her divine destiny.

Natalie was more than a coming-of-age feminist; she was an emerging humanist. Where traditional, Anglocentric Americans saw the Other in race, religion, and culture, Natalie recognized common ground. It was a perspective that would cause her to challenge conventional ideology, and push her to pursue a destiny far from Washington Square in the exotic and "uncivilized" territory of Native America.

IN THE SUMMER OF 1896, Natalie went to Europe with her brother George. She was twenty-one, and it was her second journey across the Atlantic. Natalie and George traveled to London, through the Rhine region of Germany, and across Italy. By late fall, the siblings had settled into rooms in Paris, where George enrolled at the École des Beaux-Arts and Natalie was accepted into voice classes at the revered Paris Conservatory.

It was to be a winter devoted to study and creative stimulation, but it all came to an end when Natalie suffered an acute attack of appendicitis. Mimsey boarded the first ship to France and took Natalie by train to Switzerland for medical treatment. After Natalie recovered her health, Natalie and Mimsey journeyed to Bayreuth, Wagner's home and now the mecca for all things Wagnerian, and Natalie enrolled to study the operas she had loved since childhood. Natalie's reputation as an accomplished young American pianist opened doors to Bayreuth's inner circle of musicians and socialites, and Natalie and her mother were introduced to Wagner's widow, Cosima, with whom they spent a memorable New Year's Eve 1896.[11]

Back in residence at Washington Place that spring, Natalie received an invitation from her former teacher Anton Seidl to perform a piano concerto with the Philharmonic Orchestra. Natalie, now twenty-two, was straddling two worlds: the world of the professional, paid musician, and the world of a proper single woman who lived at home with her parents. Seidl recognized an enormous talent in Natalie Curtis and urged her to take her place on the professional stage. The invitation flattered even as it terrified Natalie. She understood that although she would be equal to and respected by New York's top musicians, her professional career would be limited by her gender. She also understood that she would be expected to step down from the professional stage when she married. And if she did not marry, she would be sentenced to the life at the periphery of conventional society experienced by all single women who dared to pursue their creative passion.

Seidl's invitation to join him on the professional stage pushed Natalie's conflicts to the surface. Even in a progressive household like the Curtises', it was understood that daughters would marry and raise a family. Even an accomplished musician like Natalie was biding her time until she was betrothed. As a married woman with children, she could teach music and continue to play publicly, but not for pay. Music would become her hobby, not her vocation. Natalie's passion for music, indeed for anything, would have no place in a Victorian woman's home.

Natalie's fate as a concert pianist was not decided by intellectual debate within the Curtis family, or in private conversations with her mentors and friends. Instead, it was Natalie's obsessive demand for musical excellence that ended her dream of becoming a professional musician. A debilitating daily practice routine, coupled with the sobering reality that her artistic dreams were laden with uncertainty, broke Natalie's health, and she collapsed in the fall of 1897.

George claimed his sister's concert career ended with "a strained hand, due to over-zealous piano practice." Bridgham's account of Natalie's collapse was less specific about the cause, but he, too, acknowledged the magnitude of that moment in Natalie's life. While preparing for the most important concert of her young life, Natalie suffered nothing less than "a severe physical breakdown that made all thought of a career as a pianist out of the question."[12]

It was a line of demarcation in the life of Natalie Curtis. She was as emotionally devastated as she was physically broken. Hindsight suggests that Natalie understood the confines of the cultural prison that she, even as the daughter of progressive parents, was sentenced to accept. Natalie's physical and emotional withdrawal from the performance with the Philharmonic avoided a head-on collision between the reality that was a proper woman's place in upper-class New York society and the artistic path she had dreamed of and pursued since childhood.

Natalie had no helpful mentors and no answers, personally or professionally. What she needed was to retreat to a cabin in the woods near a place like Walden Pond where she could find solace and glean wisdom from the elders. But the elder who could have given Natalie an astute and hopeful perspective on life and art, on the individual's path and the grand scheme, her Uncle George, had been dead for five years.

Natalie's convalescence was slow. She remained in the brownstone on Washington Place, and although she was physically unable to play the piano, began to compose pieces for voice, piano, and violin. Gradually, her strength returned, and she played a little piano and sang her new songs for family gatherings. But her grand and passionate dreams of a career under the lights of the world's great concert halls were snuffed. "Whenever she played her touch was sensitive and lovely," George wrote, "and her voice, whether in singing or in lecturing, had a sweet and moving quality of its own."[13]

Natalie was an adept composer, and several of her first compositions were published by G. Schirmer: "Dearest Where Thy Shadow Falls," published in 1898, and "Song from Pippa Passes," in 1899. One long composition based on the poems of Robert Louis Stevenson, "Songs from a Child's Garden of Verses," was published in 1902.

Natalie seemed resigned to the life of an unambitious introvert. Considering the world-renowned maestros she had trained with and the prestigious concert halls she had performed in, playing a little piano and singing a few songs for an audience of close friends and family must have been as satisfying to Natalie Curtis as a trot among the stable ponies would be for a derby-trained thoroughbred. Natalie was a finely honed artist of "unquestioned brilliant promise" who seemed to have lost her confidence and gumption. At twenty-five years of age, she was grappling with the dark night of the soul.[14]

George returned from Europe and his studies at the Beaux-Arts and settled into life in New Haven. His job in the stacks of the Astor Library suited him, but the damp climate of New England aggravated his asthma, and in 1900, worn down by frequent and incapacitating attacks, George did what ailing men of means could choose to do: he quit his job, packed his bags, and boarded a train for the arid, pristine air of the American West.

The Curtis family had friends and relatives in the Los Angeles area, but George went to rural Arizona and looked for work in the small towns along the Santa Fe Railway. Although his equestrian skills were limited and his knowledge of cows nil, George was hired by one of the large cattle outfits. Life in the saddle under the big sky of the West—a life of long days on horseback, short nights on the hard ground, with meals cooked on a campfire—rehabilitated his body and stimulated his mind in much the same manner as the life on Brook Farm had restored and inspired his Uncle George.

To Bogey and Mimsey Curtis and their friends on the Eastern Seaboard, the American Southwest was an exotic territory at its best and an uncivilized, even savage frontier at its worst. The public relations department of the Santa Fe Railway was working overtime at the turn of the century to change Anglo-America's perception of the southwestern United States. In pamphlets and newspaper articles the American public was told to "See America First" and that the landscape and indigenous cultures of the western half of the continent were as exotic, dynamic, and worthy of exploration as anything found in Europe or the Middle East.

Throughout 1900 and 1901, George sent letters and picture postcards of his travels through California and Arizona home to Natalie and the family in New York. His words and images sparked Natalie's dulled imagination and diminished spirit. And although a call to adventure was not a conventional choice for a twenty-seven-year-old woman, especially if she were single and of dubious health, Natalie announced in 1902 that she wanted to join George out west.

Bogey and Mimsey, painfully aware that Natalie was not recovering her stamina and her famously energetic joie de vivre sequestered within the rooms of the Washington Place brownstone, consented to her request. George came east for a family visit in the fall, and when he boarded the train west again, Natalie was at his side.

The siblings went to Southern California and stayed with family friends near Los Angeles, where the winter weather was balmy and bright. On New Year's Day 1903, Natalie and George went to Pasadena for the outdoor celebrations and events associated with the Tournament of Roses. There, a new friend, Charles Lummis, invited them to an event showcasing Navajo singers from Arizona.

The Navajos had been invited to Los Angeles by the controversial author, editor, and outdoorsman Charles Fletcher Lummis and were camped on land near his home, El Alisal, in Pasadena. It is possible that Lummis, a political activist and journalist, had known Natalie and George's uncle George William Curtis years before in Boston. Lummis was born and raised in Massachusetts and had attended

Harvard, where his classmates included Theodore Roosevelt. By 1903, and Natalie's arrival in Los Angeles, Lummis's *The Land of Poco Tiempo* had been in print for a decade. The book was a popular success and practically required reading for Yankee tourists and everyone else who ventured to "See America First" (the phrase coined by Lummis) and make the bold journey into the Southwest.

Lummis's episodic narrative about the land of "pretty soon"—the Territory of New Mexico—introduced Americans like Natalie to the people, geography, history, and essence of the Southwest. Lummis was a disciple of the open air, close-to-the-earth lifestyle championed by Thoreau, Emerson, and John Burroughs, and advocated by Uncle George, and had walked the length of New England as an undergrad. In 1884, at the age of twenty-five, Lummis left his desk job at the *Scioto (OH) Gazette* and began a trek—he called it a "tramp"—across the American continent. Following railroad lines and wagon roads where they could be found, Lummis walked 3,507 miles in 143 days. His destination was Los Angeles, and his six million footsteps wove through natural and cultural wonders in Colorado, New Mexico, Arizona, and finally Southern California. Lummis's tramp included stopovers at the pueblos of Tesuque and Isleta in New Mexico, and his time living among the natives of these ancient villages had redirected the course of his life and work.

At dinner parties and social events at El Alisal (Place of the Sycamores) in the hills east of Los Angeles, Natalie and George were introduced to the Los Angeles artists, intellectuals, and social reformers who congregated at Lummis's home. It was a lively introduction to the rich, complicated, and many-layered cultural and political society of the twentieth-century Southwest. El Alisal was a cozy, rustic, enchanting adobe and stone home hand built by Lummis and his native friends in the oak, cactus, and sagebrush Arroyo Seco near Pasadena (later called Highland Park). The house was striking in style and character and would be recognized as among the first to exhibit the no-frills, clean, clutter-free, close-to-nature design, construction, and interior decor aesthetic of the California arts and crafts movement.

Natalie was plunged into a new visual, cultural, and intellectual environment at El Alisal. Lummis, like Natalie, was driven by a "hunger in the head," a passionate need to explore the whys and

Figure 1. Interior view of El Alisal, the home of Charles F. Lummis, ca. 1920.

wherefores of the world. Editor of *Out West* magazine, Lummis was the national spokesman for the paradise he had found in California. His clean, straightforward prose about the idyllic life and pristine landscape found out west was nearly as responsible as the Santa Fe Railway's promotion department for the mass immigration of artists, writers, health seekers, and adventurers into the Southwest in the first decades of the twentieth century.[15]

Lummis told stories about roaming the Pajarito (Little Bird) Plateau in New Mexico with the great Swiss archaeologist Adolph F. Bandelier. On foot, on horseback, and on burro, Lummis and Bandelier explored the canyon and mountain country west of the old city of Santa Fe, the region known as El Rito de Los Frijoles (Creek of the Beans) that would one day become Bandelier National Monument. "Thousands of miles of wilderness and desert we trudged side by side," Lummis wrote of his days with Bandelier, "camped, starved, shivered, learned and were glad together."[16]

Natalie had enjoyed the out-of-doors in New England and on the Atlantic coast, and she had twice crossed the Atlantic and stayed in

Paris, the Swiss Alps, and the lush German forests near Bayreuth. But Lummis described a landscape the likes of which she had never seen or even imagined, a place that was "a picture, a romance, a dream . . . a land of ineffable lights and sudden shadows . . . where the rattlesnake is a demigod, and the cigarette a means of grace . . . the heart of Africa beating against the ribs of the Rockies."[17]

At their home in the Los Angeles foothills, Lummis and his wife, Eva, held dinner parties and "noises" (salons) to which artists, writers, politicians, and activists regularly flocked. Newcomers like Natalie and George mingled with "the great, the near-great, the merely colorful, and assorted hangars-on" who on any given night could include John Muir, John Burroughs, and a California labor and Indian rights activist, suffragette, and writer named Mary Austin.[18]

Lummis and his friends were involved in the "roiling caldron of Indian rights" and with their Sequoyah League, founded in 1902, were active participants in the heated national political debate surrounding Indian reform policies. Lummis used the pages of *Out West* magazine to criticize Washington's Indian education programs, and took his grievances about federal Indian programs, especially the Indian boarding schools, to his college pal President Roosevelt. Theodore Roosevelt was frequently peeved and even outraged by Lummis and the Sequoya League's methods of activism, but to his Washington staff's chagrin, the president welcomed the provocative California writer into the White House.[19]

Through Lummis, Natalie was introduced into the society, issues, and people of Southern California. California was a foreign country with its own traditions, history, and lifestyle. Even the lively salons in Arroyo Seco had an unmistakably western flair. Lummis's wardrobe of choice (even for visits to the White House) was a Spanish bolero jacket, corduroy trousers and matching sport coat, and leather moccasins, with a wide sash around his waist, and a colored kerchief knotted about his head or neck. Khaki skirts and riding slacks, cowboy boots, Levi's, broad-brimmed hats, and colorful ties and belts were the norm for California women and men. The staid attire and formal social graces deemed proper and acceptable back in New York and Boston had no place in Southern California. Natalie had stepped into a new world, and her body, mind, and spirit responded with vigor and enthusiasm to the myth and the reality of the American West.

Lummis was not a musician, but he had been collecting and recording the folk music of the Spanish and the indigenous Indians of the Southwest since the mid-1880s. Natalie certainly asked Lummis about the region's musical traditions, and studied his notes and listened to his recordings. And she was certainly Lummis's most educated guest at the dance performance given by the Navajos at the Tournament of Roses celebration in Pasadena on New Year's Day 1903.

After several months in Southern California, Natalie was strong enough to go with George to Arizona. They left Los Angeles on the train bound for the southwestern-most corner of the United States—Yuma, Arizona. The seven-hour journey took them through snow-covered mountains and across a flat cactus-studded desert near the Salton Sea. Exactly why they chose Yuma, in the very middle of the continent's largest, driest, hottest environment, the Sonoran Desert, is not known. Yuma was, in George's words, a "humid hellhole . . . a town filled with the oft-scourings of Arizona" where the best and only lodging was found at the Hotel Gandolfo, where guests dined on rice and cabbage, and paid a dollar a night for rooms that were "not good."[20]

Lummis had traveled through the region and would have warned Natalie and George about spring on the desert. "High noon in southern Arizona. The sun is a flood of infinite fire, wherein earth and sky are saturated. The heavens are an arch of burnished brass. The blinding landscape seems the thin crust over a sea of boiling lava. . . . Touch a palm to that sand, and you shall acquire blisters as from a red-hot stove."[21]

The Colorado River and the green bosque that clung to the moisture found along its banks were the town's only inviting and attractive features. All travel around dusty, sunburned Yuma was by wagon, on horseback, or on foot. Natalie visited the state penitentiary and took notes for an article, but her interest from the start was not the so-called civilized side of the river, but the Native American community living on the reservation on the other side.

The reservation of the Yumas (Quechan, or Cochan), a Yuman-speaking tribe of desert farmers on the south side of the Colorado River, was the home to six hundred Indians. Natalie was impressed by the Yumas' peaceful, self-contained community, and that not one of their members had ever been incarcerated in the state prison. "In spite of their proximity to the town," she wrote in what was among the first of dozens of articles about the Southwest, "these Indians are comparatively free from many of the vices unconsciously acquired by a primitive people who are ignorant of new temptations."[22]

Natalie was stepping into a world rarely glimpsed by Anglo-American women—the homeland of Native America. A few women had broken ground before her: anthropologist-ethnologist Matilda Coxe Stevenson had worked with her husband in the 1880s at Zuni and other New Mexico pueblos, and Alice C. Fletcher of the Peabody Museum had begun work in the 1880s among the Sioux. But as a single white woman of education and means, traveling at her leisure across Indian Country seeking to further her understanding of the Southwest's indigenous cultures, Natalie was a pioneer.

2

LAND OF INEFFABLE LIGHT
AND SUDDEN SHADOW

> The moonlight flooded that great, silent land. . . . The
> senses were too feeble to take it in, and every time one
> looked up to the sky, one felt unequal to it, as if one were
> sitting deaf under the waves of a great river of melody.
> —*Willa Cather*

WHEN THE CURTIS SIBLINGS came to Yuma in the spring of 1903, their gear included a "talking machine," an Edison phonograph and recorder that may have been given to Natalie in Los Angeles by Lummis. The dance-songs performed with "lusty vigor" by the Navajos at the New Year's Day performance in Pasadena, coupled with Lummis's stories of the indigenous people he had met and recorded during his treks in the outback, had sparked Natalie's interest in native song, and she intended to go into the desert in search of music.[1]

Just as she had boldly introduced herself to the great maestros at the Met, and gained admittance into the inner sanctum of Wagner's family home in Bayreuth, Natalie walked across the bridge that spanned the Colorado River and introduced herself to the Yuma Indians living on the other side. Who precisely served as her guide is not known, but when she crossed the river that day, Natalie began an exploration into the heart, mind, and music of Indian America that would become her passion and her vocation for the rest of her life.

Natalie's initiation into the "primitive" world of Native America began with conversations with Indian elders. Chiparopai (also spelled

Figure 2. George Curtis and Natalie Curtis, playing a hand game with an Indian friend, ca. 1904.

Hiparopai in Natalie's writings) was an elderly Quechan woman who spoke English and Spanish. Like many Yumas, Chiparopai lived miles from the river and the white railroad town of Yuma, preferring the open desert where she could "feel the air wide around me."

Natalie met Chiparopai seated beneath a plum tree during one of the old woman's visits to relatives who lived "by the wells." Natalie told Chiparopai that she was interested in understanding and knowing the Yuma people, and asked Chiparopai if she could take notes about their conversation. Chiparopai agreed, and answered Natalie's questions with a blunt and poignant honesty. "Never mind if we are poor," the elder told Natalie in the shade of a thatched shed. "What good is life if we are not happy? . . . White people think that money is everything; we Indians think that happiness is more."

Natalie commented on Chiparopai's persistent racking cough and asked why so many Quechan were ill. "It seems as though you white folk bring poison to us Indians," the elderly woman answered. "Sickness comes with you, and hundreds of us die."

The irony was not lost on Natalie: she and her brother George had come to the desert to be healed, to live.

In her conversations with Chiparopai, Natalie learned how Indian Americans felt about Washington's assimilationist policies that banned their language, religion, and dress and forcibly placed their children in government boarding schools. Especially brutalizing to Indian children was the Bureau of Indian Affairs' (BIA) strictly enforced practice of cutting off their long hair. Chiparopai also admonished white America's preference for stiff clothes and hard collars. Natalie assured Chiparopai that not all white people agreed with federal policies regarding Indian education.

Natalie recorded Chiparopai singing "Song of the Mocking-Bird," and asked her about her tribe's spiritual beliefs. "How would we know how to live if we did not believe in something greater than ourselves?" the old woman asked Natalie. "And when we die?" Natalie asked. "Then it is all happiness," Chiparopai answered. "When we *die* we are all alike."

Natalie published an article in the *Craftsman* about her conversations with Chiparopai. She prefaced the story with the disclaimer that she, as the recorder, sought only to convey an individual Indian's opinions and thoughts about the changes brought to their world by the whites. She was not interested in conducting an academic study of Indian society or religious beliefs, but rather in learning who the people of Native America were and how they thought about their world and culture. She was also very interested in their music. "You want to know my people?" Chiparopai asked Natalie. "Live among them. See them in their fields, planting and harvesting; see them with their children; hear them sing!"[2]

Natalie took Chiparopai's counsel and, with George, traveled deeper into Indian Country to find and hear the music of the native people. They boarded the train with the bulky Edison recorder and wax cylinders and several bags of gear and headed east across Arizona. George was comfortable traveling by horse and wagon, but the Arizona wilderness had few maintained roads in 1903, and the Curtis siblings traveled by train whenever possible.

In his first years in the Southwest, George had lived and worked on a cattle ranch near Houck, Arizona. The cowboy way and a life spent close to the land and far from people fit the former librarian's temperament. As his uncle George William Curtis had done in his formative years near Walden Pond, George DeClyver Curtis, nearly thirty when he came to Arizona, began to write. Unlike his uncle, George had no ambitions to become a career journalist and had little interest in achieving a name for himself. (In 1914 George would publish his only novel, *The Wooing of a Recluse*, under the pseudonym Gregory Marword.) But George was a competent and thoughtful writer, and even when living in a tent in the outback, he regularly recorded his adventures and experiences in his diary.

In 1903 guest ranches set up to accommodate eastern dudes looking to play cowboy and to explore Indian Country did not yet exist. Natalie's first experience among cowboys and cattle was at a working ranch, probably near Houck, where life was a "hand to hand tussle with an elemental world" shaped by "scorching sun, wind, sudden cloudbursts, thirst, exhaustion, violent danger, loneliness, [and] isolation from the ties of home-women."

Unless Natalie and George were in a community like Yuma along one of the railroads that cut across the territory, or were staying at one of the Protestant missions or government schools on the reservations, Natalie's living quarters that spring and summer were exactly the same as George's.

> I have ridden with cowboys, sung with them, seen round-ups and bronco-busting, spent months amid a thousand head of cattle on one of the loneliest ranges in Arizona, devoid of all intercourse with the outside world save for visits of wayfaring Indians or stray sheep-herders seeking water at our springs. . . . When the men left to "ride the range" and I was alone in the cabin with a Colt revolver for companion; when I heard the plaintive sob of the wood-pigeon in the cedars—the prelude to the choir of coyotes who would howl at the rising moon; when I realized that should any strange man try to enter (in which case I had been instructed to "shoot") I might call forever and though the sandstone cliffs might send back my voice no human soul could hear or come—then I understood the note of utter loneliness that sounds in many a cowboy song.[3]

Natalie could never have undertaken such adventures on the southwest frontier without her brother George. Just how much of their adventures were shared in letters sent to Bogey and Mimsey is unknown, but the details of her solitary nights in an isolated cabin with a Colt revolver to keep her company were certainly omitted from the siblings' missives to their family on Washington Place.

From the cattle ranch near Houck, George and Natalie went by horse and wagon north and west toward what the early Spanish explorers and now the American anthropologists called Tusayan, or Hopiland. Their destination, the ancient mesa-top village of Oraibi, was a several-day journey across the Navajo Reservation through some of the most rugged, beautiful, harsh, and remote country in North America. Weather, the availability of water, and the physical condition and psychological stamina of brother and sister determined the speed and distance of their wagon's daily progress.

After two days of slow progress across "that Arizona wilderness of beauty known as the 'Painted Desert,'" Hopi Third Mesa rose into view on the northwest horizon. The stone and mud pueblo of Oraibi appeared carved from the stone island of Third Mesa, which soared six hundred feet into the searing blue sky. Surrounded by an ocean of sand that fell away like waves into the four directions, the home of the Hopi (or Moqui) was as exotic, primal, and spectacular as anything Natalie Curtis had ever seen.

Oraibi had a trading post as early as 1897, and by 1903 the U.S. government had built several buildings below Third Mesa near the springs and wells that provided water to the natives. By midsummer there would be small patches of green cultivated fields in the flat land below the village mesa, but in spring the sand land boasted only small flecks of color that were the fragile desert wild flowers. "The scarcity of water can hardly be conceived by those who have not been there," Natalie wrote after her first visit to Hopiland. "Every drop used in Oraibi has to be brought for a distance of two miles, one-half of which is up the steep trail, and carried all that long way in heavy earthen jars on the backs of toiling women."[4]

For nearly a thousand years, the Hopis of Third Mesa, like their tribal neighbors on the cliff-top villages on First and Second Mesas, had hauled all of their water, food, and provisions on their backs up the trails carved into the stone to their homes on top of the mesa. The Hopi were a historically peaceful tribe (their name means "quiet people" or "people of peace"), and for several hundred years they had managed to maintain a distance from European explorers and then American missionaries and other cultural invaders. But by the early twentieth century and Natalie's first visit to Oraibi, the policies of the U.S. government had begun to erode Hopi independence, and the people of Tusayan regarded the white world as wicked, and white men, and most white women, as deceitful.

Before Natalie and George departed Los Angeles in late January, Lummis may have suggested that their desert itinerary include a visit to the Hopi village of Oraibi. At that time, Lummis's Sequoyah League was launching a rigorous and covert campaign meant to undermine and expose the BIA's assimilationist policies sanctioned by Roosevelt's secretary of the interior, Ethan Allen Hitchcock. The league's efforts focused on the superintendent of Indian affairs, Charles E. Burton, at Keam's Canyon on the Hopi Reservation. Stories about overzealous BIA agents kidnapping Indian children from their homes and dragging them off to the government school had Lummis and his friends up in arms.

All of the solutions to the "Indian problem" in the United States after the Civil War advocated the same approach: the management and altering of "savages" into "civilized" Christian farmers. To implement the assimilation of Indians into the white world, the BIA opened boarding and day schools throughout Indian America. By stripping children of all outward signs of Indianness, and introducing educational programs meant to undermine and weaken their cultural identity, the U.S. government meant to bring all Native Americans into the "civilized" fold of white America.

"Kill the Indian, and save the man." The now infamous statement of Colonel Richard Henry Pratt, director of the Carlisle Indian School in Pennsylvania, pretty much summed up the federal government's agenda for Indians and Indian policy in the United States.[5]

To young Indians sent to one of the federal Indian schools, a white man's education meant learning to speak English and never *ever* speaking their native language while at school. Hair was cut short or shorn off completely, and traditional garments were burned and replaced by "citizens'" clothes—white people's trousers, shirts, and shoes. Every Indian student slept in a bed, prayed to Jesus, used a toilet, and ate only white food with a knife and fork.[6]

The remote, peaceable people of Hopiland were not spared the insensitive programs of the BIA meant to eradicate their language, culture, and religion. In 1902 Indian commissioner William A. Jones had sent out a letter to Indian agents and school superintendents, including Burton, which identified the native customs to be modified or eliminated. Long hair and traditional clothing were added to the government's formal list of forbidden behavior, which already banned use of native language or song in Indian schools. When the commissioner's rigorous instructions for assimilation of the Indians reached Burton at his office at Third Mesa, he instructed his agents to energetically, even brutally, enforce the reforms.

In April 1903, as Natalie and George made their way in their wagon across the Arizona outback toward the country of the Hopis, Charles Lummis and *Out West* magazine launched a series of articles titled "Bullying the Moqui" that specifically targeted the alleged atrocities perpetuated by Burton at his schools on the Hopi Reservation, especially at Keam's Canyon.

Lummis's inflammatory articles about Burton drew the attention of the White House. In May 1903 Lummis was granted time with Roosevelt on his presidential train as it traveled from the Grand Canyon to Los Angeles. Although Lummis had access to the president for almost two full days, and presented in detail his grievances against Burton, Roosevelt was not ready to fire his superintendent of Indian affairs.[7]

Lummis's *Out West* continued to publish stories about the mistreatment of Indian students at Burton's boarding schools. Most of Lummis's allegations of abuse were based on secret investigations by a woman named Gertrude L. Gates, and on the testimony of an Oraibi schoolteacher, Belle Axtell Kolp. Earlier in the spring of 1903, Lummis had dispatched Gates, of Pasadena, to Hopiland to collect information on Burton's activities. Gates posed as an invalid who had come to the high desert for her health, but Burton's agents became suspicious and confronted her. Gates confessed that she was in Hopiland to spy on Burton, and she was unceremoniously escorted off the reservation.

Burton's office may have been leery of Gates because she appeared on the Hopi Reservation just after the departure of Kolp, who had publically renounced Burton's education policies and resigned her teaching post in Oraibi in mid-February. Although Kolp, also from Pasadena, was not one of Lummis's spies, her eyewitness accounts of the mistreatment of Indian children in government schools helped launch the Sequoyah League's campaign against Burton. (Kolp was well versed in frontier politics and politicians—her uncle was Samuel B. Axtell, one-time governor of New Mexico and later the territory's chief justice.) Upon her return to Pasadena, Kolp wrote a lengthy deposition outlining government offences against the Hopis at Oraibi. This deposition and her experiences as an Indian schoolteacher became the basis for a series of articles Lummis wrote and published in *Out West* magazine throughout the spring and summer of 1903.[8]

The BIA did investigate Burton's activities, but cleared the superintendent of most charges. And although the situation between the federal government and Native America, especially at Oraibi, remained a tinderbox, and federal Indian policy continued to be harshly criticized by reformers all over the United States, Roosevelt insisted Lummis issue a formal apology to Burton.

Natalie and George knew about Lummis's many grievances against federal Indian policy. But in May 1903, when they pulled their horse and wagon up before the government buildings at the foot of Third Mesa, Natalie most likely did not know how she might be mistaken for yet another of Lummis's female subversives. That Natalie and George managed to move into a room in the BIA housing at New Oraibi is a testament to Natalie's compelling personality and George's gentle manner. However, the atmosphere in Hopiland was charged with suspicion and distrust, and their activities were closely scrutinized.

If Natalie had access to copies of *Out West* and Lummis's articles about Burton's "reign of terror," and if she knew about Gertrude Gates and her eviction from Indian Country, the antagonistic environment did not dampen Natalie's enthusiasm to visit the Hopis. However, it likely dampened her acknowledgment of the purpose of her journey through Indian Country—to hear and record Indian music. The singing of native songs and chants was strictly forbidden. Had a federal official asked to inspect Natalie and George's gear, they would have known that the diminutive, engaging, and educated musician named Natalie Curtis was most certainly crossing the high desert to break the law, because the wagon was loaded with crates packed with a bulky Edison phonograph.

After Natalie and George settled into rooms among the other white outsiders in the government buildings at the foot of Third Mesa,

Natalie, with George and a translator—one of the English-speaking Hopi boys who had attended a government school—hiked up the steep, exposed, cliff-hugging trail to old Oraibi. With her field notebook in hand, and dressed in what would become her desert uniform—khaki skirt, white long-sleeved shirt, lace-up leather boots, and a broad-brimmed hat—Natalie introduced herself to the villagers.

Oraibi, like each of the Hopi villages of First, Second, and Third Mesas, was a cluster of several-storied mud and stone dwellings built around small plazas perched on the narrow top of an island mesa hundreds of feet above the shimmering floor of the desert. The first Spanish priests in the Southwest built a chapel and mission near Oraibi in the early years of the seventeenth century, but the Hopis peaceably and tenaciously resisted Catholicism and maintained their own spiritual traditions. After the Spanish were thrown out of Arizona and New Mexico in the uprising of 1680, the Franciscans never returned to Hopiland. The Hopis adopted the Spaniards' sheep, burros, and horses, and when Natalie arrived in 1903, the desert landscape below Third Mesa boasted orchards of peach and apricot trees.

The Hopis were a predominantly vegetarian culture, and the daily meal included maize (corn), beans, squash, watermelons, and sunflowers. Corn was the primary food source, but among the Hopi, as among all desert dwellers, water was the supreme life source. A rainstorm was a celebrated event, and every adult and child participated in the capture, collection, and storage of the precious commodity. Hopi was and is a matrilineal, monogamous society, and Natalie was introduced to women who owned and occupied their own dwellings in the villages. Women also owned cultivated land, including some of the orchards and horses.

The village of Oraibi and the people of Hopiland surpassed Natalie's expectations. Every act of life was ceremonial, poetic, symbolic. "I was not prepared to find a people with such definite artforms, such crystallized traditions, beliefs, and customs." The music of the Hopi "astounded" her. "I had not been in Oraibi twenty-four hours before my mental picture of the scope of music faded like a desert mirage, revealing a new and far-off horizon stretching boundless as the desert itself—a new world of art."

Natalie made friends easily, and her residence below Third Mesa was soon visited by her Hopi neighbors from dawn until dusk.

Figure 3. Hopi village of Oraibi, ca. 1907.

My workshop, as I called it, was one of the "government houses" at the foot of the mesa. . . . In one of these houses I had my phonograph, and here the Indians collected daily with true Hopi curiosity to peek in at the windows, to stare at the "Pahana" [white or American woman], and to join in the fun and excitement of singing into the machine.

　　Indeed, I had but to be seen issuing from the house where I lived, to be followed by a stream of Hopis—women with babies on their backs, men on their way to the fields, children just off to school. The Indians opened my door and entered my little house as unceremoniously as they did each other's. I always welcomed them, and offered them the customary empty boxes to sit on. There were never enough to go around, and half my visitors sat on the floor. But this was Hopi style; boxes are an innovation of civilization.[9]

　In the month and a half that Natalie was among the Hopis, she cultivated relationships with everyone who would talk with her. With native guides, she traveled by wagon into the vast and often labyrinthine landscape of deep unnamed canyons, sheer cliffs, wide washes, and treacherous rock chasms to reach the desert camps and outposts where Hopi singers and storytellers were found. Natalie spent entire days on foot or in the saddle, and slept in a bedroll on the ground under the stars or in a cabin or tent near a trading post if one was nearby.

Six months after leaving New York, Bogey and Mimsey would not have recognized their daughter, the confident desert traveler. Natalie's physical and emotional strength increased with every week spent under the sky of Indian Country. Her body was healed by the landscape, and her heart had reconnected with her passion in the music of the people who called the desert home.

During one desert trek, a sandstorm engulfed Natalie and her Hopi guide and literally blew away the road. They walked into the night, and as the sky cleared and became luminous with stars, Natalie's guide began to sing. The wild beauty of the music, and the soulful, uninhibited quality of the guide's voice, astonished Natalie. Even as her classically educated ear struggled to understand the pitch and cadence of his song, Natalie attempted to sing along. "I joined my voice to that of my guide. Not a soul to hear, not one to comment or criticize—only the desert stretching broad and far, only the craggy buttes and cliffs, only the heavens and those great bright stars. What freedom to sing one's very soul out into such a wide vast night! We lifted our faces to the sky and sang."[10]

Every act of Hopi life was accompanied by song. Planting fields, grinding corn, dancing, putting children to sleep, watching the approach of the "yellow light" (dawn), the setting of the sun, rain— every season, every daily chore, was honored by song. Among the Hopis, Natalie was surrounded by music. For Natalie, whose entire life had been the pursuit of music, life *was* music. In the remote desert world of the Hopis, Natalie was among people who understood what she had always known: music was *life*.

Before attempting to talk with any of the Hopis in Oraibi, Natalie went to meet the village leaders. The most important meeting was her introduction to the elderly *kikmongwi* (village chief) Lololomai, his daughter, Noyasoya, and his sister, Ponianomsi. Lololomai (Very-Good) was about eighty years old in 1903, and was one of only a few Hopi who had traveled out of Hopiland. In the mid-1880s Lololomai had gone with the trader Thomas Keams to Washington to ask

President Chester Arthur to stop Navajo encroachment onto Hopi lands. Impressed by Euro-American civilization, Lololomai asked the federal government to open a school at Keam's trading post. By 1903, however, Lololomai's support of federal Indian schools, especially those under Superintendent Burton, had ended.

Natalie sought the elderly chief's approval of her intention to write down and also record on the Edison phonograph the songs of his people. She was taken by her interpreter, "a Hopi lad, who, although blind, led with sure foot the way up the steep, rocky trail to the village," to meet Lololomai, whom they found "seated on his house-top, spinning, for in Hopi-land it is the men who spin and weave."

After Natalie explained that she had come to talk about "something that concerns your people," Lololomai invited her to climb the ladder and join him on the rooftop. From the flat-topped roof with its 360-degree view of Third Mesa and Hopiland, Natalie told Lololomai, through her interpreter, that if Hopi songs were not written down, they would be forgotten. Lololomai understood the value of recording his people's songs, but he was fearful of repercussions against his village if Superintendent Burton learned about their collaboration. Natalie assured the chief that she would not reveal the names of collaborators, nor speak of their sessions to the whites associated with the federal government. The chief gave Natalie's work his blessing, and in late spring of 1903 Natalie began to collect and record the songs of the Hopi.[11]

Although Natalie and George were offered food and shelter in the government-issue headquarters at Third Mesa, and Natalie made friends at Oraibi and the other Hopi villages, her presence, like that of all whites, was the source of heated discussion among the Indian people. It was a volatile time in Tusayan, and at Oraibi Natalie was involved with individuals who were at the center of the political firestorm that would soon be known as the Oraibi Split.

Beginning in the late 1800s, there was disagreement among the Hopis of Oraibi as to the tribe's cooperation and interaction with white America. By 1900 the disagreement had become a rift that divided the village into two factions, the Friendlies and the Hostiles. The Friendlies, who included Chief Lololomai and his family, although ambivalent about interaction with the white world that sought to diminish their traditional way of life, believed that at least a *little* cooperation with the whites was necessary for peaceful survival. The Hostiles wanted nothing to do with the Two Hearts, the white-skinned people Hopi prophesy had predicted would come with guns and poison. (Smallpox had arrived in 1899 and was epidemic by 1901.) And when Burton and the BIA began to forcibly remove Hopi children to boarding schools, even Chief Lololomai began to question his friendly attitude toward the whites.

If Natalie knew how fractured and volatile the native community on and below Third Mesa was in 1903, she did not let it stop her recruitment of prospective collaborators. And in spite of her membership in the white race, the people of Hopiland opened their homes and shared their music and stories.

3

CAPTURING THE WIND

Single women making their way to individual destinies—who
in the home circle understands them? If they try to share
what they have found in their further reach, who wants it?

—*Elizabeth Shepley Sergeant*

BY THE FIRST OF JUNE, news reached Natalie in Oraibi that a close
friend of the family had died in New York. George was working at
a cattle ranch when he received the same news, and he traveled to
Third Mesa, packed up Natalie and her gear, and went with her to
Winslow, where they caught the Santa Fe Railway's eastbound train.

Natalie had been summoned home by Mimsey and Bogey to
sing at the memorial service of the family's deceased friend. Natalie
returned, the dutiful daughter, but it was immediately obvious to the
family that nine months in the West had changed her. She was not the
professionally ambivalent, emotionally fragile woman who had left
Washington Place last fall on the arm of her older brother. Months
spent in primitive quarters in frontier towns, in austere rooms at
government agencies, and in cowboy camps and outposts had transformed and matured Natalie.

At the memorial service, a suntanned, buoyant Natalie surprised
her family and friends by sharing several of the songs she had learned
from the Hopis. She spoke briefly about the people and cultures "so
rapidly vanishing" in the American West, and how she believed it was
important to record and preserve Indian music. That the Indians of
America had music was a revolutionary concept to most New Yorkers,

even among the Curtises' progressive circle of friends. "Cultured people in the east, except the few who were actively interested in the work of Indian welfare . . . knew little or nothing of the Indian," Natalie's younger brother, Bridgham, wrote. "To them he probably appeared as the romantic painted 'savage' of Cooper's tradition, or as the taciturn and treacherous enemy of the border warfare days, or as the debauched and grotesque outcast of the frontier town; and to them I think Natalie's relation of what she had seen and heard was a revelation."[1]

Natalie didn't so much settle into life on Washington Place as she unsettled the life of the Curtis family with her tenacious pursuit of a new mission. On arrival in the city, Natalie drafted her first article about the Southwest and handed it to one of Uncle George's colleagues, who published the piece in *Harper's Weekly*. Boldly titled "An American-Indian Composer," it was to be the first of scores of magazine articles Natalie would write about the people, music, and landscape of the American Southwest in the next two decades.

Bogey and Mimsey knew from experience with Natalie's previous self-appointed tasks that her new calling would likely not be a casual hobby, but a rigorous immersion. For Natalie to undertake her new mission, she had to overcome two substantial obstacles: she needed funding to cover the cost of expeditions into Indian Country, and she needed to find a way around the federal law that essentially undermined her ability to find and work with native collaborators during her expeditions.

Within a few weeks of returning to New York, Natalie contacted the one person who could quickly and absolutely grant her safe passage through Indian Country: President Theodore Roosevelt. By mid-July she had secured a personal audience with the president at the Roosevelt's summer home, Sagamore Hill on Oyster Bay, across Long Island from Natalie's family home in Far Rockaway. She was able to gain access to the president so easily and quickly because of Roosevelt's long association with Uncle George Curtis. George William Curtis was considered a founding member of the Republican Party, and he was also among those who, in league with Roosevelt and Henry Cabot Lodge, famously revolted against the "old-line" Republican Party at the stormy party convention in 1884 and created the Independent Republicans, aka the "Mugwumps."

George Curtis did not live to see his friend become governor of New York or president of the United States. But in his niece, Roosevelt surely saw much of his friend's charisma, creative passion, and intelligence. Roosevelt likely recognized a bit of himself as well in the diminutive person of Natalie Curtis, a woman who shared his own "tremendous capacity for work and a driving need to be productive."[2]

In Roosevelt's Sagamore Hill study, Natalie candidly outlined what she believed were the numerous injustices perpetrated by the federal government on the land and culture of the Indians of the American West. Natalie pitched her cause with unflinching conviction. The president knew that every word she uttered, every opinion she offered, was the truth as she understood it. Her Uncle George had done precisely the same in lectures and speeches and in his political columns in *Harper's*.

Natalie would look back at her meeting with the president of the United States when she "was but little more than a girl" and recall Roosevelt's capacity to consider a "radically opposite view-point." Roosevelt patiently listened to Natalie's comprehensive litany about "the benighted policies of the Indian Bureau in Washington" and its "ruthless campaign of destruction of all things pertaining to the indigenous culture of the red race." Of course, he was well versed in these complaints. Even as Natalie sat in his study at Sagamore Hill, Roosevelt's college pal Charles Lummis was publishing inflammatory articles about Superintendent Burton and about Roosevelt's Bureau of Indian Affairs in *Out West* magazine. It was a prickly subject, but something about Natalie Curtis's plea and her "straight-from-the-shoulder truthfulness"—and the exotic, strangely beautiful songs she carried from the faraway desert village of Oraibi—captured Roosevelt's imagination and his admiration.[3]

Natalie had impeccable credentials. She was a classically trained musician, the daughter of a respected New York doctor, and the niece of a friend and political ally. But perhaps of more importance to the president in 1903, Natalie Curtis was an astute eyewitness of current events in Indian Country. She had traveled into Native America and undertaken what she believed was important work in a difficult, even hostile environment. She had also managed to make friends with the elusive Hopis. And she meant to return.

"Roosevelt respected anyone, regardless of color or class, who could produce under pressure." When the twenty-eight-year-old Natalie Curtis came to his summer home to talk about Indian policy, Roosevelt recognized a person of perspicacity committed to a serious mission.[4]

Natalie told the president she planned to continue with her recording of Indian music. In defense of her law-breaking task, she insisted that any attempt to educate the native people by the white people ought to be framed and informed by a thorough study of Indian culture. "They can teach us as well as we them," she lectured the president.

Roosevelt's recognition of the value of native culture was, in Natalie's words, instantaneous:

> "I am thoroughly in sympathy with the idea of preserving and, if possible, of developing the art, the music, the poetry of the Indian," [Roosevelt] said, with that emphasis of conviction that made his decision like powerful strokes of a forging hammer beating out results. "It fits in with my policies of conservation, and I consider this question—the conservation of Indian art in our education of Indians—important enough to include in my next Message to Congress."

Before Natalie departed Sagamore Hill, Roosevelt assured her that although he did not know anything about Indian song-poems or native poetry, her effort to "keep this song literature alive" had his "immediate and hearty support."[5]

Remarkably, within hours of Natalie's departure from the Roosevelt home, the president penned and sent off several official letters, including one addressed to federal Indian agents for Natalie to carry into Indian Country. "I desire that every opportunity be given Miss Natalie Curtis to travel through all Indian reservations, and to fully investigate and report on, to me or any official under me, all matters pertaining to the wellbeing, the education, the artistic development and industries of the Indians."[6]

That same day, July 22, 1903, Roosevelt sent a letter to Ethan Allen Hitchcock instructing his secretary of the interior to consider Natalie's proposals regarding the preservation of Indian art and music. "Her desire is to see the exceptionally interesting artistic side of the life of these Indians preserved. . . . She feels—and I think she is entirely right—that the one side in which American life is weak is the artistic, and that we ought not to throw away anything which will give us a chance to develop artistically."[7]

Hitchcock and his staff, one of whom described Natalie Curtis as "an intense little person," were most unhappy about the president's instructions. Hitchcock was already disgruntled with Roosevelt's willingness to take advice and counsel from ordinary folks. Now the president was considering bringing to Congress proposals made by a person—and a woman!—Hitchcock considered to be nothing more than a do-gooder.[8]

Copies of Roosevelt's letters dispatched on her behalf reached Natalie at Wave Crest several days later. She wrote Roosevelt a thank-you note on July 29. "Though you say that your power is not unlimited, the incisive force, clarity of purpose and promptness of action with which you have met each issue in your career make us feel that any movement receives an enormous impetus by your championship."

Natalie took the opportunity to once more urge Roosevelt to make the finding of solutions to the Indian question a primary focus of his administration. She added that she would be investigating the Indian schools in the East as well as those in the American West. "I am full of plans," she wrote to Roosevelt, "but shall not take your time further."[9]

But Natalie would take a good deal more of Roosevelt's time that summer, and in many summers to come.

In spite of high-level naysayers and politically powerful disapprovers, Natalie's self-proclaimed mission had overcome a major obstacle—the federal government. Her passion was morphing into a formal vocation, but her vision still needed to secure sponsorship. Bogey and Mimsey Curtis were moderately wealthy, but they could not, or would not, finance the comprehensive project now evolving in Natalie's mind: the recording of not just the music of the Hopis and the Navajos, but of every Indian tribe in the United States.

Natalie spent the summer and fall in New York, transcribing the songs she had secretly recorded in Hopiland. She also took her presidentially sanctioned plan for a research trip to gather more Indian music and ceremonial material to wealthy family friends and colleagues from whom she hoped to garner financial support. Natalie explained to potential patrons that her mission was to preserve Indian music as close to the original form, sound, and translation as possible. Natalie's classical training and her finely tuned ear, combined with her socially gregarious and charismatic nature, made her well qualified for the task.

Although Natalie accepted the prevalent attitude of white America that the Native American world was in its twilight years, their traditions and culture all destined for extinction in the tidal wave that was the modern, industrial world, Natalie believed in the Indian world's inherent value. She also believed that white Americans, beginning with herself, had much to learn from Indian America.

LATER THAT SUMMER, on one of those "stifling days in late August when all New York panted and closed blinds," Natalie left Wave Crest and the cooling breezes found along the Long Island shoreline and went into the city to visit Charlotte Osgood Mason. Natalie and her mother had met Mason, the friendly but overbearing wife of a wealthy New York physician, in the 1890s at the meetings and lectures given by the Theosophists. Mason was a generous philanthropist and likely at the top of Natalie's list of possible benefactors for her Indian music project. When Mason asked Natalie to come to her Park Avenue apartment "on a mysterious errand," Natalie obliged.

It was only after Natalie reached her apartment that the reason for Mason's summons was revealed. "We looked from the window at a crowd that had assembled without. Standing before the front door, in the midst of the crowd, we saw an old friend—Frank Mead—fresh from the West, with the breath of the Arizona desert still upon him. Behind him in the crowd was a darker face looking out above an enormous black-and-white Apache basket urn."[10]

Frank Mead, a Philadelphia architect Natalie had met with George in Arizona, and his basket-toting friend, Yavapai (known as Mojave-Apache at that time) chief Pelia, were to be Mason's guests. Pelia was wide-eyed and awed, and moved about the luxurious apartment "as if in a dream." Once everyone settled down—Pelia was reluctant to release the basket and held it in both hands for most of Natalie's visit—Mead informed Natalie of what Mason already knew: that he and Pelia had come east so that the Yavapai chief might ask President

Roosevelt to grant the Yavapais their own reservation at an old Arizona military post, Camp McDowell. White settlers had encroached on the Yavapai's lands in the Verde Valley, and numerous requests over several years to officials in Washington for resolution of this problem had fallen on deaf ears. The Yavapai were homeless, hungry, and desperate.

It was obvious why Mason had beckoned Natalie into the city on such a humid, hot August day. Mason had surely heard all about Natalie's informal and very successful meeting with Roosevelt at Sagamore Hill, and she wanted Natalie's help in obtaining a meeting for Mead and Chief Pelia.

Had the request been for someone other than Frank Mead, and for a cause other than Indian rights, she might have been annoyed with Mason. Mead, a New Jersey native, had traveled and lived in North Africa and the Middle East, where he was influenced by architecture that reflected cultural style and indigenous design and also blended with the landscape. In 1902 he returned to the United States, gave up his position at an architecture firm in Philadelphia, and headed into the American Southwest. The dress, traditions, and architecture of Native America resonated with the iconoclastic Mead, and when Natalie met him in Arizona, he had become involved with the Indian rights movement.

Several months before the August meeting in Mason's apartment, Natalie had penned a letter that introduced her new friend Frank Mead to her new friend Charles Lummis. Mead wanted to meet Lummis and others in Southern California who shared his architectural passion for the aesthetic that would soon emerge into the Arts and Crafts movement. Mead also wanted to connect with Lummis's circle of Indian rights advocates. Natalie told Lummis that the thirty-eight-year-old Mead shared his artistic and idealistic concerns, and that he was a rare person who exemplified Polonius's dictum "to thine own self be true."[11]

Natalie agreed to help Mead and Chief Pelia meet the president, and the evening after she returned to Long Island, she sent a note to Roosevelt about Pelia. The next morning, Natalie had a response: the president would see Mead and the chief within the week.

Natalie accompanied Mead and a "well soaped and combed" Pelia and his oversized Yavapai basket to the president's home on Oyster

Bay. Pelia presented Roosevelt with the basket, a gift from his people, and then pleaded for a reservation for his homeless tribe. Mead followed Pelia's plea with a practical plan for obtaining the land the Yavapai wanted to live upon and the establishment of a reservation at Fort McDowell, northeast of Phoenix.

After listening to Mead and Pelia's impassioned pitch for a reservation for the Yavapai, Roosevelt agreed without "five minutes' hesitation" to throw his support behind their proposal. The president must have been able to look past Mead's social eccentricities, because he soon appointed Mead special agent in charge of securing the Yavapai's lands and settling disputes with the white squatters.[12]

After Mead and Pelia's late-August visit, Natalie wrote the president a lengthy letter outlining why Mead ought to be considered for the job as Roosevelt's supervisor of all pueblo Indians and allowed to set up a "model agency" in Arizona where Indian arts would be fostered. Roosevelt did not adopt nor implement all of Natalie's ideas, but he did appoint Mead his "Special Supervisor" to oversee the BIA agents and superintendents in four states and two territories in the Southwest.[13]

Reflecting on Roosevelt's ability to act decisively and quickly on matters he believed warranted immediate relief, Natalie wondered if the "red tape" that so frequently tied the hands of decision-makers in Washington was actually a regional affliction: "It is a fact that life in the West does produce 'real men.' Theodore Roosevelt owed his power of action and his driving force to the stimulus of those early days on a cattle ranch. . . . If Washington had been perched within the neighborhood of Pike's Peak instead of having been sunk in a sluggish, swampish flat, who knows but that red tape might unwind as steadily and swiftly as a stock ticker?"[14]

Shortly after Mead and Pelia's meeting with the president, Charlotte Mason offered her patronage to Natalie's Indian music project. Natalie did not leave for the Southwest immediately, but remained on the East Coast, lecturing about Indian music and the urgent need to record and preserve it. Her plea attracted another important sponsor and advocate: the New York–based businessman and philanthropist George Foster Peabody.

George Foster Peabody was a progressive thinker, social reformer, and a self-made millionaire; he is remembered by the prestigious

Peabody Awards in broadcasting, which are named for him. Peabody was a partner in the Brooklyn-based Spencer Trask and Company that during the 1880s and '90s went into business in several very lucrative fields, including electrical infrastructure and the financing and construction of railroads. Peabody was an active member of the Episcopal Church, which advocated the education of minorities, especially in the South. Beginning in the 1880s, Peabody served as a trustee and board member of several schools and colleges, including the Hampton Institute in Hampton, Virginia, a school that offered African and Native American students training in a wide variety of trades and creative skills.

Peabody may have learned of Natalie's Indian project in conversations with his colleague Charlotte Mason (who also sat on the Hampton Institute's board of trustees), or Natalie may have taken the initiative herself and told Peabody she was raising money to collect and preserve Indian music. Peabody liked the project and by the autumn of 1903 gave Natalie one thousand dollars for her next expedition into Indian Country.

With money in her pocket, Roosevelt's letter of safe passage in her hand, and brother George again by her side, Natalie returned to Hopiland in the fall. No longer afraid of Burton and his BIA police, Natalie spoke openly about her mission, and the federal agents who had made her work nearly impossible six months before now "strewed my path with courtesies and called on me before breakfast with offers of help."[15]

Natalie headed out on horseback with "only a pencil and notebook, a helpful brother, and at times some young Indian who had been to school and learned English" to find the eldest Hopi chiefs and singers. The bulky Edison and its wax cylinders were left in her room below Third Mesa. Handwritten notations were the only practical recording method in the desert outback. To accurately record an Indian song or chant on paper was a task of almost unimaginable difficulty, even for a professional musician. George was awed by his sister's gift. "Natalie's ear for music was so marvelous that she could set down, without the help of a phonograph, the strange melodies and rhythms that are so different from the white man's music; though to be sure the Indian singer might have to repeat several times before [Natalie] knew that she had the song correctly."[16]

Chief Lololomai was still living with his sister, Ponianomsi, and a nephew in their home in Oraibi. Natalie asked the chief if he would let her record his songs so that they would not be lost to future generations. "Your song is heard, then dies like the wind that sweeps the cornfields and is gone, none knows whither," Natalie told Lololomai. But if his songs were written down, his people "even to the children of their children, could know your song as if yourself were singing."

Lololomai was in his eighties, and he agreed with Natalie's assessment that his songs were destined to be lost "like a wind-blown trail." But he worried that there would be repercussions if they proceeded with the recording. Natalie shared her letter from the Great Chief in Washington, and the elder Hopi agreed to work with her.[17]

With a translator beside her, her pencil and notebook, and a wide hat to shade her face from the bright October sun, Natalie sat with the chief on his Oraibi rooftop and recorded a thank-you song sung after the village corn harvest. It was a ponderously slow chore, recording on paper Hopi words, tone, notes, and rhythm.

"In rhythmic monotone the old man crooned beside me," Natalie later wrote of that sky-touching session on top of Third Mesa. "Long and diligently I worked at the recording, with the glare of the hot sun on my paper. It was no light task to fix the chant in musical notation." Even Lololomai commented on Natalie's laborious task to make "those black marks on the paper." Natalie told the chief, "Your song is a wild blackbird to me, and it may be that the sun will move far along the sky before I have captured it."

After several hours on the rooftop, Natalie was satisfied with her transcriptions. Lololomai knelt in prayer as dusk enveloped the ancient pueblo.

> The shadows on the village street grew long. The sun was sinking. Here and there a lone Hopi was returning from below with laden burro. Soon the trail would be dotted with home-coming Indians. We sat long in silence, Lololomai, the blind boy, and I. I watched the glow enfold the desert with the mystery of dying day. . . .
>
> Silent still, the blind boy and I took our downward way upon the rocky trail. To my companion, in his night, the deepening shadow bore no import, but a twilight sadness lay upon

my spirit. I thought of the garnered Hopi corn. Will there be many more plantings of poetry and harvesting of song? Darkness closed in. But off beyond in silver glory rose the moon.[18]

Throughout the fall of 1903, Natalie recorded dozens of native singers. Her task was challenging because of the remoteness and inaccessibility of the Hopi villages, the complexity of their language, and the tonal variations in their music. She likened capturing Hopi music on paper to capturing the wind as it swept down the sides of a rock mesa. "To seize on paper the spirit of Hopi music is a task as impossible as to put on canvas the shimmer and glare of the desert. Hopi music is born of its environment. . . . There, in that wide land, under the blaze of the Arizona sun, amid the shifting color of the tinted sands and the purple-blue of the sharp-shadowed rocks must the songs be heard to be heard truly."[19]

With George, Natalie traversed Indian Country on horseback, in a wagon, and where necessary, on foot. To reach a singer in a sheep camp or in another village meant traveling across the enormous, empty, high desert of the Colorado Plateau, navigating unmarked routes that crossed ledges and canyons, streambeds, and rock shelves and circled buttes and mountains. Their path was always directed by water and the location of a spring or water cache known by the native guides.

In 1903 and 1904, and during her subsequent journey through the Southwest in 1905, nearly sixty Hopi songs were recorded in Natalie's notebook and on the phonograph. Letters home enabled the Curtis family back east to follow Natalie and George's progress across Indian Country.

"It was a long and exhausting work, physically and mentally," Bridgham wrote of his sister's recording expeditions. "As a rule her party lived in the guest rooms at the Indian Government schools, but frequently the quarters were primitive. There were long rides and drives over rough country, irregular meals—often none at all. Her health, frail at best, was seriously taxed by the hardships. . . . At times it seemed almost impossible to finish the task, but her courage and resolution never faltered."[20]

The task was daunting and the conditions difficult. Even so, Natalie was always reluctant to leave the "spiritual beauty" and the "song-poets" of the Hopi, especially Third Mesa and her friends at Oraibi. "It was sunset when for the last time I climbed the steep trail to the village of Oraibi," she wrote the evening before her departure for Williams, Arizona, and the train for home. "The level desert seemed a lilac sea, and the outlines of the craggy table-lands were sharp against the flaming sky. Many weeks had passed since I had left the railroad to take the long two-days' drive across the 'Painted Desert' to the Hopi villages. . . . To-morrow I must leave the desert and its freedom for my distant Eastern home."[21]

Natalie's sense of home was shifting with each visit to the Southwest. On one of her early visits, the Hopi gave her a name that pleased her immensely: Tawimana, "Woman Who Sings like a Mockingbird" or Song Maid. Natalie signed her Hopi name alongside her American name on Christmas cards and personal correspondence the rest of her life.

Natalie and George departed Hopiland by way of the village of Hano on First Mesa, where they met the celebrated potter Nampayo and her family. From First Mesa they headed their wagon south through the vast country of the Hopis' historic enemy, the nomadic Navajos. Natalie found the Navajos to be "industrious, independent, and fearless" with "the strength of the warrior and the simplicity of the shepherd . . . the Navajo is the true son of the silence, the awe, the grandeur of the desert." Natalie made friends among the Navajos and over the next two years would record more than ten of their ceremonial chants and songs.[22]

After her return to New York, the president summoned Natalie to "come at once" to a luncheon at the White House. It was a simple affair by Washington standards, but the just-off-the-desert Natalie, still adjusting to the noise and pace of modern life, was intimidated by the event and the guests seated around Roosevelt's table:

> I remember the entire simplicity of that luncheon—lamp chops, and for dessert baked apples—although the party was twelve or fourteen in number. The directness with which Roosevelt introduced the subject of the luncheon—the American Indian—was most embarrassing to me, who felt myself nothing but a little "snip" in the presence of gray-haired Senators and Cabinet members; for as we found our places at the table he turned his

glasses full upon me and exclaimed, with terrifying emphasis, "Miss Curtis will now sing for us an Indian grace."[23]

Natalie obliged her host and sang an Indian prayer for the senators and cabinet members, all men, seated at the long table. As the luncheon progressed, it became apparent to Natalie that Roosevelt had assembled this group specifically "to talk about Indians." He told the guests "in detail" about Natalie's translations of "Indian song-poems" and her recordings of Indian music that she had brought to his attention the year before at Sagamore Hill.

After lunch, Roosevelt asked Natalie to perform songs learned during her recent visit to Indian Country. The president led everyone into "the big ballroom, where stood the grand piano, which was quite superfluous for a rendition of Indian songs." Although unprepared, Natalie again obliged the president and performed several musical poems of the desert; she also gave an impromptu talk about her "harvestings of Indian songs" to the captive audience from Capitol Hill.

Natalie was beholden to Roosevelt, but her response to the president was more than gratitude. Natalie considered Roosevelt one of the great heroes of her time. She may, too, have seen a bit of herself in the president, if she allowed such a comparison. "Roosevelt never lost one moment's time in the accomplishment of a purpose," she wrote, " . . . he never preambled or beat about the bush; he snapped at a subject with sharp surety, and the near-sighted eyes behind the thick glasses seemed always intently focused."

Roosevelt told Natalie, "I can never afford to be in arrears with anything that I have to do; I must always be abreast or ahead of my tasks." Natalie could not have said it better.[24]

4

THE INDIANS' BOOK

There is another sort of beauty playing always about the
Pueblo country, beauty of cloud and rain and split sunlight.
. . . Everywhere peace, impenetrable timelessness of peace, as
though the pueblo and all it contains were shut in a glassy fourth
dimension, near and at the same time inaccessibly remote.

—*Mary Austin*

NATALIE SPENT THE SUMMER ON the East Coast, working on her
recordings and transcriptions at the relentless pace her family was
accustomed to, if not always comfortable with. She went to Maine
and recorded love, war, medicine, and dance songs, as well as the
hunting and creation stories of the surviving tribes of the once-great
Wabanaki nation of the Penobscots, Passamaquoddies, Micmacs, and
Maliseets. She also secured more funds, including a thousand dollar
gift from George Foster Peabody that would enable her to expand
the scope of her project to include the music of virtually every Indian
tribe in the continental United States.

In late fall, Natalie and George donned their travel clothes, packed
their khakis, boots, and broad-brimmed hats into their expedition
bags, and boarded a train for the Dakotas. It was November, and
the lovely, cool days of fall had turned into the cold, wet days of
the coming winter. It was not an ideal time of year to be traveling
into the rural Midwest, but Natalie's mission had evolved into the
writing of a major book about Indian music, and her task would not
be deterred by bad weather.

Before they headed for the Dakotas, Natalie and George made a short stopover in St. Louis to see the Louisiana Purchase Exposition celebrating Jefferson's 1804 land deal with the French and the opening of the Trans-Mississippi West. Fairgoers saw the first electric ovens and range tops, and could stand alongside the first automobiles. The Lincoln Museum, built around the log cabin where Abraham Lincoln was born, and Festival Hall, with its gold-leafed dome larger than the one on top of St. Peter's Basilica in Rome, were the exposition's showstoppers.

While George took voluminous notes, Natalie interviewed and collected songs, stories, and folklore from individuals from the Navajo, Crow, Pawnee, and Chiricahua Apache tribes who were participants in the fair's Indian exhibits.[1]

In particular, Natalie wanted to meet Chief Geronimo of the Apaches, who was featured in William Cody's, aka Buffalo Bill's, Wild West Show on The Pike (the fair's entertainment boulevard). Natalie and George found "the most famous of Apache war-leaders" making and selling bows and arrows in the Indian Department. Except for newspaper articles, very little had been written about Geronimo. The white world knew about the chief and the Chiricahua Apache people only through the dramatic and often inaccurate stories and legend-worthy accounts given by U.S. military personnel or BIA officials. Geronimo did, however, have a relationship with Roosevelt (the Apache chief would be among the luminaries to ride in the president's 1905 inaugural parade), and Roosevelt may have suggested Natalie seek out the elderly chief at the fair.

Natalie and Geronimo had no common language, but with a translator they conversed at length in the Southwest Building. Between seventy and eighty years of age, the chief, whose eyes flickered with the "tiger-flash" of a warrior, agreed to let Natalie record on paper several of his songs. The difficulties of recording Geronimo in the exposition hall were nearly as great as recording Chief Lololomai on the rooftop in Hopiland. But Natalie persevered and, with an interpreter, recorded the words and music of at least two of Geronimo's songs, one of which was "so old that none knows who made it."[2]

With notebooks bulging with new material and a lengthening list of collaborators, Natalie and George left St. Louis on November 6 on the 1 p.m. train for Chicago. Two days later, they disembarked from the warmth and comfort of the Pullman car in Sioux City, Iowa, where they did not remain even one night. They transferred their gear directly into a wagon and headed through a cold, drizzling rain to austere quarters at the Winnebago Indian agency in Nebraska.

In the next few days the rain turned to snow on the Winnebago Reservation. After several days of recording sessions with local musicians, Natalie and George left the Winnebago school and headed their horse and wagon across the frozen winter landscape to the Sioux agency headquarters at Pine Ridge and Rosebud, South Dakota. Natalie set up her workshop in a hotel and, with the safe passage granted by Roosevelt's letter, went with George in search of Sioux musicians and storytellers in town and out on the reservation.

For nearly eight continuous weeks Natalie's workshop was set up and taken down in numerous hotel rooms and government headquarters, hauled about on foot and on horseback, and packed into wagons and moved by train cars across Nebraska, the Dakotas, Wisconsin, and Oklahoma. Natalie and George witnessed ceremonies and dances rarely seen by non-Indians: the hand games and the mescal rites of the Arapahos and Cheyennes, the Antelope Ceremony and wind songs of the Kiowas, and the clandestine Spirit-Dance of the Ghost Dance religion (considered to have been "the trouble" that caused U.S. troops to massacre more than three hundred Sioux men, women, and children at Wounded Knee), still performed by the Dakotas and Pawnees.

The Curtises boarded a train for Oklahoma City. After meeting an Indian policeman, Hiamovi, a half-Sioux, half-Cheyenne who was a high chief of both the Dakotas and Cheyennes, they altered their itinerary and spent the next month among his people in Oklahoma. During the winter on the Great Plains, Natalie recorded over forty-five collaborators from six tribes, each of them named and their contributions meticulously catalogued in her notebooks.

Just before Christmas, Natalie and George departed the frigid country of the Plains Indians and headed into the country of the Puebloans, the bright, high-altitude desert landscape of New Mexico and Arizona. They spent the holidays with Charlotte Mason near Phoenix, where Frank Mead was living among the Yavapai on their new reservation at Fort McDowell.

"It was Christmas Day when Mrs. Mason and I drove in a canvas-topped cart through the Arizona desert to Camp McDowell," Natalie wrote. "Pelia [the basket-carrying chief Natalie had met in New York City fourteen months before] and his wife had driven in to the railway at Phoenix to meet us. Mr. Mead was personally conducting us to the house of the missionary agent on the reservation, and our visit to the Indians had the warmth of a home-coming."

On Christmas Day, Pelia and his tribe gathered for a night dance. Natalie, George, Mason, and Mead were the honored guests: "A huge bonfire burned on the open desert; its flames seemed to lick the deep blue-purple of the sky," Natalie wrote of that Christmas night. "Brilliant moonlight—such moonlight as Easterners have never seen—touched cactus and mesquite and lit the horizon line of hills."[3]

The New Year of 1905 found Natalie and George at the Indian school in Phoenix, where Natalie recorded students from southwestern tribes. From Phoenix, they traveled east by wagon to New Mexico, where for the next two months Natalie and George lived among the people of Zuni, Acoma, and Laguna Pueblos. By March, Natalie was out of money, and the glorious, exhausting four-month expedition through the Indian Country of the Midwest and Southwest came to an end.

Natalie returned to New York City, but she did not move back into the Washington Place home of her parents. The Curtis family also maintained a residence at 33 West 69th Street, and it was into this apartment, where her brother George and possibly Bridgham resided, that Natalie unpacked her voluminous notebooks and her weather-worn garments from her four-month expedition.

Her research and collection of Indian music were more or less completed, and Natalie's task shifted to her next goal: the assembling and editing of a book about Native American song, dance, ceremonies, and stories.

Within a month of her return to the East Coast, Natalie was writing and speaking about her experiences. In a small pamphlet published by G. Schirmer, she reproduced three of the corn-grinding songs recorded just a few months earlier at Laguna Pueblo. As she prepared the material for her book, Natalie penned articles for popular audiences about what she had seen and learned. Although she hoped her research about Indian music would earn the respect of her peers, her primary audience was not academia. Natalie wanted to preserve Indian music, but she also wanted to educate average

Americans about the federal assimilationist policies that she believed would bring extinction to Native American culture. She wrote articles for the broadly based, predominantly Anglo-American audience that regularly read *Harper's, Outlook, Craftsman*, and *Southern Workman* magazines, and newspapers like the *New York Times* and *New York Evening Post*.

By conventional turn-of-the-century standards, Natalie Curtis was a confirmed spinster when she turned thirty in April 1905. How she thought about herself as a single woman on her thirtieth birthday can only be guessed at. She had lived most of the last two years far from home in the hinterlands of the American West where an unmarried woman was able to move about and work relatively free of public scrutiny or societal disapproval. If Natalie had a romantic interest or liaison during her late twenties, in New York or out west, neither she nor her family mentioned it in their letters and diaries.

The West was a frontier for both the body and soul of those Anglo-Americans, men and women, who ventured into its vast, uncivilized landscape. In contrast, the upper-class world of New York City was still a stronghold of proper Victorian society, and a single woman like Natalie, who insisted on pursuing a vocation, even an artistic one, was treading a thin line between appropriate and inappropriate behavior.

In May 1905 Charlotte Mason came to Natalie's social and creative rescue when she offered her the use of her apartment in Washington, DC. Natalie needed a place where she could work on her Indian music book without interruption from friends and family, and she accepted Mason's offer and moved alone to Washington in late spring.

But there were numerous distractions in Washington. Natalie socialized with officials from Roosevelt's Indian affairs department and accepted invitations to society functions where she could promote Indian policy reform. Although there was a continent between them, Charles Lummis remained in frequent contact with Natalie. In 1905 he was especially insistent that she become an active member of the Southwest Society of the Archaeological Institute of America. Considering that Natalie lacked affiliation with the academic community, and that her credentials for her work among the Indians consisted of her passionate belief that native music and stories needed to be preserved, the invitation to join Lummis's circle of scientists, anthropologists, and ethnologists was precisely the sort of endorsement Natalie wanted for her work. But she declined the AIA position, telling Lummis that "every moment of my time is so absolutely taken up."[4]

But Lummis *really* wanted Natalie on the membership roster and told her so in several more letters. By 1905 Lummis had fallen from favor with Roosevelt, and he knew that her ability to get the ear of "the most powerful American" would be a valuable asset for both the AIA's and his own agendas. Natalie was likely privy to the disparaging comments and opinions of Lummis circulating drawing rooms on both the East and West Coasts. There was gossip about Lummis's indiscretions with women (he reportedly kept a log of his sexual exploits), and one California-based editor warned Roosevelt that "Lummis is awful sharp, but a consummate crank of the first water and will get you or anybody else in trouble."[5]

Never one to be swayed by gossip or to choose her friends for their social standing or political influence, Natalie was able to remain friends with Lummis and to also stay out of the trouble around him for decades. But it was not an easy friendship. Lummis continued his campaign to enlist Natalie into the AIA until December 1905, when he learned that she had joined the New York branch. Lummis wrote Natalie that he would prefer she be affiliated with the AIA's southwest chapter but added, "So long as you are in the Institute I suppose we must not quarrel."[6]

Membership in the AIA did bring validation and recognition to Natalie and her work among the Indians. The Archaeological Institute of America was twenty-five years old and had backed field expeditions and surveys by America's most eminent anthropologists and ethnologists, including Lummis's friend the Swiss anthropologist Adolph Bandelier. The same year that Natalie joined the AIA, the New Mexico–based anthropologist and AIA member Edgar Lee Hewett was in Washington lobbying for the passage of the federal Antiquities Act. Natalie may have met Hewett in Washington in 1905. If not, she would meet him in the near future. Hewett was touring the country on behalf of the AIA, encouraging cities to open local chapters and to financially and politically support the relatively new field of American anthropology.

The AIA was very good company for Natalie to keep and offered her introductions to the southwestern anthropology and ethnology community and to prominent leaders of the Indian policy reform movement. But Natalie could not stop work on her book to become a political activist. Throughout 1905, in spite of accelerated national activity around Indian rights and a burgeoning public interest in southwestern anthropology and archaeology, Natalie kept her head in her transcriptions and field notes and her hands on her typewriter.

Her book, entitled *The Indians' Book*, was completed by early 1906 and soon after accepted for publication by Harper Brothers. Natalie sent a copy of the manuscript to Roosevelt and asked him for an endorsement. Roosevelt's handwritten letter was placed at the front of *The Indians' Book*. "These songs cast a wholly new light on the depth and dignity of Indian thought, the simple beauty and strange charm—the charm of a vanished elder world—of Indian poetry."[7]

Roosevelt's words echoed the dominant sentiment among Anglo-Americans that Native America was in its last years, and that the "childlike" red race would soon vanish. This limited and racist view of Indian America would be slowly replaced by the modern understanding of the intrinsic worth and enduring vitality of Native America. Although *The Indians' Book* reflected the prevalent Euro-centric view of Indian America, it was a major accomplishment and successfully gave the American public the first comprehensive collection of native songs, stories, and ceremonies. Natalie's summaries of each tribe also introduced the general reader to the complex and numerous indigenous cultures that had existed and thrived on American soil for hundreds of years.

The Indians' Book: An Offering by the American Indians of Indian Lore, Musical and Narrative, to Form a Record of the Songs and Legends of Their Race, recorded and edited by Natalie Curtis, was published by Harper Brothers in 1907. The first edition contained colored title pages and artwork. The book was illustrated by Hinook-Mahiwi-Kilinaka, the Winnebago artist Angel De Cora. Several years older than Natalie, De Cora had already achieved considerable attention as an artist when she agreed to illustrate *The Indians' Book*. A graduate of Smith College, De Cora was a member of the American Academy of Design by the age of thirty-one, a rare honor at that time for a woman of any age or race.[8]

Harper Brothers send out hundreds of review copies of *The Indians' Book* to scholars, editors, and politicians. By the end of 1907, Natalie's position as an authority on American Indian music was well established. Her personal and professional life would never be the same.

Aware that her audience would be reading about Indian America for the first time, Natalie assembled the material in *The Indians' Book* in an accessible and reader-friendly format. Arranged by geographical location and tribal affiliation (Eastern, Plains, Lake, Northwestern, Southwestern, and Pueblo Indians), the chapter for each of the eighteen tribes began with a historical overview and summary of the tribe's religious beliefs, symbols, language, food, family, and village customs. Natalie also included contextual narratives about landscape and environment, and vignettes of her experiences among the American Indians.

The book's transcriptions of Indian songs and musical scores were rendered in Natalie's own hand and included her notes about tempo and nuance. The words of the songs were written both in their native tongue and in English translation. With the help of one of her editors, Kurt Schindler, Natalie designed a transcription system that arranged musical phrases like lines of verse and made "the song flash before the eye like the form of a stanza in poetry."[9]

There was no previous publication on Indian music or folklore to which *The Indians' Book* could be compared. The Indians were the authors of the book, Natalie stated in the introduction, and every singer, poet, dancer, medicine man, and storyteller was acknowledged by name and tribe. Natalie was simply the recorder, her task to collect, edit, and arrange the Indians' contributions.

With the release of *The Indians' Book,* Natalie's life was dominated by public appearances and speaking engagements. The book was praised by her colleagues in the upper echelon of the professional music world, including Walter Damrosch, the conductor with whom she had been smitten as a teenager. It was a heady time in Natalie's life, an intoxicating year of personal and professional adulation and affirmation. Almost a decade had passed since her physical and psychological collapse and subsequent withdrawal from the professional stage. Finally, her peers understood exactly what the gifted Miss Curtis had been doing out west all these years.

By the New Year of 1908, Natalie's head and heart longed for the uncluttered spaces and open skies of Indian Country, and she announced her plans to return to the West. George was ready to leave New York, too, and together they packed their trunks with desert khakis and riding boots, said farewells to the family at Washington Place, and journeyed by train into the land of the sun. Natalie and George arrived in Escondido, California, on January 6 and moved into rented rooms in the town of Riverside. George wanted to find work on a local ranch or fruit farm, and the next morning, after meeting a Mr. Bailey, he left Natalie in Riverside and took a four-hour ride on the mule-drawn cart of the local mail carrier to a ranch owned by Bailey's friends the Mendenhalls.[10]

Natalie had come to Riverside specifically to talk with Tawakwap-tiwa, Chief Lololomai's nephew whom she had met at Oraibi several years before. Known around Riverside by his white name, Wilson Fredericks, Tawakwaptiwa was living at the Sherman Institute with his wife and children. Natalie wanted to give Tawakwaptiwa a copy of *The Indians' Book*, in which he was a named and much-honored contributor. She also wanted to find out how her Hopi friend and his family were surviving forced relocation at the government Indian school in Riverside.[11]

Tawakwaptiwa and forty of his fellow villagers from Third Mesa had been exiled from Hopiland in 1906 by Roosevelt's commissioner of Indian affairs, Francis Leupp. The event that precipitated this exile was among the most significant altercations in Hopi history. Following Chief Lololomai's death in 1906, Tawakwaptiwa had become chief and leader of Third Mesa, the largest and most powerful of the Hopi communities. Tawakwaptiwa, like his uncle Chief Lololomai, was a Friendly and believed that compromise with Washington could be maintained without the Hopi people losing their cultural integrity. And like his uncle, Tawakwaptiwa hoped to avoid confrontation between the Friendlies and the Hostiles on Third Mesa, since he believed a split would bring the disintegration of historic Oraibi.

In the autumn of 1906, shortly after Lololomai's death, the decades-old conflict between the Friendlies and the Hostiles erupted into confrontation when the Hostiles declared that coexistence with the Friendlies was no longer possible on Third Mesa. The Hostiles, led by Youkeoma, wanted only one faction to live at Oraibi.

Figure 4. Natalie and Tawakwaptiwa in Riverside, California, 1907.

The Hopi, true to their People of Peace reputation, commenced the settlement of their conflict not with violence and weapons (although members of both groups were carrying knives, clubs, and even bows and arrows) but with an athletic contest. Late in the day on September 8, the Friendlies and the Hostiles gathered on a level stretch of hard ground northwest of the village of Oraibi. A line was drawn in the sand from east to west. Youkeoma took a position on the Oraibi side of the line and challenged Tawakwaptiwa's men to force him back over the line and away from the village. If the Friendlies succeeded, Youkeoma and his followers would leave Oraibi.

Each faction lined up behind its strongest man, a signal was given, and the great push began. After a long, hard war between the two lines of men, Youkeoma acknowledged defeat. The Hostiles packed up their families and belongings, and 298 villagers departed Oraibi. Youkeoma moved his people seven miles to the east, where they settled and built the village of Hotevilla (or Hotevila).[12]

Although the Hopi had peaceably settled their civil war, Youkeoma was arrested by federal agents and imprisoned at Fort Wingate near Gallup. In the weeks before what historians would call the Oraibi Split, Tawakwaptiwa, nervous about violence in the village, had sought the counsel of government officials, including Commissioner Leupp. Even so, after the Hostiles had departed Third Mesa, Leupp deemed Tawakwaptiwa a threat to government control of the Hopis and temporarily stripped him of his chieftainship. To avert any additional challenges to federal policies, Leupp ordered that Tawakwaptiwa and forty of his followers be sent to the Sherman Institute for four years. Leupp then authorized federal troops, augmented by armed Navajo policemen, to seize eighty-two children from Oraibi and take them to the boarding school at Keam's Canyon.

The reaction by Leupp to the Oraibi Split seemed harsh, heavy-handed, and insensitive to people like Natalie who hoped the White House was actively reforming federal Indian policies. If Natalie broached the subject or registered a complaint about events at Third Mesa with Roosevelt, it was not recorded. Roosevelt trusted Leupp, but also understood that his commissioner "though an exceedingly honest and fearless man . . . is very prejudiced when he makes up his mind."[13]

When Natalie met with Tawakwaptiwa at the Sherman Indian School in January 1908, he and his family had been living in California for two years. His hair was short, he spoke nearly fluent English, and he was delighted to see Natalie and to receive a copy of the book in which his songs were recorded. But Tawakwaptiwa was no longer the free-spirited musician of whom Natalie had written, "Of all the Hopi poets, none sings a gladder song than Tawakwaptiwa (Sun-Down-Shining) . . . a Hopi untouched by foreign influence, the child of natural environment, spontaneous, alert, full of life and laughter."[14]

Tawakwaptiwa was now a deeply disillusioned man, acutely antagonized by the white environment he had been thrust into at the Sherman Institute. The betrayal by the U.S. government that he had worked so conscientiously to accommodate had made him bitter and far less tolerant of the non-Indian world. In many ways, Leupp's effort to diffuse Tawakwaptiwa's power and Hopi tribal identity and independence backfired. In spite of the school's best efforts, the Hopis returned home determined to maintain their Hopi traditions. "I could talk like a gentleman, read, write, and cipher," Oraibi native Don C. Talayesva wrote of his education at Sherman, "quote a hundred verses of Scripture . . . debate, shout football yells, swing my partners in square dances. . . . But I wanted to become a real Hopi again, to sing the good old Katcina [*sic*] songs, and to feel free to make love without fear of sin or a rawhide."[15]

Natalie was able to remain friends with Tawakwaptiwa, and she would see him again in Hopiland (he would be released from the Sherman Institute, return to Oraibi, and reassume his position as chief in 1910). But the harmonious independence, historic self-government, and tribal unity so valued by Tawakwaptiwa and the Hopis, and so revered by Natalie, had been weakened by the interfering and insensitive hands of white men.

5

"TIME AND THE WORLD"

Put aside for a while all that mesh of complex activities
that is entangling your health, find some placid
travelling-companion and come West. I shall meet you
at the railroad with ponies and a packhorse . . .

—*Gregory Marwood, aka George DeClyver Curtis*

WHEN NATALIE AND GEORGE RETURNED to California in 1908, they found Frank Mead enjoying life in San Diego and working in partnership with the architect Irving J. Gill. Southern California's Mediterranean climate and outdoorsy, close-to-the-earth culture fit Mead's nonconformist lifestyle, and his eclectic Moorish designs resonated with the residents of San Diego. Among Mead and Gill's first important clients was Wheeler J. Bailey, for whom they designed and built Hilero, a home destined to become a landmark on the rocky bluffs north of San Diego along a wild stretch of beach called La Jolla. Bailey was the same man with whom George had struck up a conversation on his first morning in Riverside. Bailey and the Mendenhalls, whose ranch George may have worked on, and their associates and friends would become the foundation of George's social circle as he relocated his life to Southern California.

Within this circle of wealthy and creative Californians was an energetic, educated, and artistic woman named Alice Ellen Klauber, whose friendship quickly became an important anchor in Natalie's life. Alice was a native Californian, born in 1871 to a prominent merchant's family in San Diego. Like Natalie, Alice was petite and small boned, and made up for her size with a quick wit, a generous nature, and a bold, inquisitive intellect. Serene, self-assured, and dignified, Alice made friends easily.

When she met Natalie, Alice was thirty-seven years old and unmarried. She had plenty of family money and owned her own apartment in downtown San Diego where, surrounded by her sisters and her friends, she lived a happy and independent life as a single woman. Alice had traveled throughout the United States, twice been to Europe, and in January 1908 had just returned from seven months abroad, including an extended stay in Italy where she studied painting with the American master William Merritt Chase.

Alice's father, Abraham Klauber, had immigrated as a young man to California from Czechoslovakia and had built successful wholesale grocery businesses in San Francisco and San Diego. The nine Klauber children were raised in a home that valued and encouraged art, music, literature, and the finer things of American culture. Since childhood, Alice had loved to draw and paint in much the same obsessive manner that Natalie had loved to play the piano.

Although her early years were spent in the frontier town of San Diego, Alice attended high school and came of age in the "Paris of the West," San Francisco, in the progressive and active Jewish community of Oakland. Her formal training as a painter began in 1884 at the first art school on the West Coast, the Art Students League (the San Francisco Art Association), where Alice attended classes and socialized with the West's emerging artists and writers.

Although a serious student and a talented painter, a career as a painter was hardly among Alice's or any woman's options in the late 1800s. The curriculum at the Art League included a program for aspiring art teachers, but Alice had neither the inclination nor the need to become a schoolteacher. She just wanted to paint. Her parents indulged her art classes, but expected Alice to marry and raise a family. Exactly how she would combine the socially sanctioned role as wife and mother with the unsanctioned, indeed unheard-of, life of a woman painter, Alice did not know.

After completing high school in the 1890s, Alice returned to San Diego. The little town on the Pacific had boomed while the Klaubers were in San Francisco. With the completion of the Santa Fe Railway tracks into downtown and the community's connection to the rest

Figure 5. Alice Klauber.

of the United States via the comfort of the train, San Diego's population surged from 2,600 in 1880 to nearly 40,000 in 1887.

Alice came close to marriage after meeting the intense young artist Arthur Putnam in the summer of 1894. Putnam was a sculptor
who, like Alice, had studied at the Art Students League in San Francisco. When Alice met Putnam he was living with his mother on a
lemon ranch near San Diego and working as a land surveyor with
his brother George. Putnam looked like a cowboy-artist and was
charming and straightforward. According to a biographer and friend,
he was "extremely handsome, lean as a wolf, with strong, clear-cut
features . . . and large, brilliant dark eyes."[1]

The intensity of Alice and Putnam's romantic relationship was
not recorded by Alice, but they did spend one summer together
sharing their favorite pastime, exploring and drawing the flora and
fauna found in the canyons and hills near San Diego. They fell in
love, but they would not and could not marry. Alice had money and
Putnam did not. In the successful, self-made merchant family of the
Klaubers, a gifted but financially insecure artist like Arthur Putnam

was not considered an acceptable suitor for their daughter. The relationship ended when Putnam departed San Diego for Chicago and an apprenticeship with the famed animal sculptor Edward Kemeys. Although Alice and Putnam exchanged many letters, and in later years Alice corresponded with Putnam's wife, Grace Storey, Alice never saw Putnam again.[2]

At the turn of the century, the Klauber family bought nearly a thousand acres of rolling hills and canyons in the country outside San Diego. Alice called the family retreat Encanto, Enchantment, and it became her haven where she spent languid days alone painting, reading, and walking and sketching the countryside. At the age of thirty, Alice was drawn to the solitary life of a painter, but as the spinster daughter of one of San Diego's wealthiest and most influential families, she was duty bound to participate in the social and civic life of the community.

In contrast to cities on the Eastern Seaboard of the United States, in San Diego a single woman was an accepted member of Southern California's society of independent, educated, progressive, and forward-looking folks involved in building a twentieth-century cultural hub on the shores of the Pacific. Two of Alice's sisters, Ella and Leda, were artists and shared Alice's need for creative space and time. Another sister, Stella, was a photographer. Ella eventually married, as did a fifth sister, Laura.[3]

Alice did her civic duty and participated in the opening of the city's first art gallery by the Wednesday Club, a women's group, in 1905. But community art events and informal painting classes by visiting artists did not and could not nurture Alice's muse, and her development as an artist was in isolation. San Diego was a cultural backwater on the California frontier, and Alice had almost no peers beyond her sisters and the small handful of women and men painters who visited Southern California.

She did have, however, what an unmarried woman needed to undertake serious creative work: money, her own shelter and studio space, and time to herself. Alice also lived in the West, where even single women enjoyed more freedom of movement physically and socially than women in the conservative industrial centers of the East Coast. By the turn of the century, women in the American West had access to better educational opportunities and enjoyed positions of leadership in their communities. And women in western states won the right to vote decades before their counterparts back east—Wyoming in 1869, Utah in 1870, and Colorado in 1893. California would give Alice and her sisters the vote in 1911.

Alice had been born and raised in a region that in the first decade of the twentieth century was becoming very attractive to women like Natalie Curtis who sought to emancipate themselves from conventional notions of femininity. Whereas the East Coast of America was tame, familiar, domesticated, and ordered, the West Coast was the opposite. Alice offered Natalie an introduction to the refreshingly nonconformist society found in Southern California. And Natalie's arrival in San Diego gave Alice an educated and sophisticated friend who understood and encouraged her need to experience the world of art and culture beyond Southern California.[4]

With several of her siblings, Alice toured Europe in 1906. But it was just that—a tour. Alice wanted to study the work of the grand masters with contemporary masters. She wanted to experience Europe not as a woman of leisure but as an artist. The next year, as a mature woman of thirty-six, she was accepted as a student in the European Summer School of William Merritt Chase. On June 8, 1907, Alice boarded the SS *Romanic* at the Charleston Docks in Boston, bound for Punta Delgada and Naples. She traveled with a female cousin, O. Epstein, whom Alice rarely mentioned in the accounts she wrote almost daily in a small red notebook.[5]

William Merritt Chase was sophisticated, cosmopolitan, and flamboyant, and with his friend and rival Robert Henri was considered to be among the most important teachers of American artists in the first decade of the twentieth century. Chase's students included Charles Demuth, Marsden Hartley, Georgia O'Keeffe, John Marin, Rockwell Kent, and Edward Charles Volkert. In 1896 Chase had begun the Chase School of Art, which became the New York School of Art (later Parsons School of Design), with Chase and Henri the principal instructors.

Chase was a portrait painter of the first rank and was among the first American artists to paint impressionist landscapes. He knew everyone who counted in American art, and by the summer of Alice's class in Italy, he was "the reigning force among the loose constellation of painters called American Impressionists." Chase's students were taught his eclectic painting style, which employed rapid brush strokes and a strong color palette and mirrored the energy and expansion found in New York City at the turn of the century. Among Chase's students in New York in 1907 was the young Georgia O'Keeffe, who, like all of Chase's students, was in awe of him: "When he entered the building a rustle seemed to flow from the ground floor to the top that 'Chase has arrived!'"[6]

Alice was in Italy with a modern master, and also with a teacher who distinguished himself among his female students by his pronounced lack of male chauvinism. Chase encouraged women of talent to become professional artists, and almost a decade earlier had chaired the committee that made Cecilia Beaux the first woman to receive the prestigious Gold Medal in art from the Carnegie Institute.

After twelve days at sea on an ocean that was "smooth as glass," Alice and her classmates disembarked in Naples, where they were greeted by Chase's assistant, a young painter named Walter Pach. Pach, just twenty-four years old that summer, was already on the faculty at the Teacher's College at Columbia University. Pach was a gifted artist—he had met Chase while studying at the New York School of Art—and after six summer tours as Chase's assistant, he was well on his way to becoming a specialist in the new world of modern art emerging in Europe.[7]

During the first few weeks of class, Alice was intimidated by Chase and his harsh criticisms of student work. But she persevered, and by late July was among the select group that went with Chase and Pach on private museum tours or out to dinner. There was an immediate connection between the young New Yorker Walter Pach and the thirty-something Californian Alice Klauber. They gravitated to one another on class field trips in the Italian countryside and met at sidewalk cafés for long talks about art and travel, painting and painters, and life in the modern world of the twentieth century.

Everything about that summer in Italy—the instruction, the setting, the social life, her friendship with Pach—was life-changing for Alice. With Chase at the helm, Alice and her classmates went on study and painting trips to Assisi, Bellagio, Padua, Perugia, Pisa, Milan, Venice, and Verona. She also ventured out into the countryside on her own, particularly to rendezvous with two California friends, Leo and Gertrude Stein, who were spending the summer at a small villa

Figure 6. Walter Pach.

near Florence. Leo and Gertrude, and their older brother, Michael, were childhood friends of Alice's in Oakland. Michael and his wife, Sally, and their son had followed Leo and Gertrude to Paris, where by 1907 Leo and Gertrude's apartment at 27 rue de Fleurus, with its collection of canvases by unknown painters named Picasso, Matisse, and Cézanne, was the recognized epicenter of the Parisian avant-garde.

Gertrude and Leo Stein spent the summer of 1907 at the Casa Ricci in Fiesole. On several afternoons in July, Alice left the noise and heat of Florence and joined the Steins at their villa high above the Arno valley. Their back patio was a verdant oasis of potted plants and lush flowers reminiscent of Alice's home on the shores of the Pacific Ocean. Like Alice, Gertrude and Leo loved to walk, and they often hiked together across the Tuscan countryside through poppy fields and groves of fragrant olive trees. One afternoon, the Steins walked with Alice to the home of the Renaissance scholar Bernard Berenson at Settignano. Alice "enjoyed the house very much indeed but especially his books in three rooms and all over the hall."[8]

Figure 7. Leo, Gertrude, and Michael Stein.

We can imagine that on one of these excursions to the Stein's villa above Florence, Alice took along her new friend Walter Pach and introduced him to her childhood friends. Alice does not record such an event in her diary, but by late summer of 1907 Pach and the Steins were acquainted, and Pach had an invitation to visit their apartment and salon in Paris. Alice could not have known the importance of the introduction at the time, since Pach was just stepping into the swirling current of modern art, a movement for which he would soon be recognized as a major voice and authority.

Gertrude Stein would become famous for her word portraits of friends. Of Walter Pach, she wrote: "Some things are to him beautiful things, some things are to him desirable things . . . learning anything is to him a natural thing, succeeding in living is to him a natural thing, teaching any one is to him a necessary thing, teaching everything is to him a necessary thing."[9]

With Chase, Pach, and their class, Alice visited the studio and summer home of Henri Matisse near Florence. Pach told Alice he was ambivalent about Matisse's paintings, but throughout the summer, he and Alice dined frequently with Matisse and his wife, and by late summer they were friends. Alice enjoyed Matisse as a person and a painter, and after she left Italy, she regularly corresponded with the painter.

In the summer of 1907, Pach was beginning what would become a stellar career as an art critic and historian and was submitting articles and art reviews to American magazines. In August, Alice was with Pach in a bookstore in Rome when he found a copy of the latest *Scribner's,* which included one of his articles. Alice and the storeowner watched a euphoric Pach "skip around the shop" with the magazine. The article would be the first of scores of published essays and reviews by Pach that would introduce European modern art to America.[10]

In Italy, Alice was among artists who were the vanguard of the modern movement. When Chase's summer school came to a close on September 1, Alice, now fully emancipated as an artist and as a woman, did not take the boat home to America but remained on the continent. Her diary entries never acknowledged her feelings for Pach, but she confessed that the dissolution of the class and the end of the summer caused her great emotional and physical suffering.[11]

With her cousin "O," Alice remained in Europe for another three months. Walter Pach remained on the continent as well, and in October, after Alice toured Germany, Belgium, and the Netherlands, she rendezvoused with him in Paris. Gertrude and Leo Stein were back in residence at 27 rue de Fleurus, and throughout her four weeks in Paris, Alice, like Pach, was frequently a guest at their salon. The Steins took Alice to museums and galleries and may have been alongside her in the Place de la Concorde crowd that watched "the flying machine" in the sky over Paris on October 26.[12]

Alice and her cousin sailed to America from England on November 18. After a short visit with Chase at his studio at 303 Fifth Avenue in New York, Alice boarded the train for California and was home by Christmas. Alice had been away from San Diego and her family for seven months. If she pined for the stimulation and freedom found in Europe, or for the companionship of Pach, she kept it to herself.

Pach wrote to Alice even before she climbed on the boat for America. His first letter spoke of his frustration that he had not seen more of her before she departed for England. Pach, fluent in four languages, signed the letter "Suyo, ato y afmo" (Yours, sincerely and affectionately), Walter Pach.[13]

Throughout the winter and spring, Pach's letters to Alice chronicled his life in Paris among the painters and writers who were breaking bold new ground in art and literature. He told her he was still struggling to like the work of their friend Matisse, and that he had discussed his style with Claude Monet, who was also not a fan of Matisse's canvases. The Steins were almost always mentioned in Pach's letters. "The Steins send you their love," he wrote Alice from the Pension Innocenti, Florence, in August 1908, "which I need not tell you is no small thing, even though they do extend its warmth to many people."[14]

A year after they parted in France, Pach wrote Alice, "It is just a year since I missed you on my return from Amiens. Gee, I wish there were another opportunity to see you. I wouldn't let any chances get mixed with it."[15]

In San Diego, Alice was disconnected physically and intellectually from the stimulating society of artists and intellectuals she had moved among in Europe. Unwilling or unable to relocate to Paris, Alice did what she could to bring the energy of the modern art world to Southern California, and made plans to open a gallery to exhibit and sell the work of contemporary American and European artists. Pach offered his assistance, although he could not come and join her in California. Needing money, he had moved back to New York in the fall of 1908 and gone to work full-time as a commercial photographer with his father. Pach was intensely unhappy with his job and wrote Alice that he found little to like in New York City.

The content, tenor, and extent of Alice's letters to Pach can only be guessed at. Although throughout his life he collected and carefully archived all of his correspondence, nothing from Alice was found in his voluminous collection of letters. It is believed that Pach destroyed her letters when he married in February 1914.

WOMEN WHO PURSUED any creative work in the first decades of the twentieth century had to be independent, ambitious, stubborn, unconventional, and tenacious. They also had to endure the loneliness and isolation experienced by all New Women of the modern age. Having a friend to share the paradoxes of the disorderly and undomesticated New World was rare, and the arrival in San Diego of the worldly, accomplished, and kindred spirit Natalie Curtis must have seemed a godsend to Alice Klauber in the lonely winter of 1908.

George Curtis made California his home country when he bought land in the foothills of the Laguna Mountains near Ramona, twenty miles southeast of Escondido. Over several years, George constructed a house, a horse barn, and chicken coop, planted a pecan grove and a kitchen garden, plowed and planted fields of alfalfa, and became a beekeeper.

Natalie stayed with George in his rural retreat as often as she stayed in San Diego with Alice and her friends. Natalie might have been considering permanent residence in Southern California, but in 1909 her father became gravely ill, and she hurried cross-country to Washington Place. Bogey's illness was terminal, and he would be bedridden with paralysis the last years of his life. Natalie put aside her work and her dreams of a life in the West, and for nearly four years "except to fulfill the most pressing engagements near at hand . . . never left [Bogey's] side."[16]

Natalie did manage at least one visit to George and her friends (she saw Lummis, among others, in Los Angeles) and the wide-open spaces of the West in May 1910. But even as she moved into the life of an emancipated woman, she understood that in a time of family crisis, her place as an unmarried daughter was beside her mother and her father. During the years of her father's illness, Natalie was forced to make peace with her divided self, which loved and needed her nuclear family but yearned for the freedoms found among people and places far away from their Greenwich Village world. "I hunger and thirst so for a bed on the ground that, once freed, I don't believe I can ever go into New York chains again," she wrote Aleš Hrdlička. "What a problem—to have a primeval soul and one's home in New York!"[17]

While she was living in New York City, Natalie's sponsors Charlotte Mason, George Peabody, and Hollis Frissell, the principal of the Hampton School in Virginia, urged her to do for Negro music what she had done for Indian music. Natalie had recorded Negro folk songs and spirituals as early as 1904, but in 1910 she began a comprehensive study of African American music with the staff and students of the Hampton School.

Important to Natalie's survival during the years of Bogey's illness were her friendships with musicians living in New York who shared her advocacy of musical education for America's poor. Kurt Schindler, a twenty-eight-year-old Berlin-born musician and a staff conductor at the Metropolitan Opera House, had become a friend when he worked at G. Schirmer, and she sought his advice while writing *The Indians' Book*. In 1909 Schindler founded New York's MacDowell Chorus (renamed the Schola Cantorum in 1912). After Natalie returned to New York, she and Schindler joined forces to promote music education for New York City's immigrant and minority children.

Mimsey Curtis was already involved with the kindergarten reform movement that developed in tandem with the settlement house movement famously established at Jane Addams's Hull House on Chicago's West Side in 1889. Gertrude House, a settlement house associated with the Chicago Kindergarten Institute, had incorporated music in their curriculum in the early 1890s. Natalie wanted to bring music to children at the settlement houses in New York and took her idea to Mimsey and the board (on which Mimsey served as vice president) of the Mary Walton Free Kindergarten for Colored Children on West 63rd Street.[18]

With the backing of Mimsey's organization, Natalie assembled her own board of influential individuals, which included Schindler, the violinist David Mannes, the brother musicians Frank and Walter Damrosch, the patron of the arts George Foster Peabody, and the attorney and family friend Elbridge Adams, and founded the Music School Settlement for Colored People, which opened in New York City in November 1911.[19]

The men and women involved with early twentieth-century philanthropic and reform organizations were people of enormous verve, compassion, and talent. Natalie's work at the music settlement houses introduced her to several individuals with whom she would form lasting and important friendships. Among these was Charles Winfred Douglas, an Episcopalian priest and a professionally trained musician and linguist who may have served on Natalie's music school's board of directors. Douglas, a canon in the Diocese of Fond du Lac, Wisconsin, was a talented musicologist who had studied Gregorian chants in Europe among the Benedictine monks, and was among the first Americans to translate the ancient musical form called plainchant or plainsong. But Douglas's most remarkable characteristic, at least to Natalie, was his interest in and knowledge of the American Southwest.

In 1911 Douglas was the music director of the Community of St. Mary, a boarding school for girls in Peekskill, a town on the Hudson River just north of New York City. Douglas kept an apartment in Manhattan and frequently came into the city to see his colleagues Frank and Walter Damrosch and his good friend Kurt Schindler. Born in Oswego, New York, in 1867, Douglas was tall and big boned, imposing, confident, brusque, and good-humored, with an orator's voice and a preacher's shepherding bossiness. Like Natalie, Douglas was an overachieving doer and seeker. When he was in full health, Douglas was a man of tremendous energy. But also like Natalie, Douglas's passion for his work, and his relentless creative drive, frequently pushed him to exhaustion.

Much like Natalie's inaugural trip to Arizona, Douglas's first journey to the American West was precipitated by a physical collapse brought on by an obsessive work schedule. In 1893, after simultaneously obtaining degrees from Syracuse University (in music) and St. Andrew's Divinity School (where he was ordained), Douglas came to New York City to work as music curate at the Church of the Redeemer and to teach music at St. John's parochial school. In his first winter in New York, twenty-seven-year-old Douglas, overworked, exhausted, and ill, collapsed while practicing the organ one night after choir rehearsal. He was taken to Presbyterian Hospital where he lay near death with the complications of double pneumonia for nine weeks.[20]

After several months of convalescing in New York, Douglas was sent out west where it was hoped his lungs would heal in the high, dry air. Douglas boarded a train for Denver, where he met and married Mary Josepha Williams, a graduate of Gross Medical School and the joint director of a small sanatorium on Pearl Street in Denver. Dr. Jo, as she was called, was the daughter of a wealthy Detroit family with major landholdings in Colorado and Denver's first woman doctor. She owned several hundred acres of land near the Evergreen stage stop, and with Douglas built a spectacular summer home on the property they named Camp Neosho.

In the early 1900s Douglas began lecturing at Northwestern's School of Music and helped to develop the music programs at

Gertrude House in Chicago. Freed of financial concerns by his wife's wealth, Douglas traveled between an apartment in New York City and his home in Evergreen, where his only son, Frederic (Eric) Huntington Douglas, was born in 1897. Douglas sailed for England in May 1901 and spent the next year in England, Scotland, Germany, and France listening to and studying Gregorian chants and ancient plainchant. When he returned to the United States, Douglas was determined to bring the heavenly chanting music of plainsong into mainstream American liturgical music.[21]

In the fall of 1902, Douglas and his wife and son moved into an apartment in New York City on West 84th Street. Douglas resumed his duties as curate at the Church of the Redeemer, and joined Damrosch's Musical Art Society. By the winter of 1903, the canon's health broke again. After months at various convalescent centers and retreats in New York, Pennsylvania, and Massachusetts, Douglas headed out west.

For six months, Douglas lived in a tent and slept in a bedroll in the wilderness of the Rio Grande of New Mexico, on the high desert of the Kaibab Plateau, and in the deep canyons of the Colorado River in Arizona. He lived alone and with the Indians he met on his journey, including the Hopis, who adopted Douglas and named him "Tall Pine Tree." Douglas submersed himself in the culture and art of the native tribes and began to collect pueblo pottery and baskets and Navajo rugs and blankets.

Six months on the high desert healed Douglas, and in 1904 he donned his city clothes and pastoral collar and returned to work. Now a vocal advocate of Indian art and culture, and a student of Indian music, Douglas lectured to audiences in Chicago and New York about Native America. When exactly Douglas became cognizant of the work of Natalie Curtis is not known, but by 1907, and the publication of *The Indians' Book*, he had surely met her. Schindler likely introduced them. Douglas was a board member of Schindler's Schola Cantorum from its inception, and Schindler had been friends with Natalie since editing her *Indians' Book*. By the fall of 1912, Douglas's appointment book noted frequent meetings with Natalie.[22]

Bogey died just after the Thanksgiving holiday in late November 1912. George came from California and joined his mother and siblings to bury Edward Curtis in the family cemetery in Providence,

Rhode Island. Augusta was seventy-two years of age. Natalie was thirty-seven. Augusta may have hoped her spinster daughter would settle permanently in the house on Washington Place. But she knew, too, that Natalie had unfinished business—an unfinished life—on the other side of the continent. And now that George was healthy and happy in his own home in California, even Bridgham agreed that only the American West could restore Natalie's health and her spirit.[23]

Natalie and George thought it was time their mother saw for herself the country that had claimed the hearts of two of her children, and in April 1913 Natalie boarded the train west with Mimsey. For Augusta Curtis it was a journey into an exotic, foreign land. The West Coast of the United States, and the desert and mountains that served as a line of demarcation between civilized and frontier America, was still very much another country.

Mimsey had heard in detail about Natalie's adventures in the Southwest, and she may have read all or parts of George's novel *The Wooing of a Recluse*, which would be published the next winter by the Devin-Adair Company. The novel was a grand romantic monologue by an unnamed cowboy written in letters to his lover, Pandora, back in New York. The narrator's transition from a life in upper-class New York City to a cattle ranch in Arizona very much paralleled the life of George DeClyver Curtis. Although George's cowboy protagonist went east to reunite with his love, George the cowboy-writer never lived in the East again, but set down deep roots in his land near Ramona. If George Curtis ever had a gal back in New York or Boston, she lost him to his new love, Southern California.

George wrote under a pseudonym, Gregory Marwood, but his Harvard classmates, friends, and family in New York and Boston understood that the romantic novel of letters from an Arizona cowboy to his society girl back east offered glimpses into the author's own life. And throughout the novel there were passages that seemed written just for his sister Natalie.

> Put aside for a while all that mesh of complex activities that is entangling your health, find some placid travelling-companion and come West. I shall meet you at the railroad with ponies and a packhorse, and you may roam this unseeing land with as little regard for the conventionalities as when you once slide down

the roof of our icehouse. . . . I will be your guide, cook and horse-wrangler; you need only ride and be glad . . . for time and the world will be all yours if you so choose, and in the freshness of a natural life you will forget that you were once in a fair way to be an invalid.[24]

Back in California again, Natalie immersed herself in the natural life where she could, in George's words, live with little regard for conventionalities. George met Natalie and Mimsey at the San Diego railroad station, possibly with Alice Klauber, who had a car and was a good friend of both George and Natalie. Alice's extended family in San Diego included half a dozen siblings, and the Curtis women had invitations to stay in the homes of several prominent families, including Alice's mother, Theresa Klauber, who had been a widow for less than two years. Mimsey stayed a month in California. With Natalie and Alice as her companions, she explored the little city of San Diego and went out for overnight retreats in La Jolla. They also stayed with George at his ranch in the rolling hills thirty miles inland.

In late April, Natalie, George, and Mimsey motored north of San Diego with Alice to Hilero, Wheeler Bailey's weekend retreat on the La Jolla bluffs above the Pacific Ocean. Bailey, called Uncle Wheeler by Alice and Natalie, invited Alice and the Curtises to spend a few nights at the fabulous house designed by Irving J. Gill and Frank Mead.

The auto journey out to Hilero's breathtaking perch above the ocean was through a paradisiacal and pastoral landscape of green fields and wild flowers where sheep and cattle grazed. Hilero was only five years old, but it had already achieved significant national attention from builders and designers for its Moorish architectural elements, and for its museum quality collection of Native American arts and crafts. Although Natalie appreciated the collection of Indian art that decorated the walls and windowsills of the house, Hilero's greatest treasure for a musician was the red Steinway piano covered by a Navajo rug on the large first-floor portico.

Natalie wrote about their days at Hilero as "a sort of California idyl, a song of the Pacific coast." Their meals were served at long tables on the covered porches and out in the gardens. If they ate in the dining room, the enormous doors were wide open to the sounds of the surf and the sea birds. Natalie, George, and Alice, perhaps

Mimsey too, chose to leave the comfort of their beds and private
rooms and slept on the large second-floor balcony under the stars.[25]

Natalie, George, Mimsey, Bailey's relative Wheeler North, and
Alice signed Hilero's guestbook before departing on April 28. George
wrote in French and English about "Mélodie écossaise, sung at Hiliro
[*sic*], where even Auld lang syne [*sic*] has an original touch." Natalie
filled an entire page of the guest book with the musical notes and
the Navajo (with English translation) words of a Navajo peace chant,
adding "Indian thoughts inspired by a wind-swept day, and a night on
the porch of Hiliro [*sic*]—the 'Blanco Hogan' of the Pacific slope!"[26]

Mimsey departed California for New York in the first week of May.
Natalie remained on the West Coast and moved between George's
ranch and her rented rooms in downtown San Diego. By 1914 she
was living in the Palomar Apartments, a building designed by Frank
Mead and partners at the corner of 6th and Maple, within walking
distance of Alice's home in downtown San Diego. From her rooms
at the Palomar, Natalie could watch the construction of the buildings and gardens of the San Diego Panama-California Exposition
that would open in 1915. Begun in 1912, the 1,400-acre exposition
grounds of Balboa Park would define modern San Diego. Although
the exposition was to celebrate the opening of the Panama Canal, the
museums and exhibits of Balboa Park would catapult San Diego into
the twentieth century, and bring Southern California's art, history,
and natural resources national attention.[27]

Southern California was fiercely hot and dry in June and July 1913.
Natalie frequently stayed for weeks at a time on the "unseeing land"
of George's ranch. He was digging a well, installing a pump, and
trenching a pipeline that would bring water to the house. Natalie
was strong again and worked alongside George doing ranch chores
until noon. After lunch, they napped through the heat of the afternoon, and in the evenings they read aloud to one another from the
newspapers and magazines Mimsey sent from New York. "Cleared
poison oak under Merlin's oak," George wrote in his lined pocket
diary on July 18, "and read a little Dante and snoozed there in the
afternoon. N[atalie] and I walked up to the spring when the sun
went, and brought back a pail of water."[28]

With Alice, Natalie motored up and down the coast, and out
to La Jolla for overnights with Alice's friends. She also went north

to Pasadena for several days and visited Lummis. They listened to Lummis's recordings of Indian songs and discussed Washington's latest political appointments and their Indian policies.[29]

Life in California was not all play. Natalie worked on several pieces for publication including two articles about Indian music for the *Outlook*. But her benefactors, like George Foster Peabody, although pleased to know she was in good health, believed she ought to return to the East and get back to the real work that awaited her attention. Her comprehensive piece about African American musicians, "The Negro's Contribution to the Music of America," had come out in the *Outlook* in March, and Natalie needed to complete the project at the Hampton School.

If Natalie heard Peabody's call for her return to New York, she did not heed it. Instead, in the summer of 1913 she pushed deeper into Indian Country and the wild frontier.

6

SECRETS AND DUALITIES

Women are not supposed to take up much room, or to
go very far from home, or to stay away for long. They are
not supposed to be by themselves. They are supposed to
hear and obey, to come back when they are called.

—*Virginia Scharff*

WHILE NATALIE WAS KEEPING VIGIL beside her dying father in his room near Washington Square, a similar family drama was transpiring in the J. Bishop Johnson house on the tiny Massachusetts island of Nahant. On a clear day, the gold dome of the Massachusetts State House was visible from the front porch of the Johnson home on Dorothy Cove. Even so, urban Boston and the professional music world in which J. Bishop's granddaughter Carol had lived and worked for more than a decade belonged to a universe that existed far beyond the shores of the fishing community on the small island.

In 1912, when Caroline Bishop Stanley was summoned home, she was employed as a piano teacher at the prestigious Hannah More Girls' Academy in Maryland. As the only child and single daughter of a widowed, ailing mother, Carol was bound by duty and principle to leave her position as a music instructor and return to Nahant. Carol's mother, Fannie, lived in the Bishop family house on Dorothy Cove with Carol's grandmother, and Nahant's oldest resident, eighty-four-year-old Almira Choate Johnson. Coming home to care for her mother on Nahant meant Carol had to resign from one of the few professional positions available to a woman with a bachelor's degree in music in 1912. It also meant Carol, at thirty-two, was completely dependent on her family.

Carol Stanley had lived and breathed music since she was a young child. Unlike her future friend Natalie Curtis, Carol's education and departure from the bosom of the family on the island of Nahant was a hard-won accomplishment, nearly every step taken in defiance of the communal and familial tide of expectation. Carol's father, Edwin Stanley, had died on Nahant in the 1880s when Carol was a small child, and Carol and her mother had gone to live with her grandparents in their house on the beach. Grandmother Almira was widowed in 1896, so by the turn of the century, the J. Bishop Johnson house had become the domain of two widows and a serious-minded young girl who wanted only one thing in life: to play the piano.

The history of Nahant island was the story of the extended Johnson family. There were two distinct and separate Johnson lineages, and Carol's mother's family was related to the latecomers, the Maine-based Johnsons, who had come to the island in the mid-1800s. The first Johnsons predated Carol's family by two centuries, and were listed among the first three families to settle the island in the 1600s. In spite of their lack of residential longevity, Carol's family was considered island royalty, especially since her grandfather's first wife, Caroline, was a Johnson of the first pedigree.

Carol's maternal grandfather, known around the island as J. Bishop, came to Nahant from Maine with several of his brothers. By the mid-1800s the Johnson brothers had a thriving fish business, and J. Bishop built a family home at the corner of Willow and Valley Roads beside the Johnson fish market, a short walk from the waters of Massachusetts Bay.

Carol was born on December 16, 1879. By that time, there were Johnsons belonging to one of the two Johnson families in every classroom, business, and neighborhood in the village of Nahant and out along the island's shoreline. The dual lineage of the Johnson name befits the island, as Nahant is a place of dualities and twins, of mirrors and magnification, and the island's history is laced with stories of the seen and unseen, above and below land and water. The name Nahant was derived from the Indian word *nahanteau* (twins), and the island is actually two islands, Little and Big Nahant, that are connected by tombolos, isthmuses, that flood at high tide. Before

Figure 8. Forty Step Beach, Nahant, Massachusetts, 1906.

the raised cart road was built in the mid-1800s, islanders could only reach the mainland and the neighboring town of Lynn on horseback or in buggies when the tide was out. This limited and rhythmic accessibility created a community where business revolved around the tide tables.[1]

In the earliest accounts of fishermen and sailors there was frequent mention of a peculiar optical illusion, called doubling, seen on the sea near Nahant island. When certain weather and cloud conditions existed, ships and landmarks appeared to be mirrored in the cloud ceiling. This doubling was so endemic to Nahant that early historians included illustrations of the phenomenon, and poets wrote of the mirrored and magical world above and below Nahant.

Nahant was a place of doubles and also of secrets. Along the coast-line where the land has been battered and shaped by the waves of the Atlantic there are numerous caves and secret passages: Spouting Horn was so named because of the sound the sea makes at it crashes through this formation on the rocky cliff on the island's eastern tip. Swallows' Cave is a deep channel seventy-two feet long and eight feet high that opens into the sea and is accessible only by climbing down rock cliffs to the cave's entrance at low tide. Nearer the center of the island, on the high land near the village proper, is the Witches'

Cave, where several women eluded capture and prosecution during the Salem witch trials in 1692.

Caroline Bishop Stanley was in body and in spirit a *Nahanteur*. She had a twin brother, Edward, who lived only two months. Caroline had an older brother who died during childbirth, so after her twin died, Caroline was raised an only child. In true mirroring style, Carol was named for her grandfather J. Bishop Johnson's first wife, Caroline Johnson, who had died in childbirth thirty years before.

Although the public death record confirms that Carol's twin died in February 1880, there was never again an acknowledgment in private or public accounts that Carol's mother had given birth to twins. We assume that Carol was told about her twin brother, but the keeping of such a secret would not have been out of character among the Johnsons or any other family with deep roots on the island of Nahant.[2]

Carol's childhood on Nahant in the 1880s and '90s coincided with the island's heyday as the resort and second-home community of Boston's elite. As the northeast seaboard was transformed by American industry and Boston became crowded and dirty, city folk looked east across the water to rural Nahant, a pastoral island of peace and quiet untouched by industrial America. The island off the shore of the bustling town of Lynn was a quiet backwater during the New England winter. But each summer, Nahant's population more than doubled with day-trippers from Boston who came in droves on the daily ferries, and seasonal residents who moved into their grand cottages for the summer.

In 1821 Colonel Thomas H. Perkins and William Paine bought East Point, the "Ram Pasture," and built a fine hotel. By 1903 the island boasted fourteen hotels, several of which were grand affairs that catered to the ultrawealthy. On Nahant the Brahmins could escape the heat and pollution of the city, and often a stay on the island prompted visitors to build second-home "cottages" along the beaches and up in the village. Although Boston's Brahmins brought to the island the culture and money of Boston high society, they shed the posturing and formalities inherent to urban life. The family breadwinner could continue to commute to his work on Beacon Hill or near the state house and commons while his wife and children could soak up the healthy sea air and sun while swimming and boating, or riding horseback at the stables.

The island's part-time residents included Boston's most prominent families. Samuel A. Eliot, father of Charles W. Eliot, the future president of Harvard, kept a residence on the island, and the family of George H. Mifflin of the publishing house spent summers in their home on Nahant. Natalie's uncle George's close friend Henry Wadsworth Longfellow, the iconic American poet, was perhaps Nahant's most famous resident. Longfellow lived in Cambridge and taught at Harvard, but beginning in 1850, he came each summer with his family and lived in their home directly across the cove from Carol's grandfather's fish market. Another friend of George Curtis's, the statesman Henry Cabot Lodge, was a child on Nahant. Lodge's father, John E. Lodge, had come to the island in the 1830s, and after he married Anna Cabot in 1842 and moved to Beacon Hill to raise their two children, he returned to build a grand summer house on Nahant. As a U.S. senator, Henry Cabot Lodge retreated to Nahant for solitude and respite from politics. Although busy with the matters of Washington and the world, he served as Nahant town moderator for twenty years and remained a trustee for the Nahant public library for over four decades.

Lodge was not a progressive Republican, like Theodore Roosevelt, but aligned himself with the conservatives who dominated the Senate when Roosevelt was president. Although often at political odds, Lodge was a welcomed friend at Roosevelt's home, Sagamore Hill, and Roosevelt came to Nahant to visit Lodge at his family retreat.

AROUND NAHANT, Caroline Stanley was the local girl who excelled on the piano. In 1894, when Carol (called Carrie as a child) was fifteen, she played "Smiling Springtime" at the Nahant graduation exercises. There were only three graduates that year (all of the children on Nahant attended one school), but the whole town turned out for the event, which included orchestral performances, several violin and piano solos, including Carol's, six student recitations, and an address titled "The Nation's Progress" by graduating senior Charles Cabot Johnson.[3]

Carol Stanley graduated Nahant School in a similar ceremony in 1899 and entered Mount Holyoke College the next fall. But the Massachusetts women's college didn't offer the level of music instruction Carrie wanted, and in the autumn of 1900 she transferred to the New England Conservatory of Music in Boston.

Figure 9. Pleasant Street School, Nahant, 1880s. Carol Bishop Stanley is in the front row, second from right.

The New England Conservatory of Music was undergoing dramatic growth in the first years of the twentieth century. In Carol's third year, the conservatory moved out of cramped quarters in the South End of Boston and into a new building near the Boston Symphony Orchestra's headquarters. The school began an affiliation with Harvard, and in June 1903, when the conservatory's new Jordon Hall and its modern, elegant, and acoustically perfect stage and auditorium opened, the New England Conservatory boasted, and rightly so, that it could compete with any music school in the world.

Indeed, by 1906 even the *New York Observer* touted the conservatory's formidable offerings, telling New Yorkers that "Boston is the recognized musical center of the country" where is found "the New England Conservatory of Music, the best equipped institution of its kind, and in quality of work rivaling kindred institutions in foreign countries."[4]

Carol and her classmates were the first to occupy the conservatory's new residential housing on Hemenway Street, which was an easy block's walking distance from the school's offices, class and rehearsal

Figure 10. New England Conservatory of Music on Franklin Square, Boston.

rooms, and library and bookstore on the corner of Huntington Avenue and Gainsborough Street. The conservatory was in the heart of Boston's music world, and the school's population boomed to almost two thousand students. Carol studied piano with George W. Proctor and music theory with the young American composer Harry N. Redman. She joined the staff of *The Neume*, the conservatory's yearbook, and in the fall of 1903 was the seventy-eighth member inducted into the Zeta chapter of Alpha Chi Omega, a national sorority dedicated to attaining "the highest musical culture and to cultivat[ing] those principles that embody true womanhood."[5]

Conservatory student musicians performed solo recitals and participated in the school's orchestra and chorus in public performances throughout the school year. Jordan Hall hosted the Boston Symphony Quartet's six public concerts a year, and the Apollo and

Figure 11. New England Conservatory of Music graduates, 1905.
Carol Stanley is in the third row, second from right.

McDowell Clubs and the Choral Art Society also held their annual
concert series at the conservatory's signature facility.

Nahant island native Carol Stanley was being educated at one
of the finest conservatories in America. She was also learning the
realities of modern urban life. And every day from 1900 until her
graduation on June 20, 1905, Caroline Bishop Stanley was being
indoctrinated into the ranks of the twentieth century's New Women.

The Johnson family was comfortably middle-class, but Carol's
mother, Fannie, was not wealthy, and at least a portion of Carol's tuition and board was paid for by her grandmother Almira. Carol likely
received additional tuition monies from Almira's Brahmin family
or from the Edward C. Johnson family, with whom Carol lived in
the summers during her college years. Carol earned money teaching piano lessons on Nahant, and also worked as the nanny for the
Edward Johnson family when they came to stay at their summer
house on the island. The E. C. Johnsons, relatives of Carol's grandfather's first wife, Caroline, were the wealthy owners of the Boston
dry goods house C. F. Hovey & Co.

The E. C. Johnsons moved in Boston's most exclusive social circles. Their daughter, Carol's step-cousin Charlotte Howe Johnson,

married Curtis Guild Jr., and when he became the forty-fifth governor
of Massachusetts in 1905, the Edward Johnsons attended every gala
event and social function at the governor's mansion. But even among
the proper Brahmins, daughters could wander from the straight and
narrow and fall into the wilder side of society. When Carol was a
single woman living and working in Maryland, she learned that
Edward Johnson's daughter Mary Frothingham Johnson, her cousin
and former piano student, had eloped with a count named Vittorio
Oriandini Guidi. The Boston gossip columnist had a field day with
the humiliating announcement, saying the count "was cutting quite
a wide swath in Boston and Brookline society" and although he was
the "social lion of the hour" was in fact a sewing machine salesman.[6]

When young Mary Johnson ran off with and married the Italian
sewing machine salesman at the Providence, Rhode Island, Episcopalian church, she personified the improper, independent, headstrong,
unchaperoned New Woman the Victorian Brahmins of 1907 feared
and shunned. The news of her elopement served as a reminder to
all families with single daughters: keep the girls at home until they
marry, and supervise their interactions with all potential suitors, even
titled ones.

Carol was twenty-six and a self-supporting music teacher at the
Hannah More Academy near Baltimore when the gossip about the
new Countess Guidi reached her apartment on the strictly guarded
grounds of the oldest Episcopalian girls' school in America. If Carol
had a love interest in Reisterstown, she knew better than to share the
details of her social life with the Stanley-Johnson clan back in Boston
or out on Nahant island. Such was the paradox of the educated,
single woman at the turn of the century: to keep the family peace,
she kept the extent of her ambitions and independence to herself,
and although she was frequently crossing the boundary between the
Victorian and the modern world, she still longed for family approval
and support. Dualities and secrets were second nature to Carol, and
she kept her explorations into the frontier of the New Woman to
herself, and spoke of her professional and personal concerns only
with a small circle of colleagues and confidants.

Natalie Curtis and Canon Winfred Douglas were among the friends
with whom Carol could talk of her life as a single woman and of her
love of music. With no record of their early friendship, it is impossible

Figure 12. Canon Charles Winfred Douglas.

to determined whom Carol met first, Douglas or Natalie. In November 1906 Cardinal Gibbons of Baltimore held a high mass to confirm ninety-one novitiates at St. John's Church in Frederick, Maryland. It was a gala event that included an orchestra and chorus. Carol B. Stanley was a member of the professional choir that performed at the mass, which was attended by dozens of ministers from various denominations and by politicians, military officers, and college presidents from the Baltimore region.[7] Winfred Douglas had just accepted the post as music director at the Community of St. Mary and moved with his family to Peekskill, New York. Was Father Douglas in Baltimore for the gala high mass in November 1906, and if so, was he introduced to the young music teacher, Carol Stanley of Nahant?

The next fall, in October 1907, the *Baltimore Sun* announced that the Hannah More Academy had opened the scholastic year with more than a hundred women students. The school's new teachers included a member of the music department, a Miss Carol B. Stanley.

Living and teaching at the Hannah More Academy was as good as it got for a young female music teacher, and Carol remained on the resident staff for five years. She might have stayed another ten, but in the late fall of 1912 Carol learned that her mother, Fannie, was dying of carcinoma of the uterus. Carol resigned her position at the academy and returned to the Johnson House on Nahant.[8]

Through the next winter and spring, Carol cared for her bedridden mother and kept house for her elderly grandmother Almira. In early June, when Nahant gardens began to bloom and the islanders anticipated the return of the summer tourists and seasonal residents, Fannie fell into a coma.

On Sunday, June 8, 1913, when Carol was tending her comatose mother, unusually ominous clouds began to gather in the sky over Nahant island stretching to the coastal town of Marblehead on the mainland. By early afternoon a great storm moved into Massachusetts Bay. As the day turned dark and the winds surged, Carol, like all her neighbors on Dorothy Cove, tied down everything around the house and yard.

The daily steamer, the *General Lincoln*, was approaching Nahant's Bass Point wharf with a full load of Bostonians preparing to disembark for a Sunday afternoon on the pier or on one of the island's lovely beaches. When the steamer was ten minutes out, the storm broke. The captain pulled the *General Lincoln* away from shore and, in gale-force winds, turned the steamer stern first into the storm and then let it be carried down the coast.

From her mother's bedroom window, Carol may have watched the *General Lincoln* reverse its course as the flags marking the channel across the harbor were blown from their moorings. The Johnson house shutters slammed and banged, and anything not tethered and secured was thrown into the air. Carts on the road to the village were overturned by the wind, and dust clouds reduced visibility on the island to a few yards.

With the very first clap of thunder—a violent, concussive sky-splitting crack—a bolt of lightning struck the Johnson house, traveled one of the house's vent pipes down three stories, and exploded in the first-floor lavatory. The bolt instantly reversed and shot back up the staircase, ripping the woodwork as it ascended to the roof, where it splintered shingles and tore off the saddle board.

Neighbors who had seen the lightning strike fought the winds and torrential rain to reach the Johnson house to see if anyone was hurt. Carol and the eighty-five-year-old Almira were shocked and traumatized by the ferocity and scope of the lightning strike but physically unscathed. Fannie remained unconscious throughout the violent storm. Several hours later, however, Fannie Johnson Stanley passed away.

As reported in a local newspaper, Dr. Cusick, the family physician, was of the opinion that the "shock of the bolt" and the ferocity of the storm had not hastened Fannie's death.[9]

Fannie was buried in the tiny cemetery on Nahant. Carol, an unemployed woman of thirty-four, remained on the island for the next year, living with and caring for her grandmother, teaching piano lessons, and wondering what she would or could do with the rest of her life. Her mother's brother, Otis, and his wife and two daughters lived in town, and Carol knew virtually everyone who lived in the village or in the grand summer homes out along the shoreline. Even so, Nahant island was no longer Carol's home of choice.

Carol's grandfather had been a man of determination and vision, and his hard work as a fisherman and market owner had brought him wealth. Her grandmother, Almira Choate Estes Johnson, also had her own family money. She was the granddaughter of Ebenizer Choate, a relative of the New York lawyer and statesman Joseph Hodges Choate. The Choates had been part of the seasonal community on Nahant island since the first grand hotel was built on East Point by Colonel Thomas Perkins in the 1820s. As the granddaughter of one of the wealthiest and most respected dignitaries on the island, the middle-aged spinster Carol Stanley had no real financial or social worries *if* she settled down within the Johnson family domain on Nahant.

But Carol could not settle down on Nahant. Her heart remained focused on Boston, Baltimore, and the world of professional music she had been part of for a brief, wonderful decade. She continued to interact with musicians at the music settlement houses, specifically Boston's South End Music School, about which Natalie wrote in 1911. Carol practiced and sometimes performed with local orchestras, and volunteered and played piano at the Seaman's Bethel of the Boston Port and Seamen's Aid society in North Boston. But on most days during the year after her mother's death, Carol was isolated as a woman and a professional musician in the family house on the quiet beach of Dorothy Cove.[10]

If Carol did indeed know Natalie Curtis and Winfred Douglas by 1913, her desire to return to the world beyond the island was likely intensified by their stories of the people and places of Arizona, New Mexico, Colorado, and California. However, Carol kept her thoughts and yearnings to herself and remained on Nahant, the obedient granddaughter, until Grandmother Almira's death the following year. After that, the second half of Carol's life would begin with an epic journey into the deepest, most remote and unforgiving wilderness yet found in the American Southwest.

7

CREATING A BRAVE
NEW WORLD

You either have to be utterly common place or else do
the thing people don't want, because it has not yet been
invented. No really new and original thing is wanted:
people have to learn to like new things.

—*Willa Cather*

IN 1913 NEW YORK CITY was fertile ground for radical discourse
and social experimentation, a place where American intellectuals
interested in new ideas about politics, society, the arts, and women
found energy and voice. The hub of this radical New World—the
Greenwich Village salon of Mabel Ganson Dodge—was located near
Washington Square just a few blocks from Natalie's family home.

Mabel Dodge was born in Buffalo in 1879, the daughter of a
wealthy industrialist. In the first decade of the twentieth century,
Dodge and Alice Klauber had several friends in common in Italy and
France, although neither woman makes mention of ever meeting
the other in Europe or America. Dodge lived in Florence for several
years beginning in 1905, and she dined and socialized, as Alice did,
with the Bernard Berensons at their villa in the Tuscan countryside.
Dodge became friends with the Steins in Italy, and her visits to their
famous Paris salon in 1911 completely transformed her ideas about
men, women, art, and life.

When Dodge returned to America in November 1912, she moved
into an apartment on Fifth Avenue near Washington Square and
within the year established her own salon for weekly gatherings of
Greenwich Village bohemians and radicals. Dodge was a feminist, or
on her way to becoming one, and as a New Woman was determined
she would not be bound by traditional roles and ideas. Like the
New Art and the New Psychology, the New Woman was creating an
innovative paradigm that denounced the Victorian social barriers and
gender limitations that had repressed their parents' generation. Like
Stein in Paris, Dodge and her Greenwich Village crowd of "capital-
ists, anarchists, artists, writers, and actresses" debated sex and society,
marriage, monogamy, the work of men and women, and child care
and were imagining and creating a modern society that encouraged
personal, professional, and artistic freedom.[1]

Some historians claim it was "the restlessness of women" that
caused "the development called Greenwich Village, which existed
not only in New York but all over the country." The New Woman
was to be independent, self-defined, and physically capable, and not
to be at the mercy of her biology. She was to determine the direction
of her own life, with or without a man, and could assume positions
of power in politics, education, and reform movements.[2]

As Natalie, Alice, Carol, and Mabel Dodge had learned by 1913,
the New Woman was not an easy persona to integrate into their daily
lives. In spite of their best efforts to be independent and self-directed,
women in the early twentieth century, even those with education and
money, were conflicted and even hindered by the deeply ingrained
need for a husband, for security, and for acceptance in their family
and a place in society.

It is not known whether Natalie knew of her neighbor Mabel
Dodge and her Greenwich Village salon, but several years later, in
1917, the two women's paths were destined to cross two thousand
miles away in an adobe casita near the plaza of old Santa Fe.

BEFORE NATALIE AND MIMSEY departed New York for California
in 1913, they, like most everyone in New York City, witnessed the
most important event in the history of American art: the opening of
the International Exhibition of Modern Art, known as the Armory
Show. Held in the cavernous halls of the 69th Regiment Armory in

New York City, the exhibition introduced European and American modern painting and sculpture to an artistically naïve and largely ignorant American public.

The Armory Show's major organizers were the American painters Walt Kuhn and Arthur B. Davies, and Alice's friend Walter Pach, a painter and an emerging American authority on modern art. Pach was living again in Paris, where he was often found at the home of Leo and Gertrude Stein, and also at the residence of their older brother, Michael. The Steins were involved with the Armory Show from its inception. Leo, "at the pinnacle of his reputation as the first prophet of the new art" (many considered Leo to be the discoverer of Picasso), assisted Pach in the securing of loans from Parisian art dealers.[3]

Pach was the Armory Show's chief European liaison, loan, and sales agent. Throughout 1912 he approached and secured loans from the best European moderns, many of whom were his close personal friends, and he was directly responsible for securing the exhibition's most scandalous pieces: Marcel Duchamp's *Nude Descending a Staircase, No. 2*, Matisse's *Blue Nude*, and Brancusi's *Sleeping Muse*.

The show brought to the United States the first major exhibition of modern art, and the 1,250 works by three hundred American and European artists included the most innovative of the Europeans, including Cézanne, Duchamp, Matisse, and Picasso. Four thousand people flocked to the Armory Show's opening night on February 17, 1913, to view the finest examples of Symbolism, Impressionism, Post-impressionism, Neo-Impressionism, and Cubism. But even urban and progressive New Yorkers were not ready for modern art. The exhibit's month-long run in New York City, and the subsequent exhibitions at the Art Institute of Chicago and at the Copley Society of Art in Boston, shocked the American public, unleashed vociferous outrage from the press, and ultimately altered the course of art history in America.

The New American Art movement emerged from the same soil and at the same time as the New American Woman. And like the New Woman, the New Art that invaded America via the Armory Show would be the object of public distain and ridicule for many years before it gained widespread acceptance.

The year before the momentous opening of the Armory Show in New York City, Alice Klauber once again left the peaceful but

Figure 13. Robert Henri (*standing center*) and class, summer 1912,
Spain. Alice Klauber is third from right.

artistically unchallenging environment of San Diego for Europe. In
June 1912 she sailed for Spain with the iconic American artist and
teacher Robert Henri. Henri was a member of the "Ashcan" group
of painters, New York realists who rebelled against both "the dead
hand of tradition and the foreign hand of Paris Modernism." Henri
would become one of the first American painters associated with
the moderns, and with his cohorts advocated a New Art with a new
ideal of beauty—the common and nonheroic people and activities
of everyday life.[4]

Henri was a member of The Eight, a group of painters whose New
York exhibition in 1908 caused a sensation in American contempo-
rary art. In 1910 Henri and The Eight organized the larger Exhibi-
tion of Independent Artists that included Rockwell Kent, George
Bellows, and several other contemporary art renegades who, like
Henri, challenged the academic traditions defined and defended by
Alice's first teacher, William Merritt Chase.[5]

In Henri's class, and to some extent in Chase's classroom in
Italy five years earlier, Alice was an observer of the aesthetic power
struggle unfolding between the dominant artists and teachers of the

American modern art movement. Chase was ideologically opposed to all the modernist movements, American and European, and did not care for the narrative subject style favored by Henri's Ashcan group. Although a leader and a force in contemporary art, Henri was not himself a fan of the American avant-garde movement that was influenced and ultimately eclipsed by the European moderns Pablo Picasso, Albert Gleizes, Constantin Brancusi, Jacques Villon, Henri Matisse, and others.

In 1911 Henri and the members of The Eight formed the Association of American Painters and Sculptors. Henri, the organization's first director, and the association initiated the conversation in 1912 that gave birth to the Armory Show. Henri might have been the grand master of the International Exhibition, but in 1913 he was jostled from power and directorship by a colleague, the painter Arthur B. Davies.

ON JUNE 7, 1912, Alice, Henri and his wife, Marjorie Organ (called Margie "O" or simply "O"), Henri's assistants Randall Davey and Wayman Adams, the painters Meta Gehring and Esther Stevens Barney, and the dozen other members of Henri's summer class boarded the *Carpathia* in New York, bound for Gibraltar. Just six weeks earlier, the *Carpathia* had become the most famous rescue ship in the world when it was the first to reach the *Titanic*'s survivors on the night of April 14. Alice and her traveling companions were on the *Carpathia*'s first transatlantic crossing since that fateful night when the ship had reversed it course to Europe and returned to New York with its decks filled with passengers rescued from the Atlantic.

Alice's crossing ended uneventfully at Gibraltar on June 14. During the next month, Alice and the rest of the group followed Henri across a sweltering hot Spain, stopping to paint in Granada, Seville, and Madrid. In Cordova in late June, after sketching the famous mosque, Alice lunched with Gertrude Stein and Alice B. Toklas on the old square. Stein and Toklas had been in Spain for almost two months, visiting the same cities, art museums, and architectural landmarks that Alice and Henri's class were touring. The relentless Spanish summer heat was inhibiting the class's progress and rearranging itineraries. On a particularly steamy noon in Cordova, Alice met Stein and Toklas at a sidewalk café. The upcoming Armory Show dominated art news on both sides of the Atlantic, and with Walter Pach orchestrating the

Figure 14. Robert Henri on board the
Carpathia, June 1912.

selection of artwork to be sent from Europe to New York, we can imagine Stein shared with Alice details of Pach's life in Paris.[6]

The next day, the group went on to Madrid, Segovia, and Toledo, where the class painted for the next several weeks. Stein and Toklas went to Seville, where Stein suffered a severe attack of colitis that prompted the two women's quick departure for Gibraltar and the cooler breezes found along the Mediterranean.[7]

Throughout the summer, Henri lectured on art, literature, theater, and philosophy and instructed his students to get away from their canvas and experience the world. His lessons continued after class around dining tables and in outdoor cafés. One of Henri's favorite themes was the challenge of the solitary life necessary for the serious artist. "Few have the courage and stamina to see it through. You have to make up your mind to be alone in many ways."[8]

Alice, forty-one that summer, knew all about the solitary life of an artist, and had experienced the numerous ways in which a single woman of a certain age felt alone. Like Natalie, Alice knew that immersion in creative work was the only antidote to her ennui. "And dont [*sic*] get discouraged," Henri told Alice. "Don't let discouragement stop you. You can't afford that. Work . . . work all the time."[9]

Throughout their months in Spain, Alice talked art and life with Henri during long train rides, at tables in sidewalk cafés, while walking through cathedrals and museums, and at her easel in the studio. Henri preached that "life and art cannot be disassociated" and encouraged his students to be "all wrapped up in life" because an artist's education took place as much out of the studio as in the studio. He advocated a new freedom of expression and sense of adventure, and even as his students studied the grand masters, Henri reminded them to make their own art. "[The masters] made their language," Henri told his painting students. "You make yours."[10]

Alice took copious and meticulous notes that recorded verbatim Henri's wit, philosophy, and wisdom. She understood the historic importance of her conversations with Henri, and after she returned to the United States, she transcribed his informal talks, lectures, and her personal journal entries about her time with the great teacher into a single notebook labeled "Robert Henri lectures."

As she had in 1907, Alice remained in Europe after the class disbanded in early fall. During her month-long stay in Paris, Alice saw the Steins many times. If she met with Walter Pach, in public or private, she did not record the meeting in her travel journal. Henri and Margie "O" also stayed in Paris and did see Pach that October. Pach was still single but within the year would become engaged to Magdalene (Magda) Frohberg, a young German woman he became acquainted with the same summer he met Alice in Florence.

Alice returned to San Diego proselytizing Henri's contemporary art ideology. She also returned home inspired and eager to begin new work in her La Jolla studio. She continued to be the driving force behind a small gallery downtown that promoted local artists. But after her trip to Spain, Alice was ready to bring contemporary, even modern, art and artists, including Henri, to Southern California. Alice's instincts were aligned with the times, since San Diego and Southern California were precisely poised to begin the transformation from a frontier backwater to a nationally recognized center of contemporary art and culture. And Alice was perfectly positioned to assist in that transformation.

The construction of the exhibit halls, grounds, and gardens of San Diego's Panama-California Exposition at Balboa Park dominated Southern California's civic agenda for several years. The November 11, 1911, ground breaking on Balboa Park's 1,400 acres of treeless hills and barren canyons set in motion three years of construction and beautification that would profoundly alter the persona of San Diego and environs. The grounds of the park underwent extensive landscaping, with the natural sagebrush and chaparral hillsides transformed into a lush landscape with the planting of several thousand trees, including hundreds of fragrant eucalyptus. San Diego harbor was rebuilt and improved, the trolley system was enlarged, the streets of downtown were paved, and the Santa Fe Railroad built an attractive new Spanish Colonial depot.

The designing of the Panama-California Exposition at Balboa Park instigated an interest in and rebirth of Southern California's Spanish architectural traditions, and also brought to San Diego Mediterranean and Moorish designs like those first employed by Frank Mead and Irving J. Gill at Bailey's Hilero house in La Jolla. The towers, archways, gardens, domes, reflecting pools, and fountains of the new park brought a romance and refinement to the scruffy frontier of San Diego. The California Building with its Spanish-Moorish tower and Cabrillo Bridge, designed by Gill, which spanned deep Cabrillo Canyon and connected the town to the park, became iconic landmarks on the twentieth-century San Diego skyline.

By the spring of 1913 and Natalie's return to the West, Alice was involved with two challenging projects. The first was a little book of Henri's teachings based on her notes and journal entries from her summer in Spain. The second was the creation of Balboa Park's fine art exhibition, which was scheduled to open to the public in early 1915.

In April, Alice sent off to Henri a typed and edited manuscript of the lectures he had given in Spain. Alice asked him for his opinion of the transcriptions, and of her twenty-two-page introduction to the text. She also asked Henri if he would grant her permission to publish the manuscript.

Henri, in Ireland with a class for the summer, was evasive about publication. After months of correspondence, he admitted to Alice that Margery A. Ryerson was just then working on a book that promised to be the complete collection of his lectures and criticism.

Henri did not want Alice's manuscript published ahead of Ryerson's, but more importantly, he had instructed Ryerson to withhold publication of her book until after his death. Disappointed, Alice scrapped her book project and tucked her notes and manuscript into a drawer.[11]

AS ONE OF SAN DIEGO'S most accomplished painters with personal connections to important art dealers and prominent artists in America and Europe, Alice was named chairman of the Fine Arts Department of the Panama-California Exposition. This role thrust Alice into the forefront of the most important event in Southern California cultural history to date. Alice edited the official exhibition catalogue and also participated in the selection of art and artists for the exposition. She met and worked with Edgar Hewett and the anthropologists, archaeologists, and artists, many of whom, like Hewett, were from Santa Fe, brought to San Diego to create the buildings and exhibitions in Balboa Park.

Charles Lummis may have provided the first link in the historic chain that connected the art and archaeology community of San Diego with its counterpart in Santa Fe and the soon-to-be-state of New Mexico. In a conversation in 1911 with Colonel D. Charles Collier, the director-general of the San Diego Exposition, Lummis had learned that Collier was looking for a director of the Balboa Park exhibitions. Lummis suggested Collier consider Lummis's friend and camping buddy Edgar Lee Hewett for the job. Hewett was the director of both the Museum of New Mexico and the School of American Archaeology housed in the old Palace of the Governors on the plaza in Santa Fe.

Collier took Lummis's advice and hired Hewett as director of exhibitions. Hewett, widely known as "Doctor Archaeology" and called "El Toro" (the bull) by friends and foes alike, was given the daunting task of overseeing the vast ethnology and art exhibits that would highlight the culture, art, and lifestyle of the Mayan and Aztec Indians of Mesoamerica and the Native Americans of the southwest United States. The theme of the San Diego exposition was "the Progress of Man and his achievements in the completion of the Panama Canal." With his second wife, Donizetta (his first wife, Cora, died in 1905), Hewett began to commute between Santa Fe and San

Diego as he directed the planning and building of the ambitious Science of Man exhibitions. With an initial budget of $100,000 granted by the Smithsonian for the anthropology exhibits, Hewett planned five grand rooms that would tell the story of man's evolution and development.[12]

Hewett brought in Alĕs Hrdlička, the director of physical anthropology at the National Museum of Natural History in Washington, to develop the exhibit on human evolution. Hrdlička was a Bohemian-born physician and a physical anthropologist who had become friends with Natalie in Washington, DC, in 1912. Hrdlička liked the gutsy ethnomusicologist immediately, and their friendship was anchored in their like-mindedness concerning the reformation of Washington's Indian policies.

Hrdlička was one of the first of dozens of high-profile experts in American archaeology, ethnology, and art Hewett drafted into service to create the exhibitions that became the fair's headliners. Anthropology received top billing at the Panama-California Exposition and deservedly so. More than five thousand specimens of ancient pottery, apparel, and tools were brought from around the world into the Museum of Man. Hewett was also responsible for the Science of Man exhibits, for which Hrdlička spent three years literally searching the world for artifacts and fossils to display in the Primal Man, Java Man, Neanderthal Man, and Cro-Magnon Man exhibits.

As director of exhibits, Hewett supervised the Indian Arts Building, the California Building's Mayan exhibits, and the Painted Desert, an open-air, mini–theme park complete with replicas of Taos Pueblo and a cliff dwelling that would be "staffed" by natives of Hopi, Zuni, the Rio Grande Pueblos, and from the Navajo and Apache reservations. (The Painted Desert was underwritten by the Santa Fe Railway, which was vigorously promoting the Southwest, especially New Mexico, "The Land of Enchantment," in national publicity campaigns.)

In twentieth-century New Mexico, art and anthropology coexisted as professional and creative communities, and the activities and goals of the artists and the scientists frequently overlapped in mutually beneficial civic projects and public events. Hewett solicited members from both disciplines, and Balboa Park profited from inspiration from New Mexico's visual artists and expertise from the state's anthropologists and archaeologists. Hewett imported Santa Fe–based painters Carlos Vierra and Gerald Cassidy to create the permanent murals for Balboa Park's Central American and Science of Man exhibits. The ethnologist John Peabody Harrington was hired to create models of Indian villages and homes in the Indian Arts building, and the New Mexico–based artist Kenneth Chapman, considered to be the leading authority on pueblo pottery, partnered with Jesse Nusbaum, Hewett's six-foot two-inch, twenty-six-year-old photographer and all-around assistant at the Mesa Verde excavations, to create the life-sized villages and dwellings of the Painted Desert outdoor exhibit. When the fair opened in 1915, Hewett's, Chapman's, and Nusbaum's New Mexico friends, the husband and wife potters Maria and Julian Martinez of San Ildefonso Pueblo, were in residence and gave daily demonstrations of native ceramic art at the Painted Desert village.[13]

FROM HER RENTED ROOMS at the Palomar Apartments, Natalie could view the progress of Hewett's exhibitions, and walk across the boulevard to Cabrillo Bridge and stroll through the new pedestrian-friendly grounds of Balboa Park. With so many colleagues and friends involved daily with the exposition—Alice, Hewett, Hrdlička, Lummis, plus Maria and Julian Martinez, and the very elderly Geronimo, who participated in the Painted Desert exhibitions—Natalie frequently visited the park and offered her expert advice to whoever would listen.

In Natalie's opinion, the "live" demonstrations of Indian arts and crafts at the Painted Desert villages did not do native art justice, and she suggested privately to Alice that a showcase be created where the fair-going public could view exemplary examples of American Indian art. With Hrdlička, Natalie designed an Indian Art Industries exhibit that would explain and display Indian ceramics, particularly the work of her Hopi-Tewa friend Nampeyo, Navajo blankets and rugs on loan from the collection of Canon Winfred Douglas, plus a selection from Frank Mead's collection of rare Navajo silver. Natalie also proposed an exhibit devoted to the handcrafts and artwork of Angel De Cora's students at the Carlisle Indian School.

It was not a practical proposal and Natalie knew it. She admitted to Alice that even if the exhibit appealed to Hewett, she and Hrdlička had estimated their Indian Art Industries display would cost a thousand dollars. With the war in Europe draining funds from American philanthropists, Natalie confessed she did "not feel competent to raise so much money," and the idea was scrapped.[14]

In spite of the national publicity blitz by the Santa Fe Railway and the Fred Harvey Company promoting the beauty and cultural treasures endemic to the American Southwest, in 1913 the capital "city" of Santa Fe was considered by most Americans too primitive and foreign to hazard a visit. It was the town's exotic, nonconformist qualities, however, that made it a haven for artists, archaeologists, and ethnologists who used Santa Fe as a base camp for their explorations of the vast country and multicultural people of New Mexico.

If they had not yet heard talk about the new "expat" colony of artists and intellectuals taking root in old Santa Fe, Natalie and Alice certainly learned of it from Hewett and his team of creative and scientific overachievers who came from New Mexico to build Balboa Park. Hewett became friends with George Curtis, likely through their common pal Alice, who was a member of the San Diego chapter of the School of American Archaeology. Hewett is mentioned in George's diary as early as May 1913. Natalie socialized with Hewett when he worked in San Diego, but it is possible she had met El Toro several years earlier, perhaps through Lummis at an AIA meeting, or as early as 1906 when Natalie and Hewett were both temporary residents of Washington, DC.

With Hewett and a dozen other Santa Fe luminaries actively involved with creation of the Panama-California Exposition, it was fitting that the fair organizers invited the new state of New Mexico to submit a plan for their own building and exhibitions in Balboa Park. The New Mexico state legislature responded enthusiastically to San Diego's call for "something different" and enlisted Ralph Emerson Twitchell to oversee the state's displays, and chose the architects and brothers Isaac H. Rapp and William M. Rapp to design the New Mexico Building.

For inspiration, the Rapps viewed Santa Fe artist Carlos Vierra's paintings of mission churches. In particular, they studied the design of the two-hundred-year-old Franciscan monastery and church of San Esteban del Rey perched on the island mesa of Acoma Pueblo. The two-story adobe chapel flanked by two bell towers, the only

Figure 15. New Mexico Building, Balboa Park, 1916.

Franciscan mission to survive the Pueblo Revolt of 1680, became the Rapps' model for the New Mexico Building in Balboa Park.[15]

Jesse Nusbaum oversaw construction of the New Mexico Building, and Twitchell designed and oversaw the creation of the building's exhibits depicting the long history of New Mexico and its people. The completed structure was a stunning and historically accurate copy of the Franciscan mission church at Acoma. Hewett, the Rapps, Twitchell, Vierra, Nusbaum, and all of the New Mexicans who assisted in the design and creation of the Mission Revival masterpiece in Balboa Park knew they had participated in something special.

In 1915 Hewett proposed to the New Mexico legislature that a building of nearly identical design be re-created on the Santa Fe plaza. The proposal was approved, and in 1917 a second reconstruction of the Acoma church (incorporating designs from six of New Mexico's Franciscan mission churches) would open its doors as the Museum of Fine Arts.

Alice threw her prodigious energy into organizing the Fine Arts Department and also into assembling her energetic and influential women friends into a committee, the Women's Board, whose purpose was to bring to Southern California the first major show of modern American art. With the financial support of the San Diego community, Hewett wanted the art show to have the status boost of a high-profile general director. Exactly when Hewett learned of Alice's access to American contemporary art star Robert Henri can only be guessed, but by 1914 Alice and Hewett were negotiating with Henri about overseeing the fine art exhibit at Balboa Park.

Alice had been exchanging newsy, chatty, and informal letters with Henri since the end of their European trip in 1912. She repeatedly urged Henri and "O" to come for an extended stay in San Diego, and after a particularly severe winter in New York, the Henris finalized their plans to visit Alice's home on the Pacific Ocean in the summer of 1914. "Looking forward to California as a place where the sun will warm me up to the right heat of production," Henri wrote Alice. "Where I can luxuriate in work, sunshine, fruit, flowers, good food, not have to dress, not entertain or be entertained, nothing but work and sun and the afore said."[16]

In the same March letter, Henri told Alice that in February Walter Pach had married Magdalene "Magda" Frohberg in a small, private ceremony in New York City.

The Henris planned to remain on "the other edge"—the West Coast—for seven months. Alice arranged for Henri, Margie "O," and "O's" sister, Violet, to lease a house near her own studio in the rural beach village of La Jolla. (The Henri's Richmond Court cottage was not far from Bailey's cliff-hugging Hilero and was designed by Frank Mead's former partner and Hilero's co-builder, Irving J. Gill.) While living in La Jolla, Henri used Alice's studio for public demonstrations and also to work on his own paintings. Henri did ten portraits in Alice's coastal studio, one of which, an oil "sketch" of his wife, titled *Marjorie "O,"* Henri gave to Alice. He signed the drawing: "dedication to Miss Klauber, a souvenir of the summer of 1914."[17]

During that summer Hewett met Henri in San Diego and asked him to cochair, with Alice, the California Building's fine arts exhibit. Still smarting from his loss of influence and power with the Armory Show the year before, Henri welcomed the personal and professional reception he received in Southern California, and agreed to curate and manage the fine arts exhibition.

For Balboa Park's fine art exhibit Henri assembled forty-nine works representative of American modern art. Seven of the invited artists were from the original eight "Ashcan" painters who had shown together in 1908: George Bellows, Maurice Prendergast, William Glackens, George Luks, Guy Pene DuBois, John Sloan, Carl Sprinchorn, and Henri. (Everett Shinn did not exhibit at Balboa Park.) All of Henri's invitations were to artists whose work embodied what he considered to be *American* modern art—Joseph Henry Sharp, Childe Hassam, and Ernest Lawson, among others—not the European-style Henri disliked and that was favored by the Stieglitz group, John Marin, Max Weber, Marsden Hartley, and Alfred Maurer.

With Henri's urging, Hewett sent an invitation to Arthur B. Davies, the director of the Armory Show who had elbowed Henri out of power a few years before. Davies declined to submit a canvas to the Balboa Park art show. Henri was not surprised and told Hewett that Davies "was not essential to the success of the exhibition."[18]

As chair of the Fine Arts Committee, and a founding member of the San Diego Archaeological Society, which sponsored the fine art show, Alice assumed charge of the gallery and supervised installation of the paintings, all of which followed very precise color and design instructions given to her by Henri. It was a small but noteworthy exhibition, especially because it gave major American painters the opportunity to, in George Bellows's words, "show on the other edge" for the first time.

At midnight on New Year's Eve 1914, President Woodrow Wilson, on the other edge of the continent in Washington, pressed a button that lit the buildings, plazas, avenues, pavilions, fountains, and gardens on the fairgrounds at Balboa Park and officially opened the Panama-California Exposition. Among the dignitaries who witnessed Balboa Park's grand opening was Theodore Roosevelt, who was a passenger in the first automobile to cross Cabrillo Bridge.[19]

The Balboa Park art exhibition precipitated the birth of Southern California's art colony. Both can be attributed to Henri's visit to San Diego and the efforts of Alice and other women artists who were versed in and moved within the American contemporary art movement. Henri's influence on these women was substantial. Alice's classmate in Spain Meta Gehring married another of Henri's students, Bert Cressey, and moved to Southern California in 1914. The painters Henrietta Shore and Esther Stevens, also Henri's protégées and friends of Alice's, settled in Los Angeles and San Diego. "Their

Figure 16. California Tower, Balboa Park, 1915. Oil painting by Alice Klauber.

activities encouraged the birth of the region's culture as we know it today."[20]

Shore would help found the Los Angeles Modern Art Society in 1916, and after the Balboa Park exposition, Alice would be a founding member of the La Jolla Art Association and the San Diego Art Guild and be instrumental in the opening of the Fine Arts Gallery in San Diego.

8

DESERT EUPHORIA

The desert will take care of you. At first it's all big and
beautiful, but you are afraid of it. Then you begin to see
its dangers, and you hate it. Then you learn how to
overcome its dangers. And then the desert is home.
                    —*John Wetherill*

IN THE SPRING OF 1913, after several months of easy living in the
California sunshine at George's ranch and at her apartment in San
Diego, Natalie was ready to don her desert boots, wide-brimmed
hat, and khaki riding skirt and return to the desert outback. Discussion began among Natalie's friends on both coasts about itineraries
and possible expedition routes in the Arizona canyonlands. Winfred
Douglas was part of this discussion from the start. Douglas was living
in Peekskill, New York, where he continued to serve as director of
music at the Episcopalian boarding school for girls, St. Gabriel, at
the Community of St. Mary. Located at the top of a small mountain
overlooking the Hudson, the cloistered Community of St. Mary was
a haven for Douglas's overworked colleagues, such as Natalie's friend
Kurt Schindler, who used a cottage at St. Mary's for weekend retreats
away from the bustle of New York City.

Douglas and Schindler shared an uncommon expertise in and
enthusiasm for ancient and obscure musical traditions. Douglas, a
member of Schindler's Schola Cantorum board of directors, was col-
laborating with Schindler on the editing of sixteenth-century Spanish

motets. Like Schindler, Douglas had spent much of his professional life researching ancient liturgical songs and folk music, and after his studies among the Benedictine monks in Europe and England, he had become an American authority on Gregorian chants and plain-song. Schindler advised Douglas on his ongoing effort to translate and adapt the English texts called "plain-chant" and was helping Douglas locate obscure sources for songs of the Crusades (only available in French) and English madrigals.

In the winter of 1913 Schindler was already working extraordinarily long hours when he accepted the position as choral director for Temple Emmanuel in Manhattan. With the demands on his time and energy that accompanied the phenomenal success of his Cantorum (formerly the MacDowell Chorus), Schindler was courting physical collapse. In the first week of March, just before Easter, Schindler's hectic rehearsal and performance schedule, and the daily management of his chorus of 250 singers, put the thirty-one-year-old in bed with exhaustion. Douglas, famously guilty of wrecking his own health with an unsustainable work ethic, told Schindler he needed to get away from the city, hop the train to Peekskill, and recuperate in the peace and quiet of Douglas's residence at St. Mary's.

Douglas was in poor health himself that spring, overwhelmed by the weekly commute between his home in Peekskill and his apartment at 127 West 87th Street in New York. By March, the canon was looking ahead to the summer break and the Douglas family's annual return to their palatial, two-story, seventeen-room log home at Camp Neosho (named for Dr. Jo's mother, Mary Neosho Williams) near Evergreen, Colorado. But even at Camp Neosho, Douglas had a full work schedule, since he was the founder and the director of the Evergreen summer music conference.

As he had in the past when his health deteriorated, in the spring of 1913 Douglas returned to Camp Neosho. While his friend Schindler recuperated in New York, Douglas spent a month in the Rocky Mountains. He sent letters to his young friend (whom he addressed as "My Dear Boy"), urging Schindler to consider making the trip west for a long stay in the Douglas's home in the Rocky Mountains. In March, Douglas began to plan the Arizona sojourn that would, he hoped, include Natalie, and he invited Schindler to "join some of us in as much as you will of the Desert Journey."[1]

The "some of us" on the roster for the desert journey that would cross Navajoland to Canyon de Chelly and culminate at the Hopi pueblo of Walpi were Douglas's teenage son, Eric, a friend and guide named Ted Whitaker, Natalie, Natalie's San Diego friend Alice Klauber, and Kurt Schindler. By late spring Douglas, an experienced outdoorsman and a natural, eager, if sometimes overbearing camp leader, became the self-appointed expedition point person and general organizer of the itinerary, outfitters, guides, and supplies.

George Curtis did not sign up for this excursion with his sister. He had animals, gardens, and a ranch to tend, and it was hellishly hot in Southern California that year, the temperature most days soaring to over one hundred degrees. George and his neighbors were on a twenty-four-hour fire watch from midsummer until late September. "The country is like tinder," George wrote in his diary, "a fire coming up the valley or starting at the roadside, would take the house." George could not leave his ranch and risk the safety of his home and livestock.[2]

The departure date was set for late July. Natalie advised Alice on expedition necessities and preparations. Her own camping gear had been packed away for years in one of George's sheds on the ranch, and with his help, Natalie aired out blankets and sleeping bag, ordered supplies, mended garments, and readied it all for train and eventually horse travel.

Douglas wrote an apprehensive Schindler in New York that their expedition would commence the last week of July or in very early August. He assured Schindler, the definitive city slicker tenderfoot around horses and everything to do with the desert and camping, that all the necessary camping gear would be provided by outfitters. All Schindler had to do was climb on the westbound train and make his way to Colorado.[3]

Although a native Californian and avid outdoorswoman, Alice, like Schindler, had never ridden horseback across the high desert of Arizona or camped there. Alice trusted Natalie and her knowledge of the outback, but she was ambivalent about following a stranger, even an ordained one, into the wilderness. George may have assured Alice that she would be in capable hands. Although he could not vouch for Douglas's wilderness skills, George could and did vouch for Natalie's.

With Douglas, Natalie planned their three-week sojourn so as to conclude their expedition at Third Mesa in Hopiland where Natalie planned to rendezvous with Theodore Roosevelt at the Snake Dance on August 21. With Roosevelt's public announcement of his and his sons' plans to attend the Snake Dance, and his promise to write three articles for the *Outlook* about his summer adventures in Arizona, the remote village of Walpi anticipated "such crowds of white people as no Hopi mesa had probably ever before beheld." A historic number of tourists would likely make the rigorous trek across the nearly roadless, amenity-barren Arizona desert just to watch the ex-president watch the Hopi Snake Dance in late August. Even so, Natalie welcomed the chance to introduce her friend to Hopiland and, with Douglas, coordinated their expedition route so as to be in camp below Walpi during the third week of August.[4]

The Roosevelt family expedition into the Arizona outback began on July 14, several weeks ahead of Natalie and Douglas's. With his sons, Archie, nineteen, and Quentin, fifteen, and their cousin, Harvard undergrad Nicholas, Roosevelt began the six-week expedition at the South Rim of the Grand Canyon. Their itinerary would take them down into the canyon, across the Colorado River, and north to Kayenta, where, with guide John Wetherill, they planned to cross the dangerous and challenging Rainbow Trail to reach the legendary Rainbow Bridge, one of the most remote landscapes in North America. From here, the Roosevelts would traverse the desert southwest to Walpi on top of First Mesa.

It was to be an epic expedition, but it was exactly the sort of physically demanding journey Roosevelt yearned for in 1913. Eight months before, he had lost his bid for a third term in the White House in a humiliating defeat to Woodrow Wilson. Although Roosevelt had enjoyed the public's veneration after he survived an assassination attempt, his former party members and legions of political allies were furious with him because he ran as a Progressive and spoiled the chances of the Republican candidate, incumbent William Howard Taft, at beating Wilson.[5]

Roosevelt had spent the winter of 1913 hunkered down at Sagamore Hill, isolated, lonely, and depressed. He kept himself in the public eye, at least on paper, by writing a column for *Outlook* magazine, for which he was a staff member. When the Armory Show opened in February, Roosevelt decided to go see for himself what all the fuss was about. He chose March 4, the day of Wilson's inauguration, to investigate the "bedlam of aesthetic debate" that was the International Exhibition of Modern Art in New York City.[6]

In the two weeks since it opened, the Armory Show had attracted record-breaking crowds, caused traffic jams throughout midtown Manhattan, and received the kind of newspaper copy that was every publicist's dream. Widely ridiculed and satirized by the press, hailed as a "Chamber of Horrors," the show's headliners, Matisse and the Parisian painters, were dubbed *enfants terribles*. The single most notorious work in the show, Marcel Duchamp's *Nude Descending a Staircase*, brought to America by Walter Pach, was likened to an "explosion in a shingle factory."[7]

Not one scared off by controversy, Roosevelt entered the vast hallways of the 69th Street Armory determined to come to his own conclusions about modern art, and to write down his thoughts in a review for the *Outlook*. Roosevelt's guides through the cavernous galleries were Henri's rival and nemesis Arthur Davies, the painter Walt Kuhn, and the American muralist Robert W. Chanler. Chanler's brother, William Astor Chanler, had lived in Wyoming (where his friends included Butch Cassidy and the Hole in the Wall Gang) and had soldiered with Roosevelt's Rough Riders. Robert Chanler painted the American West, and during his tour of the Armory Show, Roosevelt stopped and gazed a long while into Chanler's mural of a ceremony called the Snake Dance in a faraway Indian village called Walpi.

Roosevelt must have felt a familiarity with the exotic, primitive scene and people depicted in Chanler's painting. Natalie had told him stories about the Hopis and their cliff-hugging villages, and Roosevelt had read her accounts of sunset meetings with old chief Lololomai on a flat roof under the open sky of Oraibi. Perhaps all that modern and even unsettling futurist art surrounding Roosevelt in the Armory made it apparent that what he needed to reconnect with his sense of purpose was time alone under the wide sky found in the primitive outback of the American Southwest.

At fifty-four, Roosevelt was looking for redemption and distraction. Throughout his life he had turned to physical tests of endurance in the great outdoors to overcome disappointments and setbacks. In the spring of 1913, Roosevelt accepted an invitation to visit Brazil and explore the Amazon River, a larger-than-life trip that would commence in the fall. He also announced to his sons Archie and

Quentin that in July they were going with him on an expedition deep
into the Arizona desert.

The Roosevelt family pack trip began with a predawn descent on
horseback into the Grand Canyon in the light of the nearly full moon
on July 15. Their route through Navajoland traversed the canyon and
ascended the North Rim into the Kaibab National Forest, crossed
the Colorado at Lee's Ferry, and finally headed northeast across the
harsh, bald, and breathlessly hot sandland plateau toward Kayenta.
By Roosevelt's account, they passed herds of buffalo and Navajo
sheep, confronted venomous rattlesnakes, and cooked supper over
campfires beneath sunsets that turned the heavens ruby red before
fading to a pale turquoise.[8]

This was what a world-weary, politically wounded, middle-aged
Roosevelt had come to the Southwest in search of: an encounter with
the primordial universe.

In late July, Kurt Schindler shed his starched white dress shirt and
elegant black tails, put away his sheet music and conductor's baton,
and with a duffel bag carrying new khakis and oiled-leather lace-up
boots, climbed on the train in New York and commenced the journey
to his own encounter with the Southwest. Schindler arrived in Mor-
rison, Colorado, on July 26 and, following Douglas's instructions,
took Skerrett's automobile service from the depot up into the Rocky
Mountains to Camp Neosho in Evergreen. Douglas was away on
business, so Schindler spent a week walking the mountain trails and
enjoying the fragrant pine forest sanctuary that was Camp Neosho
before catching the train to Colorado Springs, where he connected
with Douglas and his fifteen-year-old son, Eric.[9]

The three took the Santa Fe train south to Albuquerque and west
to Williams, Arizona, where they met up with Douglas's friend Ted
Whitaker and at least one guide who went with the men on the
stage up to the Grand Canyon. After several days on the South Rim,
Douglas and his son left Schindler, Whitaker, and their Navajo guide
at the canyon and hopped the stage to Holbrook, where Natalie and
Alice would disembark their train at the Santa Fe depot on Friday,
August 8.

Climbing on the train bound for Arizona with her camping gear was,
for Natalie, the final leg of a long-anticipated homecoming to Indian
Country. For Alice, however, departing the genteel and civilized city

of Los Angeles with bags that carried only those clothes and personal items deemed necessary for survival in the desert was unsettling.

Alice may have kept her ambivalence about the expedition from Natalie, but she admitted in her diary the imbecility of undertaking such a rigorous trip with strangers. She had never met the expedition's leader, Canon Douglas, although she had heard all about the good and able musician-priest from Natalie and George. Alice had also heard about New York conductor sensation Kurt Schindler from Natalie and read about him, too, as Schindler's chorus was receiving rave reviews and national attention. Even so, except for Natalie, Alice was about to depart civilization with complete strangers.

Alice loved to be alone in nature and sought solitude on La Jolla's rocky shoreline and in the hills and scrub desert outside of San Diego. She had thrice sailed across the Atlantic for extended, even rigorous travels through Europe and the Mediterranean. But the physically demanding journey by horseback she was about to undertake with Natalie into the remote, uninhabited, dangerous, and still very much uncivilized southwest wilderness was an extreme adventure the likes of which the forty-two-year-old Alice had never attempted.

That first night, Natalie and Alice left California and rode the Santa Fe train across a bright, moon-infused desert to Arizona. Alice was unable to sleep in their shared Pullman car, her discomfort as much psychological as material. "I felt sick enough to ponder the imbecility of undertaking the trip with strangers," she scribbled in her small journal. The next afternoon Alice's spirits were lifted by thundershowers that cooled the smoldering desert, and her well-being and optimism returned when the train stopped for supper at the comfortable, immaculate, and professionally staffed Harvey House in the tiny outpost of Ashfork, Arizona. After dinner and a tour of the Harvey House Indian Curios room, Natalie and Alice reboarded the train at dusk and continued east to their rendezvous in Holbrook with Douglas.

As their train came into Holbrook, the moonlight on the desert, and the absolute stillness of the night, cast a surreal quality onto their arrival. Alice and Natalie's midnight train was met by the good Canon Douglas, who alone (Eric was asleep) carried their bags to their room in a hotel. The hotel was not on a par with a Harvey House, and Holbrook was nothing more than the Santa Fe depot by the single track and a dirt street with a few stores, a bank, and a post office. If Alice had concerns about the quality of their lodgings, and was still harboring doubts about the wisdom of following the priest into the outback, Douglas assuaged her unease and discomfort when he brought the women a late supper in their room.

A night of sleep in a lumpy bed in a third-rate hotel completely refreshed Alice. With Natalie, she breakfasted with Douglas and Eric. After a day of errands and preparations that included a visit to the bank, and a last laundry and bath, Natalie and Alice went with the Douglas men to meet Schindler's train.

It was a happy and much-anticipated reunion for Natalie and Schindler, who had not seen one another since Natalie left New York with Mimsey last winter. Alice had heard all about the brilliant and eccentric musician Kurt Schindler. Even so, his appearance and demeanor astonished her. After meeting him at the Holbrook depot that evening, Alice wrote: "With all N.C.'s hints and suggestions [I] was not prepared in fullness—curious, sensitive, attenuated being— looks like a Navajo (Zuni) Indian who had just crawled out of a sunless cavern completely bleached out + with a much quickened interest in his fellow man which a Navajo would succeed much better in hiding."[10]

The Curtis-Douglas entourage enjoyed one last supper in civilization at a small Holbrook diner called The Cottage. And then, with two teams and a wagon carrying their camping gear, a wrangler friend of Douglas's named Ted Whitaker, and several more saddle horses and pack animals, the two women and four men left Holbrook for the open desert. At eight in the evening, Saturday, August 9, their journey began much like Roosevelt's three weeks before under the surreal light of the quarter moon, with Mercury, the evening star, sparking in the west for an hour after sundown.

They struck north for Ganado and the settlement at Hubbell's trading post, where they would camp a few nights among the folks who attended the annual late-summer Navajo fair. It was a trek that would take the horses and wagons four days following the tracks of previous teams that had made this journey before them. Even with the fine quarter moon lighting their way, Douglas and Whitaker lost the trail several hours out, and they had to retrace their tracks for several miles. They made camp where they found the trail again, and even

Figure 17. Desert Expedition, July–August 1913. *Left to right:* Eric Douglas, Kurt Schindler, Alice Klauber, Natalie Curtis, Winfred Douglas.

though it was impromptu, and they'd lost several hours looking for the route north, everyone slept well. The dawn was a fine one, and before breakfast Alice slipped away with her sketchbook to make a drawing of the sun lighting the sky over the empty, silent Arizona sandland.

Douglas, Natalie, and Whitaker had traveled between Holbrook and Ganado and were familiar with the route to Cottonwood Wash and a campsite Douglas had used two years before. To Alice's eyes, though, the landmarks that marked the trail across the desert were often imperceptible, and she, like Schindler, had to abandon all notions of self-reliance and place her fate in the hands of the expedition leader.

Early in the afternoon on their first day out, Alice and Natalie shed their travel skirts for more appropriate desert riding apparel—split skirts of heavy cotton—and left the wagon and rode horseback alongside Douglas, Eric, and Schindler. Schindler was stoically managing blisters, sore muscles, sunburn, and chafed surfaces after a long, hot day in the unfamiliar embrace of a western saddle. On previous trail rides, Natalie had come to terms with the nongenteel aspects of riding astride a horse. But Alice had never ridden a western saddle and had to quickly adjust her sense of propriety. "Don't like it astride a bit," she wrote in her journal, "and couldn't ride side-saddle in my skirt if I could get a side saddle."[11]

The horses and wagon followed a route that was never more than tracks in sand or ruts through arroyos, and that took the riders up steep mesas, across slick rock, and around jagged stone outcroppings to Twin Buttes. They were in the fantastic country of the Desierto Pintado, the Painted Desert, the region the Navajo called Halchíítah (Among the Red Areas). At six thousand feet above sea level, the huge swath of eccentrically eroded and multicolored sandstone, clay, and volcanic rock was brilliantly striated. The hues and forms of the desert changed hourly with the movement of the sun and the shadows of the clouds. It was fine country to be swallowed up in, and a visual feast for a painter. Alice likened the landscape to the Holy Land and remarked how the colors of the desert belonged in a Jules Guérin painting.

Each day they moved farther into the wild. Natalie welcomed the transformation wrought by desert life. She, like Douglas, knew the Colorado Plateau outback would work its magic on Alice, Schindler, and young Eric, even as it had on her and George a decade ago. The physical and emotional challenges endemic to wilderness travel on horseback, and the confidence and resiliency earned as those challenges were successfully met and overcome, were life altering. Natalie wrote, "For us the sordid bargaining of our narrowed city lives, the fret and whirl of petty currents that bear us so far from our inner goal—all were forgotten in that enchanted land."[12]

Dawn on August 12 came with a soft, pastel-colored sky and a herd of Navajo goats wandering into their camp near Indian Wells. Alice was the first to dress and leave the tent she shared with Natalie, and she hiked a sand hill and completed a sketch before Douglas even made the breakfast fire.

Desert life settled into a comfortable routine. Expedition members became accustomed to their assigned tasks and chores, and confident in their riding and camping abilities. Douglas and Whitaker pushed the horses and riders north, their destination Hubbell's trading post, a two days' ride in the wide riverbed of the Pueblo Colorado Wash that cut through the hard desert of the Diné to Ganado.

Schindler took to wearing a bandana tied about his head Navajo-style. Douglas rode with his shirt sleeves rolled to his elbows, but

Natalie and Alice kept their sleeves buttoned down around their wrists, their shirt collars up, and their necks wrapped with bandanas. Sunup till sundown, everyone lived beneath a broad-brimmed hat. Even with so much precaution, the sun exposure at this altitude was extreme and even dangerous, and three days into the desert, everyone was sunburned somewhere on their body.

A drenching thunderstorm late on the afternoon of August 12 sent the expedition up and away from the Pueblo Colorado Wash, which became a raging river with flash flood waters. They found shelter in the cedar trees on the side of a mesa, and after several hours the storm cleared and left the red desert fragrant beneath a perfectly formed double rainbow. Douglas and Whitaker led them in the approaching dusk to a camp on a hill near a dramatic volcanic mountain that the men climbed at sundown. Alice and Natalie remained by the campfire, listening to the haunting songs of Navajo shepherds camped nearby. After dark, when Douglas and the men had returned from their hike up the volcanic cone, one of the Navajo singers came to their camp and exchanged songs with Natalie.[13]

Traders and ranchers, anthropologists, adventurers, and adventurous tourists frequented the route Douglas and company were following between Holbrook and Ganado. The Diné, the Navajos, who lived in family groups scattered across their 25,000-square-mile reservation, were becoming accustomed to *Bilagaana* (non-Navajo) horse and wagon expeditions crossing Navajoland. Even so, encounters on such an enormous frontier were infrequent and remarkable. The usually reserved Diné often approached Natalie and Douglas's entourage. White women were rare in this remote country, and Natalie and Alice were a curiosity to the natives they encountered on the trail.

On August 13 they rode into Lók'aah niteel (Wide Reeds) and Hubbell's trading post at Ganado. After four days on horseback in the glittering monotony of sun, rock, sky, and horizon, in a land where mesas floated like islands in a sand sea, coming into the Ganado valley was like riding into modern civilization. Of course, Ganado was not *modern*: the homestead of John Lorenzo Hubbell, known by everyone as Don Lorenzo, was one of very few parcels privately owned within the boundaries of the gigantic Navajo Reservation. It had amenities like water, fresh food, and buildings that boasted

Figure 18. Hubbell's trading post, 1890s. John Hubbell is holding the rug.

wood floors and glass windows, but the post was extremely isolated, fifty miles west of Gallup and sixty-five miles northeast of Holbrook.

The red stone and log trading post served as the stage stop, post office, supply store, farm and ranch outfitter, wool warehouse, stable and blacksmith, and trader of wool, goat, and sheep skins and the finest Navajo blankets, rugs, and silver. Ganado also provided modern medical services at the first and soon largest Indian mission and hospital, which had been built by the Presbyterians in 1901.

The waters of the Pueblo Colorado River filled a reservoir that irrigated fields of alfalfa, wheat, oats, and barley, a vineyard and an orchard of fruit trees, and the Hubbell family's kitchen garden. The trading post also kept chickens and hogs, sheep, goats, cattle, saddle horses, and a small flock of peafowl to keep the rattlesnakes away.[14]

For horse and wagon travelers in 1913, riding in off the desert to Hubbell's in mid-August was akin to finding an oasis in the Sahara. Don Lorenzo was a friend of both Douglas's and Natalie's (Natalie and George had stayed with the Hubbells on previous trips), and he arranged for their group to camp in a prime location in the trees near the trading post, and to take several meals a day in his family's house.

This gave Natalie and company the best of both worlds—the privacy and space of their own tents at a distance from the busy trading post, and the cool and comfortable porches, dining and sitting rooms of the Hubbell family home.

The thick-walled stone and mud dwelling housed a private museum of native crafts and was decorated floor to ceiling, and across the vigas of the ceiling itself, with Indian baskets, carvings, ceramics, and textiles. The paintings of contemporary artists who had stayed with the Hubbells were displayed throughout the home, and the shelves of the library in the grand salon held signed editions of America's best authors, including Mark Twain and Zane Grey. And every floor in the house boasted the finest examples of Navajo rugs found anywhere in the world.

Like Louisa and John Wetherill's trading post and home more than a hundred miles to the northwest in Kayenta, Hubbell's was a destination that outback travelers planned their itineraries around. Don Lorenzo had lived nearly all his life among the Navajos and spoke their language and understood the subtleties and complexities of their culture. Like the Wetherills' near Monument Valley, the Hubbell home was a gathering place for archaeologists and anthropologists, writers and artists exploring the country of the mysterious Diné.

The Hubbell dinner table was usually a hub of energetic conversation, and Natalie and Douglas looked forward to evenings with Don Lorenzo. However, in 1913, following the death of Don Lorenzo's wife, Lena Rubi, the atmosphere around the trading post was somber, and Natalie's group hardly socialized with Hubbell.

They camped in the cedar trees of Ganado for three nights. The ground was flat and hard, and pockmarked by petrified wood and cactus, but there were the luxuries of ample shade and plenty of water for washing and bathing. Although Natalie, Alice, Douglas, and Eric enjoyed a daily dip in the Pueblo Colorado River, Schindler had become a devotee of the cowboy way and continued to take his daily bath in the camp's Dutch oven.[15]

Six hundred Navajos and Hopis came to Ganado on August 13 and 14 for the annual Indian fair. There were two days of races and contests on horseback, and in the evenings there was storytelling around campfires. When word got out around the trading post and camp that Natalie was the woman who collected Indian songs, more than twenty Diné came to her and Alice's tent wanting to share chants and stories.

On Monday, August 15, Natalie, Douglas, and friends struck their comfortable camp in the cedar trees and said good-bye to their horses, which were left in Don Lorenzo's barn. They were to continue north to Chin Lee (Chinle) in Don Lorenzo's "Ford machines." It was thirty-five miles of very slow going on a primitive road north through the wild and lovely Nazlini Canyon, home to a community of small black bears sacred to the Navajos. To their west, across a wide ocean of buff-colored sand and low featureless plateaus, was Hopiland. Below the horizon to their east were the cool pine-covered slopes of the Chuska Mountains that marked the Arizona–New Mexico border.[16]

Recent rains had packed down the sand, but the wheels of the two Model Ts, considered good desert vehicles because of their four-cylindered, twenty-horse-powered engines, were no match for the thick clay and mud. The drivers had to navigate the road's high centers, deep arroyos, and scrabbled inclines, and Alice and Natalie commented that horses and wagons were a better choice than the lurching, swerving Ford machines. Navajos came and went on horseback, and travelers in wagons passed by the noisy automobiles, both groups destined to arrive hours ahead of Natalie and Alice's company.

They were driving due north to the great Canyon de Chelly, the labyrinthine canyon where sixty years before the Navajos hid from Kit Carson and the U.S. military in the ancient, inaccessible cliff villages abandoned long ago by the Anasazi, the ancestors of the Hopis. Douglas had explored Canyon de Chelly before, but it would be an inaugural visit for Natalie.

The two Fords and their eight passengers arrived at John Kirk's trading post near Canyon de Chelly in the late afternoon. Kirk's log and stone store was tucked into cottonwood trees against a small bluff a half mile from the entrance to the great canyon. Even so close to the massive stone labyrinth, the pastoral landscape surrounding the trading post gave travelers no clue about their proximity to the legendary canyon.[17]

Douglas had arranged for new drivers and guides—Ken Shelly, a Navajo from Fort Defiance, and a second guide named Brady—to accompany their group into the canyon. After an hour in the trading post, where Natalie, Schindler, and Alice talked with the locals who

Figure 19. Spider Rock, Canyon de Chelly, 1873.

came in to trade and to have a cup of Arbuckle's coffee, Douglas shepherded everyone into the automobiles, and with new supplies of food and a load of dry firewood, they drove into the canyon.

There would have been nothing that Douglas or Kirk or their guides could have told Alice, Natalie, and Schindler that would have prepared them for the hauntingly exquisite beauty that was Canyon de Chelly. It was dusk when they passed through the stone-walled gateway into the heart of the canyon. Sheer, smooth, red and gold stone rose hundreds of feet into the air on either side of the cottonwood-lined river. Until they departed the canyon two days later, all Natalie and Alice would see of the Arizona sky was the slice of blue held between the stone rims of Canyon de Chelly's vertical walls.

Darkness fell and a million stars crowded the sky above the canyon. The automobiles drove through a tunnel of darkness that followed the river, the skilled Navajo drivers careful to keep the automobiles' tires from the canyon's famous yellow quicksand that was known to suck vehicles into muck so deep they vanished completely.

The full moon finally reached the sky beyond the stone rim and flooded the canyon with a luminous, otherworldly light. They set up camp on a high ledge of fine dry sand alongside a great bluff that gleamed in the moonlight. On the flat surface of smooth stone, Natalie, Alice, Douglas, and the men ate a late supper of bread and mackerel, olives and grape juice, with a nightcap of hot chocolate. The night was too beautiful and clear for tents, and no one bothered to even unpack the tarps, but slept in bedrolls on the open ground in the shade made by an enormous stone monolith. Alice lay awake and stared into the radiant nightscape that surrounded her, listening to the sound of horses hobbled somewhere in the canyon.[18]

Dawn came in a soft blush of color to the canyon rims. An hour later, the hot rays of the sun reached down the southwestern walls. The floor of the canyon was smooth white sand, and the river, lined by lush groves of cottonwood and fruit trees, wound through a chasm edged by sheer stone walls, rock towers, and polished buttes that stood more than eight hundred feet above the canyon floor.

They saddled up the horses brought in by the guides and rode deeper into the canyon past summer hogans, cornfields, orchards of peach trees, and small corrals of horses and goats that belonged to the Navajos who lived in the canyon. Their destination was the White House ruin tucked on a ledge under an immense stone overhang. After scrambling about the old pueblo, they rode up the tributary of Cañon del los Muertos and from a stone ledge in the shade pondered the gruesome fate of Navajos who were slaughtered by the Spanish in Mummy Cave several hundred feet above them.[19]

Two days later, Natalie, Alice, Schindler, Douglas, Eric, and Whitaker reemerged from Canyon de Chelly. At Kirk's trading post they purchased supplies, repacked and organized their gear into the Model Ts, and headed west for Keam's Canyon, Hopiland. It was Sunday, August 18, but after ten days in the outback, the calendar of the "civilized" world ceased to have meaning. Alice's journal entries, like her sense of time, had become untethered from dates and days of the week. Alice and Schindler now understood what Natalie and Douglas knew: when you traveled into the deep outback of Indian Country, conventional time became irrelevant. Hours and days were measured by the movements of the sun and the moon, and time was of significance only in relation to the distance one needed to cross between sunup and sundown.

Natalie flourished in the primordial landscape, and delighted in the days and weeks spent "wandering, roofless and free, over the sun-scorched deserts . . . for in them we quite lost the trail of the twentieth century and of our materialistic and commercial civilization. . . . Even the wrinkles and crow's feet that lined our white faces . . . were burned away. In the silence of the desert and the sweep of pure winds our souls were washed clean, till we too seemed true children of the Earth-Mother and the Sky-Father."[20]

9

WALPI RENDEZVOUS

The spell of the desert comes back to me, as it always will
come. I see the veils, like purple smoke, in the cañons, and
I feel the silence. And it seems that again I must try to
pierce both and to get at the strange wild life of the last
American wilderness—wild still, almost, as it ever was.

—*Zane Grey*

THE ROAD TO KEAM'S CANYON angled across the high desert to the
south and west from Chinle, directly into the ocean of buff-colored
sand plateaus. The same day they left Kirk's at Canyon de Chelly,
Natalie and Douglas's expedition left the mixed blessings of the Ford
machines and transferred onto horses, with a team and wagon once
again carrying their camping gear. The weather was cooler and they
were able to ride fifteen miles to Salina Springs, where they set up
camp in a thicket of cedar trees above the spring. The next morning,
August 18, they rode off the high plateau east of Low Mountain
and followed Jadito Wash toward Peach Orchard Springs, Keam's
Canyon. By noon, they rode down rock and sand bluffs into a herd
of goats grazing in the peach trees, and stopped before the trading
post owned by Don Lorenzo and run by his son Lorenzo Hubbell Jr.

An ancient village site of the Hopis, by 1913 Keam's Canyon was
as anglicized as any community found in Indian Country. The BIA
offices were within sight of the notorious Keam's Canyon boarding
school that Natalie, Lummis, and scores of other Indian rights activists had condemned for years.

Superintendent Leo Crane was not a fan of Natalie Curtis's work among the Indians and would not have welcomed her arrival to Keam's Canyon. However, in August 1913 Crane had been briefed by Washington officials that Natalie and her friends were slated to rendezvous with Theodore Roosevelt at the Snake Dance at Walpi. Crane and his agents were instructed to accommodate Roosevelt and Curtis and to provide an office at Third Mesa where the ex-president and the ethnomusicologist could meet.

Agent Crane had served as superintendent of the Hopis for only two years, yet his tyrannical style of management (he continued to send Navajo policemen into the Hopi villages to round up school-children) and his palpable animosity toward all Indians, who, in his estimation, lived "on a moral plane little above their livestock," made him deeply disliked in Tusayan. Crane was suspicious of traders like Hubbell and the "open-mouthed" tourists, curio hunters, actresses, authors, and moving-picture fans who revered all things Indian. And Crane absolutely *detested* the annual heathen affair called the Snake Dance that brought hordes of Indian-loving outsiders into whatever Hopi village was sponsoring the ceremony. Crane wanted outsiders kept outside, and the "immoral" Hopis kept under his firm, civilizing hand.[1]

A persistent and bothersome thorn in Agent Crane's side was Natalie's collaborator and friend Tawakwaptiwa, now the *kikmongwi* of Old Oraibi. The Oraibi Split of 1906 had precipitated social and political realignments among the Hopis, and Chief Tawakwaptiwa was seen as both a hero and a scoundrel among his own people. Crane detested Tawakwaptiwa and was particularly perturbed by the adulation and recognition Miss Natalie Curtis had given Lololomai's nephew in *The Indians' Book*.

Even if Crane had no patience for her work in preserving Indian music and culture, he understood the place of privilege Tawimana (Song Woman) Natalie Curtis held in Hopiland. He would be out-wardly courteous and helpful to Natalie and her traveling compan-ions, but he would be relieved when the spectacle of the Snake Dance was over and all meddlesome outsiders, famous and not, departed Indian Country.

After Natalie's friends enjoyed a leisurely stopover at the Hubbell Keam's Canyon store, they remounted and rode east eleven miles

across a well-used but very rocky road to Polacca, the outpost below
the imposing rock promontory of First Mesa. The sand drifted in
deep dunes across the road that wound up and down treacherous
ledges and bald rock outcroppings. It was obvious to Alice why
the Ford machines were left at Canyon de Chelly: a dozen autos a
week were stranded on this road, defeated by the steep ascents or
swallowed up by sand that reached to their hubcaps.

Natalie, Alice, Douglas, and the others reached First Mesa in the
afternoon. In the shade of a large peach orchard they set up tents,
tarps, and their outdoor kitchen within walking distance of the stone
trading post, yet another establishment owned by Don Lorenzo
Hubbell. They would remain at this camp beneath First Mesa for at
least the next week.

It had been eight years since Natalie had trod the trail up to the
Hopi villages of Walpi and Sichomovi and the Tewa-Hopi village
of Hano on the slender island of rock that was First Mesa. She was
eager to see Nampayo and before dusk led everyone but Alice (who
confessed to her diary that she was cross, tired, and of no help any-
way) up the narrow path to Hano, perched on the mesa six hundred
feet above the desert floor. The sinking sun cast purple and rose hues
onto the desert below the trail, and the air was fragrant with the scent
of cedar fires and burnt sage. As they ascended the mesa, the dusk
silence was laced with the calls of ravens, the bells of goats, and the
shouts of the village children.[2]

Natalie took Douglas, Schindler, Eric, and Whitaker directly to
Nampayo's home, where they were warmly welcomed by Nampayo
and her family. Nampayo was nearly blind now, but continued to
make pottery with her daughter Nellie. Nampayo's pottery, like that
of the Tewa artist Maria Martinez at San Ildefonso Pueblo in New
Mexico, had become the gold standard by which Native American
ceramics were evaluated. With the publicity boost brought to her
pottery by the Indian Department of the Fred Harvey Company
and the Santa Fe Railway, Nampayo's ceramics were collected by
museums and by connoisseurs of fine Indian arts and crafts.

After a quick tour of Hano in the soft light of the August dusk,
Natalie and Douglas led Eric, Schindler, and Whitaker back down
the mesa. Later that night, from the warmth of her bedroll on the
open ground below First Mesa, Natalie pondered the fragility of

Figure 20. Walpi, First Mesa, Arizona, ca. 1907.

the traditional life of her Hopi friends. Nampayo's pottery and the craftwork of other emerging native artists were bringing collectors directly into the villages and communities of Native America. Staring up at the stars twinkling through the branches of the peach trees, Natalie wondered if it was possible to stop or even slow "the tide of Anglo-Saxon iconoclasm that would sweep the Hopi Indian villages from their ancient sites."[3]

Natalie's desert idyll ended the next morning. Roosevelt and his expedition were coming in on horseback from the north, and the news of the former president's arrival moved through the native and nonnative communities on and below First Mesa like an electric current. After weeks without even a passing thought about the condition of her appearance, Natalie was suddenly conscious of her disheveled clothes and tangled hair.

"Weeks in the Arizona desert do indeed restore one to an atavistic, primitive state in outward appearance as in inner peace of mind," Natalie reflected. "I was travel-stained from head to foot, and on the front of my khaki riding-skirt flared with placid disregard of all conventions a large round circle of black axel-grease, where the camp wagon had branded me for my affront of trying to climb in over the front wheel."

Alice, Douglas, and Schindler understood how important Natalie's appointment with Roosevelt was to her. But with each of them looking equally rumpled and unkempt—skin sun dried and burned, hair matted under hats, lips chapped, boots scuffed, shirts discolored by sweat and horsehair—Natalie's sudden need to be presentable, indeed *professional*, became the subject of much camp humor. Douglas and Schindler thought the grease stain decorating the front and center of Natalie's riding skirt made a fine Indian sun symbol, and ought to be left alone. But if she insisted on removing the grease stain, the men told Natalie nothing short of a bath in gasoline would do the job. Burning the skirt seemed a more prudent solution.

Natalie left her unsympathetic compadres beside the breakfast fire and marched off alone in search of gasoline. In the BIA buildings at Polacca, agency workers were mopping floors and scrubbing surfaces "for Roosevelt." Next door at the schoolhouse, the teacher was cleaning up the students and the classroom for the president, and had no time to help Natalie with her stain. She did, however, offer Natalie the use of any cup she could find. After locating a handle-less vessel in the school's kitchen, Natalie went outside and found a man standing beside his parked automobile.

"I need gasoline," Natalie told him, gesturing at her skirt. After telling Natalie she was welcome to as much gasoline as she could extract from his auto's tank, the man quickly left to join the crowd gathering on the far side of the mesa to greet Roosevelt's expedition as they rode in from the desert.

Natalie had no idea where the vehicle's gas tank was located and was accepting defeat when a horse and rider appeared.

"Presently a handsome and deep-tanned young cowboy in blue overalls passed me, leading some horses," Natalie later wrote of that August morning. "I wonder if you could get me some gasoline from this car? . . . I am allowed to have it. You see, we are all trying to clean up in honor of Colonel Roosevelt—he is expected today some time."

The young man smiled, dismounted, and within moments "lay in utter chivalry under the car, milking the gasoline into my cup." He soon slid out from under the auto, handed Natalie the handle-less cup filled with gasoline, gathered up the horses he was leading, remounted his horse, and with a tip of his hat trotted away.

Carefully balancing the cup with the precious cleaning agent, Natalie walked back toward the camp in the orchard. As she crested a low rise, she stopped: "A stalwart figure on a cow pony was riding up the hill, alone and unattended; without any flourish of trumpets, Colonel Theodore Roosevelt had arrived! His sunburned face was partly shaded by a big Stetson hat, a red bandanna fluttered at his throat, and he too looked as though gasoline might improve his khakis. I waved my sombrero and cried, 'Hail to the chief!'"

Roosevelt had arrived at First Mesa. Undetected by his great herd of fans, only the tiny, tanned, smiling Natalie Curtis welcomed the president to Hopiland. Theodore Roosevelt enjoyed a Big Entrance before a large, boisterous, adoring crowd—Henry James described him as "the mere monstrous embodiment of unprecedented and resounding Noise"—but on this particular August morning under the hot sun and brilliant cerulean sky of Indian Country, Theodore Roosevelt rode into the outpost at Polacca the iconic western loner. Even his doting and protective sons were not with him.[4]

Roosevelt recognized his friend immediately and leaned down from his saddle to grasp Natalie's outstretched hand. It was so like Roosevelt, Natalie would later say, to appear where no one expected him "ahead of the rest of the world."[5]

The night before, while Natalie had contemplated the universe from her bedroll under the peach trees, Roosevelt had done much the same on the hard ground of a mud flat in the desert north of First Mesa. With his sons Archie and Quentin and his nineteen-year-old cousin Nicholas, and with John Wetherill and two Navajo guides, Roosevelt had ridden three days through the mountains of Black Mesa and down across the roadless country of low cliffs and blood-red buttes between Kayenta and Walpi. After six weeks on horseback, camping on rims, in pine forests, and under the great Rainbow Bridge in canyons so untouched by humans as to be unnamed and unmapped, Roosevelt had become immersed in what Natalie fondly called the desert dream. "Only those who live and sleep in the open," Roosevelt wrote in his notebook, "fully realize the beauty of dawn and moonlight and starlight."[6]

After several minutes of casual chat, Roosevelt told Natalie she needed to meet his son and turned in his saddle and called out

Figure 21. Theodore Roosevelt, Kayenta, August 1913.

for Archie. A few moments later, the handsome cowboy-knight in overalls who had filled Natalie's cup with siphoned petrol rode up alongside his father. "We have met to-day before," a smiling Archie said to a speechless Natalie.

There was almost no gasoline in Natalie's cup, as it had quickly evaporated into the dry air. But Natalie didn't care anymore about cleaning up her skirt. No explanations were necessary. She was among kindred spirits.[7]

Winfred Douglas, wondering what had become of Natalie and her quest for petrol, wandered over to the schoolhouse and found her with the Roosevelts. After introductions, it was agreed that Natalie and Douglas would meet with Roosevelt the next day in the Indian agency near the school where Agent Crane had set aside spacious quarters for Roosevelt. Douglas had seen the Snake Dance in 1911, and Roosevelt wanted context before witnessing the ceremony. He also asked Natalie if she would accompany him on his tour of Walpi. Roosevelt had only a few days to absorb Hopi culture and draft his *Outlook* article about the people of Hopiland. Natalie agreed to help.

Figure 22. Theodore Roosevelt at Walpi, August 20, 1913.

Roosevelt actually had plenty of expert consultants with him at First Mesa. He was traveling with John Wetherill, surely the most knowledgeable and revered guide in Navajoland. Don Lorenzo Hubbell had come to Polacca from Ganado to assist Roosevelt during the Snake Dance. Hubbell was a personal friend of the Roosevelts, and had visited the family in February during a trip to Washington for a meeting at the BIA. John, as Roosevelt called Hubbell, had also served as a driver and guide for various legs of the Arizona expedition.[8]

Later that day, Natalie took Alice and Schindler to see Second and Third Mesas. They rode twelve miles up and down a steep and difficult road to Second Mesa, where they visited friends of Natalie's at the village of Shongopovi. As the afternoon passed into the evening, Natalie, Alice, and Schindler pressed on to Third Mesa, where Natalie hoped to reconnect with Chief Tawakwaptiwa at Old Oraibi.

They spent the night at New Oraibi, a community of federal-issue dwellings and offices at the base of Third Mesa. Natalie was distressed by New Oraibi's lack of indigenous architectural characteristics, and by the U.S. government's continued insistence on funding and constructing buildings artistically and practically out of synch with Hopiland. The traditional thick-walled, flat-roofed dwellings stacked several stories high, with shaded overhangs and terraces, had for centuries successfully served the Hopis as they worked, played, socialized, and celebrated in every season of the year. At New Oraibi, the traditional Hopi village was replaced by rows of impractical pitched tin-roofed dwellings with too many windows that were frying-pan hot in the summer and ice cold in the winter. Natalie had hoped to find improvements in the federal government's management of Indian Country. Instead, she found the feds had continued their campaign to weaken the traditional cultures and lifeways of Native America.

After a night in one of the government buildings of New Oraibi, Natalie woke Alice and Schindler at dawn and led them up the steep foot trail to see Tawakwaptiwa at his home in Old Oraibi. To Natalie's great sorrow, she found Tawakwaptiwa was the chief of a diminished pueblo. The once-vital village where Natalie and Chief Lololomai had sat and watched sundown from a rooftop was disintegrating back into the dust of Third Mesa. Natalie blamed the community's ruination on the U.S. government's relentless insistence that Hopi children be forcibly taken from their homes and placed in

Figure 23. Alice Klauber and Chief Tawakwaptiwa,
August 1913.

boarding schools whose goal was to obliterate the cultural heritage of
Indian America.

In spite of the community's deterioration, the Hopi of Third
Mesa continued to perform the Flute Ceremony. Natalie, Alice, and
Schindler joined the mostly native audience to watch one of the most
poetic of the traditional Hopi dances. The drama was an invocation
of water for the springs below the pueblo, and dancers were dressed
as symbols of the sun, the rainbow, and the blossoming earth. The
Flute Dance was of keen interest to Kurt Schindler, who incorporated folk music and indigenous rhythms into his own compositions.[9]

While Natalie was at the Flute Ceremony at Third Mesa, Douglas,
who had lived among the Hopis a decade before, assumed the role

of cultural tour guide for Roosevelt's entourage. With his son, Eric, Douglas retrieved Roosevelt from his rooms in the well-scrubbed schoolhouse and walked the colonel, his two sons, and cousin Nick up the trail to the villages on top of Third Mesa. Roosevelt, who had several days before successfully crossed the infamously difficult and nerve-testing Rainbow Trail to reach Rainbow Bridge, remarked on the precipitousness of the very narrow and steep cliff-hugging path.[10]

Douglas took the Roosevelt's to meet Nampayo and her family. Nampayo's husband was an old friend of Douglas's, someone, he explained to Roosevelt, to whom he owed much. Winfred Douglas was a man who inspired great loyalty among his friends, and equally great animosity among those who disliked him. What Roosevelt's personal opinion of Canon Douglas was can only be guessed. His *Outlook* article shared only professional comments about Douglas. Cousin Nick, however, *loathed* Father Winfred Douglas, whom he had met on this very mesa in 1911.[11]

Douglas was a gregarious extrovert, confident and outspoken about his professional and intellectual accomplishments, and ever ready to offer pastoral counsel, comfort, and assistance. Nick Roosevelt had encountered Douglas at the 1911 Snake Dance at Walpi when he was in high school in Phoenix, and he thought the canon was an "insufferable idiot" who "held forth in stentorian tones" as he explained the Snake Ceremony to a woman friend who was "the most remarkable bird" the teenager had ever seen. "She was attired in less than knee length skirts, was middle agish, stout, bespectacled and cock-like, had her hair piled mountain high over her forehead, wearing upon it a minute green Alpine hat, on the top of which sat in an attitude of possible premeditated flight, an enormous bird."

In 1911 Douglas had apparently been in Hopiland with one of his more eccentric friends, likely a European. Whoever she may have been was of no concern to Nick: he did not like the canon in 1911, and his opinion of Douglas would not improve in August 1913. Nick, like Roosevelt's sons Archie and Quentin, guarded the former president's privacy, and thought Douglas didn't deserve so much access to Roosevelt. As Nick saw it, Douglas was able to get close and "get his claws" into Roosevelt only because he was traveling with Roosevelt's friend Natalie Curtis, "apparently a real person, and a woman of great good sense."[12]

Natalie, Alice, and Schindler returned to the peach orchard at the base of First Mesa and spent the afternoon resting in camp. While they napped in the shade, John Hubbell took Roosevelt up First Mesa. Roosevelt had been invited to a private meeting with the Snake priests in their kiva, the ancient heart of Walpi.

The meeting between the Snake priests and the man they called the Great White Father from Washington lasted only a quarter of an hour that hot afternoon on August 20. Roosevelt's descent by ladder into the kiva was the climax of an extraordinary personal journey through Indian Country. In the sacred subterranean chamber, the Snake priests had been preparing for the Snake Ceremony for nine days. Roosevelt knew there would be snakes—*lots* of snakes—but he was unprepared for the large number of *poisonous* snakes slithering untethered and uncontained about the kiva floor throughout his audience with the priests.

The smoky, dimly lit kiva was decorated with eagle feathers, animal skins, lightning sticks, and paintings of snakes. Roosevelt sat on a blanket in the middle of the chamber with his back just eight feet from "thirty-odd rattlesnakes, most of them in a twined heap in one corner, but a dozen by themselves scattered along the wall." There was also a ceramic pot "containing several striped ribbon-snakes, too lively to be left at large." One man spoke English and translated the priests' greetings and Roosevelt's questions, but the conference in the kiva that afternoon was mostly silent. Roosevelt did his best to mimic the priests' nonchalance about the venomous participants, which were mostly kept to one side of the kiva by a snake watcher who used a fan made of eagle feathers to redirect those reptiles which wandered too close to Roosevelt. "Every move was made without hurry and with quiet concern," Roosevelt wrote, noting that the religious life of the Hopi contained relics of "an almost inconceivably remote and savage past," but also "a mystic symbolism which has in it elements that are ennobling."[13]

Archie, Quentin, and Nick greeted Roosevelt when he climbed out through the top of the kiva into the blindingly bright pueblo plaza "burning with enthusiasm."[14]

The remainder of that afternoon and long into the evening, the schoolhouse below First Mesa functioned as Roosevelt's impromptu office. Nick served as clerk and timekeeper for the droves of dignitaries, politicians, and celebrities who appeared to pay their respects to the ex-president. Governor George W. P. Hunt of Arizona came to Polacca from Phoenix with a press entourage of photographers, motion picture people, and a writer from *Collier's* magazine. Even though he was the wounded Republican-turned-Progressive spoiler, a photo op with Roosevelt was highly valued by politicians.

Natalie's scheduled appointment with Roosevelt commenced in the evening, after everyone (Natalie, Alice, Douglas, Schindler, and Whitaker, plus the Roosevelt clan) trekked up First Mesa at dusk to observe the Antelope Dance, a ceremonial precursor to the Snake Dance. Douglas joined Natalie and Roosevelt at the schoolhouse for a discussion that lasted long into the night. Roosevelt wanted Natalie's and Douglas's input on the *Outlook* article he was drafting about the Hopis. But Natalie had her own agenda, and as Roosevelt well knew from a dozen meetings at Sagamore Hill and in the White House, she was not easily deterred.

Natalie bluntly asked Roosevelt what right the U.S. government had "to stretch forth an autocratic hand arbitrarily to change the village life of this ancient and peaceful folk?" She then proceeded to lecture him on the function and design of the historic Hopi villages that for centuries had existed in harmony with their natural surroundings. Natalie complained about buildings like the schoolhouse they sat in, designed with no eye to either beauty or usefulness, that the BIA forced upon the Hopis. And, she asked Roosevelt, just when *would* the feds study the Indian culture they sought to change? "Until some great foundation like the Carnegie . . . or Rockefeller shall endow funds for a study of this kind," Natalie concluded, "and until the whole matter of white-man control of Indians can be lifted out of politics, our efforts at Indian education are bound to be like the rain-shedding roofs in the desert—misfits in spirit as in fact."[15]

Roosevelt had heard these grievances from Natalie before. But that August night he was hearing them while sitting in a BIA schoolroom at the base of First Mesa, deep in Indian Country. In *The Indians' Book* Natalie wrote that one would only understand Hopi music when it was heard in the environment from which it was born, in the wide land, amid the shifting color of the tinted sands and the purple blue of the sharp-shadowed rocks—the very landscape Roosevelt had been immersed within for the last six weeks. That evening, Roosevelt had stood on the lip of the mesa and watched dusk descend to the haunting rhythm of the Antelope Dance, and that afternoon he had shared with dozens of snakes the packed mud floor of a kiva that echoed with the chants of the Snake priests. Roosevelt had stepped into the heart of Native America and he had been changed by it. Roosevelt assured Natalie he would use the power of his pen to educate the American public about Indian culture, "for somehow people do listen to me."

Roosevelt had drafted "Across the Navajo Desert" about his trip from the Grand Canyon to Kayenta and Rainbow Bridge. He read the article aloud to Natalie and Douglas and asked for corrections or suggestions. Natalie offered a few changes to strengthen the text. "I was amazed at the electric snap with which the Colonel would grasp a suggestion," Natalie later wrote, "and without a moment's hesitation put it into a written form far clearer and more succinct than the suggester could have supplied."

The article, penned in longhand, would be mailed to the *Outlook* offices in New York from Hubbell's at Ganado the next evening. Natalie was impressed by Roosevelt's productivity while traveling on horseback through the outback, and asked him when and how he had found the time and circumstances in which to write. Roosevelt smiled and commented that he liked "the strenuous life."

Before dawn on August 21, with the steady light of two morning stars, Mercury and Venus, glimmering over the desert, and with the glow of the night fires of Walpi flickering on the rim of the mesa above them, Natalie, Alice, Douglas, Eric, Schindler, and Whitaker left the warmth of their bedrolls and made a pot of coffee over the campfire. Before leaving the schoolhouse the night before, Natalie promised Roosevelt she would come for him before sunrise, and together they would walk up the steep, dark trail to Walpi. (Archie, Quentin, and Nick were not housed with Roosevelt, but camped nearby with John Wetherill.) In the half-dark, Natalie dressed, filled a thermos with coffee, and went to find Roosevelt. But Roosevelt's room was empty, and as she walked back to the camp in the peach orchard, Natalie reminded herself that one must indeed get up *very* early to keep up with the colonel.[16]

Natalie and her campmates skipped breakfast and scrambled up to the summit of First Mesa. They found Roosevelt high on a stone

ledge silhouetted against the "yellow line" of the dawn. With his
two sons and cousin, Roosevelt, led by John Wetherill, had ridden
on horseback up the First Mesa trail. Roosevelt brushed off Natalie's
apology for being so tardy, but accepted her thermos of hot coffee.
As the sun rose above the horizon, the mostly Hopi crowd waiting
on the edge of First Mesa cheered the return of ceremonial runners
as they completed a six-mile race.

With sunrise came the first trickle of what would become the
great flood of visitors to First Mesa. The Snake Dance would begin
around 5 p.m., and throughout the day hundreds of white tourists
and dignitaries ascended the vertigo-inducing trail to Walpi. Nick
Roosevelt estimated some eight hundred people made the climb to
the old village and that the audience was four times as large as that
which attended the Snake Dance in 1911.[17]

Alice and Schindler were introduced to Roosevelt that morning.
Alice liked Roosevelt immensely, and she thanked him for his good
work for the Indians and for America. Alice had carried her copy of
The Indians' Book in her saddlebag for eleven days, and she asked
Roosevelt to inscribe it. Inside the front page he penned: "In a Hopi
Indian pueblo . . . To Alice Klauber with all good wishes, from The-
odore Roosevelt, Walpi August 21, 1913."[18]

Nick Roosevelt ignored Douglas when they stood face-to-face on
Walpi, but he was impressed by and eager to be introduced to Kurt
Schindler, "the terrific genius so much spoken of at the Opera House
in New York's musical circles." Schindler knew Nick's sister, Lorraine
Roosevelt Warner of Boston (whom Nick thought Natalie resembled in size and demeanor). Like everyone else standing around
Roosevelt, Schindler had spent weeks traveling by horseback across
the Arizona desert, and the usually pressed, shaven, and showered
Schindler scarcely resembled the conductor toasted by New York's
effete music circles. Schindler, introduced to the Roosevelts "as being
no tenderfoot," was as brown as the natives, and although he "wore
the costume of a musician" (his hair hung below his ears and was tied
down with a bandana), the morning Nick met him, Schindler "had
apparently forgotten to put on a shirt."[19]

After lunch, Natalie, Alice, Douglas et al. left the shade of the
orchard and walked again up to Walpi. By mid-afternoon, all the dirt
roads leading to First Mesa were crowded with people coming for

the Snake Dance. "They came on foot, in wagons, and on horseback, and from the mesatop we watched the automobiles crawling over the sand like an eruption of ugly and alien beetles. Such a heterogeneous crowd as flocked from all directions to watch the Colonel watch the Indians!"[20]

Natalie had been assigned a seat beside Roosevelt, his sons, and Governor Hunt, front and center to the ceremony that would be performed on the plaza. Douglas, Alice, Schindler, and their camp-mates, like John Wetherill and Don Lorenzo Hubbell, had to find a place in the great mob. The crowd around the plaza became so large that people climbed up onto the rooftops and lined the village's rock walls. The pueblo's small plaza ended abruptly in a sheer drop to the desert floor hundreds of feet below, but dozens of spectators, anxious for a view of the dance and the former president watching the dance, took positions along the mesa's dangerous precipice.

The whole scene on Walpi reminded Nick of the Republican Convention. Reporters, photographers, and "moving picture men" joined the "mob of the idle curious and the near great." Before the Roosevelts reached their assigned seats at the base of a wall to one side of the plaza, the colonel was stopped several dozen times by men and women asking for an autograph, or reaching out to shake his famous hand. Roosevelt obliged everyone.

Natalie walked into Walpi alongside Roosevelt. In the last two weeks of camping, she had somehow managed to keep one outfit free of desert grime, dust, mud, horsehair, and axle grease, and she floated into the Snake Dance wearing a pristine white cotton shirt and skirt, her face shaded by an enormous white hat. The clicking sound of rapid-fire Kodak cameras followed Roosevelt's entourage as it moved through the narrow walkways of the Hopi village. By Nicholas's estimate, they were photographed exactly sixteen million times.[21]

Before the dance commenced, the crowd, now stacked three stories high on ledges and rooftops surrounding the plaza, was given a preliminary speech about the sacredness of the ceremony and instructed that there was to be silence throughout its duration. The speaker was an Indian service official. Douglas and Natalie actually instigated the preperformance cultural lecture, although they had suggested Roosevelt stand and address the crowd before the ceremony. This idea was quickly nixed as inappropriate.[22]

Figure 24. Snake Dance, Walpi, August 21, 1913. Theodore Roosevelt and Natalie Curtis (in white hat) are in the center of the second row.

Figure 25. Natalie, Theodore Roosevelt, Quentin and Archie Roosevelt, and Governor George W. P. Hunt, Snake Dance, Walpi, August 21, 1913.

The ceremony commenced when the snakes—the same serpents seen by Roosevelt on the floor of the kiva the day before—were brought into the plaza in bags by the Snake priests and placed in the *kisi*, a shallow pit covered with a board that represented the underworld. The snakes' arrival in the crowded plaza was followed by the solemn line of chanting Antelope and Snake priests. Two Antelope priests accompanied each individual Snake priest as he was given one of the snakes and proceeded trance-like around the plaza. The rattlesnakes were first carried in the priests' hands. When the snakes were transferred to the priests' mouths, the assisting Antelope priests helped the dancer support the weight of the snake and also stroked and calmed the rattlesnakes with feathers. (Roosevelt saw several dancers bitten by snakes, but the priests did not seem to suffer ill consequences from the poisonous strikes.)

As the mass of onlookers pressed in within an arm's length of the dancers and their venomous partners, the procession of Snake and Antelope priests chanted and stomped four times around the plaza.

At the end of the spirited, dramatic ceremony, the snakes were tossed down into a circle. With their bare hands, each of the Antelope priests retrieved half a dozen snakes each and dashed out of the plaza with them and down the steep sides of First Mesa to the desert floor, where they released the sacred reptiles into the four directions.[23]

As the mob of spectators climbed down from their perches on Walpi's dwellings and walls, Natalie said her farewells to Roosevelt. She hoped to see him back east after his trip to South America later in the fall. Natalie wove her way out of the throng pressing in to see Roosevelt and found Alice and Douglas. After regrouping with their campmates, they walked across the mesa to Hano to watch the sunset from Nampayo's home.

The legions of white people headed back to their autos and civilization, and Hopi First Mesa returned to normal. Roosevelt and his family packed up their expedition gear, said farewell to their horses, Navajo guides, and their very good friend John Wetherill, and piled into John Hubbell's two Ford machines to drive into the night to Ganado.

Natalie and Douglas's expedition remained in Hopiland another week. Natalie set up a workshop at their campsite near Polacca, and many Hopi friends came to share stories and songs with her in the shade of the peach trees. One of the Snake priests who had sat with Roosevelt in the kiva, named Harry, was an old friend of Natalie's, and he spent an afternoon telling stories and singing with Tawimana and her white friends. Natalie sang almost as many songs for the Hopis as they sang for her. Schindler scribbled notes throughout Natalie's sessions with native singers. When he returned to New York, he planned to incorporate the native melodies and folk rhythms of Hopiland into his own compositions.

On the morning of August 24, Canon Douglas held an outdoor mass in the orchard near their campsite. After an Episcopalian service under the wide Arizona sky, Natalie, Alice, and the men packed up camp and walked the trail to Hano one more time to say good-bye to Nampayo.

Over the next few days they camped in the open country near Second and Third Mesas. Natalie wanted to connect with several Hopi singers, including Chief Tewaquaptewa, who came to see her when she returned with her group and set up camp below Old Oraibi. Alice

Figure 26. Ted Whitaker, Alice Klauber, Kurt Schindler, Natalie Curtis, Winfred Douglas, and Hopi chief, First Mesa, August 1913.

carried *The Indians' Book* in her saddlebag, and on the same page signed by Natalie and Roosevelt, the chief wrote *Kwaptiwe*, "Hopi Chief/Orababi/August 24, 1913."[24]

During one of these private sessions with the Hopi chiefs and priests, Alice received her Hopi name—Koiyahoinim. Ted Whitaker was also given a Hopi name, but no one's diary recorded what that name was.[25]

After several days in the village of Hotevilla, the community founded by the Hostiles who departed Oraibi in 1906, Natalie and friends rode east to the Toreva Spring and camped near Second Mesa. At the ancient Hopi village of Shongopovi, they were invited to observe the Flute Ceremony. The ceremony beside the spring at Shongopovi was rarely if ever viewed by outsiders. Douglas later wrote about the procession and dance, and he became credited as perhaps the first white man to see this particular Hopi ceremony.[26]

News and letters from the outside world awaited Natalie, Alice, and the others on their return to the BIA offices in Polacca. After a final stop for supplies at Hubbell's trading post, they rode southwest out of Tusayan into the Painted Desert of the Navajos. It was very hot. The monsoons had passed, and the dry landscape shimmered with ghostly mirages as they rode southeast for Indian Wells. After a

final night under the open sky of the high desert, they packed up the
horses one more time, and their great journey across Indian Country
came to an end the next afternoon when they rode into Holbrook.

After a fitful night in hotel rooms that felt confining and airless,
they carried their gear and bags to the Santa Fe Railway depot and
boarded the eastbound train. Two hundred miles east across the
desert, the train stopped at Laguna Pueblo, New Mexico. Everyone
disembarked except for Schindler, who was to remain on the train
bound for Chicago and New York. After twenty-two days of fel-
lowship on the desert, Natalie, Alice, Douglas, Eric, Schindler, and
Whitaker had developed the bonds known by all who share the trail
through a beautiful and dangerous land. Saying farewell to Schindler
was difficult.

Natalie intended to spend a few weeks at Laguna visiting friends
and working on her field notes, and she set up her tent near the old
section house, where she was a guest of the Marmon family. Alice,
who wanted to explore the pueblo and sketch and paint the people
and landscape, remained in Laguna with Natalie. Douglas had one
more destination on his itinerary, and with his son and Whitaker,
he left Laguna and rode eighteen miles across the New Mexican
desert to Acoma, the Sky City Pueblo, whose mission church was
the architectural template for the New Mexico Building under construction at Balboa Park. The men spent several days exploring the
massive rock islands of Acoma and its neighbor, Enchanted Mesa.
During this expedition, Douglas found and successfully climbed a
legendary trail that led nearly straight up the side and onto the top
of Enchanted Mesa. Douglas would be hailed as the first white man
to locate and climb the ancient "lost" trail of the Acoma Indians.
Whether the trail was actually lost, and whether Douglas was, in
fact, the first white man to find and ascend that trail, remain open to
discussion. However, Douglas's membership in the elite Explorers
Club was in recognition of two "firsts," both of which occurred on
his expedition with Natalie in 1913: his witnessing of the sacred Hopi
Flute Ceremony and his ascension of the difficult and unmarked
trail to Enchanted Mesa. From its inception in 1905 until 1981, the
Explorers Club recognized the feats and adventures of men only.
That Natalie and Alice may well have been the first white women
invited to attend the Hopi Flute Ceremony, and that they witnessed

Figure 27. Southwest point of Mesa Encantada (Enchanted Mesa) near Acoma, New Mexico, ca. 1900.

the ceremony twice, on August 23 at Third Mesa and on August 26 at Second Mesa, was never honored or officially recorded.[27]

On Thursday, September 4, their grand desert dream came to an end. Natalie and Alice said good-byes to Douglas, Eric, and Whitaker at the Laguna station and watched them depart on the 4:30 train for Denver. Their farewell was blessed with a good omen from the Snake gods: thunder rumbled from clouds over the western horizon, and the promise of rain scented the wind ahead of the storm. Later that evening, Alice went by wagon with the Marmon boys through pouring rain to the depot and boarded the 11 p.m. train for Los Angeles. Natalie remained in New Mexico. Alice hated to leave her alone at Laguna, but knew Natalie wanted and needed to "get a bit of real work done here when there's no interruptions."[28]

The heat that dogged Natalie, Alice, and company across the Arizona desert had been bearable because of the relief brought by the seasonal monsoon thunderstorms. Southern California was suffering the same intense heat that summer, but was not blessed with the rain that fell on the neighboring state of Arizona. Alice returned home to San Diego through a parched landscape. The country surrounding George Curtis's ranch was a tinderbox by late summer, and on September 16 a terrific wildfire swept across the top of the valley near George's house. George fought a fierce wind and cleared dead brush from around his house and beehives, and his little ranch was spared.

It was still hellishly hot and dry in late September, but a drizzle of rain finally dampened the fires, and George was able to work on his ranch "without the demonic image of smoke on the horizon." On the night of the full harvest moon, October 15, Natalie returned to California on the train. George retrieved her and brought her to the ranch. Over the next several days they unpacked Natalie's bags, aired out her gear, and then repacked and stowed the camping equipment in his shed.[29]

Later that week, Natalie and George together read Roosevelt's article "The Hopi Snake Dance," which was published in the October 18 issue of *Outlook*. Roosevelt praised Natalie's work collecting Indian music and reiterated her plea to the federal government to create an educational system that would perpetuate Indian poetry and music. Roosevelt also gave American readers a detailed and colorful recounting of his experiences among the Hopis, especially about his time in the "grey twilight" of the kiva of the Snake priests where he encountered the "symbolism and dark savagery" of their "elder world."

Perhaps because Roosevelt was still assessing his feelings about the modern art seen at the Armory Show, he commented on the importance of Nampayo's ceramics and the Native American aesthetic. "A great art must be living," he wrote, "must spring from the soul of the people; if it represents merely a copying of an imitation, and if it is confined to a small caste, it cannot be great."

It must have made Natalie smile when Roosevelt suggested in his article that the federal government needed to design and construct dwellings appropriate to place and culture, and challenged the decision to force the Hopi off their mesa-top villages and into white man's–style communities built "precisely like some ten million other cheap houses."

Even Washington outsider Frank Mead, Natalie and George's eccentric friend who had found an appreciative audience for his

North African and indigenous American building designs, received a nod from Roosevelt. "Mr. Frank Mead . . . has done admirable work of the kind by adapting Indian architectural ideas in some of his California houses."

Roosevelt's six weeks of submersion in Indian Country, particularly his three days and two nights at Walpi and his conversations with Natalie at the schoolhouse at the foot of First Mesa, had transformed his thinking. "Give [a Hopi] a chance to lead his own life as he ought to," Roosevelt wrote, "and realize that he has something to teach us as well as to learn from us."[30]

10

"A FINE WOMAN TO BE OUT WITH"

> The personality of which she was so tired seemed to let go of her. The high, sparkling air drank it up like blotting-paper. It was lost in the thrilling blue of the new sky and the song of the thin wind in the piñons. The old, fretted lines which marked one off, which defined her . . . were all erased.
>
> —*Willa Cather*

ALMIRA CHOATE JOHNSON DIED in her bed of heart complications in March 1914. She left her spinster granddaughter, Carol Stanley, the house built by J. Bishop Johnson across Dorothy Cove from Longfellow's former residence. Almira also left her unmarried granddaughter a sizable bank account. With a home and money of her own, her grandmother gave Carol what she as a Choate and as a married woman always had: security.

At thirty-five, Carol had earned the means and the right to live out her days as a respected woman in the community on Nahant island. But Carol was not interested in living out her days as the island's spinster music teacher. The staid life of nursemaid and helper that had defined the last two years had left her tired, dissatisfied, and restless. She held on to an image of life beyond the woman's sphere of home and community service, and yearned to return to the stimulation and challenge she had known in Boston and Baltimore. The house on Dorothy Cove and the security of her own bank account were gifts of incalculable value to a single woman, but Carol had experienced too much of the world beyond her family. She still wanted to do something with her music and with her life. And whatever that something was, it was not found on Nahant.

The Lynn and Nahant Street Railway connected the island to the mainland trains into Boston, and Carol had continued to socialize with professional colleagues and friends during her mother's illness. She had also worked as a volunteer at two organizations in Boston—the South End Music School, where she interacted with Natalie and Canon Douglas, and the Boston Port and Seaman's Aid Society. As the daughter and granddaughter of fishermen, Carol understood the travails of seamen and their families, and gave piano concerts for boarders and visitors at the Seaman's Bethel in Boston's North Square. The Seaman's Bethel was a Methodist and Episcopalian charity organization founded by the "Sailor Preacher" Father Edward Thompson Taylor in the 1820s. Like the South End Music School, the bethel was staffed by mostly female volunteers from Boston's wealthier families who worked to improve the moral, religious, and living conditions of Boston's working-class folks.

Natalie wrote about Boston's South End Music settlement school in the *Craftsman* in 1911, and may have met Carol during one of her tours of Boston settlement houses. Natalie and Carol were probably not aware that their ancestors may have known one another years before: Natalie's uncle George Curtis entertained Joseph Choate, a relative of Carol's great-grandmother Elizabeth Choate, at his home in Ashfield, Massachusetts, decades before Natalie and Carol were born.[1]

Boston was populated with friends from Carol's school days at the New England Conservatory of Music. Carol also had Brahmin relatives and Nahant friends living on Beacon Hill: her father's first wife's relatives, the Edward C. Johnson family, several Cabots, Lodges, and a few Lowells whom Carol had known since childhood when they lived or summered on Nahant. But Carol was not a Brahmin, and her social circle, although educated and worldly, was made up of musicians and intellectuals, not heiresses and business barons.

Carol continued to play piano on the professional stage, although her opportunities were limited while she lived out on Nahant. Even though she was in her thirties, and past the conventional age when women married, by the fall of 1914 Carol was dating a professional musician. Carol was no beauty, but she was witty and smart, and had pleasant, attractive features and a good fashion sense. She also had enough money to be considered independently wealthy.

Carol's family on Nahant, specifically her mother's brother, Otis Johnson, feared the musician courting his niece had his eyes, not on Carol, but on her very attractive inheritance. Details of the liaison are scant, but Carol evidently had a serious affair with a violinist with whom she shared the Boston concert stage. By Carol's own account, the affair ended scandalously (the violinist may have eloped with a wealthy society patroness), and Carol's friends, and possibly her family too, suggested she needed to leave town.[2]

Winfred Douglas may have been among those friends who urged Carol to sever ties with Boston, and he may have helped orchestrate her departure from New England by recommending that she join the staff at the Kindergarten Institute in Chicago. By late fall of 1914, Carol closed up her Nahant home on Dorothy Cove, packed up her belongings, and departed Boston for Chicago.

From Douglas and Natalie, Carol had heard dozens of stories about desert expeditions and Indian ceremonies, about cultures and landscapes as foreign to Nahant island as the civilizations found along the Nile. Carol never recorded when the suggestion was first made that she go with Douglas on a journey into Indian Country, but in the spring of 1915, after a winter in the Midwest, Carol traveled to Evergreen, Colorado, where she embarked on a journey to Arizona with Douglas. She couldn't have known it at the time, but her introductory journey with Douglas into the American Southwest would change the course of her life and, in doing so, would significantly alter and influence the lives of dozens of other people, some of whom would leave bold and transformative marks on Southwest history.

Sometime in late May 1915, Carol and Douglas took the train south and west from Denver to Durango and eventually Mancos, Colorado. From the narrow-gauge station in Mancos, they journeyed across the country below Mesa Verde and the cliff dwellings famously "discovered" by John's brother Richard Wetherill and his brother-in-law Charles Mason in the winter of 1888. From Cortez, they headed into McElmo Canyon and reached the San Juan River near Bluff. They continued downriver to the bridge at Mexican Hat and the last leg of their journey south and west across the Utah-Arizona

Figure 28. The Wetherill Trading Post and home, Kayenta, Arizona, ca. 1912.

desert to Kayenta and their destination, the home of Louisa and John Wetherill.

Douglas had become friends with the couple on previous expeditions in the Four Corners country. In 1915 Douglas was a defense witness for an upcoming trial in Denver, and on this trip with Carol he had come to see Louisa Wetherill about locating other witnesses living on the Ute reservation. Douglas stayed a few days at the Wetherills' discussing the trial with Louisa (John Wetherill was not in Kayenta but on an expedition with a group in the outback), and then he left Kayenta for Utah.

Carol, a guest at the Wetherills' throughout Douglas's meetings with Louisa, must have impressed Louisa because Carol did not leave with the canon, but remained her houseguest for the next few months. Living at the Wetherills' trading post home provided Carol with an extraordinary introduction to Indian Country. As Roosevelt and his family had learned in the summer of 1913, Louisa's home in Kayenta was a desert palace in the heart of the most spectacular landscape in all of Indian Country. Louisa, like her husband, had achieved legendary status among the Navajos and Utes who lived on this high desert, and among the white people who wanted to experience one of the last great American frontiers.

Louisa Wade Wetherill was known as Asthon Sosi, Slim Woman, among the Navajos. She had lived in Kayenta with her husband, a trader, backcountry guide, and internationally known amateur archaeologist, since 1910. Louisa's stone house on the red desert twenty-four miles south of Monument Valley hosted adventurers, traders, writers, archaeologists, and former presidents. All expeditions to the great Rainbow Bridge began and ended at the Wetherills', and nearly all of these were led by John.

On August 14, 1909, John Wetherill, and his companions Dr. Byron Cummings and William B. Douglass, entered the historic record as the first white men to reach Rainbow Bridge. Outback insiders knew that it was Louisa Wetherill who enabled their "discovery," since in November 1908 she had convinced the Navajo known as One-Eyed Man to guide her and John to the legendary stone rainbow the Navajo called Nonnezoshe. Louisa's securing of a Navajo guide was nothing short of extraordinary. Nonnezoshe was sacred to the Navajo, but the Diné had forgotten the appropriate prayer for the great bridge, and normally no Navajo would venture near it.[3]

Louisa Wetherill was a respected *Bilagaana* among the native people of the Four Corners region. Born in 1877 in Nevada, Louisa grew up in Mancos, Colorado, near the ranch of her future husband's family. She spoke nearly fluent Navajo and was known and trusted by the Navajos, Utes, and Paiutes she had lived among since childhood. After witnessing Louisa's interactions with the Indians who came to trade at the Wetherills' post during his stay in Kayenta, Roosevelt commented that she was not simply versed "in archaeological lore concerning ruins and like, she was also versed in the yet stranger and more interesting archaeology of the Indian's own mind and soul. . . . [Louisa] not only knows [the Navajos'] language; she knows their minds. . . . They trust her so fully that they will speak to her without reserve about those intimate things of the soul which they will never even hint at if they suspect want of sympathy or fear ridicule."[4]

The Wetherill outpost at Kayenta was a desert oasis. Louisa diligently watered a garden that included Virginia creeper and rosebushes shaded by a large stand of box elders and a front yard that boasted a grass lawn. For eastern dudes who might forget they were

Figure 29. Louisa Wade Wetherill and Sitsosie, a Navajo guide and friend of the Wetherills, Olijato, 1909.

in the middle of a very hot and dry desert that received only a few inches of rain a year, Louisa posted a "Keep Off the Grass" sign alongside her fragile green lawn.[5]

At Kayenta, Carol had a room in a dwelling unlike any she had seen in New England. The floors of the Wetherill home were packed dirt softened by Navajo rugs. The walls were decorated with more

Navajo tapestries and replicas of Navajo sand paintings, Indian baskets and artifacts, and dozens of original paintings given to Louisa
and John by the artists who had stayed with them. The roof was
constructed of poles packed with earth, and to keep debris from
sifting down onto food and drink, lengths of unbleached muslin
was tacked to the ceiling over the dining table, which frequently
accommodated ten or more guests. Like their counterparts at the
Hubbells' in Ganado, the Wetherills' bookshelves were crammed
with books on Southwest history and archaeology.[6]

The home of Louisa Wetherill was, in Roosevelt's words, a delight
to the senses, "clean, comfortable, with its bath and running water,
its rugs and books, its desks, cupboards, couches, and chairs, and the
excellent taste of its Navajo ornamentation."[7]

Kayenta was the gateway to the most iconic landscape of the
American Southwest: Monument Valley and its otherworldly landscape of sculpted red buttes, stone needles and towers, obelisks, and
colossal spires began a few miles to the north. Comb Ridge and El
Capitan, Church Rock, carved the horizon to the northeast, and on
the horizon to the south was the great limestone rampart of Black
Mesa, whose rock fingers reached fifty miles across the desert to the
Hopi mesas. Fifteen miles to the west of Kayenta, a primitive road
crossed Marsh Pass into verdant Tsegi Canyon (Navajo National
Monument), where John Wetherill had stumbled upon the cliff ruins
of Kiet Seel in the 1890s and located the Anasazi cliff dwellings of
Betatakin in 1909.[8]

The small cluster of stone and mud-chinked cedar post buildings
that was the Wetherills' home was an island outpost surrounded by a
wilderness of sand and rock. Perhaps this was why Carol felt at home
in Kayenta: she was well accustomed to island living, and to windows
that framed views of infinity.

Carol was living in a land of legendary places and people. Zane
Grey's novel *The Rainbow Trail* was published in 1915, the same
summer that Carol came with Douglas to the Southwest. Grey's
story, set in Hopi and Navajo land, introduced urban readers to the
rugged canyonlands of Arizona. Two years before Carol moved in
with the Wetherills, Grey had stayed in those same rooms and had
gone with John Wetherill to Nonnezoshe. Grey scratched his name
into a stone near the base of the bridge, and three months later his

signature was found by Roosevelt and his sons when they followed Wetherill to the sacred monument.

Natalie's and Douglas's descriptions of Arizona's space, color, and hot light could only partially prepare Carol for her experiences at the Wetherills'. Carol learned what Louisa had come to know as a young woman: from this hard country came beauty.

The Wetherills' home became the headquarters and supplier for the surveyors and archaeological teams studying and excavating the cliff dwellings and Anasazi sites in Tsegi Canyon and in the canyon-lands along the San Juan River near Bluff, Utah. In 1909, before beginning work at Balboa Park, Edgar Hewett and Jesse Nusbaum had stayed here and traveled with John Wetherill into the vast unmapped country Hewett was surveying for the Archaeological Institute of America.

When Carol arrived for her several months' residency, the Wetherills' outpost was the base camp for a young Harvard PhD, Alfred V. "Ted" Kidder, who with Samuel James Guernsey was completing a second season of fieldwork in the caves and ruins near Marsh Pass. Ted Kidder was an affable, good-humored, bearded fellow who had been on Hewett's field teams in Bluff and McElmo canyons, and at Mesa Verde. Kidder had also worked at Hewett's archaeological field school (frequently visited by Hewett's pal Charles Lummis) in the cliff dwellings of the Rito de los Frijoles on the Pajarito Plateau in northern New Mexico.

If Carol's residency overlapped with Kidder's at the Wetherills' that spring, they surely talked about goings-on in and around Boston, where Kidder lived with his wife. They may have also talked about the land of enchantment, New Mexico, where Kidder had spent several summers in the canyon, mesa, and pine-forested mountain country west of Santa Fe near a town called Española. Kidder loved all things New Mexican, and he may have sparked Carol's interest in the ancient pueblo country of the Rio Grande Valley. Within the year, Carol would be in Santa Fe, and like Kidder, Lummis, Hewett et al., she would be smitten by the enchanting country of New Mexico.[9]

The first automobiles that used the rough wagon roads broken by John Wetherill and his partner, Clyde Colville, reached the Wetherill trading post and the farthest-flung post office in the United States in 1914. With the motorcars came a different type of visitor into the country of Monument Valley: auto tourists, who, Louisa said, were "impatient of delay, frightened of hardship, desiring the comfort of settled places." The Wetherills, like the Hubbells, had been negotiating the desert in Model Ts a few years before the first tourists. But as Natalie, Alice, Douglas, and their co-travelers learned in 1913, even with the best of drivers behind the wheel, auto travel across sand dunes and rock ledges on roads that were nothing more than trails was laborious and slow going. Most people came to Kayenta on horseback or, as Douglas and Carol did in the spring of 1915, by horse and buggy.[10]

Douglas and Carol journeyed to Kayenta because Douglas was a subpoenaed witness in the trial of Tse-ne-gat, also known as Everett Hatch, the young son of Chief Polk (Billy Hatch) of the Utes. The year before, in March 1914, Tse-ne-gat was charged with the robbery and murder of Juan Chacon, a Mexican shepherd, near Navajo Springs, Colorado. After a warrant was issued for his arrest, Tse-ne-gat had gone directly to Louisa for advice. After hearing his story, Louisa was certain the young Ute had been set up by the real murderers, and she told him to go directly to the Ute Mountain Indian agent in Colorado and tell his story. While en route from Kayenta to the Ute agency, Tse-ne-gat was told by an agency policeman that no one would believe he was innocent. Afraid that he would be jailed when he reached the Ute agency, Tse-ne-gat went into hiding in the vast Indian Territory of the Four Corners region.

Through the fall and winter of 1914, a federal posse unsuccessfully searched for Tse-ne-gat on the Ute, Paiute, and Navajo reservations. In February 1915 violence erupted between a frustrated posse composed of three Colorado sheriffs and twenty-six armed cowboys and Chief Polk's tribe living in teepees in Cottonwood Gulch near Bluff, Utah. The sound of gunfire brought over fifty more armed white men from Bluff and Blanding to the posse's aid, and several dozen Ute warriors camped on the San Juan River with Chief Posey rushed to help Chief Polk. The Battle at Cottonwood Gulch lasted only twenty-four hours, but several members of the posse were killed, and dozens of Utes and white men were wounded. One Ute warrior and two Ute women were killed, and a young Ute child was wounded.

Chiefs Polk and Posey and their warriors escaped into the desert, and the Utes and their allies, the Paiutes, declared a state of war with the U.S. government, warning that any whites who came near their camps would be shot on sight.

In the winter of 1915, while Carol was planning her first trip to the American Southwest from the civilized comfort of a Chicago apartment, a posse of fifty Navajo policemen was assembling to pursue Polk and his band of Utes. But even the Navajos could not locate and apprehend the renegade Indians. Frustrated and fearful, the local BIA agents requested help from Washington, and by spring 1915 the Four Corners Indian uprising was handed over to Brigadier General Hugh L. Scott of Virginia.

Because Louisa was trusted by the Utes, Paiutes, and Navajos, the Indian agents working with General Scott suggested she travel into the now very hostile territory of the Utes, find the camp of Chief Polk and his family, and convince them to bring Tse-ne-gat in for what the feds promised would be a fair trial. General Scott even promised to protect him from both the white posse and the Navajo police.

Louisa agreed to intervene and put out the word among her Navajo and Ute friends that Scott could be trusted. Chief Polk and his family came into Kayenta and, after consulting with Louisa, took Tse-ne-gat to Mexican Hat, an outpost on the San Juan River, and surrendered him to General Scott.

Figure 30. Louisa Wetherill and Utes, Kayenta, June 1915. The woman in the doorway may be Carol Stanley.

Newspaper writers across the United States recounted in colorful detail the Bluff War and the Battle of Cottonwood Gulch, and the hunt for Tse-ne-gat. To readers in Boston and New York, even in Chicago, the West was yet a wild place, and the region called the Four Corners a frontier where untamed and hostile Indians roamed free. In June 1915, when Carol traveled by buggy with Winfred Douglas from the train depot in Mancos, Colorado, across the mountains and canyonlands to Kayenta, Arizona, she was moving into a region whose residents, both Indian and white, were still reeling from the violence at Cottonwood Gulch.

It was a nervous and even dangerous time in Indian Country, and tourism was not encouraged. Exactly how it came to pass that Douglas left Carol alone with the Wetherills—whether this was an impromptu arrangement made after Carol met Louisa, or was the plan from the beginning of their journey—in a time of such hostility, it speaks volumes about the Wetherills' reputation in the Four Corners. It also reveals a good deal about the character of Carol Stanley.

In June 1915, in the pages of the only diary ever kept by Louisa Wetherill, Carol emerges into the written record of the American Southwest. Louisa's diary chronicles her quest to locate the Indian witnesses and interpreters Tse-ne-gat's attorney needed brought to Denver. The trial would begin on July 6 and time was running out, so after Douglas left Kayenta, Louisa decided to go into Ute country herself, locate the witnesses and interpreter, and get everyone including herself onto the train for Denver in time for the opening arguments.

Louisa departed Kayenta at supper time on Saturday, June 26, in a buggy packed with enough supplies and provisions for a four-day, fifty-mile journey across the desert to the Ute agency at Navajo Springs. This was no journey for a tenderfoot. Louisa would be roughing it, following leads to Ute camps where there would be no amenities like those found at trading posts. In spite of the challenges, Louisa invited Carol to accompany her and Emma Charley, a young English-speaking Navajo, and John Chief, a friend of the Wetherills.

Like Natalie's and Roosevelt's camping expeditions, Carol's outback adventure began in the long shadows before sunset. Louisa's buggy with Carol and Emma Charley, followed by John Chief and several horses, headed north past El Capitan and into the dusk. Before dark engulfed the desert, the light of the full moon illuminated the landscape. Carol's first camp in Indian Country was on a sand hill at the edge of Monument Valley. They did not pitch tents, and from her bedroll under the open sky, Carol gazed at a dreamlike moonscape of stone spires. She was ecstatic, and even Louisa remarked in her diary about the beauty of the June moon on the landscape.

The next day the weather was hot, and deep sand made for slow progress. They were following a road—faint tracks obvious to Louisa but barely perceptible to Carol—that wound around the monolithic buttes, stone arches, and rock islands. After sundown cooled the desert floor, they continued to push on, and the moon rose and lit their way to Spencer's store in Goodridge. Louisa's son, Ben, and her husband, John, met their buggy and helped them set up camp. Since leaving Kayenta two nights before, Louisa's party had crossed more than forty miles of desert.

Louisa was surprised and delighted to find John and Ben at Spencer's, since they had been gone a month, guiding a Yale professor through the canyons of the Colorado River. Carol likely met John Wetherill for the first time that night, although she would have known of him from reading the popular writings and stories of Zane Grey and Theodore Roosevelt.

The next morning, Monday, June 28, Ben Wetherill and John Chief rode south to Kayenta. John Wetherill joined Louisa, Carol, and Emma Charley bound northeast across the desert for Bluff. The heat was worse than the day before, and when they found grass and water for the horses at Lime Creek, they stopped for a long lunch break. There was no shade to be found for miles, so Carol and Louisa stretched a tarpaulin from the buggy to a sage bush, and everyone crawled under and ate lunch under the tarp that protected them from the blistering sun.

Louisa wasn't feeling well that afternoon, and when they reached Bluff at supper time, she was put to bed by their hosts, the Perkinses, friends who lived near the San Juan River. During the twenty-mile journey that day Carol had moved from the seat of the buggy onto the back of one of John Wetherill's horses. It was her first time in a western saddle, and very possibly her first time on a horse. Although Nahant had an equestrian community with stables that served the island's summer residents, Carol's family did not keep horses. With John and Louisa's calm encouragement, Carol rode cowboy

Figure 31. Carol Stanley in the desert.

style—astride—across a sand, cactus, sage, and stone plateau six thousand feet above her sea-level home on Dorothy Cove. "Miss Stanley is a fine woman to be out with," Louisa wrote in her diary that evening in Bluff. "She has been riding horse back a good deal today so is pretty tired as she has never ridden before. She done fine though."

A fine woman to be out with. Although she did not know it, the sunburned, muscle-bruised, and saddle-sore Yankee music teacher had received the supreme compliment from Louisa Wetherill.

Winfred Douglas was also at the Perkinses' home in Bluff that night. The next morning after breakfast, Douglas left in an automobile with Frank Hyde and a Mr. Cornell of Bluff, both of whom, like Douglas, had been subpoenaed by the defense to appear as witnesses at the trial of Tse-ne-gat. Douglas would accompany them to Durango, where they were all to catch the train for Denver.

Louisa still had to locate several Ute witnesses and also an interpreter before she could follow Douglas to Denver. After a messenger told Louisa that Chief Polk was camped above McElmo Canyon and that he was very anxious to talk with her, Louisa, Carol, Emma, and John Wetherill headed out in the buggy and on horseback. The road to McElmo Canyon was terrible, and it took four hours for them to cross ten miles. Exhausted, they slept that night on the open ground beside the buggy. In the morning, they were found by Polk's men, who led them to the Ute camp on a mesa high above McElmo Canyon.

For the next several nights, Carol and the Wetherills stayed in the camp of Chief Polk and his family, and went with them to Navajo Springs below Ute Mountain where the Sun Dance ceremony was to be held. Hundreds of Utes and Paiutes came to see this dance, and at sunset on the last day of June, Carol stood with Louisa and gazed out at the teepees of the Indian village where dancers in beaded costumes were gathered for the ceremonies. "It was a beautiful picture to see them riding here and there," Louisa wrote, "and the beautiful red and gold clouds over the blue mountain, and to hear the drum beating, and the whistles blowing, and the Indian singing the Sun Dance Song."

Carol woke before dawn and walked with Louisa and John into the Ute village to watch the Rising Sun Ceremony. The dancers had been dancing for two days and a night without water or food, and one by one they went mad and fainted to the ground.

Louisa's search for witnesses led them from camp to camp across the Ute reservation. Carol was a natural horsewoman, and by July she preferred the saddle to the buggy seat. Louisa asked Carol several times to witness her conversations with agency personnel and telegraph operators, and to listen in on and witness telephone calls to officials. After several more days of riding and camping, Louisa located the witnesses she needed, including Chief Polk's wife, who was subpoenaed to appear in Denver, and also secured a trustworthy interpreter for those witnesses.

On the Fourth of July, Carol was in the tiny frontier town of Mancos, Colorado, where Louisa and John had grown up and met. The community of ranchers and traders celebrated Independence Day with contests and games, pistols and firecrackers. Businesses and adobe houses were decorated with American flags and red, white, and blue bunting, but the Fourth of July in this small Colorado town bore no resemblance to the annual Yankee extravaganza Carol had known back in Boston and out on Nahant island.

Carol said good-bye to Louisa at Mancos and, with John Wetherill and Emma Charley, headed back across the desert to Kayenta. Louisa and Tse-ne-gat's mother took a Pullman car from Durango to Denver. Louisa was bored and lonely in the city, although Winfred Douglas, his wife, Dr. Jo, and other friends of the Wetherills came to visit her at the Kaiserhoff Hotel. The trial commenced on July 6, and after three days of testimony and seven hours of deliberation by the jury, Everett Hatch, aka Tse-ne-gat, was found innocent of murder.[11]

The verdict cited a lack of evidence against the young Ute, and later accounts by those in the courtroom said the jury was particularly swayed by the strength of the testimonies given by the defense witnesses, specifically the statements given by a pair of Mormons from Bluff who insisted the boy was innocent. These two Mormons may well have been Frank Hyde and Mr. Cornell, the subpoenaed witnesses who traveled with Winfred Douglas from Bluff to Denver.[12]

Carol left Kayenta by midsummer. She eventually went back to Chicago and worked at least temporarily at the Chicago Kindergarten Institute. For Christmas that year she may have visited Nahant. She may have seen Natalie in New York and told her of her life-changing experiences with the Wetherills in Indian Country. Carol left no diary, so we can only speculate about the details of her life in the months after she left Kayenta. However, from the moment she left the Southwest, Carol was planning her return. And when she does return nine months later with Natalie, Carol, like Natalie, is determined to make the Southwest her home country.

11

THE CITY DIFFERENT

With a burro to ride and a burro to drive,
There is hardly a man so rich alive.

—*Alice Corbin*

IN 1916 SANTA FE, ALTHOUGH now the capital of the brand-new state of New Mexico, was still situated in a region of the United States that most Americans deemed exotic at best and primitive and downright dangerous at worst. In March of that year, "civilized" Americans in Boston and New York were reading about the jaw-dropping exploits of the Mexican *bandito* Francisco "Pancho" Villa and the raid by his guerilla band of armed revolutionaries on the town of Columbus in southern New Mexico. Seventeen Americans were killed by the Villistas, and a small army under General John J. Pershing went into Mexico in pursuit of the guerillas. New Mexico's National Guard was serving as border patrol, but Americans were discouraged from traveling in southern New Mexico.

New Mexicans themselves were appalled by the exaggerated news accounts and blatant misinformation making headlines back east. "Supposedly intelligent persons" mistakenly reported that Villa's guerillas were encamped in canyons near Santa Fe, and that his Zapata bandits were terrorizing Albuquerque's streets. Although hundreds of miles of mountains and desert lay between the Mexican border and Santa Fe, to a New Yorker or Bostonian reading about Pancho Villa in the newspapers, all of New Mexico was under siege.[1]

H. H. Brook and C. B. Ruggles, the owners of Cliff Dwelling Pack Outfitters, which guided archaeologists and tourists across the mountains and into the canyons of the Pajarito Plateau west of Santa Fe, worried that their fledgling business would be ruined by inflammatory headlines in eastern newspapers, rubber-stamped their outgoing mail with their own headline: "This region [Frijoles Canyon, Los Alamos Ranch, and the Ramon Vigil Ranch] is 400 miles from the Mexican Border and the war cloud causes less interest here than in New York City. Not the least uneasiness need be felt in visiting this wonderful country."[2]

Regardless of the headlines and the belief among the gentry back east that New Mexico was the home of desperados and banditos, on April 10, 1916, Miss Natalie Curtis of New York City and Miss Caroline B. Stanley of Boston arrived in Santa Fe for what they planned to be an extended stay. The ladies' appearance in the capital city, and their registration at the Hotel De Vargas, was noted in the "Personals" column of the *Santa Fe New Mexican*. Throughout the spring and summer, as news of the Villistas' guerilla raids, arrests, and hangings dominated the front pages of the *New Mexican*, the comings and goings of Carol and Natalie—numerous camping excursions in Indian Country, day visits to the pueblos along the Rio Grande—were documented in the newspaper's gossip and social columns.[3]

Natalie and Carol visited the popular tourist sights in the old capital city and explored the quaint streets and small shops near the historic plaza, but they were not in Santa Fe for a vacation. They had come to New Mexico to make permanent homes and to begin new lives in this country.

After Carol departed Kayenta in the summer of 1915, she returned to Chicago and worked on the teaching staff at the Chicago Kindergarten Institute, where Winfred Douglas lectured and also was a member of the board of directors. In partnership with Northwestern University, the institute had begun a postgraduate program in music education, and Carol may have been considering a long-term teaching position there. In the fall of 1915, she went to the meetings of the Musical Education League of Chicago and became an active member of Chicago's suffragettes.[4]

In Chicago, Carol had opportunities for permanent employment in a welcoming community of like-minded professional women. But

Figure 32. Hotel De Vargas, Santa Fe, ca. 1920.

she could not forget what she had seen and felt in Kayenta and in Indian Country and, with Natalie, made a plan to return.

In 1914 Natalie heeded the call of duty and left George's ranch in California and returned to New York City to continue her work on Negro folk songs. The project, underwritten by George Foster Peabody and the Hampton Institute, pleased many of her friends and colleagues, including Charlotte Mason. Everyone hoped Natalie would do for American Negro music what she had done for American Indian music with the publication of *The Indians' Book*. Throughout 1914 and 1915, and until her departure for Santa Fe in April 1916, Natalie traveled throughout the American South collecting folk songs, spirituals, and poems. This collection would eventually fill the four volumes titled *Negro Folk Songs*, published by G. Schirmer in 1918 and 1919.

Natalie's brother Bridgham and her mother, Mimsey, still lived in New York, and Natalie had a comfortable apartment on West 76th Street in the same neighborhood as Winfred Douglas. New

York City was a stimulating environment in 1915, and the epicenter of American cultural change. Natalie had many friends living in the city, including her outback expedition pals Douglas and Schindler. Schindler's compositions and choral arrangements were now laced with the peculiar rhythms and atonal chants and songs heard during his 1913 journey through Indian Country, and the concert programs of his Schola Cantorum juxtaposed variations of Hopi and Navajo music with Bach, Mozart, and Schubert.[5]

Years before, while working on *The Indians' Book*, Natalie had shared several Indian melodies with her former teacher Ferruccio Busoni. In February 1915 Natalie traveled to the Academy of Music in Philadelphia to hear Busoni's use of those melodies in his composition *Indian Fantasy*. With her friend Percy Grainger, the Australian composer and folklorist, she listened to the Philadelphia Orchestra rehearse *Indian Fantasy* under the direction of Leopold Stokowski. Busoni himself played the piano for what was an emotionally charged performance for Natalie.[6] "With the first bars of the orchestral introduction the walls melted away, and I was in the West, filled once again with that awing sense of vastness, of solitude, of immensity."[7]

One year later, she made her return to the immense vastness with her friend Carol Stanley, who, like Natalie, was determined to create a home in the Southwest, specifically in Santa Fe. The capital of New Mexico was on the cusp of historic change. Statehood in 1912 had prompted the Anglo-driven Chamber of Commerce and Women's Board of Trade to launch formal campaigns to attract new residents and more tourists to Santa Fe.

Natalie likely suggested to Carol that they go to Santa Fe because she had many colleagues and friends here, with Hewett the energetic hub of Anglo society. Hewett's establishment of the School of American Archaeology and the Museum of New Mexico in Santa Fe in 1909 had turned the ancient city into home base for legions of anthropologists, ethnologists, geologists, and linguists migrating into the state. And Hewett's promotion of New Mexico artists, architecture, and cultural riches at the San Diego exposition in 1915 had prompted cross-country train travelers to add stopovers in Albuquerque and Santa Fe.[8]

By 1916 Santa Fe was touting itself as the "Granada of America" and, in league with the Santa Fe Railway and the Fred Harvey Company, was aggressively promoting New Mexico as a destination with natural and cultural sites that rivaled those found in Europe and the Mediterranean. The exhibitions at Balboa Park had developed an appreciation and understanding of Southwestern arts and crafts among the American public, and the Harvey Company's Indian Buildings along the Santa Fe Railway offered collectors and tourists easy access to Native American wares. Instead of a primitive, dangerous backwater, New Mexico was now hailed as America's pristine backyard with stunning and spectacular scenery, charming villages and pueblos, and indigenous cultures still connected to the land, a retreat in the American West that offered peace and renewal to those weary of modern, industrial, urban life.

Charles Lummis and Edgar Hewett went so far as to predict that Santa Fe, the headquarters for the Archaeological Institute of America's School of American Archaeology, would soon take its rightful place alongside the world's great cultural centers of Athens, Rome, and Jerusalem.[9]

While working on the Balboa Park exhibits, Hewett had also managed to supervise the renovation of the old Palace of the Governors on the Santa Fe plaza which had commenced in 1909. In his absence, Hewett left the renovation in the able hands of Jesse Nusbaum, Sylvanus Morley, and Carl Lotave, and by 1913 the renovated Palace of the Governors gave the Santa Fe plaza a historic landmark worthy of national attention.

At the Hotel De Vargas, Carol and Natalie had rooms just a block from the heart of old Santa Fe, the Palace of the Governors, and the plaza that dated to the arrival of the Spanish in 1610. Narrow dirt roads and foot trails led from the plaza into neighborhoods of adobe dwellings with flat roofs of packed dirt. Seen from a distance, the buildings of Santa Fe seemed carved from the earth. The village was watered by the *Acequia Madre*—the Mother Ditch—and there were lush vegetable and flower gardens, orchards of mature fruit trees, and graceful cottonwood and elm trees shading the neighborhoods and *caminos* nestled in the foothills and canyons of old Santa Fe.

The Sangre de Cristo (Blood of Christ) Mountains rose twelve thousand feet into the sky above Santa Fe. The town itself sat at nearly seven thousand feet above sea level, and was blessed with a clear, clean, dry, high-altitude climate. Never too hot, never too cold, the salubrious air of old Santa Fe was scented with mountain pine and aspen, and canyon sage and cedar. Even at midsummer, the nights were cool, and in winter the noon sun was bright and warm, and lunch could be taken out of doors.

It was the climate that attracted Santa Fe's first colony of expats. Tuberculars and others with chronic respiratory complaints left the East Coast and Midwest and checked into Santa Fe's Sunmount or St. Vincent's sanatoriums. Patients often arrived on stretchers, gasping for a last breath. In New Mexico, lungers found their breath and recovered their health, and in Santa Fe's thin, dry air and pristine atmosphere, most didn't just survive, they thrived.

St. Vincent's Sanatorium was built in 1911 near St. Vincent's Hospital located alongside St. Francis Cathedral a few blocks from the plaza. Sunmount was under the tutelage of Dr. Frank E. Mera, who with his brother, Dr. Harry P. Mera Jr., bought the tent-city sanatorium in 1902. Perched on a hill just north of the old plaza, by 1916 Sunmount was more health resort than hospital. Patients could be housed in spacious cottages with their families for months at a time. The main house had modern medical facilities, but also had ample and comfortable space for the frequent and numerous social events sponsored by Sunmount's residents. These included poetry readings, evening lecture programs with local archaeologists and artists (many of whom were former patients), and performances by the Sunmount thespian group.[10]

Sunmount's patient population included numerous artists and writers who, after experiencing the light and life of the Indian-Spanish community nestled up against the foothills of the Sangre de Cristos, remained in Santa Fe and became permanent residents. When Natalie and Carol arrived in the spring of 1916, the Sunmount's roster of convalescing residents included the nationally known poet Alice Corbin. On April 1, the *New Mexican* noted the recent arrival in Santa Fe of Mr. and Mrs. William Penhallow Henderson of Chicago. William Henderson was a painter of considerable success and national renown. Alice Corbin, his wife, was a respected poet and a founder and associate editor of *Poetry* magazine, one of the most influential and important literary magazines of the time.

Corbin was thirty-five when she was diagnosed with advanced TB. With her family, she left Chicago, "the warm center of her world," for

Figure 33. Alice Corbin and William Penhallow
Henderson.

New Mexico, "the ragged edge of the universe." "I had been thrown
out into the desert to die," she wrote of her March 1916 exile to Santa
Fe, "like a piece of old scrap-iron, or a rusty Ford."[11]

With their nine-year-old daughter, Little Alice, Alice and Will
Henderson moved into a cottage at Sunmount where it was believed
Big Alice might die. But with the care of the staff and the healing
attributes of the clear air of Santa Fe, Alice Corbin recovered from
tuberculosis. Instead of ending her life in "desolate exile," Corbin
"found a new world of beauty."[12]

Like a dozen other creative artists and writers who convalesced at
Sunmount, Alice and Will Henderson were enamored of the people
and lifestyle of the quaint town of Santa Fe, and invigorated by the

variety and the vitality of the indigenous cultures thriving in New Mexico. The Hendersons moved out of Sunmount and into a primitive adobe dwelling on the mostly uninhabited Telephone Road (so named for the telephone line that used its right of way), and in the next few years built a comfortable home where they raised their daughter, pursued their art and craft, and became the nucleus of Santa Fe's art colony.

Natalie had suffered respiratory ailments since she was a child, and at forty-one, her health continued to concern her family and friends. She spent the winter of 1916 in California, and was in good health when she arrived in Santa Fe in April. However, in the months that followed, Natalie and Carol embarked on several strenuous expeditions, and by midsummer Natalie would take a room at St. Vincent's Sanatorium for a few days of rest and recuperation.

Natalie and Carol were introduced to the Hendersons that summer, perhaps by their common friend, Edgar Hewett. At the Hendersons' adobe home on the renamed Camino del Monte Sol (Road to the Sun Mountain, the name used by the locals) there could always be found a friendly and energetic group of artists and archaeologists sharing coffee, conversation, or cocktails. As Alice Corbin regained her health, she promoted Santa Fe as a writer's colony and, imagining a dynamic new literary arts center in the West, encouraged her many literary friends to come out to New Mexico and visit her splendid home.

The American writer Willa Cather and her companion, Edith Lewis, came to Santa Fe in the summer of 1916. Cather and Lewis had visited Mancos and Mesa Verde the summer before, and had traveled on the same Denver and Rio Grande narrow-gauge railroad from Denver, up and over La Veta Pass, and across the valley to Durango which had brought Carol and Douglas to Mancos a few months ahead of them. In Mancos, Cather heard the story of John Wetherill's brother's discovery of Mesa Verde while looking for lost cattle in the canyons below the cliff dwellings. With Lewis, Cather spent a week climbing about the unexcavated cliff dwellings in the rough country of Mesa Verde's Cliff and Soda Canyons.[13]

During her stopover in Santa Fe, Cather visited the villages and pueblos of the Española Valley and explored Taos and the small villages found in the mountains north along the Rio Grande. Cather was working on the first draft of *My Ántonia*, but the landscape and people of the Southwest had cast their spell on her, and she had begun to gather the material that would become *The Professor's House.*

Santa Fe's population and infrastructure were undergoing a historic transformation the spring that Carol and Natalie unpacked their bags in the Hotel De Vargas. The new Museum of Art, designed by the same Rapp brothers who had designed the "Cathedral in the Desert," the New Mexico Building at Balboa Park, was under construction on the northeast corner of the plaza. The new art museum, as it was colloquially called by the locals, was under the direction of Edgar Hewett, who was also the director of the School of American Archaeology (which in 1917 changed its name to the School of American Research). In Santa Fe, artists and archaeologists shared the same professional and social circles.

Hewett and the chamber of commerce were energetically promoting Santa Fe as "The City Different." Hewett's New Mexico exhibits at Balboa Park had aroused national attention in the art and culture of New Mexico, and capitalizing on the popularity of all things New Mexican, he invited nationally known artists to spend a summer in Santa Fe. The chamber of commerce helped visiting painters find inexpensive housing, of which there was a plethora, and Hewett offered artists work and exhibit space free of charge at the Palace of the Governors. Artists and writers began to arrive in droves. Santa Fe, like Paris, promised artists and intellectuals an inexpensive Bohemian life unrestrained by traditional social rules and mores. "No paved streets, no automobiles, one sewer line. . . . A passenger could ride all over town in a horse-drawn taxi for a quarter."[14]

The word was getting out: In New Mexico, a new society based on art and creativity was flourishing within and alongside some of the oldest and most picturesque indigenous communities found in North America.

Although the new art museum would give the community its first real exhibition space, the residential artists valued Santa Fe's primitive qualities as much as its exquisite sunsets and sparkling vistas. In 1916 New Mexico, there were few automobiles and only a handful of roads that could accommodate them. Transportation of people and goods was by horseback, in buggies and wagons, and on the backs of burros. Electricity, indoor plumbing, telephones, and central heating were rare in private homes and most businesses. Spanish was spoken more than English, and although the tourists' hotels, restaurants, and upscale shops and businesses located around the plaza had the amenities and services found in modern America, the persona of Santa Fe and environs was still that of the frontier outpost at the end of the Santa Fe Trail.

Hewett's tactics to attract a colony of artists to Santa Fe were very successful. Several years before the new museum opened in November 1917, the studios in the Palace of the Governors were home to Balboa Park artists Gerald Cassidy, Donald Beauregard (who was with Wetherill, Cummings, and Douglas when they reached Rainbow Bridge), and Carlos Vierra (who with his wife remained in Santa Fe after recovering his health at Sunmount), and to Santa Fe part-time and full-time residents William Penhallow Henderson, Paul Burlin, and George Bellows, among others. And in the summer of 1916, after much effort, Hewett brought American art headliner Robert Henri to Santa Fe.

Hewett initially wanted Henri's advice about the contemporary art exhibit that would open the art museum in 1917. But by the fall of 1915, Hewett wanted to convince Henri to come to Santa Fe and set up his painting studio in one of the spaces at the renovated Palace of the Governors. Having Henri in residence would bring the Santa Fe art colony and the formation of the new art museum national attention. After months of correspondence, the Henris accepted Hewett's invitation and made plans to arrive in New Mexico by midsummer of 1916, for a several months' stay in old Santa Fe.[15]

AFTER ALL OF THREE DAYS in the comfortable and civilized accommodations of the Hotel De Vargas, Carol and Natalie packed up their gear and struck out for the Pajarito Plateau west of Santa Fe. Their destination was the Pajarito Club at the Ramon Vigil Ranch, a few miles and several canyons from Edgar Hewett's cliff-hugging field school in El Rito de los Frijoles.

The Pajarito Club, a small, rustic guest ranch tucked into Pajarito Canyon, had been owned since 1913 by four Michigan-based partners: Roy D. Chapin and Henry Joy, executives of the Hudson Motor Company and the Packard Motor Company, respectively; and the brothers Paul and David Gray, Detroit bankers. The Pajarito Club was built primarily as a vacation retreat for its wealthy owners, their families, and friends.

The Ramon Vigil Ranch and the Pajarito Club were managed by a fifth partner, Ashley Pond, who lived with his wife and three children at the club. Pond was a former member of Roosevelt's Rough Riders, who, after coming to New Mexico to recover his health, had become an avid outdoorsman. Pond's dream was to start a boys' school in New Mexico where young men from back east would be educated in the great outdoors.

In April 1916, when Natalie and Carol made their first visit to the Ramon Vigil Ranch, Pond and his Detroit partners were very much at odds, financially and otherwise, about the purpose and future of the Pajarito Club. Was it to remain a rustic outpost for private expeditions, or ought the club become a luxurious dude ranch that catered to paying guests? This country was the same plateau that Charles Lummis had hiked and explored with Adolph Bandelier before 1900, and within the 32,000 acres of the Ramon Vigil Ranch were dozens of unexcavated archaeological sites, including prehistoric cliff houses. Pond wanted the partners to invest in improvements to the existing lodge and cabins so the club could accommodate more guests. But the Detroit partners wanted the ranch they rarely used—the Gray brothers had yet to lay eyes on the place—to cost them no money until they figured out what they wanted to do with the remote property. At the very least, Pond thought the owners ought to visit the ranch and appreciate the truly spectacular piece of New Mexico real estate they owned.

Exactly what Natalie and Carol knew about the Pajarito Club's status during their first stay at the ranch is unknown. They likely chose to stay at the guest lodge because of its proximity to Hewett's field school in nearby Frijoles Canyon. Although archaeological teams rented the rustic cabins of the Pajarito Club during their fieldwork at sites on the Pajarito Plateau, ranch guests were more often wealthy visitors from back east looking to explore the New Mexican wilderness for a week or two.

The canyon of El Rito de los Frijoles, in which Hewett and his students and colleagues had spent years excavating cliff ruins and ancient pueblo villages, was a six-hundred-foot-deep cut in the massive

Pajarito Plateau on the southeastern flank of the Jemez Mountains. Named Pajarito (Little Bird) by Hewett, the region was considered to be one of the richest locales of archaeological sites in the West, and perhaps in the world.

Located in the piñon and ponderosa pine country west of the Rio Grande at the base of the Jemez Mountains, the plateau had been formed by two massive volcanic eruptions more than a million years ago. The crater from those eruptions was an enormous grassy bowl known as the Valles Caldera, or Valle Grande. Over millions of years the landscape surrounding the caldera was eroded and carved into a rugged plateau with steep, narrow canyons wedged between elongated mesas of porous rock that extended like fingers away from the crater.

To reach the Pajarito Plateau, Natalie and Carol likely hired one of the vehicles owned by E. J. Ward's Rocky Mountain Camp Company. Ward's outfit had been taking visitors into the outback on horseback since 1910 and in automobiles since 1914, and his drivers were considered the most experienced with New Mexico's famously dreadful roads. If the weather held, it took three hours to drive the twenty-seven miles from the Hotel De Vargas to the Pajarito Plateau. If it rained or snowed, or an axle broke, it could mean spending the night camped alongside the road.[16]

The Denver and Rio Grande narrow-gauge railroad—affectionately known as the Chile Line—did serve Santa Fe at Guadalupe Station, and travelers for the Pajarito could take the little train north and west to Otowi Station on the Rio Grande, connecting with a wagon or an automobile to cross the river at Buckman and continue into the steep canyons of the Pajarito. But for most travelers, it was more convenient to hire a car and a guide and be driven from Santa Fe to the plateau.

The automobile and wagon road for the Pajarito Plateau followed the Pojoaque Wash to the pueblo of San Ildefonso on the Rio Grande, the same village where Natalie's friends, the famed potters Maria and Julian Martinez, lived. From here the road angled south along the river until it reached the "town" of Buckman, which was just a cattle corral, lumber-loading platform, and small depot where the Chile Line, which began in Utah, reached the end of the line in the deep bottom of White Rock Canyon. The river crossing there,

Figure 34. Julian Martinez, Ceremonial Cave, Rito de los Frijoles, Bandelier National Monument, 1910.

the Buckman Bridge, a rock and timber assemblage no wider than a single vehicle, had served Hewett, Lummis, Kidder, Chapman, Nusbaum, and legions of Pajarito-bound explorers and archaeologists for nearly a decade.

From Buckman Bridge, wagons and autos began the steep ascent to the Pajarito Plateau on the old Buckman sawmill road, a narrow, rutted, rocky trail that climbed nearly straight up the canyon on switchbacks across stone shelves. Ward's drivers were accustomed to the ledge-hugging road that clung precariously to rims hundreds of feet above canyons, but the journey to the Pajarito Plateau and the Pajarito Club was often an exhausting and nerve-wracking affair for their passengers.

In the spring of 1916, one of the Rocky Mountain Camp Company drivers was a former Jemez Mountains forest ranger named Richard LeRoy Pfäffle. Roy Pfäffle owned a livery stable in Española and guided dudes on horseback into the outback of northern New Mexico and Arizona. He also drove visitors from Santa Fe to the Ramon Vigil Ranch, and Pfäffle could have been the driver behind the wheel of the Rocky Mountain Camp Company's Oberlin touring car that carried Natalie and Carol to the Pajarito Plateau in the third week of April 1916.[17]

Pfäffle was compact and athletic, a handsome, talkative bachelor cowboy in his early thirties. Years later, Carol's friends would remember that she and Pfäffle first met on the platform of the Denver and Rio Grande Railway station in the small town of Española, New Mexico. Canon Douglas and his son, Eric, were in Santa Fe several times that summer, and engaged Roy Pfäffle's services on expeditions into Indian Country and to the Grand Canyon. Carol could have met Pfäffle through Douglas, or vice versa. However they first met, the music teacher from Boston and the cowboy guide from Iowa liked one another in a way that changed everything for each of them by early summer.[18]

Natalie and Carol liked the rustic quality of the Pajarito Club and returned for extended stays several times that spring. They rode over to Hewett's excavation sites in Frijoles Canyon, and went with guides, likely Pfäffle, on horse camping trips in the Jemez Mountains. Anticipating a summer in the outback, Natalie wanted her own equipment, and she wrote George to send her bedroll and camping gear stored in his ranch shed.[19]

The Detroit owners of the Pajarito Club and the Ramon Vigil Ranch were becoming more and more frustrated with Pond's management style, which they believed was costing them money. Pond may have shared details of the struggles with his Michigan partners with Natalie and Carol, or they may have heard rumors about the pending dissolution of the partnership from Pfäffle or others who worked in the Santa Fe tourist business. Natalie and Carol were looking for a place in New Mexico where they could put down roots, and as the gossip about Pond's potential departure from the Pajarito Club escalated, the two friends began to talk about what they would do if they were the managers of the guest ranch on the Pajarito.

Because the Ramon Vigil Ranch was wedged between canyons containing some of the most extensive archaeological sites found in the Southwest, and the Pajarito Club was only a few miles from Frijoles Canyon, there was already discussion about making the guest ranch into a cultural center that would offer visitors historic context to the cliff dwellings and ancient villages of the Pajarito. In 1914 Pajarito Club owner Roy Chapin had vigorously pushed for the passage of House Bill No. 14739, which would have established the National Park of the Cliff Cities on the forest service lands surrounding the Ramon Vigil Ranch. The bill did not pass, but by 1916 Chapin, the only one of Pond's partners who had made the trek to New Mexico to see the ranch, was still interested in how the Pajarito Club could be a destination for tourists visiting Frijoles Canyon and other ruins under excavation by Hewett and company.

How Natalie and Carol came to know about Chapin's interest in developing the Ramon Vigil into a cultural center is not known. But by May, Natalie was eager to share their ideas and plans for the ranch with her brother George and told him in letters that he needed to come to New Mexico. Immediately.

On May 19, Alice Klauber and her friend Mrs. Heinricks drove out from San Diego to visit George at his ranch. During her visit, Alice learned that George did not want to go to New Mexico. She would have sympathized with his reluctance to leave his ranch: he was still digging wells and wrestling with the ranch water system, was building an apiary, and was at war with gophers. But Alice had stopped over in Santa Fe at least once, and she knew all about the special aura of New Mexico; she understood Natalie's enthusiasm for the life and people of Santa Fe. In addition, she, like George, had made friends with New Mexico artists and archaeologists when they worked on the exhibitions for the Balboa Park fair. Everyone who went to New Mexico became enamored of the place. And in 1916, something special was happening in Santa Fe.

On May 20, Natalie sent two telegrams to George insisting he get on the train for New Mexico. In his journal George swore about Natalie's summons, but, bound by duty and love to his sister, and perhaps a bit curious about what she was so eager to talk with him about, he packed his bags, left the ranch animals, garden, orchard, and beehives under the care of a neighbor, and jumped on the stage north to Los Angeles, where on Monday, May 22, he caught the 9 p.m. train for Lamy, New Mexico.

Alice may have been tempted to go with George on this impromptu excursion, but she remained in San Diego. Since Henri would be in Santa Fe by mid-July, Alice was making plans to be in the City Different by late summer when she could rendezvous with her former teacher and friend.

The Santa Fe train was running four hours late, and George's rail excursion across the Arizona–New Mexico desert was hot and tedious. Two days later, he disembarked at Lamy, and the heat and discomfort of the train car dissolved into the cool, clear New Mexico morning. A bus took the train passengers on a road that wove across the sage- and piñon-studded foothills into Santa Fe. Natalie met George on the plaza, and after unpacking his bags at the hotel, they met up with Carol (whom George called Caroline) and walked to the Rocky Mountain Camp Company stables, where they saddled up horses and went out riding in the hills above the old town.[20]

Even the reluctant tourist George found the landscape and people of Santa Fe irresistible, and on the first evening he was enchanted by the setting sun that turned the landscape into "a fairy land of purple mountains." The next morning, he was up early for a stroll around the plaza. With Carol and Natalie, he found Hewett at his office in the Palace of the Governors, and they went for a tour of the new art museum under construction across the road.

During the next week there were supper parties under the stars, morning horseback rides into the foothills, and leisurely afternoons spent wandering adobe neighborhoods with Carol and Natalie. In spite of himself, George fell under the spell of the people and the mystique of old Santa Fe. "Starlit air or some sweet influence, soothed me earlier to sleep," George wrote in his diary. "The sacred mountain at dawn was still wrapped in clouds."[21]

Natalie had also summoned the Curtis family's financial adviser, Elbridge Adams, to Santa Fe, and he arrived from New York on May 29. Natalie wanted Adams's advice about the ambitious proposal she and Carol were preparing for Roy Chapin and the Pajarito Club owners in Detroit. George and Carol remained in Santa Fe while Natalie took Adams on the Chile Line to Buckman, where they were met by a car that took them up the mesa to the Ramon Vigil Ranch.[22]

Natalie and Carol were about to propose to Chapin that the Pajarito Club be developed into a major Indian arts, crafts, and cultural center for the Pajarito Plateau. Frank Mead was part of the professional team Natalie was assembling. Adams would serve as legal counsel, and as such, Natalie and Carol wanted him to carry their proposal to Chapin in Detroit and negotiate on their behalf.

The idea to build a cultural center to showcase Indian art and history had been a topic of conversation between Natalie and her friends long before she came to New Mexico in 1916. "Before we ever saw Pajarito," Natalie wrote Chapin, "we had in mind the creation of a centre in the Southwest for people of culture, who, nevertheless, know little of the interest (historical, artistic and ethnological) nor of the beauty and value of this Spanish-Indian part of the United States."[23]

Early in 1916, Natalie, Frank Mead, George, and likely Alice had discussed the creation of an Indian art and crafts ranch in Southern California. Although Balboa Park had generated significant interest in Indian art and culture, Southern California lacked indigenous attributes important to their concept, and by spring the consensus was to find a location in the Rio Grande district of northern New Mexico where the landscape, the density of archaeological sites, and the vital life of the puebloan people provided the perfect combination of scenic and cultural attractions.

It was an ambitious undertaking, but after touring the Ramon Vigil Ranch and reviewing their formal plan, Adams believed that the women's proposal was sound and agreed to take it to Chapin. Adams left Santa Fe in late June—George had departed New Mexico several weeks earlier—and presented Natalie and Carol's ideas to Chapin in his office at the Hudson Motor Company.

Roy Dikeman Chapin was a Michigan native who at the age of twenty-eight had directed the consortium of engineers and merchants that founded the Hudson Motor Car Company in 1908. Chapin was an enormously powerful individual in the American auto industry, but he was also approachable and "friendly to an exceptional degree" with a "gift of participating in another's outlook as though it were his own." After meeting with Adams, Chapin was genuinely interested in Natalie and Carol's proposal for his remote New Mexican ranch. After Adams's visit, Chapin penned a letter to Natalie telling her that he liked the women's ideas about the development of the Pajarito, and that he wanted to meet with Frank Mead as soon as possible.[24]

Natalie and Carol received news of Chapin's interest in their proposal in a letter from Adams carried to them in the saddlebag of a cowboy who found the women camping somewhere in the outback. Natalie hastily penciled a short response to Chapin telling him that she and Carol were on a camping expedition and that she would contact Mead as soon as they returned to "quasi civilization" in mid-July. Natalie apologized to Chapin for the condition of her letter that "goes to Santa Fe in a guide's pocket."[25]

Upon their return to Santa Fe, Carol remained in residence at the Hotel De Vargas, but Natalie, who was not feeling well, stayed in bed in rented rooms on Buena Vista Street. Both women corresponded with Chapin, and by July he invited Natalie and Carol to come to Detroit.

Winfred Douglas and Eric were in Santa Fe several times that summer, and they hired Pfäffle to be their outfitter and guide on at least two expeditions into Indian Country. Douglas was an informal consultant for the Pajarito project, and his name was mentioned in at least one letter to Chapin because he was an old friend of the Gray brothers, the Detroit bankers who had yet to visit New Mexico.[26]

Ashley Pond was not included in the flurry of letters passed back and forth between the women in Santa Fe and the ranch partners in Detroit. Chapin's insistence that Pond not be privy to their discussion about the ranch's future bothered Natalie and Carol, who had become friends with the "kindly and good-hearted" Pond and his family. Although they did not want their plans to offend him or damage their relationship, negotiations between Natalie, Carol, and the Detroit partners proceeded without Pond's knowledge until August, when Chapin finally wrote to Pond of the women's plans.[27]

The ladies' plan would transform the Pajarito Club's lodge and cabins into the headquarters and outfitter for the ethnologists, archaeologists, writers, artists, and tourists who wanted to be immersed in the great canyons, mesas, and mountains of the Pajarito Plateau. To maintain the pristine beauty of the country, all expeditions would be by foot or horse only. The mission of the new Ramon Vigil guest ranch would be to celebrate and promote the art and culture of the Indian Southwest. The finest Native American arts and crafts would be displayed in a museum and sold in the museum shop. All new construction or renovation at the Pajarito Club would employ the architectural style championed by Frank Mead in Southern California and applauded by Roosevelt in his 1913 *Outlook* article. Natalie sent Chapin photographs of Mead's Spanish-Indian buildings in the event that he was unfamiliar with southwestern style.[28]

Chapin told Natalie and Carol that their plans "fit in very closely with what all of us, as owners, have in mind." Chapin's only reservation had to do with finances, since his partners weren't looking to spend more money on their rustic hunting camp. Even so, Chapin thought a meeting with Mead would advance a plan that would be mutually satisfactory.

Providentially, by late summer Ashley Pond informed his Ramon Vigil partners that he and his family were going to leave the Pajarito Club in the fall. Pond had long held the dream of starting a boys' school in the New Mexico outback, and in late summer of 1916 he had struck a deal with the owner of the adjacent Brooks Ranch to create an outdoor school that would promote "a sound mind and a healthy body." By fall, Pond planned to formally open the Los Alamos Ranch School on a high mesa just a few miles across the Pajarito Plateau from the Pajarito Club.

After several lengthy camping expeditions with Carol and friends, Natalie's health was failing again, and by August it was decided that Carol would journey alone to Detroit to meet Roy Chapin. Armed with detailed plans for a cultural center and Indian heritage museum on the Ramon Vigil Ranch, Carol climbed onto the train from Lamy to Chicago and Detroit on August 16.

Unfortunately, recent telegrams from Nahant had brought Carol the devastating news that her inheritance had been squandered by poor management. Carol still owned the Johnson house on Dorothy Cove, but with her bank account now greatly diminished, she needed a secure situation. Carol's new twist of misfortune added urgency to negotiations with Chapin.

Adams had introduced their plan and opened the door for Natalie and Carol to negotiate with the Detroit men. Now it was up to Carol to convince these captains of industry that their proposal and credentials were solid, and that she and Natalie, with the advice and input of friends and advisers that included Mead, Douglas, Hewett, Adams, Lummis, and Alice Klauber, could develop the Pajarito Club into a cultural center.

Carol evidently gave Chapin a professional and convincing presentation, because he told his partners that he was "tremendously impressed" and found Carol Stanley to be very attractive and to have a charming personality, "quite the type that we all desire to have in charge of the property." After Carol departed Detroit for Santa Fe, Chapin wrote Henry B. Joy and the Gray brothers—all of whom were vacationing on Cape Cod—that they needed to seriously consider underwriting the cost of the proposed heritage center. "While you plutocrats are enjoying sea breezes, I am sitting here sweltering in the heat, trying to put our Pajarito Ranch on the map. . . . Something has transpired that looks as though it might be particularly interesting."

Carol socialized with Chapin's wife and, by the end of her visit, was comfortable enough with Chapin to tell him that her once-sizable inheritance had been lost to mishandling and negligence by the estate executor. "Neither Miss Curtis or Miss Stanley have any income of any great amount. Miss Stanley had hoped to finance the scheme such as Miss Curtis has outlined, from her inheritance, but she discovered very recently that the Executor of her Mother's Estate had dissipated practically all of the funds and she is now in a position where her income is not enough to keep going and as she puts it very plainly,—she must go to work."[29]

It was a grand scheme for a unique piece of real estate in the New Mexico wilderness, a scheme that needed considerable funding from a small group of investors who lived in the modern world of automobile production and high finance. Chapin seemed confident enough in Natalie and Carol's management abilities, but his partners were reluctant to finance such a grandiose project on a remote mesa on the ragged edge of the New Mexican frontier with two single women at the helm.[30]

12

REMARKABLE TIME, REMARKABLE PLACE

> Looking back, it is as if these men and women knew
> of their place in history even as they sat around the
> evening campfires at Puye and Rito. . . . Magic itself
> informed the early years of [Hewett's] school.
>
> —*Marjorie Lambert*

THROUGHOUT THE SUMMER and fall of 1916, Santa Feans observed
the daily progress of the massive pueblo-mission building that was
the new art museum emerging from the sandy dirt on the northwest
corner of the plaza. The museum's Saint Francis Auditorium was a
jaw-dropping feat of brick construction that lifted over two stories
above West Palace Avenue. The auditorium's ceiling was held up
by massive timber beams and carved corbels that were hoisted into
position by cables. When the museum opened in November 1917,
it promised to change the skyline of the old city and become the
cultural, artistic, and social hub of twentieth-century Santa Fe.

Just a short walk across Lincoln Avenue from the new museum,
the colony of artists in residence at the Palace of the Governors
was industriously preparing for a late-August group show of New
Mexico landscapes and portraits. To Hewett's delight, Henri was in
residence and working in the old Palace, and had also agreed to hang
the late-summer exhibition, which would include his Balboa Park
compatriots Carlos Vierra, Gerald Cassidy, and Kenneth Chapman,

and additional artists new to Santa Fe like the New York modernist Paul Burlin, who had been one of the youngest artists to exhibit at the 1913 Armory Show.

Hewett's art exhibitions at the Palace of the Governors, and soon at the Museum of Fine Arts, implemented Henri's "open-door" policy that allowed any artist working in New Mexico to participate in public shows. Modeled on the exhibition practices favored by Paris artists, which removed the critic as gatekeeper and encouraged a nonacademic, nonjuried environment, this policy let the artists themselves choose what to exhibit. Henri and Hewett's "open door" at the old Palace and a year later at the new art museum instigated a considerable migration of prominent painters to New Mexico, and the formation of the Santa Fe modernists' movement by 1920.[1]

Alice joined her expat pals in Santa Fe in August, arriving at Guadalupe Station at high noon on Saturday, August 12. Even with so many friends and colleagues living within a few blocks of the narrow-gauge railroad depot, no one met her train. Alice made her way to the Hotel De Vargas, checked in, enjoyed a light lunch in the hotel dining room, and, still unable to connect with Natalie or Henri, set out to see the little town.[2]

Alice walked across the plaza to the Palace of the Governors and found the front doors locked. She was told that everyone—the Hewetts, the Henris, Natalie, and her friends—had left town and driven out to see the dances at Santa Clara Pueblo. Alice wandered the charming alleyways and dirt roads of Santa Fe and perused the small shops around La Fonda and the plaza. She was just beginning to feel lonely when Natalie telephoned her at the hotel. Natalie and Carol Stanley, whom Alice had not yet met, were recovering from a strenuous expedition to Acoma and Zuni Pueblos during which they both came down with "a queer dysentery" that had placed them in beds in a Gallup hotel for five days. Carol apparently was on the mend, but Natalie had been bedridden and staying in rented rooms on Buena Vista Street for most of the past three weeks.[3]

Alice went in search of Henri and found him taking in the pleasant evening from a chair on the front porch of his rented abode on De Vargas Street. Henri was sharing the house with his wife, Margie "O," his sister-in-law, Violet, their friend Lucy, and several dogs. Henri told Alice that Hewett took care of everything, and that everyone in the Henri household was quite satisfied with life in the little capital. Alice ate supper with the Henri clan, and then walked with them to the plaza to people watch. A rustling in the trees heralded a drenching downpour that sent them scurrying to the Hotel De Vargas. Soaked to the skin, the Henris called for a buggy and said good-night to an equally sodden Alice. Alice retired to her room, changed out of her drenched clothing, and wrote in her diary what a truly glorious first day it had been in old Santa Fe.

The next morning, Carol, who kept her Santa Fe residence in the Hotel De Vargas, knocked on Alice's door and introduced herself. Carol was in the company of a woman named Dorothy Kent, and they invited Alice to go with them to Tesuque Pueblo northwest of Santa Fe.

Dorothy Kent's home was in Tarrytown, New York, a community on the Hudson River seventeen miles south of Peekskill, where Winfred Douglas lived. Dorothy was a twenty-six-year-old painter and a classically trained violinist. She was the younger sister of the up-and-coming artist Rockwell Kent, who, coincidentally, had been a friend and classmate of Walter Pach's at the New York School of Art. Rockwell Kent was among those who, with Pach, had joined Henri and the other members of the Ashcan school of "realist renegades" in the 1910 Exhibition of Independent Artists.

Dorothy Kent had studied painting with Homer Boss in New York. Through her association with Boss, and with her brother, Rockwell, with whom she had a famously contentious relationship, Dorothy was tangentially involved with the birth of the Society of Independent Artists in 1916. At the same time that Henri and Hewett were advocating an "open-door" exhibition policy in Santa Fe, Pach, Boss, Kent, and their circle of New York modern artists, writers, and musicians were drafting the society's "no-prize, no-jury" mission policy. Dorothy, like her brother, would participate in the society's first exhibition at Grand Central Palace, New York City, in 1917.[4]

On her third day in Santa Fe, Alice met her "Santa Fe self which is a new woman." Santa Fe Alice rose early and stayed out with friends until close to midnight. She sketched in her notebook and painted watercolors of the streets and people of old Santa Fe. She dined with the Henris and the Hewetts, and the new museum's construction foreman, Jesse Nusbaum, whom Alice had become friends with in

San Diego. She went to the movies with the Henri clan, and with Natalie, Carol, and Dorothy Kent. Alice was reading Lummis's *Land of Poco Tiempo* and took her book to a bench among the hollyhocks in the Palace of the Governors courtyard near Henri's studio, where he was working on a portrait of a puebloan, Willie Begay.[5]

On Wednesday, August 16, the same day that Carol climbed on the Santa Fe train bound for Chicago and Detroit and her meeting with Chapin, Alice and a friend, Miss L. W. Wilson, took the Chile Line northwest from Santa Fe on the first leg of a long day's trip to reach Hewett's field camp at Puye near Santa Clara Pueblo. The summer monsoons had filled the Rio Grande to flood level, and after Alice climbed off the train and crossed the river at the Buckman Bridge, she was met by Crescensio Martinez, who would take her by wagon to Hewett's camp.

Crescensio, the brother of Julian Martinez, was a gifted self-taught watercolorist. Alice had met Crescensio several years before at Balboa Park. He was now working in a studio near Henri's in the Palace of the Governors and, with Awa Tsireh (also known as Alfonso Roybal), also of San Ildefonso Pueblo, Fred Kabotie of Hopi, and Ma-Pe-Wi of Zia, was part of the first wave of pueblo artists whose work would bring national recognition to contemporary Native American art.[6]

From Buckman Bridge, Crescensio and his horse and wagon took Alice twelve miles north along the Great River via the lands of San Ildefonso and Santa Clara Pueblos, and then west into Santa Clara Canyon and the cliff dwellings under excavation by Hewett at Puye. As dusk fell, Crescensio pulled the wagon up to a camp at the base of massive cliffs. There were two snapping bonfires, and some fifteen people—all relatives of Crescensio's—moving between a dozen tents. Alice joined them and shared her picnic supper in exchange for hot coffee. It was a congenial and lively camp at the foot of the cliffs, but it was not Alice's final destination. After supper, still in her traveling skirt and laced boots, with duffel bag in hand, Alice followed Crescensio on foot up the dark cliffs. They climbed a ladder straight up the stone walls, and followed the deep grooves of ancient trails across narrow ledges of volcanic rock to the ridgetop camp of Dr. Archaeology, Edgar Hewett.

Alice was welcomed into a camp community of more than twenty students and professional archaeologists. After an hour beside their campfire under the sparkling star-filled sky of the Pajarito Plateau, Alice was taken to her tent. She climbed into her bedroll and within minutes collapsed into sleep.[7]

The men and women sitting around the campfire that night were participating in a summer field school that would be remembered as a charmed chapter in the story of archaeology in the American Southwest. On the high ledges of Puye and in the canyon of El Rito de los Frijoles, which she would visit several days later, Alice was among the world's most rarefied assembly of archaeologists. It was a remarkable time in a remarkable place. "Most of those who came to study, work on, and contribute to Hewett's programs at Puye . . . and the Rito de los Frijoles . . . were to become giants in the field of American anthropology and also legends in their own lifetime."[8]

Hewett's field schools and their sponsoring organization, the School of American Archaeology, were "peopled with giants." Adolph Bandelier, Alice Fletcher, and Charles Lummis all worked with Hewett's school in some capacity. Jesse Nusbaum, Ted Kidder, Kenneth Chapman, Sylvanus Morley, John P. Harrington, Donald Beauregard, F. W. Hodge, Neil Judd, Maude Woy, Barbara Friere-Marreco, even San Ildefonso potters Maria and Julian Martinez, worked alongside El Toro, the enigmatic, domineering, forceful bull who was Edgar Hewett.[9]

The field school's day commenced at dawn with breakfast served at a long plank table under a large canvas tarp. On her first morning at Puye, Alice went with Hewett's team to an excavation site where she watched the unearthing of a large ceramic vessel. After a picnic lunch, Alice climbed a narrow trail down the cliff side to a cave where two young Santa Clara potters, Romana and Maximiana, were teaching Hewett's students the fundamentals of traditional pueblo ceramics. At five o'clock, Alice, Hewett, and his crew ascended the cliff back to camp. Alice had tea in Donizetta Hewett's tent and participated in the hour-long Spanish class before supper. Evening was spent, once again, around the campfire under the wide, star-studded sky.

Each day for the next week, Alice's routine was the same. She often accompanied Hewett on his treks to various excavation sites, including one six-mile hike across several canyons and up a cliff ladder to a site on a neighboring mesa. Hewett was excavating a large kiva, and he asked Alice to sketch petroglyphs and artifacts as they were found.

Alice departed Hewett and his field school at Puye late in the afternoon of August 23. She went by a wagon to San Ildefonso Pueblo, where she spent the night on a hillside beside Maria and Julian Martinez's home. Maria gave Alice breakfast and a tour of the old pueblo before she went on foot to the depot at Buckman, where she met the narrow-gauge train that took her up the Rio Grande Gorge to Taos.

After several days of hiking into the mountains and sketching the Spanish villages near Taos, and touring and sketching Taos Pueblo, Alice climbed back on the little train and traveled back down the gorge to Española and Santa Fe. It was Saturday, August 26, and Carol Stanley returned from her trip to Detroit on the same afternoon.[10]

Alice, Carol, and Dorothy Kent joined Hewett, Henri, and most of Santa Fe's residents at the opening of the exhibit of New Mexican paintings by Henri and the other artists in residence at the Palace of the Governors. Natalie, however, remained in bed, as she was still not feeling well, and her circle of close friends began to quietly discuss moving her into one of the local sanatoriums.

Also absent from the festivities surrounding the art show opening were Winfred Douglas and Roy Pfäffle, who were making their way

Figure 35. Alice Klauber at the home of Julian and Maria Martinez, San Ildefonso Pueblo, August 1916.

back from weeks in the outback. In early August, Douglas and son, Eric, had gone with Roy on a trail-scouting expedition through New Mexico and Arizona that ended at the Wetherills' in Kayenta. From Kayenta, John Wetherill had taken Douglas, Eric, and Roy across the infamously brutal Rainbow Trail. Roosevelt and his sons, the party of Zane Grey, and a few dozen lesser-known but no less intrepid individuals had similarly followed John Wetherill into the notorious canyon country to Nonnezoshe, the great Rainbow Bridge.

After several days of hard riding, walking, and scrambling across the hot, steep, slick rock ledges of the high plateau, the party stood beneath the bridge. On August 24, Pfäffle and the Douglases added their names to the fabled registry tucked in the rocks. It was likely Pfäffle's and Douglas's first visit to the sacred arch, but it would not be their last.[11]

The August pack trip Roy Pfäffle took with the Douglas men was historic in the annals of modern Southwest expeditions, since they were the first to travel by horseback from Santa Fe across Navajo and Hopi country to Rainbow Bridge. Pfäffle and other guides routinely took horses and riders on the train from Lamy to Gallup, where they disembarked, packed up, and headed by horseback into Indian Country. Pfäffle's historic outing with Douglas and his son began on horseback in Santa Fe and continued north and west across New Mexico into Navajoland, and west and north across Arizona to Kayenta. It was an epic achievement—they rode nine hundred roadless miles in twenty-eight days, and successfully blazed a trail through Cañon del Muerto at the east end of Canyon de Chelly. Pfäffle and Douglas mapped a route from Santa Fe to Canyon de Chelly that would become the standard for horse expeditions in the next decade.[12]

In late August, Natalie was still bedridden with a lung disorder, and with the lingering effects of the nasty germ picked up on her trip with Carol into the outback in July. Although Natalie remained involved in the discussions about the Pajarito Club's future, Carol realized that if Chapin and his partners agreed to their proposal, Natalie could not possibly live on the plateau and manage the ranch. Carol, alone, would have to go oversee the Pajarito Club for the winter.[13]

Carol, Alice, Douglas, and all of Natalie's Santa Fe friends were anxious about her ill health. On the last day of August, Alice and Carol went to St. Vincent's and made arrangements for Natalie to move into one of hospital's private rooms. The next day, they moved her into the sanatorium.[14]

St. Vincent's was near the old plaza just off the corner of Palace Avenue and Cathedral Place, and in 1916, with seventy-five beds, it was Santa Fe's largest hospital. Private rooms were furnished with home-style beds, rocking chairs, and wide windows with a view of Palace Avenue or the cathedral gardens. Visitors were welcome, and Natalie had many during her convalescence. One person in particular, Paul Burlin, remained by her bedside.

Over the spring and summer of 1916, Natalie and Paul Burlin had fallen in love. Carol knew the extent of their relationship because she was with Natalie when the courtship began. Burlin had gone on camping trips with Carol and Natalie's friends, and when Natalie moved out of the Hotel De Vargas, she had rented rooms in a little house in the same neighborhood as, if not alongside, Burlin's casita on Buena Vista Street. But Alice had only just met Burlin a few weeks before, at the Palace of the Governors where he had a studio near Henri's, and she did not grasp his significance to Natalie until she walked into Natalie's hospital room early one morning and found the artist sitting beside her bed.

It was obvious to Alice that Burlin was devoted to Natalie. In the next few days, he was never gone long from her room at St. Vincent's, and Natalie was delighted by his presence and his attention. Alice slept one night on the sofa in Natalie's room at the hospital and visited her several times each day, but throughout Natalie's four-day internment Burlin was the first to arrive at her room in the mornings and the last to leave at night.

At first glance, they seemed an unlikely couple—she was forty-one, he was just thirty that summer—but Natalie and Burlin had much creative and intellectual common ground. Burlin was a nationally known artist who had studied in New York and Europe before leaving the world of modern art to embark on a solo adventure in the American West. The son of an English father and a Polish mother, Isadore "Paul" Burlin was raised in New York City and London, and

Figure 36. Paul Burlin.

studied at the National Academy of Art and the Art Students League. In his twenties, Burlin traveled through Europe, where his work was influenced by the European avant-garde, especially by Cézanne's composition and Matisse's use of color.

But it was during his first journey to the American Southwest in 1910 that Burlin, just twenty-four, encountered what would be the most significant influence on his art: the landscape, culture, and spirituality of indigenous Native America. Burlin came to the Southwest looking for a pristine landscape and primitive culture. He found both in New Mexico. Armed with a gun given to him by New York friends, Burlin traveled by horse and wagon through the Southwest outback and "learned to sing out of doors just to keep the demons away."[15] Although nervous about the remoteness and isolation, and intimidated by the Indians and Hispanic Americans he encountered in New Mexico, Burlin fell in love with the unspoiled frontier.

Burlin kept a residence on 51 West 10th Street in New York, but after 1913 he spent a substantial part of each year in what he referred to as the simple, unpretentious town of Santa Fe. He always rented the same tiny adobe dwelling on the corner of Buena Vista and College Streets (later Old Santa Fe Trail), and he was among the first of the New York painters and expats to move into the studio space provided by Hewett in the renovated Palace of the Governors.

By 1916 when Burlin met Natalie, he was a knowledgeable and competent outdoorsman, and he became part of the regular gang of good friends with whom Natalie and Carol went into the outback. Roy Pfäffle was frequently the guide on their informal jaunts in the deep, vast network of canyons on the Pajarito and to the high country of ponderosa and aspen forests in the Sangre de Cristo and Jemez Mountains.

During the days of Natalie's convalescence, Alice and Burlin became acquainted in conversations in the hospital, and over lunches and informal suppers at eateries on the plaza. Alice became interested in Burlin's very modern, often dark and somber art and went to view his new canvases at his studio at the Palace of the Governors.

On Monday, September 4, while Natalie recuperated in her room at the sanatorium, her friends gathered for an end-of-summer luncheon at a café on the plaza. Carol, Dorothy Kent, the Henris, Alice, Paul Burlin, and the newly returned Roy Pfäffle and Canon and Eric Douglas all recounted their summer travels and discussed departure itineraries and autumn plans. On Tuesday, Alice was at the Palace of the Governors and watched Burlin, Carlos Vierra, and Will Henderson hang "the Taos Group" in one of the galleries. By Thursday, Natalie moved out of St. Vincent's and, with Alice and Paul Burlin, went by automobile out to the Pajarito, where Ashley Pond helped move Natalie into one of the cottages in the canyon. In the cool quiet of the ponderosa forest, she planned to read, write letters, walk, and sleep until she was fully recovered. Pond knew of Natalie and Carol's negotiations with Chapin and his partners, but he was looking forward to the opening of his boys' ranch school, and Pond and Natalie were able to maintain their amicable relationship.[16]

After a visit with the Henris and the Hewetts in Santa Fe, Alice caught the Santa Fe train from Lamy to the Grand Canyon, where she spent a few days hiking and sketching. Then she headed for San Diego and her home on the Pacific.

Natalie remained at the Pajarito Club until late September. During her weeks on the high plateau, she wrote Chapin several letters reaffirming her and Carol's interest in building the cultural center at the Ramon Vigil Ranch. Burlin may have stayed at the Pajarito Club for all or part of Natalie's convalescence and journeyed with her back to Santa Fe on September 27. Natalie's return to the capital was mentioned in the "Personals" of the *Santa Fe New Mexican*, where it was also noted that she planned to join an expedition to the Grand Canyon in two days. Natalie would not return to New Mexico for the winter, but would continue on to San Diego, where she would spend the winter.[17]

Natalie wrote Chapin that she was planning to take the train and meet Carol and other friends at the Grand Canyon in mid-October. Unbeknownst to Natalie, Carol had left Santa Fe six days earlier with Roy Pfäffle.[18]

Roy Pfäffle and several other guides from the Rocky Mountain Camp Company had left Santa Fe on horseback on September 13 for another trail-blazing expedition through Indian Country. Roy's July journey with Douglas had created a buzz among the outfitters and guides who worked around Santa Fe, and Roy was happy to share what he and Douglas had learned. Roy also wanted to scout additional routes between Santa Fe and Canyon de Chelly via Chaco Canyon and Washington Pass (Narbona Pass) to Luckachukai. Carol and Dorothy Kent must have proven themselves adept campers and proficient horsewomen, because they were invited to ride with Roy and the other professional guides on an arduous three-week-long adventure in the outback.[19]

Their whereabouts for three weeks were not recorded in anyone's journal or letters, and it is not until October 2, in Gallup, New Mexico, that the expedition reemerged into recorded history. On that day, at two o'clock in the afternoon, in the small railroad town on the edge of the Navajo Reservation, Caroline Bishop Stanley of Boston, Massachusetts, married Richard Leroy Pfäffle of Santa Fe, New Mexico. The Reverend David A. Sanford of Gallup's Episcopalian Church of the Holy Spirit officiated. The reverend's wife, Mary

Sanford, and the bride's good friend, Miss Dorothy Kent, witnessed the ceremony. The McKinley county clerk entered the bride's date of birth as December 16, 1884, her age thirty-four. Carol was actually born in 1879 and was thirty-six, but no one at the impromptu ceremony, including the math-challenged clerk, seemed concerned about the age of the suntanned, saddle-and-trail-toned bride.

Roy Pfäffle was recorded as being thirty-one years of age, although his stated year of birth was 1882, making him thirty-three. The age of the bride and groom was surely of less interest to the witnesses gathered in Gallup that October afternoon than the fact that the new Mr. and Mrs. Pfäffle were both born on December 16. What Roy knew of Carol's life story is unknown, but at some moment during their six-month courtship, she must have mentioned to him that he shared a birthday with her and her long-lost twin, Edward.

Two days later, the newlyweds and the other members of the expedition returned on the train to Santa Fe. The success of their trip by horseback from Santa Fe to Chinle received a glowing write-up in the *New Mexican* on October 5. However, the newspaper story did not include the Gallup marriage. That announcement would wait until Carol sent off personal telegrams and letters about her marriage to friends and family back in Boston and Nahant.

Three weeks after the fact, Carol and Roy's secret marriage was formally announced in the *New Mexican*. The new Mrs. Pfäffle, "well-known in musical circles in the east," was introduced to Santa Feans as a member of the Choate family of Massachusetts. Roy Pfäffle was already well known in northern New Mexico, since he had worked for several years with the forest service in the Jemez Mountains above the Pajarito, and then as a guide with the Rocky Mountain Camp Company.[20]

By late October, Roy had severed his ties with the Rocky Mountain Camp Company, and the Pfäffles moved to Española, where Roy had a livery stable and the couple hoped to open their own business. Chapin had sent Carol a warm letter of congratulations after he learned of her marriage to Pfäffle, but he had also told her that because his partners were ambivalent about the cultural center, the project was shelved. With Roy's reputation as one of the region's premier guides, and with Carol's social connections back

Figure 37. On the trail to Rainbow Bridge, ca. 1924.

east, it seemed reasonable that the Pfäffles could attract sufficient clientele to build a viable outfitting business. Even out in the tiny railroad town of Española.

Before joining up with the Rocky Mountain Camp Company, Roy had operated a small outfitting business out of the Oñate Hotel in Española. Roy also had family in the town: his widowed mother, Margaret, known as Gaga, and two younger sisters, Marie and Lois, had been living at the Oñate for several years. Carol had met Roy's family and was aware that his mother and sisters depended on him financially and personally. But exactly how all their lives would mesh after Carol moved into the Oñate with the other Pfäffle women, no one could say.

In early November, Carol and Roy packed up their horses and rode west into the Arizona outback for a honeymoon in Indian Country. Their destination was the Wetherills at Kayenta. The couple

Figure 38. Rainbow Bridge, ca. 1920.

retraced the route they had taken in September, and also scouted trails and campsites north and west from Chinle across Hopiland for their new outfitting business. Several weeks later, the Pfäffles rode into Kayenta. Just eighteen months had passed since Carol had learned to ride a horse with Louisa and John Wetherill, but that New England music teacher was long gone. The new woman known as Carol Pfäffle was very much at home on the bright, hot desert of Navajoland, and with John Wetherill and her new cowboy husband, she rode across the Rainbow Trail to the legendary bridge on the far side of the world.[21]

13

A RARE THING

Becoming Oneself

On the other side of the Sangre de Cristo Mountains there
is a great welter of steel and flame. . . . I know nothing of it here.
—*Alice Corbin*

THE UNITED STATES FORMALLY entered World War I on April 6,
1917. The American effort to mobilize what would by 1918 total over
four million military personnel immediately affected all U.S. industry
and business. Detroit auto companies, including Pajarito Club owners Roy D. Chapin and Henry B. Joy, cut their automobile production in half and reconfigured their factories to serve the war industry.

In late 1916 Hewett proposed that his field school become a private corporation under the State of New Mexico. This new entity
would continue to conduct field schools and respond to the research
mandates of the Archaeological Institute of America, but the change
in status would allow Hewett to go after much-needed financial support. In December 1916 the institute unanimously approved Hewett's
proposal, and the School of America Research (SAR), with headquarters in the Palace of the Governors, was incorporated in early 1917.
However, America's entry into the European conflict brought the
Pajarito field schools and all excavations in the Southwest under
Hewett's auspices and SAR to a halt, since "the services of the staff

and all the facilities of the School and Museum were promptly placed at the disposal of the Governor and the State Council of Defense."[1]

Santa Fe's new art museum was pushing toward completion and its scheduled opening in late November, although the museum staff and space were redirected to serve the activities of the local Red Cross and the Women's Naval Auxiliary. Patriotic rallies were held on the plaza in front of the Palace of the Governors and the new museum, and the Santa Fe art community channeled its prodigious creative energy into the war effort. Alice Corbin became director of publicity for the Santa Fe Women's War Effort, and her husband, Will, with Sheldon Parsons and Paul Burlin, learned from Taos artist Ernest L. Blumenschein how to use their skills with paint and brush to create "range-finder paintings"—detailed landscapes of the French countryside to be used by army machine gunners to develop target, distance, and range assessment skills.[2]

In January 1917 Carol and Roy Pfäffle opened their outfitting business at the Oñate Hotel in Española. Advertised in newspapers and tourist brochures as the most experienced guide service for major expeditions to Chaco Canyon, the Natural Bridges of southern Utah, and Mesa Verde in Colorado, the Pfäffles' business, like all tourist-based endeavors in the Southwest, received a substantial boost when the United States entered the war. Wealthy Americans canceled their trips to Europe and the Mediterranean and instead booked vacations to the American West, many for the first time. It took a war overseas, but the cultural and natural wonders of the Southwest were finally getting the attention that Lummis had been clamoring for since he first uttered "See America First" in the previous century.[3]

Española was a quiet, pastoral village on the Rio Grande near its confluence with the Chama River, and was flanked by the tribal lands of the Tewa pueblos of Santa Clara to the south and San Juan to the north. The only horse, wagon, or automobile road between Santa Fe and Taos passed through the center of town, and Española was linked to Colorado by the narrow-gauge tracks of the Denver and Rio Grande Railroad. The oldest foot and wagon routes to the Four Corners and Indian Country followed the Chama River valley north and west from Española to Abiquiú, and the wonders of the great Pajarito Plateau and the Jemez Mountains were accessible by horse through the canyons and mesa country to the south and west of town.

Figure 39. Carol Stanley Pfäffle, 1920.

Headquartered at the Oñate Hotel, the Pfäffles' outfitting company was located at the gateway to Indian Country. Clients arrived by the D&RG railway and stayed at the hotel before and after their expeditions with Roy into the outback. Although Carol often went on these expeditions into the country she loved, her primary job was business manager. The Pfäffles needed to expand their clientele, so beginning in 1917 Carol went each winter to Chicago, New York, and Boston to give lectures about her experiences in the American West to friends and former colleagues, hoping to sign them up for their own adventure in New Mexico.

Carol supervised the daily operations of the hotel where Carol, Roy, and the extended Pfäffle family also made their home. Carol's mother-in-law, Gaga, not only lived with Carol and Roy, she worked for them, too. For Carol, and for her in-laws, it was an uncomfortable and complicated family arrangement from the start.

Roy Pfäffle had taken care of his mother and younger sisters, Marie and Lois, since the violent death of his father, Frederick Harley Pfäffle, in a train wreck near Avoca, Iowa, in 1907. Fred Pfäffle was a fireman for the Rock Island Railroad, and after his death, Roy's mother and sisters left Council Bluffs and went to live with Roy on his homestead in South Dakota. Times were tough, and in 1910 twenty-six-year-old Roy gave up his job clerking at a store, boarded up his homestead, and moved with his mother and sisters to the home of relatives in the frontier ranching community of Sapello, New Mexico. Roy found work as a cowboy on ranches near Las Vegas, and eventually became a forest ranger in the mountain country near Santa Fe and Española.[4]

When Carol Bishop Stanley of Boston met Richard LeRoy Pfäffle of Council Bluffs at the Española railroad depot, they were the embodiment of the western story romanticized in a dozen dime novels. She was the educated and genteel lady of the East who had left everything to find something of her own out west. He was the penniless son of German immigrants with little formal education and no experience of the modern, urban world. The match shocked Carol's and Roy's families, although among their friends in Santa Fe the marriage was really not all that remarkable. Carol was in middle age, her inheritance had been reduced to pennies, and she was alone. She could not or would not return to Nahant. Carol needed a partner in New Mexico if she was going to make a home there. Roy Pfäffle was in his early thirties, handsome and well spoken, industrious, self-reliant, as popular with the men as with the ladies, and skilled as a guide and horse wrangler. Although he had a wild streak—he loved to play poker—he was liked and respected in social and business circles around Santa Fe and northern New Mexico. Everyone knew Roy had taken good care of his widowed mother and sisters for a decade, and by 1916 he was ready to have a partner in his life.

Roy's elopement with the educated, middle-aged spinster with the odd, *r*-less Boston accent brought significant challenges to his mother's household in Española. Overnight, the home and business of Roy Pfäffle was run by his new wife, and Gaga's diaries reveal now and again a mother-in-law's repressed disgruntlement with the haughty, strong-willed, aristocratic eastern lady who stole her son's heart and moved into her family's home.

In the winter and spring of 1917, while Carol was figuring out married life with her new husband and his family in New Mexico, Natalie was in San Diego preparing to marry Paul Burlin. Burlin, himself suffering from tuberculosis, spent most of the winter of 1916–17 in the warm climate of Southern California. By January, Natalie and Burlin had discussed their intention to marry with George, who was given the task of telling Mimsey of Natalie's engagement plans. George had met Burlin the summer before in Santa Fe and heartily endorsed his sister's engagement to the young painter. But George was a Californian now and lived by the relaxed status quo found in the new society of the "other edge," the West Coast. He knew Mimsey and the Curtis family back east would not necessarily celebrate Natalie's engagement to Paul Burlin.

Early in 1917 Natalie and Burlin traveled cross-country together to attend the opening of an exhibition in New York City of Paul's new work alongside that of Man Ray. Although the New York reviewers liked Burlin's Santa Fe work, Natalie's family, especially her mother, was ambivalent about his modern style. Mimsey was also ambivalent about her daughter's engagement to Burlin.[5]

Natalie announced that she and Paul wanted to be married in New York City. Burlin had colleagues and friends from his art school days living in the city, and some of his immediate family (with whom he was not close) still resided in New York; and almost all of Natalie's friends and professional colleagues lived in or near Manhattan. New York seemed the natural choice for their wedding.

Natalie's plan to marry in New York City garnered a tepid response from the Curtis family. Although Mimsey and her siblings *liked* Burlin, there were several matters that inhibited their support of him as Natalie's choice for a husband. He was not wealthy, and although highly respected in the modern art world, he hardly made enough income to support himself, let alone a wife. Burlin was also ten years Natalie's junior, and he was an immigrant. A Jewish immigrant.

The Curtises, for all their social-reformist agendas and liberal, progressive political alliances, were members of New York's elite old-money crowd. Mimsey made it known to Natalie that her marriage to Burlin would be an awkward affair in her hometown, and the discussion about a Curtis-Burlin wedding ceremony in New York ceased. Even their engagement was kept a secret. Mimsey later admitted to George that she had been greatly relieved that Natalie quickly understood the potential awkwardness of the event and did not pursue a New York City wedding where "the Montagues and Capulets would not blend."[6]

If Natalie was disappointed in her family's understated but potent upper-class snobbery, or was surprised by the undercurrent of anti-Semitism flowing just beneath the polite surface of New York's intellectual elite, she never said so publicly. With Burlin, Natalie returned to California and the welcoming environment of George's rural ranch and Alice's home in San Diego. By late March, Natalie and Burlin were happily residing in bohemian Santa Fe, where their unlikely romance didn't seem so unlikely.[7]

Carol was delighted to have Natalie back in New Mexico, and left her mother-in-law in charge of the Oñate to spend nights with Natalie in Santa Fe. Española and the Oñate Hotel did not offer Carol much opportunity for intellectual or creative stimulation, and she sometimes went alone to Santa Fe for evenings with Natalie and their friends.

Natalie attempted to explain to family and friends her love for Burlin and the life they shared in faraway New Mexico. She told her Aunt Nat that with Paul Burlin she had at last found the "Great Happiness" in a relationship that was born in the out-of-doors where, in "the enforced and inevitable intimacies of camp-life, people come to know each other through and through." Her husband-to-be took such good care of her, Natalie said, that she believed she would never again be ill. She and Paul shared an "affection based on sound friendship, mutual aims and absolute intellectual and spiritual rapport," and Natalie assured her Aunt Nat they would have an enduring happiness "even without riches." Natalie's letter to her aunt was written during a visit to Carol's new home in Española. The two friends found comfort in their similar situations, and shared thoughts and feelings about their family's reactions to their decisions to marry years "after first youth." Perhaps hoping to give her forthcoming New Mexico marriage context, Natalie told her Aunt Nat that she was staying with "a dear friend of mine, a Boston Girl who is married and living out here."[8]

Carol well understood the camaraderie and intimacies developed during outback expeditions, having herself fallen in love with and married her cowboy guide after knowing him for just six months. And as Carol may have done several months before, Natalie defended her choice for a husband to friends and family back east. "Of course my family would have liked me to marry a *rich banker*! or some version of the well-to-do and 'tried [tired?] businessman' but I could never have been really happy with anyone but an artist of some kind, because my whole make-up demands that kind of understanding."[9]

Natalie penned similar letters to friends, including her patrons, Peabody, Mason, and Frissell, each of whom was surprised but ultimately supportive. But they were worried, too. Worried that Natalie would not return and complete her work on Negro folk songs, although she assured everyone that, with Paul by her side, she would return to the South and resume her study.

THE ROBERT HENRIS returned to Santa Fe in June 1917 and moved into the Safford house at 601 Palace Avenue. Planning to remain in Santa Fe until the art museum opened in late November, Henri set up a studio in the adobe dwelling. He wrote Alice that Santa Fe was "more beautiful and delightful than ever."[10]

During his second summer in Santa Fe, Henri immersed himself in the domestic and artistic life of the small town at the foot of the Sangre de Cristos. His home was a pleasant walk from the old plaza and the Palace of the Governors. Henri shared the house and yard with his wife and her sister, their friend Lucy, also a painter, Hilda the cook, Flossy the feline, Patsey [*sic*] the canine, four burros "whose names I do not know," plus "a chorus of bees, wasps, bumble bees, lizards, children of the Earth [Jerusalem crickets], horned toads and etc. etc."

The new art museum was close to completion, and the anticipation and planning for its grand opening gave Santa Feans a happy distraction from the distressing news of the war. But like other towns across America, Santa Fe's social agenda was dictated by the organizations and activities involved with the war effort. Henri described to Alice the Cowboy Ball, a benefit for "the Navy boys" held at the Armory, for which "we, the 'art colony'" made posters that were awarded to the best costumes. "It was a success," Henri wrote, "and the costumes make a good spectacle notwithstanding my own opinion that having a cowboy costume party in cowboy country is like taking coals to Colgate."[11]

Henri's studio on Palace Avenue was within walking distance (as was most everything in Santa Fe) of the rustic, three-room adobe Paul Burlin rented on the hillside corner of Buena Vista and Old Santa Fe Trail. The Henris, like most people in town, knew Burlin and Natalie Curtis were engaged (by 1917 Natalie and Burlin may have been cohabitating in the little house on Buena Vista). There was no date set yet for the wedding, but Natalie and Burlin's relationship was the talk and toast of the town. Henri wrote Alice in mid-June, "Yes, there are nuptials in the air at Santa Fe—It's no secret and both bride and Burlin are radiantly transformed. May they be blessed with much happiness and not a large family!"[12]

The marriage of Natalie Curtis and Paul Burlin took place at high noon in the federal courthouse a few blocks north of the Santa Fe plaza on July 25, 1917. It was a quiet and simple affair conducted by Supreme Court Justice Clarence J. Roberts. Carol and Roy Pfäffle and a friend from San Diego, Alice E. Chaffee, witnessed the brief ceremony. Although the marriage license had been obtained five days before, Alice Klauber did not or could not make it to Santa Fe for the wedding. After the ceremony, the wedding party joined friends at one of the restaurants on the plaza for a celebration that lasted into the evening and included nearly everyone in Santa Fe's expat community of artists, archaeologists, tour guides, politicians, physicians, and shopkeepers.

Henri wrote Alice a comprehensive description of Natalie's wedding, and in his missive about the happy day, he took the opportunity to express his feelings about desert khaki: "Miss Curtis (Mrs. Burlin) looked fine. I hardly knew her out of kaki (however that is spelled) and I should advise all women never to wear kaki except when roughing it very roughly, and even then I see no reason to have to wear such a colorless color. They looked happy and I hope they will make a great go of it."[13]

Henri told Alice that the Burlins' honeymoon was "in the Penitentes country," a nickname for Rio Arriba County and the region
of northern New Mexico where the mysterious and once-forbidden
Catholic folk religion Los Penitentes (the penitent ones) had thrived
in rural communities since the late 1700s. In 1917 the Hispanic villages of the Rio Grande near Española, north along the Chama
River, and throughout the mountains near Taos still had active albeit
clandestine Penitente organizations that met regularly in their local
moradas (meeting places). During his years in the forest service,
Roy Pfäffle had worked with and earned the trust of dozens of local
ranchers, many of whom were Penitente *hermanos* (brothers). With
friends active in the village moradas, Roy knew more than most
Anglos about the Penitentes. The Pfäffles' Oñate Hotel was likely
where the Burlins spent at least part of their "Penitentes country"
honeymoon. They may have gone with Roy and Carol by auto (if
Paul was hoping to paint) or by horseback to visit the moradas in
Alcalde on the Rio Grande or in villages like Abiquiú on the Chama
River. Burlin's painting titled *Penitentes' Santuario* dated "before
1918" may have been painted during the August honeymoon.

A Southwestern-style wedding announcement designed by Natalie
and Paul celebrating the iconic mountains, mesas, and pueblos that
were the beloved landscape of their new life was sent out to friends
and colleagues on both coasts by early August. Charles Lummis,
although working as an adviser on the new museum and frequently
seen in Santa Fe and New Mexico, a place he referred to as "my own
country," was not in town for Natalie's wedding. Nor was he aware
of her romance with Burlin. Upon receiving the wedding announcement Lummis wrote: "Dear Natalie Curtis Plus: As the Spanish say:
'When least you expect it up jumps the jack-rabbit!' . . . I had no
prevision of any such news as I have just received. But I am surely
glad now, as always, of any good fortune or happiness that comes to
you." Lummis hoped Natalie and Paul's celebrating would "get over
as far into the wilderness" as his home near Los Angeles so that "we
shall have the pleasure of having you under our roof."[14]

In late summer, Mimsey sent out her own announcement
of Natalie's Santa Fe wedding. Her mailing list included more
than a thousand names, and it included Paul Burlin's friends and

acquaintances. Mimsey wrote George that "Paul's list included many Goldberg's, Frybergs . . .—not in the Social Register."[15]

As the Great War raged on overseas, the tourist business in the Southwest continued to thrive. The Pfäffles' Oñate Hotel was filled to capacity, and Roy took a succession of expeditions into Indian Country throughout the summer. In late August, Carol went with him on horseback to the Hopi Snake Dance at Walpi. The conflict in Europe was a vague and distant concern for people on the reservations, although the war had brought a noticeable surplus of cash to Indian Country. The U.S. government needed wool for uniforms and blankets, and by late 1917 Navajo sheepherders had more money in their pockets than ever before. However, the Navajos and Hopis were losing their loved ones in a war with another sort of enemy. In the year since Carol and Roy had crossed Navajo and Hopi land on their honeymoon trip, a smallpox epidemic had decimated entire Hopi and Navajo families, and their losses and grief hung like a dark cloud over Indian Country.[16]

On the road across Hopiland, Carol and Roy crossed trails with a Santa Fean named Nathan B. Stern. Stern was a land developer, and in the late summer of 1917 he was coincidentally the manager of Roy Chapin's Ramon Vigil Ranch on the Pajarito. During a trailside conversation under the hot sun of the high desert, the Pfäffles learned that Stern was on his way to join his regiment in California and was bound for France within a month. Stern needed—actually was legally bound to find—someone to move onto and manage the Pajarito Club.

Stern realized that the Pfäffles had precisely the skills and experience needed to manage the remote guest ranch, and then and there he asked Carol and Roy if they would relocate their outfitting business to the Pajarito Plateau and assume the management of the Ramon Vigil Ranch.

Carol and Roy were understandably nervous about accepting the position. Their business was doing very well out of the Oñate in Española. The Pajarito Club was a magnificent guest ranch, but it was located in a very remote canyon on the high plateau of the mountains. Roy had worked as a forest ranger in the Jemez Mountains and well knew how the Buckman road was terrible to dangerous in any season.

But how could they say no? Just one year ago, Carol and Natalie had prayed for the opportunity to manage and live at the Pajarito Club. The Pfäffles could hardly pass up the chance to run an outfitting business from the heart of the greatest archaeological region in North America.

Stern had to know their decision that day, and before they climbed back into their saddles and rode into their respective horizons, the Pfäffles and Nat Stern brokered a deal and sealed it with a handshake under the big sky of Hopiland.[17]

By early November, Carol and Roy moved to the Pajarito with mother Gaga and Roy's sister Lois. During their first two weeks on the plateau, the Pfäffles had a full house with thirty-six guests in the main lodge and cottages of the Pajarito Club. It was an auspicious beginning, and seemed to indicate that neither the war nor the colder weather diminished America's fascination with the ancient, untouched-by-modern-time world of the Pajarito Plateau.[18]

The Museum of Art opened with great fanfare and grandiloquence on Saturday evening, November 24, 1917. The old Algodones Bell in the Acoma Tower of the museum announced to Santa Feans and to the several hundred visitors to the City Different that the day of celebration had arrived. The dedication exercises would take place over several days, but an enormous crowd of more than two thousand people came to the opening evening gala. Hewett, master of ceremonies, spoke briefly, and then the crowd inside St. Francis Auditorium and outside on the road sang "The Battle Hymn of the Republic." And the new art museum's doors were thrown open.[19]

Before the first speaker (Dr. David R. Boyd, president of the University of New Mexico) took the podium in the auditorium, the crowded hallways and reception rooms of the museum echoed with an emotionally charged rendition of "America" sung by the several thousand visitors filling the halls and courtyard—a moment of spontaneous gratitude for the young men from New Mexico and all over the United States fighting overseas.[20]

Alice came to Santa Fe and attended the museum's opening night with the Henris, the Burlins, and the archaeologists and artists she had met in San Diego when they worked on Hewett's exhibitions at Balboa Park—Jesse Nusbaum, Ken Chapman, Carlos Vierra, George

Figure 40. Burros and wagon loaded with firewood in front of the Museum of Art, Santa Fe, New Mexico, ca. 1918.

Bellows, and a dozen others. Hewett, now director of both New Mexico's Museum of Art and San Diego's Museum of Man, had sent out hundreds of invitations. Roosevelt was personally invited to attend the opening ceremonies, but declined. He wrote Hewett that he had promised his family he would not travel over the holidays (it was Thanksgiving weekend).[21]

Although she missed Natalie's Santa Fe wedding, Alice was very much involved with the San Diego wedding of George DeClyver Curtis to Josephine (Lora) D. Jones on September 8, 1917. Alice provided the flowers for the bride, who was twenty-seven years old and staying at the Palomar Apartments. Alice may have also arranged the couple's honeymoon lodgings at her friend Miss Chase's bungalow in La Jolla. If Natalie and Paul traveled to San Diego for George and Lora's wedding, George, who was forty-six when he married, did not mention it in his diary.[22]

In the months before the museum's opening, Henri, anticipating the surge of artists and archaeologists who would come for the celebrations, asked Alice to ship him some liquor because Santa Fe was now a dry town. Alice, daughter of a prominent California merchant, always brought Henri gifts of cigars and cigarettes. But in the fall of 1917, he sent Alice a very specific gift list, and before she left San Diego for New Mexico, she shipped Henri eight bottles of American gin, four bottles of Italian vermouth, and five boxes of Melachrino cork-tip cigarettes.[23]

Throughout the fall the Henris hosted spirited preopening dinner parties at their casa at 601 Palace Avenue for the painters and archaeologists working in and around the Palace of the Governors and the new art museum. Henri's association with the new museum brought many nationally recognized painters to Santa Fe. Prominent contemporary artists George Bellows and Leon Kroll came in late summer to tour and paint northern New Mexico, and also to help Henri assemble the art exhibit at the museum. Bellows, a former student of Henri's at the New York School of Art, set up a studio in the old Palace. Leon Kroll came to Santa Fe from Colorado Springs to rendezvous with Bellows and Henri, and managed to paint several canvases in between the socializing and festivities.

Kroll's canvas *Santa Fe Hills*, Bellows's *Chimayo*, and several of Henri's painted during the summer and fall of 1917 were included in the art museum's opening exhibition. Alice had at least one painting in the opening exhibit, whose roster of artists was a virtual who's who in American art: Henry Balink, Donald Beauregard, George Bellows, Oscar E. Berninghaus, Ernest L. Blumenschein, Paul Burlin, Kenneth Chapman, Edgar S. Cameron, Gerald Cassidy, E. Irving Couse, Katherine Dudley, W. Herbert Dunton, William Penhallow Henderson, E. Martin Hennings, Robert Henri, Victor Higgins, Alice Klauber, Leon Kroll, Ralph Myers, Arthur F. Musgrave, Sheldon Parsons, Bert G. Phillips, Grave Ravelin, Julius Rolshoven, Doris Rosenthal, Joseph H. Sharp, Walter Ufer, Carlos Vierra, and Theodore Van Soelen. After the show many of the artists donated their paintings to the art museum, thus beginning the museum's superb collection of twentieth-century art.

Henri's letters to colleagues back east left no doubt as to his passion and enthusiasm for the new museum and the emerging art colony of Santa Fe. "Santa Fe may do the rare thing and become itself," he wrote to the painter and new San Diego resident Henry Lovins. "The painters are all happy. The climate seems to suit well both temperaments—to work or not to work—and here painters are treated with that welcome and appreciation that is supposed to exist only in certain places in Europe. Being of the 'to work' temperament myself, I am having a fine time."[24]

Walter Pach did not leave his desk in New York City and travel to Santa Fe to review and critique the three hundred canvases by forty contemporary artists, nearly all of whom were well known to him. Pach may have passed up the opportunity to chronicle the opening of a major art museum in the American West (still a frontier on the maps of most New Yorkers), and probably peeved a few of his art world colleagues like Henri and Bellows, but the editors of the *New Mexican* did their best to make up for the lack of national press coverage. The newspaper's columnists effusively expressed the local sentiment that Santa Fe's museum was worthy of national if not international attention and that the opening exhibition "ranks with the Carnegie gallery in Pittsburg, the Chicago Art institute, the Corcoran Art gallery in Washington and others." Although the Museum of Art in Santa Fe invited such comparison, the editor added, it was so artistically and architecturally unique, so completely in a class by itself, as to be an institution "without parallel in the country."

Natalie spoke to a full house in St. Francis Auditorium (which seated more than 600) on Tuesday morning, November 27. She gave a lecture about Indian music and ceremonial dance, and introduced San Ildefonso pueblo dancers, who performed the Eagle Dance on the auditorium stage.[25]

A photograph of Natalie Curtis Burlin taken at that time captured the confident forty-two-year-old newlywed astride her horse on the street near the new museum. Dressed in formal riding clothes, laced boots, and a broad-brimmed hat (but no khaki), Natalie, like her hometown of Santa Fe, seemed to have done the rare thing and become herself.

Figure 41. Natalie Curtis Burlin, Santa Fe, 1917.

The photograph became Natalie's 1917 Christmas card and was mailed to friends and family on both coasts. The copy she sent to Lummis was inscribed "To Mr. Lummis, Sage of the Southwest the thought of whom Dwells in the 'New Museum' at Santa Fe and in the hearts of many friends."[26]

14

"A COUNTRY OF THINGS IN LIGHT"

> I found out that the sunshine in New Mexico could
> do almost anything with one: make one well if one felt
> ill, or change a dark mood and lighten it. It entered
> into one's deepest places and melted the thick, slow
> densities. It made one feel *good*. That is, alive.
>
> —*Mabel Dodge Luhan*

ON A BRIGHT AFTERNOON IN mid-December 1917, Natalie and Paul Burlin were visited by the New York socialite Mabel Dodge Sterne, who had come to Santa Fe by train the night before. She came with her husband, the painter Maurice Sterne, who was a friend of Paul Burlin's from New York City. Sterne was also a former student of Robert Henri's, and he had arrived in New Mexico in October and set up a studio in a small adobe just across the road from the Burlins' home at the corner of Buena Vista and Old Santa Fe Trail.

When Mabel and Maurice walked into the Burlins' front room, Alice Corbin was on the Taos daybed knitting a khaki sweater for the Red Cross. Alice Corbin and Natalie warmly greeted Mabel Sterne, but their welcome fell on deaf ears. Mabel had been in the capital less than twenty-four hours, and in spite of her husband's best efforts, had already decided she disliked the little city. "Santa Fe was the strangest American town I had ever seen. In that bright December sunshine the plaza was a queer mixture of oddities. There were wood-carts drawn by burros, with the short lengths of piñon wood made into square piles and set in sort of high cages, and these were led by dark Mexicans. . . . I saw only two or three automobiles. People rode horseback or drove two-seated buggies. . . . The only Americans I saw who looked like people I was accustomed to, were the shopkeepers in the few stores I went into."[1]

Mabel especially loathed the obligatory social call to her husband's friends the Burlins, whom he praised as "pioneers." For two months, Maurice Sterne had been enjoying the people and environment of Santa Fe, and had encouraged his wife to join him in New Mexico and begin a new life in the town at the foot of the Sangre de Cristos. But Santa Fe's expat community did not resonate with the thirty-eight-year-old Mabel.

"Going across to tea at the Burlins . . . was the first really tiresome thing that happened," Dodge wrote of her first day in New Mexico. "There was a good deal of bright paint about—yellow and blue—and Paul Burlin's modernist paintings here and there on the walls. Natalie Curtis, his wife, was a little old doll that had been left out in the sun and the rain. She had faded yellow hair, cut in a Buster Brown bob, and faded blue eyes. Paul was much younger and looked fresher. He had curly red hair above a round forehead, and the absent, speculative thoughtful look of an intelligent Jew."[2]

Mabel, who had yet to experience firsthand the effects of New Mexico's high altitude sun and year-round aridity on the skin, hair, health, and overall disposition of those who lived in the Southwest, was stiff-necked, ill humored, and unsmiling throughout the visit. She was aggravated and bored by the tea-time talk of modern writers and *Poetry* magazine (Alice and her co-editors, Harriet Monroe and Carl Sandburg, had recently produced a special issue of *Poetry* devoted to Indian chant and song and its influence on modern American poetry), the wartime efforts of the Santa Fe Red Cross, and the Burlins' and Hendersons' plans to spend Christmas Eve and Day at Santa Domingo Pueblo.

Before Mabel and Maurice Sterne departed the Burlins', Alice Corbin suggested they come tomorrow for tea at the Hendersons' home, just a few steps away on the Camino del Monte Sol. Mabel did not respond to the invitation but instead announced, to her husband's surprise, that she planned to motor up to "a place called Taos"

Figure 42. Mabel Dodge Luhan.

the next day. And so she did. Thus began Mabel Dodge Sterne's (later Mabel Dodge Luhan) very high-profile and famous life in Taos, New Mexico.[3]

In spite of her unfriendly behavior and comments, Mabel Dodge Sterne knew there was a good deal more to Natalie Curtis Burlin than faded hair and dry skin. Mabel was enormously interested in primitive cultures and was certainly aware of Natalie's extensive travels into and writings about Indian America. Mabel's home at 23 Fifth Avenue in Greenwich Village was only a few blocks from Natalie's family home on Washington Place. They may have not met face to face until that December day in Santa Fe, but Mabel and Natalie surely knew something of each other's activities.

Mabel also had a home in the town of Croton-on-Hudson, New York, just a few miles from Winfred Douglas's home at St. Mary's in Peekskill. Douglas certainly spoke of Natalie's book and adventures in the Southwest to Mabel, as he was at least partially responsible for Mabel's interest in and inaugural journey to New Mexico. Years later, she mentioned Douglas when she described her first trip to the "little known neighborhood" of the Southwest: "I armed myself with letters of introduction to several individuals who stood out in that unknown and unexplored land. Among them, one was to Ford Harvey [relative of Fred Harvey] and another to Lorenzo Hubbell. These letters were both given me, after some effort to find people who had been to New Mexico, by a priest named Father Douglas who had lived near a tribe named Hopi. . . . He had told me strange, wonderful stories about those people."[4]

Mabel later claimed that she went so quickly to Taos because Santa Fe was too tame and conventional. But Santa Fe in 1917 could hardly be accused of either of these characteristics. For Mabel, the real problem with Santa Fe was its population, however small, of erudite, creative, and audacious New Women who were already making their mark on the place. Mabel needed her own space to make her mark, and the day after the insufferable tea party at the Burlins', Mabel Dodge Sterne motored up to Taos with her soon-to-be-ex-husband, Maurice, and her son, John Evans, and began her own new life.

The Burlins' home on the hill, at the corner of a narrow dusty lane called Buena Vista and the rutted dirt road that would later be formally named Old Santa Fe Trail, was in the beating heart of the Santa Fe art colony that flourished almost overnight after the Great War ended in November 1918. Within a stone's throw of Natalie and Paul's front door lived the British painter Arthur F. Musgrave, who, like Alice Corbin, had come in 1916 for a stay at Sunmount, recovered his health, and settled into life in Santa Fe. The painter Louise Crow lived next door to the Burlins, and Sheldon Parsons, the Hendersons, Will Shuster, and Carlos and Ada Vierra all made their homes in adobe houses close by.

Marsden Hartley came for a stay at Mabel's new Taos salon in the spring of 1918. Paul Burlin knew Hartley in New York, and he went with Mabel to meet Hartley's train at the Lamy station on June 10. Alice Klauber's friend, and Gertrude's brother, Leo Stein had recently begun his own infatuation with New Mexico. No longer on speaking terms with his famous sister, Leo was living full-time in New York City. After his pal Mabel moved to New Mexico, it was Leo who encouraged Hartley to go out west and visit her utopian world in Taos. Stein joined Hartley at Mabel's that summer and loved everything about Taos. But Hartley tired of the town and their hostess, and in late summer moved down to Santa Fe and into the casita next to the Burlins in the vibrant Buena Vista neighborhood of artists, writers, and musicians.[5]

With Natalie and Paul Burlin, Hartley toured the pueblos of the Rio Grande and met Natalie's many native friends. Hartley was a member of Alfred Stieglitz's "soil-and-spirit" group of artists who believed that the spiritual essence of the new American modernism would be found in the American soil. Natalie's long-held belief that Indian music, song, and ritual were a pure and original American art form paralleled Hartley's philosophy of an "essential reality" found in the landscape and people of the Southwest. With Natalie and her husband as sympathetic and educated guides, Hartley traveled into the remote Indian and Spanish American country of northern New

Figure 43. Marsden Hartley, Randall Davey, and John Sloan on the patio of the Palace of the Governors, 1919.

Mexico. Hartley stayed only two years in Santa Fe, but the landscape, like the indigenous people, forever changed him as an artist and a person. "New Mexico is essentially a major sensation, for my eye, at least," he wrote. "The sense of form in New Mexico is for me one of the profoundest, most original, and most beautiful I have personally experienced. It must be 'learned.' . . . It is not a country of light on things. It is a country of things in light."[6]

Santa Fe was as welcoming to the women artists, writers, and archaeologists (although there were few female archaeologists before 1920) as it was to the men who flocked there during and after the war. The author and playwright Mary Hunter Austin arrived in Santa Fe in early November 1918. Austin was in town to investigate land laws and customs of the Native Americans and Hispanic Americans of New Mexico, and Natalie and Alice Corbin were among her first consultants. Within a few weeks of her arrival, however, Austin's sociopolitical energies were rechanneled into more civic artistic endeavors when she offered to help Santa Fe establish a community theater like the one she had begun in Carmel, California.

With Austin's assistance and direction, the same artists, writers, and archaeologists whose skills and energies built the new art museum created the first Santa Fe community theater. The opening season featured productions written and produced by locals, including the crowd-pleasing one-act spoof entitled *Tranquilina, An Archaeological Absurdity in One Fragment, Discovered, Excavated and Decoded by Waldo C. Twitchell*. The boundaries between the New Mexico art and archaeology communities had always been blurred, and by 1918, on- and offstage, the merging of Santa Fe's scientific and artistic colonies was a fait accompli.[7]

That same year, Austin wrote the introduction for *The Path on the Rainbow*, an anthology of Indian songs and chants. Contributors included Natalie, Alice Corbin, Matilda Coxe Stevenson, John Peabody Harrington, and J. Walter Fewkes. Austin's introduction noted the "instinctive movement of the American people is for a deeper footing in their native soil" and praised Natalie, Alice Fletcher, Frank Cushing, and Washington Matthews for "the clarity and sincerity of their literal translations" of Indian poetry, music, and dance. "I know of no task so salutary to the poet who would, first of all, put himself in touch with the resident genius of his own land."[8]

The art and anthropology communities merged in the husband-and-wife team of Natalie and Paul Burlin when they created a dance-drama called *The Deer Dance*. Natalie wrote the musical score based on adaptations of San Ildefonso Pueblo deer, buffalo, and eagle dance ceremonials, and Paul designed the sets and the costumes. Although it was performed locally, the Burlins' dream to bring the production to New York and Boston never materialized.

ALTHOUGH THE PAJARITO PLATEAU was less than thirty miles from Santa Fe, the newly renamed guest ranch, the Rancho Ramon Vigil, where Carol and Roy now lived was so removed from the modern world as to be in another country. The winter of 1918 was warm with almost no measurable snowfall, and the road from Pajarito Canyon to Buckman, where Carol retrieved mail, supplies, and arriving guests, of which there were several dozen, remained dry and passable. But even dry, the journey to and from the ranch was hazardous for horses, wagons, or automobiles. And even with a bridge over the Rio Grande at the Buckman depot, there was no guarantee that a vehicle or horse could cross the river.

The Buckman Bridge was famous for disappearing. If the river was high, the bridge was often washed out, carried downstream by the waters of the Rio Grande. Without the bridge, the only way a vehicle or wagon could cross the river was on the open trestle of the D&RG Railroad. To access the trestle "bridge" the driver of a car would back up so as to align the tires with the railroad track and "bump its way across the ties with the river swirling ominously below."

Even when the Buckman Bridge was intact and above water it was an unstable, worrisome structure, especially for first-time visitors to the Pajarito. Once across the Rio Grande, the road to Carol and Roy's guest ranch cut up the very steep and very high mesa on the other side. For the Pfäffles' guests, just getting to the Rancho Ramon Vigil was a test of nerves. "The original road went in from Buckman, across wobbly old Buckman Bridge, then slantwise in what looked deceptively like one straight gash up the formidable escarpment of the Pajarito Plateau in a two mile stretch of ruts and rock called Buckman Hill."[9]

In spite of the challenges involved with reaching the guest ranch, throughout the winter and spring of 1918 the five guest rooms in the two-story main house and the thirteen rooms in the eight cabins were filled with lodgers who paid twenty-one dollars a week for the privilege of a bed and meals on the remote plateau. Many of these folks were friends, or friends of friends. Charles Lummis was among Carol's first guests and came twice in December 1917, his second visit coinciding with Carol and Roy's birthday party on December 16. Mother Gaga's birthday was on December 17, so Carol and Roy's birthday cake included candles for Gaga, and there was plenty of sparkling burgundy for Lummis and the ranch guests.[10]

In January, Hewett's friend, and patron of the new art museum, Frank Springer came for several days, and Natalie and Carol's attorney and business advocate, Elbridge Adams, made his way up the plateau with several Rothchilds and one of the Rockefellers. With Roy and Carol as guides, the Adams entourage spent the week touring Frijoles Canyon and other archaeological sites on the Pajarito. Natalie's horse, Buck, was stabled with Carol and Roy's horses on the plateau, and the Burlins and the Hendersons came to the plateau for horse excursions and overnights. Charles Lummis returned in March during Easter and went "Penitente hunting" with Carol and Roy and a crowd of unnamed friends that may have included the Hendersons and the Burlins.

Except for expected and routine car and truck troubles—overheated engines, blowouts, punctured tires, and burst radiators—it was an uneventful winter. Gaga and a friend did get stranded in their car on Buckman Hill one afternoon and had to walk home, and several guests became temporarily lost while hiking about the canyons. But Roy and Carol managed to find everyone and return them safely to ranch headquarters before dark.

In April and May, a Boston acquaintance of Carol's and Natalie's from the South End Music Settlement School in Boston, Mary Cabot Wheelwright, came with a friend to stay at the ranch on the Pajarito. Carol's personal staff now included Alice Pring, an Englishwoman who joined the household that winter as Carol's maid. Gaga, Carol, and Alice worked dawn to dusk on laundry, dishes, meals, and guest entertainment and transportation needs. Gaga's diary records that a young man from Denver named "Erick" worked as Roy's ranch hand throughout that winter and spring. The diary does not reveal the man's full name, but he may be Eric, Canon Douglas's

Figure 44. Carol Stanley Pfäffle, Jack Lambert (*far right*), and Eric Douglas (*second to left*) at Rancho Ramon Vigil, 1918.

Figure 45. Carol Stanley Pfäffle and expedition at Los Alamos Ranch School, ca. 1925.

son. As managers of a guest ranch, Roy and Carol's daily routine was a relentless repetition of mundane but necessary chores. Carol fled the plateau for overnights in Santa Fe with Natalie, and for ten days in February she went alone to Denver to stay with the Douglases in Evergreen.[11]

The lack of snow and the January heat wave (Gaga recorded the temperature on the house porch at ninety degrees on January 2) meant a *very* dry spring. Roy, having worked as a forest ranger in this country, well understood the implications of a snowless winter. The streams of the Pajarito canyons would be low flow at best, bone dry at worst. And with drought came the threat of forest fires.

Throughout the winter and spring, Carol kept Roy Chapin and his partners, who were looking for a buyer for the Rancho Ramon Vigil, apprised of the ranch's activities. Chapin was living in Washington, DC, serving on the War Department's Highways Transport Committee. Henry Joy was a captain with the U.S. Signal Corps and was also living in DC. The Gray brothers remained in Detroit.

Carol hated bothering Chapin with trivial issues, but when the drought lowered the water table on the plateau and the ranch wells began to run dry, she was forced to share the dire news with him. "We are, frankly, terribly nervous about the water," Carol wrote Chapin after she returned to the Pajarito from Denver in late February. "All there is in the whole canyon is a tiny bit in the well near the tennis court. We serve on the table and for bathing, weird dark brown fluid which naturally scares most of our guests, and has lost us some. Boiling fails to improve its color, and our immaculate Mother Pfäffle has been reduced almost to tears because one new comer asked if her pitcher might be 'cleaned occasionally.'"[12]

It seemed like divine intervention when, in late February 1918, Roy was asked to accompany a wealthy Denver mining magnate, James R. Thorpe, on a property tour in the Tesuque hills near Santa Fe where Thorpe wanted to build an upscale resort. Thorpe liked what he saw and on April 18, 1918, bought 152.8 acres of land from the family of William Scoville and Edith Pulitzer Moore. This property in the piñon-juniper foothills of the Sangre de Cristo Mountains four miles from the plaza of Santa Fe, named Bishop's Ranch, included the chapel and retreat once used by the French Jesuit archbishop Jean-Baptiste Lamy.

It was a spectacular location for a guest ranch. Unlike the rustic and isolated Rancho Ramon Vigil, Bishop's Ranch had the luxuries of electric lights and heating systems, indoor plumbing, landscaped gardens, orchards, and *water*. (The estate had two lakes on the property.) Before Thorpe even placed an offer on the Tesuque property he asked the Pfäffles if they would like to oversee the creation and management of his new Bishop's Ranch, soon renamed Bishop's Lodge.[13]

Carol immediately wrote Chapin that she and Roy were considering Thorpe's offer. They still owned the small outfitting business in Española, and Carol told Chapin that Roy thought they could feasibly run a "circuit business" and manage all three operations.

The Rancho Ramon Vigil became an untenable situation even for the resolute Pfäffles when the plateau wells went dry in early March. "Our sword of Damocles has fallen," Carol wrote Chapin. "The well has gone dry, and now, with a house full of people, we are hauling water from nearby canyons."[14]

An Española sheep rancher and businessman, Frank Bond, and his brothers purchased the Ramon Vigil from Chapin and company by late April, and Carol, Roy, Gaga, Roy's sister Lois, and most of the Pfäffles' employees moved down to the new Bishop's Ranch by May.

In the spring of 1918, while talking to a local bear hunter and outfitter named C. B. Ruggles in front of the Capital Pharmacy near the Santa Fe plaza, Roy was introduced to a young cowboy named Jack Lambert. Ruggles knew Roy and Carol were setting up the new Bishop's Ranch and suggested Roy consider Lambert as a ranch hand. When Roy learned Lambert was a seasoned cowboy and outdoorsman, he invited the Santa Fe newcomer to join him for lunch at a local diner.

Everett Vey "Jack" Lambert was all of twenty when he met Roy Pfäffle in Santa Fe. Born in Okarche, Oklahoma, in 1898, Lambert had spent several years living on his horse. As a teenager he worked as a cowpuncher, pack guide, camp cook, taxi driver, even a bridge builder (on the Green River) as he made his way across the desert and mountains of the Southwest. The ruggedly handsome Lambert was tall and thin, even tempered, courteous, and thoughtful. When in the company of ladies, he was a perfect gentleman, and he was as comfortable on a horse in the deep outback as he was in a corral filled with high-maintenance, wide-eyed dudes just off the train from the East.[15]

Figure 46. Jack Lambert and Roy Pfäffle.

Jack Lambert, like Roy Pfäffle, was a self-educated, self-made, self-reliant man born and raised in the hardscrabble country of the Great Plains. Roy and Jack liked each other immediately, and over lunch at the diner near the plaza, Roy offered Lambert a job at the new Bishop's Ranch. Lambert accepted, and thus began a twelve-year partnership between Lambert and Roy and the extended Pfäffle family.

Roy and Jack were still pulling boards off the windows and renovating guest cabins when the first guests arrived at Bishop's Ranch. Carol oversaw the daily management of the ranch while Roy and Lambert organized and packed up expeditions, often from Roy's livery stable in Española, and headed out into the Four Corners Indian Country. Bishop's Ranch guests went on auto and horse trips to Chaco Canyon, Canyon de Chelly, the Natural Bridges of Utah, and through the Mesa Verde region. That first year Roy led at least two groups on epic pack trips to Kayenta and the Rainbow Bridge between May and August.

Charles Lummis came to see Bishop's Ranch in July and, with Carol and Roy and their Overland touring car, went up to the

Pajarito. The Pfäffles continued to maintain the lodge at the Rancho Ramon Vigil for the Bond brothers, and with Lummis, they hiked Frijoles Canyon during the day and stayed nights at the former Pajarito Club.

Roy Chapin came with his wife and three-year-old son, Roy Jr., in October for a two-week retreat at Bishop's Ranch. Carol had become friends with Chapin's wife, Inez, during her trip to Detroit, and the Pfäffles accompanied the Chapin family on an auto tour of northern New Mexico that included an overnight at the Pajarito Club. The rumors of an armistice dominated conversations that October, and during dinners with guests and family at the Bishop's Ranch, Chapin shared an insider's view of the war, and also read aloud from "some very interesting speeches" brought from his office in Washington.

Mr. Hubbell, either Don Lorenzo or one of his sons (Gaga's diary entry does not specify), came from Ganado to visit the Pfäffles at the new Bishop's Ranch several times that fall and winter. Hubbell's first visit coincided with Carol and Roy's anniversary party, and Hubbell joined the Chapins and the other Bishop's Ranch guests in dining and dancing with the Pfäffles and the ranch staff late into the night. Hubbell returned again before Christmas and was a guest at Carol and Roy's birthday party on December 16.[16]

Roy's anniversary present to Carol that year was a grand piano—the first piano she had had in New Mexico—which was placed in the Bishop's Ranch main house. Carol played an informal concert on October 16 for the guests, who included Judge and Mrs. Abbot, who had a ranch in Frijoles Canyon; the Chapins, who were departing for the East in the morning; and Hubbell. A perfectly sublime fall evening of music and friends came to a sudden end when Carol fainted. Although Gaga commented in her diary that "we had a time bringing her to," she provided no further details about Carol's collapse. Carol fainted several more times in the next weeks and was bedridden with influenza after Christmas.

Now that Carol had a piano in the house, she offered music lessons to neighbor children and friends. She also gave her teenage sister-in-law, Lois, voice and piano lessons. Lois, however, was an unenthusiastic student and preferred horse or auto excursions in the mountains to afternoons inside the lodge at a piano with her older brother's wife. Like her mother, Lois resented Carol's executive position in Roy's businesses (Carol kept the books and dictated the house budget) and was critical of her shopping holidays to Denver and Chicago.

A good bit of Lois's disgruntlement with her sister-in-law was really a teenager's declaration of independence. Lois frequently left the ranch in Tesuque to horseback ride with friends or go into the movies in Santa Fe. Lois especially liked to do anything in the company of Jack Lambert, who, although only three years her senior, was not considered a proper suitor, at least by Gaga, Roy, and even Carol.

The Great War came to an end on November 11, 1918. Santa Feans, like folks in towns and cities across America, awoke at dawn to loud whistles that announced the signing of the armistice and the cessation of hostilities. The bells of the capital churches and the new museum joined the shrill whistles from city hall and the Santa Fe Water and Light Company.

By midmorning, there were boisterous demonstrations around the plaza and "every motor car in town was in motion, and every one of them decorated with bunting." Children on "wobbling cycles" joined the throngs of people who carried the flags of the United States, Italy, and France through downtown Santa Fe, past the art museum and around the plaza, and Carol and Roy drove into Santa Fe by midday to confirm the news and to celebrate with friends.[17]

The end of the war marked the end of an era in Santa Fe and the American Southwest. The sense of a frontier landscape separated geographically and temperamentally from the rest of the United States and the world would rapidly diminish within the next year, and a great surge of visitors and new residents would make their way to the Land of Enchantment.

IN 1920 NATALIE RECEIVED a small inheritance and with it purchased the three-room adobe casita near the corner of East Buena Vista Street and Old Santa Fe Trail that she and Paul had been living in for several years. After adding a small kitchen and purchasing a few handcrafted and locally made benches, chairs, and tables, the Burlins settled very comfortably into married life.

The little house and its "hand's breath of land" sat on a hill and had fine views to the north and east of the roads to the plaza and of the foothills of the Sangre de Cristos. Although considered modern by New Mexico standards—the house had running water and indoor plumbing, a telephone and electric lights, and its three quaint rooms "fashioned with a wand" in true Santa Fe style—the Burlins' adobe was not, by a Greenwich Village New Yorker's criteria, much to write home about. Indeed, had Natalie's Washington Place family come to Santa Fe and stepped through the rough wood doorway into her mud and timber, dirt-roofed abode, they would have been appalled.[18]

Natalie's adobe in old Santa Fe would not have shocked George, though. Like Natalie, George Curtis had slept in the mud, stone, and wood dwellings that were home to the Southwest's native peoples, and he had lived in rustic cabins and tents in far-flung cow camps. Natalie suggested that George come and stay with her and Paul in Santa Fe, although her only guest room was the breezeway between rooms in which she and Paul often slept in the summer. But George couldn't get to Santa Fe. He and his wife, Lora, had their hands full with their ranch.[19]

Although Henri did not return to Santa Fe until 1922, he continued to send his friends and colleagues to New Mexico. In the summer of 1919, after listening to several years of Henri's incessant, effusive praise about the light and character of New Mexico, the artist and teacher John Sloan decided to undertake the arduous cross-country auto trip "to investigate the situation in Santa Fe." Sloan convinced a friend, Randall Davey, to join him on this adventure, and with their unenthusiastic wives, the two painters drove a 1912 ninety-horsepower Simplex chain-drive touring car from New York to Santa Fe in 1919.[20]

"It was a great day for John Sloan when he discovered New Mexico," Walter Pach would later write about Sloan and company's arrival in Santa Fe. "But it was also a great day for New Mexico."[21]

By 1919 Sloan was nearly as prominent in American art as Henri. He was one of the Ashcan Eight painters, was a founder and president of the Society of Independent Artists, and had exhibited alongside Henri in the Independent Exhibition in 1910 and the Armory Show in 1913. Sloan was also a close acquaintance of Walter Pach, who had been his student in 1906 when Sloan and Henri were instructors at the New York School of Art.

Sloan and Davey liked the light, the landscape, and the people of Santa Fe. They also liked Hewett's and the art museum's open-door exhibition policy, Santa Fe's nonacademic creative environment, and the exceptional community of artists who welcomed them with open arms. And once they climbed out of the noisy, cramped, dusty touring car, their wives took a liking to Santa Fe, too.[22]

Within a week, Hewett set Sloan and Davey up in studios at the Palace of the Governors and helped them find comfortable quarters to rent near the plaza. Dolly and John Sloan loved their summer in Santa Fe and became seasonal residents, returning every summer for the next thirty years. But Randall Davey and his wife, Isabel, liked Santa Fe so much they wanted a permanent place of their own, and in 1920 they bought the historic house and orchard of Candelario Martinez at the top of the Santa Fe canyon east of town.

Alice Klauber had met Randall Davey in the summer of 1912 when the twenty-five-year-old Davey was Henri's affable and capable assistant in Italy. When he arrived in Santa Fe in 1919, Davey was a nationally known and award-winning painter enjoying much success on the American art scene. He had exhibited in the Armory Show in 1913, and in 1915 won the Julius Hallgarten Prize of the National Academy of Design and honorable mention at Balboa Park's Art Exhibition. Davey had studied architecture at Cornell, and he personally directed the enlargement and restoration of the structure that had served as Santa Fe's first sawmill in 1847. Located near the entrance to the Santa Fe National Forest on what became Upper Canyon Road, the Davey home became a favorite gathering place for Santa Fe's burgeoning colony of artists, writers, musicians, and archaeologists. Although Davey continued to teach semesters at the Chicago Art Institute, he and his wife and son made Santa Fe their primary residence.

Davey became one of Santa Fe's most devoted residents, and surely spoke for the Burlins, Hendersons, Pfäffles, and a few dozen other New Mexico expats when he wrote: "I wouldn't trade my life here where I can hunt, shoot, ride, for all that committee going and bootlicking you've got to do in a city for anything. An artist might starve for food here, but he'll starve spiritually in a place like New York."[23]

Although Natalie had finally found a devoted partner with whom she could share her love of the land and people of the West, and now had a home and place of her own in the affirming and stimulating environment of Santa Fe, she kept her promise to Frissell,

Peabody, and Mason and returned to the East and resumed her study of African American music. In 1918–19 Natalie's complete study was published in four volumes titled *Negro Folk-Songs*. As she had in *The Indians' Book*, Natalie included cultural context and background information on the words, tunes, and symbolism of African American music, music she believed was an essential and vital part of modern America's life and culture.

Kurt Schindler added Natalie's arrangements of Negro spirituals to the Schola Cantorum program in New York in July 1918. Eighteen months later, Frank Damrosch and the Musical Art Society of New York performed two of Natalie's concert arrangements of African American Christmas songs in their annual Christmas program.[24]

In 1919, while Natalie was back in New York City working on her books of Negro music, Carol contacted Winfred Douglas and, with his assistance, enrolled Roy's sister Lois in the private school run by the good sisters at St. Mary's in Peekskill where Douglas was music director. Although Carol was friends with the wranglers and cowboys that worked for her, and had herself dramatically eloped with a cowboy just a few years before, she hoped Lois would not marry a cowboy. At least not for a few years. Everyone around Bishop's Ranch knew that Jack Lambert was sweet on seventeen-year-old Lois. Only physical separation would avert premature matrimony.

Gaga and Carol did not agree on much, but they agreed that Lois needed to be sent east to finish high school, and by the fall of 1919 Lois Pfäffle was sent to live in Peekskill under the watchful tutelage of Canon Winfred and Dr. Jo Douglas.

Jack Lambert drove Lois to the station at Lamy to catch the train for Chicago. He did not, however, stay to watch Lois depart: "Poor Jack," Lois wrote her mother, "he didn't stay until the train left. He just went down and then left."[25]

During her first months in Peekskill, Lois was introduced to the art and culture of New York City by the Douglases and by Dorothy Kent, who was at home in nearby Tarrytown. Lois stayed with the Douglas family over Christmas, and also remained with them for the summer holiday. She became an adept urban traveler and went weekly by train or motorcar into New York for lunch, shopping, and evenings at the movies. She went to numerous Carnegie Hall events with the Douglases and with Dorothy Kent and was frequently in

Figure 47. St. Mary's, Peekskill, New York, where Winfred Douglas lived and where Lois Pfäffle was sent to finish high school.

the audience for Schindler's choral concerts. During her first winter at St. Mary's, Lois met Natalie for the first time at Dorothy's home, where Natalie often came to ice skate on the Kents' pond.

In March 1920 Lois went into New York with Kent and the Douglases to visit Natalie at her studio. They braved a cold and pouring rain to have tea with Jesse Nusbaum and Frederick Webb Hodge, friends of Natalie's and Douglas's whom Lois may have already met in New Mexico. Nusbaum lived in Santa Fe and was a frequent camper on the Pajarito Plateau. Hodge had worked at Frijoles Canyon in 1910 alongside Hewett and Nusbaum, and returned to the Southwest each summer for extended fieldwork. A prominent anthropologist and writer, and the former director of the Bureau of American Ethnology, Hodge edited the massive *Handbook of North American Indians.* When Lois met him at Natalie's in 1920, Hodge was the director of the New York Museum of the American Indian and with Nusbaum was working during the summer months on the excavation of Hawikuh at Zuni Pueblo in New Mexico.[26]

Although Carol and Roy orchestrated Lois's separation from Jack Lambert, within a year of his arrival Lambert had become indispensable to the Pfäffles and was essentially a full partner in their outfitting business. He had also become Carol and Roy's most trusted friend. As such, in the next decade Lambert, like Carol, would witness and suffer the personal and professional consequences of Roy Pfäffle's escalating gambling and alcohol addiction.

Roy, like most men who came of age as a cowboy or homesteader, learned to play cards at a young age. He was good at poker, but he lost as much as he won, and as his gambling became habitual, so did his drinking. In late 1919 James Thorpe, owner of Bishop's Ranch, fired Roy Pfäffle as his ranch manager, claiming Roy was mismanaging the new guest ranch. In fact, Bishop's Ranch was doing very well at the time. Thorpe may have heard about Roy's poker escapades and hoped that by firing him he was distancing Bishop's Ranch from the seedier side of northern New Mexico.

However, it is also possible that Roy's dismissal was a defensive move by Thorpe, because at that precise time, November 1919, the Pfäffles, in partnership with Lambert, were assembling the funds with which to purchase property in Alcalde, where they planned to build their own guest ranch. The Pfäffles' attorney, Francis O. Wilson of Santa Fe, was negotiating a deal with the family of Elias Clark for several historic and decrepit adobe buildings and 34,000 acres of land bordered by San Juan Pueblo and the eastern bank of the Rio Grande.

It was a spectacular location for a guest ranch. Alcalde, a tiny Penitente village four miles north of Española, was located on the road that connected Santa Fe to Taos through the tectonic chasm called the Rio Grande Gorge. Although more than a thirty-mile drive over rough roads to Santa Fe, Alcalde was located near the confluence of the Chama and Rio Grande Rivers, and the Clark property had unimpeded access to the best horse and auto routes north and west to Colorado and Arizona Indian Country. The Sangre de Cristo Mountains dominated the length of the eastern horizon, and the Jemez Mountains and the Pajarito Plateau, a half day's ride across the lands of three Tewa pueblos (San Juan, Santa Clara, and San Ildefonso), rose above the river valley to the south and west.

The purchase of the Alcalde property, at least partially underwritten by loans from friends and private investors, was completed by February 1920. With Lambert, the Pfäffles began the colossal task of rebuilding the decrepit dwellings, outbuildings, and corrals. Carol planted flower and vegetable gardens, furnished and decorated the adobe casitas in the style and manner she had admired at Louisa Wetherill's home in Kayenta, and renovated the historic hacienda into a rustic but charming ranch headquarters.[27]

Carol and Roy named their guest ranch San Gabriel. The name paid homage to San Gabriel del Yungue, the first Spanish settlement in New Mexico, established four miles downriver from the Pfäffles' ranch in 1598. But Carol was also honoring her own migration story. The Episcopalian school of St. Mary's in Peekskill, New York, was built on Mount San Gabriel, high above the Hudson River. It is possible that during a visit to Winfred Douglas's home at the school on Mount San Gabriel, Carol had begun to imagine her journey to the Wetherills and a new life in the Southwest.

By spring, Carol had produced a brochure about San Gabriel Ranch that became part of the Santa Fe Railway's postwar campaign promoting tourism in the Southwest. The ranch letterhead was graced with the simple "Little Bird" petroglyph found in abundance in the ancient villages on the Pajarito Plateau. During their three years at the Rancho Ramon Vigil and Bishop's Ranch, Carol had assembled a large mailing list, and she sent out announcements of the new guest ranch to former and prospective clients and to friends in Chicago, Boston, New York, and Southern California. By summer of 1920 the dude ranch called San Gabriel was on the map.

San Gabriel's resident staff included the most experienced cow punchers, dude wranglers, wilderness guides, and automobile drivers and mechanics found in New Mexico: horse wranglers Jack McKinley, Alfred "Slim" Jarmon, and Sandy MacLean; driver, auto mechanic, and guide and historian Orville Cox; and two cowpunchers remembered only by their nicknames, Shorty and Weary. Roy had worked alongside most of these men in the forest service and the Rocky Mountain Camp Company, and with Jack Lambert as ranch manager, and Carol as general manager and bookkeeper, San Gabriel had an excellent and respected foundation. Carol's English maid, Alice Pring, and Roy's mother, Gaga, also moved to the new ranch.

Five years had passed since Carol's arrival at the Wetherills' trading post. Since that time, she had lived in hotels and rented rooms in Santa Fe, and at ranches and outposts in some of the most remote and

Figure 48. Roy and Carol Pfäffle, San Gabriel, ca. 1922.

beautiful settings found in the Southwest. But until San Gabriel on the Rio Grande, Carol had not lived in a place she could call her own.

Lois graduated from St. Mary's in the spring of 1921. After saying her good-byes to Dr. Jo and Canon Douglas, who she would see out west within a month or so, Lois boarded the train for home. Her mother had come to visit Lois in New York, but Lois had not been back to New Mexico in two years. Jack Lambert was waiting exactly where she had left him—on the train station platform in Lamy, New Mexico. Jack still had eyes only for Lois. Lois was nearly twenty-one and, after seeing a bit of the modern world, knew what she liked and whom she loved, and several weeks later, on June 23, Lois married her favorite cowboy, E. V. "Jack" Lambert.

15

DEATH IN PARIS

One will never remember
A greater thing when one dies
Than sunlight falling aslant long rows of corn,
Or rainy days heavy with grey sullen skies.

—Alice Corbin

THE BURLINS SPENT EACH SUMMER in their simple adobe home in old Santa Fe, but Natalie's speaking and lecture engagements, and Paul's need to participate in the contemporary art world, necessitated long absences from New Mexico. If Natalie and Paul Burlin came for a retreat at Carol's dream ranch on the Rio Grande, it was never recorded.

Unfortunately for Paul Burlin and his contemporaries in the modern art movement, after the Great War the American public retreated to the intellectual and artistic conservatism popular in the years before the war. Even back east, the progressivism initiated by the Armory Show fell from favor as Americans sought to return to prewar normalcy. Like the paintings of his avant-garde colleagues, Burlin's ultramodern, somber canvases became the target of violent verbal attack by critics in New York and Philadelphia. Burlin had weathered harsh criticism before, but by 1920 he had lost all patience with American conservatism, and possibly with its not so subtle anti-Semitism as well. Bohemian Santa Fe and the clean, uncluttered faraway atmosphere of New Mexico had given his artistic spirit space and refuge in the years before the war. But in late 1920 even Santa Fe was feeling too American for Burlin, and he told Natalie he wanted to move back to Europe where modern art was celebrated instead of chastised.

Burlin departed for Paris in the winter of 1921. Natalie remained alone in New York to promote her new book, *Songs and Tales from the Dark Continent*. In May, she sailed for Europe and joined her husband in London. Burlin was reenergized by Great Britain, but Natalie was unable to engage her artistic passion in soggy England. Before leaving America, she had told her family that she wanted to expand and revise *The Indians' Book*, but in London, Indian music and the physical and spiritual landscape from which it came, like Natalie's three-room adobe house on the hill in old Santa Fe, seemed to belong to a former life.

Mary Austin was in London promoting *The Trail Book*, and during a conversation with her Santa Fe neighbor, Natalie realized how her mind and heart atrophied when she was not engrossed in creative work. "I know I have been rather spineless here," Natalie wrote Mimsey, "but I can't seem to get up steam."[1]

Natalie ached for her work, her home, and her sense of purpose, all of which were deeply rooted in the soil and people of the American Southwest. But she soldiered on, the supportive wife, and in July went with Paul to Paris to set up house in the City of Lights.

After the war, Paris quickly established itself as the cultural capital of the world, and the Burlins joined the migration of English-speaking expatriate artists and intellectuals drawn to the city's beauty and history, and to the respect accorded the arts by the French. In Paris, Paul Burlin was welcomed into a community of painters who were publicly celebrated for their innovation and experimentation. And Natalie found an enthusiastic audience for her work with American Indian and Negro music.

Life in postwar Paris was a perfect fit for the Burlins. Natalie wrote to George Peabody of the city's pulsating atmosphere, "full of artists, musicians, all bustling with ideas and new expression" that she found "encouragingly purposeful." The Burlins moved into a comfortably appointed pension on the rue Jeanne d'Arc and settled into a stimulating and satisfying community of like-minded artists and intellectuals. The Burlins were introduced to the movers and shakers

Figure 49. Natalie Curtis Burlin, ca. 1921.

of bohemian Paris by a friend of Paul's, the French painter Albert Gleizes, and his wife, Juliette. Gleizes was the recognized founder of Cubism (he cowrote with Jean Metzinger the movement's treatise, *Du "Cubisme,"* in 1912), and was among those modern French painters brought to America and the Armory Show by Walter Pach. Gleizes had joined Pach, John Sloan, George Bellows, Rockwell Kent, Homer Boss, Maurice Sterne, and other friends of Natalie and Paul's to organize, in 1916, the American version of the French Society of Independent Artists.[2]

In the spring and summer of 1921, Albert Gleizes guided the Burlins through Paris. Natalie, who spoke French with adequate fluency, also went with Paul into the French countryside. Although its population and landscape was war-ravaged and scarred, she was encouraged by the spirit of the French people, and by the palpable intellectual excitement surrounding the artists and writers working in Paris. "Everybody in the art-world is here," Natalie wrote to Peabody and to her family back in the States, "and it is a great source of inspiration and development to us both."[3]

By midsummer, Natalie's creative ennui was replaced by the effervescent fire that always presaged a new chapter in her work. In the canvases of Picasso, Braque, and the French moderns Natalie saw striking similarities to the abstract art and design elements of Indian America. She wrote Mimsey about these French painters who had "broken away from representation *completely* and *entirely*," and used nothing in their paintings that recalled a visual object "any more than designs on Indian pottery look like visual rain-storms, or real corn-fields."[4]

Paris was also experiencing a modern movement in music. Futurist instruments used in a concert at the Théâtre des Champs-Elysées were to Natalie the musical equivalent of modern painting. Natalie penned an article for the *Freeman* titled "A Futurist Experiment" about industrial society's need to nurture and embrace the spiritual and emotional complexities of the individual. She understood the need of contemporary musicians to throw off the shackles of the past and make "music unfettered by the present orchestral limitations." But she concurrently recognized how humans living in the postwar world were overwhelmed and numbed by the sterility of modern machines. Music continued to be a source of healing. "There is a cosmic music . . . all about us," she wrote, "full of beauty to which we arc only half awake."[5]

Gleizes personally presented Natalie's books about African American and Indian music to French publishers. She was invited to lecture to Paris audiences about her life and work among the Indians of America, and by midsummer European editors expressed interest in translating and publishing new editions of her books.[6]

In early September, Alice joined Natalie in Paris and moved into a small hotel on the Left Bank for a several months' stay. Alice was in Paris to attend with Natalie the International Congress of Art History held at the Sorbonne in September and October. Alice was the appointed secretary for the American delegation, which counted only four delegates (tiny Belgium had seventy-eight representatives): Harvard music professor Edward Burlingame Hill; respected but conservative painter Cecilia Beaux, who was in her seventies; secretary Alice Klauber; and the American delegation chairman, Robert W. de Forest, president of the Metropolitan Museum of Art. (For reasons never understood by Alice, Chairman de Forest did not make it to

Paris for the meeting.) Natalie had been invited to give a lecture at
the Sorbonne about her work in American folk music, but she was
not an official delegate to the conference.

Alice's California friends Michael and Sally Stein, like Michael's
sister, Gertrude, were still living in Paris. Leo Stein remained in
America, exploring the bohemian colonies of Taos and Santa Fe.
After his first visit in 1918, Leo, smitten by New Mexico, bought his
own adobe casita in Taos and began to work in "the only landscape
. . . where Nature is as aesthetic as Art; the only landscape that can
compete with the great painters."[7]

In Paris, Walter Pach was a valued and popular member of the
artistic and literary coterie that passed in and out of Gertrude Stein's
salon at 27 rue de Fleurus. After the war and throughout the 1920s,
the home of Stein and Alice B. Toklas was the favored territory for
the American expats Stein called "the lost generation" (Ernest Hemingway, F. Scott Fitzgerald, Juan Dos Passos, Sherwood Anderson,
et al.) whose work would become synonymous with the great literature of the twentieth century.[8]

Within several days of her arrival in Paris, Alice received a telephone call from Magda Pach, Walter's wife, asking her to come to
their apartment before they left on an autumn trip to Germany.
Magda and Walter Pach had a six-year-old son and a stable and satisfying life in Europe. Alice spent just one hour with the Pach family, but the visit was enough to renew their friendship. Alice found
Pach to be a happier and "better rounded off" man than the person
she had known years before. Now thirty-eight, he was among the
world's most authoritative and influential writers about modern art.
Following their brief reunion, Alice and Walter Pach began a spo-
radic, tender, and respectful correspondence about art and life that
continued into the 1940s.[9]

In October, Alice and Natalie went "by bus, car, + taxi" to see
Michael and Sally Stein at their spacious and airy apartment on the
rue Madame. Like Leo and Gertrude, the Michael Steins had been
collecting modern art since the early years of the twentieth century,
and the walls of their Paris apartment showcased the finest modern
painters. (In 1906 the art collection in their San Francisco home
included the first three works by Matisse brought to the United
States.) Although Alice remained a close friend of Michael and Sally

Stein, her 1921 diary does not mention a visit to Gertrude and Alice Toklas, whom she had last seen when they lunched in Italy in 1912. Natalie and Paul Burlin saw Leo Stein several times in New Mexico, but if Natalie ever met Leo's famous sister Gertrude in 1921, it was not recorded.[10]

Throughout the fall, Paul Burlin left Paris for extended painting and sketching outings in the French countryside. Alice and Natalie shared the glittering days of a very warm autumn in Paris with long walks along the Seine, leisurely lunches at sidewalk cafés, and evenings at concerts and the opera. They took cabs, buses, and trains in, around, and out of the city to visit the grand historic sites, famous gardens, and museums of Paris and its environs. They were joined by their friend Alice Chaffee, who was in Paris for several months (and who with Carol and Roy Pfäffle had witnessed Natalie and Paul's vows before the justice of the peace in Santa Fe four years earlier).

The meetings of the art history congress began the third week of September, and for the next several weeks, the two Alices and Natalie attended dozens of talks and lectures at the Sorbonne. On Monday morning, October 3, Natalie was scheduled to deliver her much-anticipated lecture about American folk music. In the weeks before the event, she was uncharacteristically nervous about her presentation. Unlike most of the English-speaking presenters, Natalie had decided to give her paper in French. Juliette Gleizes assisted her with the translation and coached her pronunciation. Even with Juliette's expert help, Natalie remained anxious about the event, and confessed in a letter to Peabody that it was "a petrifying job to give a talk in a language not your own."[11]

But Natalie wasn't just nervous about speaking to an international audience in French. She was uncomfortable about the order of the program, which placed her lecture directly after Professor Hill's. Edward Burlingame Hill was a composer and assistant professor of music at Harvard, where he had graduated in 1894, one year after Natalie's brother George. Hill's students would include several who would achieve considerable fame, notably Leonard Bernstein. Natalie respected Hill, although he, like fellow American delegate Cecilia Beaux, was an academic, a traditionalist, and a confirmed conservative on artistic matters. Hill's and Beaux's opinions on American art were diametrically opposite Natalie's, and their speeches to the

Sorbonne congress would venture that America was too young to have its own music or art traditions.

Beaux, an accomplished portrait painter and the first woman elected to the National Institute of Arts and Letters, made no secret of her disgust for the French moderns. She especially disparaged Gleizes and the Cubists, whose work she found "irritating, violent, exaggerated, and produced by mad idiots." Once while standing before a canvas in a Paris gallery, Beaux remarked to the woman standing next to her that the avant-garde painting "looked like nothing but a map with odd splashes of color stuck about." The woman was Gertrude Stein, and their conversation ended with Stein's curt retort "This is realism, a still life group."[12]

Natalie knew that Hill's lecture would assert that American composers (including him) were incapable of creating music that could be characteristically called American because America had nothing resembling its own music. In a private conversation, Hill told Natalie that "the reason we haven't any great music in America is because we have no folk music. I suppose you'll say we have?"[13]

Natalie told the professor that America certainly did have its own folk music and that her presentation would dispute the premise of his lecture. But later that night, Natalie realized she could not in good conscience get up before the audience at the Sorbonne and bluntly contradict and possibly embarrass Professor Hill. Hill was the formal American designate in music. Natalie was just an American in Paris who had been invited to talk about her self-directed work among the American Indians and Negroes. Natalie went to the presiding officer and asked to be removed from the program. He refused. American folk music, he told her, was of particular interest to this year's assembly, at least among the non-Americans.

Natalie and Alice sat together in the audience and listened to Hill deliver his address. Hill had made one modification to his thesis: instead of his rigid declaration that there was no folk music in America, he explained that while there was folk music *made* in America, it belonged to the Indians and the Negroes, and thus was not *American* folk music.

Hill's insulting, elitist, and racist doctrine provided Natalie with the fuel she needed to deliver the lecture of her life. Natalie took the podium and gave the speech she had so carefully rehearsed in French.

But she added an impromptu response, in French, to Hill's claim that Indians and Negroes were not American. Natalie's twenty years in the field collecting and absorbing the stories, songs, myths, art, and life of Native and African Americans came with her onto the Sorbonne stage where she, by the accounts of those present, spoke eloquently and passionately about American art and music.

Natalie dismantled Hill's assertion that Negroes and Indians were not Americans, pointing out that American Negroes, "good enough 'Americans' to die for American ideals in our wars," had a long tradition of folk music and songs "that are the very voice of our South."

Natalie had long harbored resentment at "the notion that only New England with Harvard College [not forgetting it was her Uncle George and both brothers' alma mater] at its 'hub'" was considered American. "All America is not New England—it is an agglomeration of races that has given us a folk-lore almost as rich and diverse as that other agglomeration of races that we call Russia." The music of America, she told the multinational audience, was not found in universities and schools "but out in the great expanse of territory that stretches from the Atlantic to the Pacific Oceans, and from Canada to Mexico."

Halfway through her speech, the French and Belgian delegates were enthusiastically nodding their heads with approval. "I didn't mean to get into any kind of controversy," Natalie would later tell friends, "but when I sang those songs about the American maize, about the big, hot American sun that rides his turquoise horse across our Rocky mountains; those chants that have come out of *America* itself—the audience was literally electrified."

Professor Hill's myopic assertions about what exactly could be called American music were dismantled by a diminutive, spirited, self-taught, self-directed scholar whose credentials as an ethnomusicologist had been earned over two decades in the farthest reaches of the American outback. Natalie was sorry that her speech had "tread all over Mr. Hill's toes," but the audience's response to her performance—she sang several Indian songs and demonstrated the use of Indian rattles—and the groundswell of support immediately following her speech alleviated her misgivings. Her speech may have offended Hill and his conservative colleague Cecilia Beaux, but the international delegates showered Natalie with compliments and praise. "We not only know you—we felt you," a Greek woman told

Natalie. "You should go all over this world with this voice from the America that we do not know."

Although Professor Hill's theories had been summarily dismissed by Natalie's fervent and informed remarks, Natalie's gentle charm, sincerity, and great, grand, genuine love of America and Americans won Hill's respect. "We parted very good friends," Natalie wrote in her missive about the event, "even though [Hill] accused me of saying the 'schools and universities had never done anything for music in America'!"

Natalie was resolute in her belief in the value of the people, landscape, and music of indigenous America. "I feel so proud of the wonder and force of the American background," Natalie summarized in her letter home, "the big hinter-land of our Country that is so striking in character, so forceful, so dynamic, so red-blooded. It's not what the European-educated composers do that counts, but the thing that's of the land itself, the thing that's in the soil."[14]

Alice returned to her hotel (she had moved into the Hotel de L'Univers on the rue Croix-des-Petits-Champs) and that night, alone in her room, wrote in her diary how Natalie's presentation "went off with her usual finesse." For the next three weeks, Natalie basked in the afterglow of her performance at the Sorbonne. There was renewed interest from editors and publishers for a French version of *The Indians' Book*, and Natalie talked about returning to her work on American folk music. After the conference ended, Alice and Natalie, often with the Gleizes and the Steins, lunched at cafés (their favorite was the Medici Grill), browsed bookshops, listened to music, and strolled the boulevards. Paul Burlin, who had set up a studio in Marseilles, spent most of that gloriously sunny October painting in the French countryside.[15]

On Sunday, October 23, the unseasonably balmy weather overnight turned cold and rainy. Paris was famous for such a quick change of seasons. Young Ernest Hemingway, experiencing autumn in Paris for the first time that October, wrote how the bad weather "would come in one day when the fall was over. You would have to shut the windows in the night against the rain and the cold wind would strip the leaves from the trees."[16]

Alice went out that first cold, wet evening with friends to see a performance of *The Three Musketeers*. When they emerged from the theater, Paris was deluged with rain, and after a long, chilly wait by the curb, Alice found a taxi and gratefully reached the warmth of her tiny hotel room. The next morning, she slept in and wrote letters to her sisters in California. Just about the time she thought she ought to call Natalie and ask her to join her for lunch, Alice was summoned to the phone in the hotel lobby. She picked up the phone expecting Natalie to be the caller. But it was Natalie's "hotel woman," and in French and broken English, the woman told Alice that Natalie had been hurt. Worried and confused, Alice returned to her room, dressed, and went by taxi to Natalie's hotel. It was only when she reached Natalie's rooms that Alice understood that Natalie had been hospitalized the night before with very serious injuries.[17]

The previous day, while Alice was at the theater, Natalie had spent the afternoon with friends and then taken a bus across Paris back to her hotel. At 5:45 p.m., at the corner of the boulevard du Mountparnasse and the rue Campagne-Première, Natalie got off the bus. It was dusk and pouring rain, and as she walked into the street, a motor car struck her down. The driver, a Dr. Poujand speeding down the boulevard to a medical emergency, never saw the petite woman in the rain near the bus stop.[18]

From Natalie's hotel, Alice telegraphed Paul Burlin in Marseille. The authorities had tried to reach him the night before, but had sent the message to the wrong address. Alice telephoned the Gleizes and with them went to the hospital, where they all expected to find an injured but stable Natalie resting in a bed. Instead, they learned that Natalie had never regained consciousness and had died two hours after the accident.

Albert and Juliette Gleizes went to meet Paul's train. Numb and dazed, Alice, alone in the hospital room with Natalie's body, wondered why, the day before, she had had no presentiment of the accident. "It is unbelievable that Natalie should have been snuffed out like that and I dining within two blocks and no premonition of any sort . . . I was walking . . . feeling happy!"[19]

In the terrible hours and days that followed, Juliette Gleizes calmly and compassionately guided Alice and a grief-stricken, nearly dysfunctional Paul Burlin through the French police reports and official documents, and the planning of Natalie's cremation and memorial service. Even as Alice suffered and grieved Natalie's passing, she understood that Natalie's quick death was precisely the way Natalie would have wanted it. "Natalie died without knowing anything of the pain and distress of it all," Alice wrote to Mimsey Curtis. "She looked in death serene and beautiful—her slight smile, the great tranquility of the room in which she rested, the beauty of the flowers banked about her would have meant much to you as they did to me. I went often, and I stayed long alone with her for the very peace it brought me and I am sure that the veil that separates us is a very thin one. She never feared death and said that she hoped the end would come quickly when it did come. The dear blessed girl has gone without pain or suffering."[20]

Natalie's memorial service was held on All Saint's Day, October 31, at the Père Lachaise Cemetery in Paris. Albert Gleizes read selections from Mercereau, "Come raggio di sol" was performed beside the coffin, and the hymn "Abide with Me" was sung twice by the mourners. After the service, Alice, Alice Chaffee, Michael and Sally Stein, and Albert and Juliette Gleizes walked alongside Paul Burlin behind the coffin the several miles to the crematorium. Some fifteen thousand people came out to honor Natalie that cold day.[21]

In the weeks after Natalie's death, Paul Burlin stayed in the Gleizeses' home. Alice was cared for by Michael and Sally Stein.

News of the tragedy reached George in a telegram from his sister Connie on October 28, five days after Natalie's death. At the time, George and Lora were on holiday in La Jolla, dining and taking in the sea air with several of Alice's friends, the Hillyers and the Nivens, and a Miss Mary Bickel. The day after the telegram with the horrible news reached him, George received a last letter from Natalie written in Paris on October 7. And several days later, George and all of the Curtis family received a final missive from Natalie, written on October 16, which shared the details of her phenomenal success at the Sorbonne.

George was "knocked all of a heap" by the news of the brutal accident and wrote in his diary that he "felt dull and stupid" as he went about the chores and duties of the ranch. The random senselessness of the accident, and the sudden loss of his cherished sister and best friend, devastated George Curtis. He wrote his younger brother, Bridgham, "What a brilliant mind, what character, what driving force, with the tender sympathy and understanding that found the best in everyone, and gave her power to help people to help themselves. The world seems to me dingy and mean, without her. What a blind, brutally stupid waste there is in her taking-off. . . . It's enough to make the human race hold an indignation meeting and pass resolutions of censure."[22]

The Curtis family found some consolation in recalling Natalie's calm acceptance of life and death, and her unshakable belief in what her Indian friends called the Great Spirit. "She never had the slightest feeling about death," Mimsey told George in a letter, "and would be perfectly willing to go at any moment—except to leave Paul. I never met a person so sure of the circumstance of the soul."[23]

Paul Burlin confided to Mimsey he had never known happiness in any abundance until he met and married Natalie. To Paul, Natalie was a saint and "self abnegation was the key note of that sweet gentle woman—my wife."[24]

With Natalie's younger sister Connie, Mimsey climbed on a boat to France and helped a bereft Paul pack up Natalie's possessions. Alice assisted however she could and then, on November 17, said farewells to Mimsey and Connie, who accompanied Paul, carrying Natalie's ashes, on the ocean voyage back to America.[25]

Winfred Douglas was called upon to conduct the private graveside service at the family cemetery in Providence, Rhode Island. George and Lora did not come east, but her brother Bridgham, her sisters, Connie and Marian, and childhood friend Bessie Day stood graveside with Mimsey and Paul Burlin. Canon Douglas made a few remarks about the life and person of Natalie Curtis Burlin, and Paul placed Natalie's ashes into her father, Bogey's, grave. And it was done.

In the next months and years there were a dozen concerts and events given in Natalie's honor on both coasts and in Santa Fe. At the memorial service held at the Hampton Institute, Elbridge Adams spoke about Natalie's unique character, and read a letter from Kurt Schindler announcing the establishment of a Hampton scholarship in Natalie's name.[26]

Theodore Roosevelt had died two years before Natalie. At sixty years of age, his death was considered premature for such an energetic and vital man who brought so much to his world. When Natalie learned of Roosevelt's death, she remembered how he had presaged his death in 1913. "I have only about six more years of the strenuous life before me," Roosevelt told Natalie during a conversation in the shade of the peach trees below First Mesa. At that time, Natalie found Roosevelt's "unconscious measuring of his days" fatalistic. Six years later, she had a new understanding of Roosevelt's words. "Though his going was untimely and tore a gap in American life that no other personality can fill, it seemed characteristic. Decrepitude and age were not for him, whose mind and body so loved hard work and hard play."

In the months following Natalie's death in Paris, her final musings about Roosevelt's life and death offered her friends and family a comforting perspective as they grappled with her sudden and untimely passing at the age of forty-six, the zenith of her life as a woman and a creative artist. "And so [she] will remain in our minds a powerful figure vibrant with life to the end, even as we saw [her] on the Hopi buttes at dawn—up and on the mountaintops before the world was half awake."[27]

16

CITY OF LADIES

They do as they please, they say what they think, and
nobody cares, for everyone is busy doing likewise.
—*Mabel Dodge Luhan*

EXACTLY WHEN AND HOW Carol learned of Natalie's death is not
known. Winfred Douglas may have wired the Pfäffles with the awful
news. Just two months before, the canon and his son had stayed at
San Gabriel following a month-long outing with Roy in the "savage
desert" of drought-parched Arizona. Roy and Douglas were once
again trailblazing (this time across Hopiland to Kayenta and the
Rainbow Bridge, south across the Kaibab plateau and into the Grand
Canyon, a route that included a nerve-wracking human and pack
animal crossing of the new suspension bridge over the Colorado
River). Carol and Roy's sister Lois, who had lived with the Douglases in Peekskill, were practically kinfolk to Douglas and his wife,
Dr. Jo. And Roy, who was "always patient" with Douglas "around
the horses," and with whom Douglas had now twice crossed the
character-testing Rainbow Trail, had a special place in the canon's
life. "I had a whole month of comradeship with Richard," Douglas
wrote to his wife at the end of the 1921 expedition, "who is to me
the perfect man friend—one in ten million."[1]

In late autumn of 1921, the *Santa Fe New Mexican* and *El Palacio*,
the publication of the Museum of New Mexico, published lengthy
obituaries of Natalie, and a local memorial was organized by Carol
Pfäffle, Alice Corbin, and their friend and part-time Santa Fean

Elizabeth Shepley Sergeant. Bridgham Curtis's farewell to his sister, given several weeks before at her memorial service in Providence, was read by Alice Corbin at the service in Santa Fe, attended by a multitude of Natalie's many friends and colleagues from the Santa Fe Society of the Archaeological Institute, Hewett's School of American Research, the Fine Art Museum, the pueblos of the Rio Grande, and the extended community of Santa Fe artists and archaeologists.[2]

Paul Burlin did not attend the Santa Fe memorial, and he would never return to Santa Fe and the house near the sandy corner of Buena Vista and Old Santa Fe Trail. After traveling back to the United States with Mimsey and Connie Curtis, and interring Natalie's ashes in the family plot in the North Burial Ground in Providence, Paul went back to Europe and set up a studio in Germany, where he could live and work "where most of the 'modern' painters sell." The people and place of New Mexico, once the source of creative and personal inspiration and affirmation, became synonymous with everything Burlin had loved and lost when Natalie died.[3]

By June 1922, Burlin rented Natalie's first and last home to Witter Bynner, a Harvard-educated poet and scholar who had worked at *McClure's* magazine, where he was a colleague of Willa Cather's. Although Bynner was acquainted with Robert Henri and John Sloan in New York, it was Alice Corbin who convinced him to visit Santa Fe. During his early spring stopover in the capital, Bynner fell ill with influenza. Alice urged him to move into Sunmount Sanatorium, where, she assured him, he would be safer than in a New York trolley car. After six weeks at Sunmount, Bynner wanted to remain in old Santa Fe, where he found a community of resourceful people "washed clean of the war. . . . I was writing to friends who lived on another planet." Bynner learned that the Burlins' former home in the Hendersons' neighborhood was for rent, and he moved into the house by June.[4]

Bynner loved Natalie's "little shack" and its "three quaint rooms" on sight and wanted to make the adobe his own, but he couldn't afford Paul Burlin's asking price of $2,500. While waiting for Burlin to lower the price, the house was bought out from under Bynner by Margretta Stewart Dietrich.[5]

Dietrich, like Bynner, was new to Santa Fe, and had come with her sister, Dorothy Stewart. Dietrich was a Bryn Mawr graduate and classmate of another New Mexico newcomer, Elizabeth Shepley Sergeant. She was also the wife of the former governor of Nebraska, the current president of the Nebraska Women's Suffrage Association, and had a sizable income with which she was buying and renovating Santa Fe properties.

Like Bynner, Dietrich fell in love with Natalie's "sweet little old adobe house" and its undulating walls plastered with "pinkish mud from La Cienega." For the next three years, Dietrich rented the dwelling to an indignant Bynner, who believed the house was meant to be his. Bynner relentlessly pestered Dietrich to sell him the adobe, and in 1925 she relented and sold it to him.[6]

Bynner lived happily for the rest of his life in the house in the midst of the "mumble jumble of chumminess" that was Santa Fe's art and archaeological community. Bynner also purchased the adjacent property and enlarged the Burlins' small hillside lot to a full acre. He eventually transformed Natalie's three-room casita into a palatial compound of more than twenty-five rooms in several multistoried buildings. Over the next four decades, Bynner and his partner, the writer Willard "Spud" Johnson, hosted frequent and legend-worthy parties in the house. The once-humble casita of newlyweds Natalie Curtis and Paul Burlin was destined to become a Santa Fe landmark listed on the National Register of Historic Places.[7]

In September 1922, when Bynner was still just a renter, Mabel Dodge Sterne brought D. H. and Frieda Lawrence to visit. The Lawrences were just off the train from the east, and because it was a long and challenging drive to Taos through the Rio Grande Canyon, Mabel asked Bynner to accommodate them all for the night. Bynner welcomed Mabel and her friends, and Frieda and D. H. Lawrence spent their first night in New Mexico in Natalie's adobe a few blocks from the Santa Fe plaza. Although Bynner and the Lawrences were destined for a famous falling-out with Mabel, everyone had a lovely time that evening. Bynner and the Lawrences became friends, and within the year, much to Mabel's ire, Bynner would travel with them to Mexico.[8]

Leo Stein, now a seasonal resident of Taos, had encouraged his friend Lawrence to come to New Mexico and immerse himself in what Stein considered a transcendent landscape. Lawrence was not disappointed and was captivated by Santa Fe and Taos. "New Mexico was the greatest experience from the outside world that I have ever had. It certainly changed me forever. . . . The moment I saw the brilliant, proud morning shine high up over the deserts of Santa Fe, something stood still in my soul, and I started to attend."[9]

In May 1922, the Museum of Art opened its first annual exhibition of western artists. The seventy-eight artists included local favorites John Sloan, William Henderson, J. H. Sharp, Sheldon Parsons, Will Shuster, Willard Nash, and Californian Alice Klauber. Alice did not return to Santa Fe for the gala opening, but remained in self-imposed exile in Europe.[10]

After Natalie's death, Alice remained in damp, dreary Paris until mid-December. She was not sleeping well, and hoping to escape the depression and listlessness that had dogged her since Natalie's accident, she departed Paris for Lyons and Marseilles, and eventually Florence, a city where she had been happy years before. But Alice was restless and unfocused, and soon left Italy for Germany. Her melancholy would persist for two years, and she would spend those years a nomad in Italy, Spain, Germany, Switzerland, northern Europe, England, and France. "So may this shadow on my soul," Alice wrote in a poem, "Lift away when I am whole."[11]

In the fall of 1923, while traveling through Belgium and France, Alice was reading *The Ladybird*, D. H. Lawrence's newest collection of novellas (published in the United States under the title *The Captain's Doll*). In her diary she quoted Lawrence several times. "A man can only be happy following his own inmost need." "Exactly, I will lay down the law for nobody, not even myself. The thought of death and the afterlife saves me from doing any more. . . . As the thought of Eternity helps me."[12]

Neither contemporary literature nor the great art and architecture of Europe consoled Alice. She was in her mid-fifties, and the sudden death of Natalie initiated soul-searching reflection on her past, present, and future. Alice began to write poetry about love and loss, nature and death that would be privately published in 1928.

Three years after Natalie's death, at the end of 1924, a much older, well-traveled, and certainly transformed Alice moved back to America and her home in San Diego. Like everyone who had known and loved Natalie, Alice would never be completely at peace with Natalie's abrupt passing. But as her poetry revealed, Alice did

come to an appreciation of death as the eternal mystery, and life—
and love—as precious and fleeting. Although she kept the details
and names to herself, and her letters to male friends like Pach were
destroyed or lost, Alice left intimations in her poetry about her love
life and discreetly alludes to romances that even in middle age continued to frame the landscape of her heart. In "Relapse" she wrote:

> I make each day a weary task,
> To close my heart to him, as then!
> And now, as punishment but ask
> It break, and let him in again.

And in her poem "Tryst":

> I feel the sweet unclosing leaves
> Refreshing in the limpid dew.
> I hear the lily sigh. She grieves
> That I should wait the night for you.[13]

In the month after Natalie's death, Carol Pfäffle went into the
desert to grieve. After the guest season of 1921 ended, Carol, possibly
with Roy, left San Gabriel Ranch and went to Hopiland and the Grand
Canyon. One November morning, in the Harvey Curio room at Hopi
House on the South Rim of the canyon, Carol had an extraordinary
encounter with several Hopi singers. Carol shared this chance meeting
with Elbridge Adams in a letter written on her forty-third (and Roy's
thirty-sixth) birthday. "Just after news came of Natalie's death I met
a Hopi whose uncle was Natalie's teacher for some time. I told him
of her death. After a long silence he said 'But she cannot die. She is
singing now—somewhere with her Hopi friends.'"

In spite of the room being filled with tourists, the Hopi elder and
his friends began to softly and reverently chant in the Harvey gift
shop. Carol recognized the songs—Natalie had taught them to Carol
years before. When the singers were silent again, the elder Hopi told
Carol, "[Natalie] sang like Indian. Have to have spirit of Indian for
white woman to sing that way."[14]

Adams shared Carol's letter with the story of her serendipitous and
affirming encounter with the Hopi singers with Mimsey Curtis, who

sent it on to George. Carol wrote the letter as winter descended on the Rio Grande Valley. At the time, she was struggling to maintain a hopeful attitude about San Gabriel Ranch and its large mortgage, about her husband and his late-night poker games, and about her mother-in-law, Gaga, who, she confided to Adams, "while the dearest mother that ever lived, is a born pessimist."

Friends back in New England were concerned about Carol's decision to live in rural New Mexico. "My good friends write with a kind of worry and suggestions that my life is not as rich as they might wish it to be," she wrote Adams. Carol wanted to pack up her friends and "put them down in this blessed valley where they may see for themselves how wonderful my life is."

San Gabriel would be quiet until the start of the tourist season in late March. The New Mexico winter and the absence of guests offered a welcomed respite for Carol and Roy, Gaga, and newlyweds Jack and Lois Lambert. Even so, empty beds and idle saddle horses meant there was no income, and if the spring and summer did not bring a full house of dudes and dudettes, it could mean foreclosure on the Pfäffles' 34,000-acre dream ranch on the banks of the Rio Grande.

Figure 50. Carol Stanley Pfäffle and Jack Lambert, Canyon de Chelly, ca. 1922.

In spite of everything, Carol was very much in love with Roy and his "Coeur de Lion," and told Adams she would not let their life be ruled by petty concerns and financial worries.

At San Gabriel, the only apparent remnant of Carol's former life in Boston was the Steinway grand piano in the hacienda's front room. Carol played music for the ranch guests and taught piano to the Spanish American children at San Juan Pueblo and at the local mission school. Carol and Roy traveled to Chicago and Boston at least once each year. To her friends and former colleagues back east, Carol had chosen an unconventional husband and a tenuous, even risky lifestyle. But it suited Carol.

"Think of us having music," Carol wrote at the close of her birthday letter to Adams, "going quail and duck shooting, riding over the foothills and getting a good long breath to last us over what we pray may be a grand rush from early spring to late fall."

Perhaps it was Carol's unwavering optimism in the face of so much uncertainty that prompted her pueblo neighbors to christen her with the Tewa name T'apokwj, Sun Lake.[15]

IN SANTA FE AND ALL of northern New Mexico, the 1920s saw a tide of tourists and new residents, and each year Carol and Roy's prayers were answered and a grand rush of guests did indeed descend upon San Gabriel Ranch from early spring until late fall. The Pfäffles' ranch on the Rio Grande was featured in virtually every national article about New Mexico tourism, and San Gabriel Ranch received top billing in the travel brochures produced by the Santa Fe Railway. Carol commissioned Gustave Baumann, a German-born painter and printmaker who had joined the Santa Fe art colony in 1918, and whose work had won a gold medal at the Balboa Park exhibition, to design woodcuts for the San Gabriel Ranch pamphlet. Each December, the Pfäffles commissioned New Mexico artists to create custom-made Christmas cards (including two by Alice Corbin's husband, William Henderson, that featured Roy and his horse) to send to friends, family, and former and prospective clients.

With Natalie gone, Carol no longer had a room in which to stay overnight in Santa Fe. Because ranch guests often arrived on the late train and needed to remain in Santa Fe before driving on to Alcalde —a several-hour trip in one of the ranch Packards—and because Carol

Figure 51. San Gabriel Ranch Christmas card by
William Penhallow Henderson, ca. 1925.

often wanted time away from the guest ranch, in 1926 the Pfäffles
leased a four-room apartment from the Baca family at 537 Canyon
Road. The Pfäffles' pied-à-terre was just over the garden wall from the
Prada property under renovation by Margretta Dietrich, and was within
walking distance to just about everything and everyone in Santa Fe.[16]

The Santa Fe art colony was flourishing. Artists and writers were
no longer just summer residents with temporary studios in the palace
or rented rooms near the plaza, but were buying plots of land and
constructing or renovating their own permanent dwellings. Building

with adobe was inexpensive. Mud and adobe bricks, rough-cut lumber, and ponderosa beams for ceiling vigas made up a home builder's materials list. The rustic, handmade artisan quality that was revered as Santa Fe style was doable by even the novice adobe mason. By the 1920s Carol had become proficient with adobe construction, having worked alongside the local crews renovating Bishop's Lodge and San Gabriel Ranch, and was comfortable with every step in the process from adobe brick making to hand-plastering exterior and interior walls with mud made with the colored sands of local arroyos.

The town of Santa Fe was expanding into the foothills, especially along the Camino del Monte Sol where the Hendersons lived. In the early 1920s Santa Feans watched with amusement the building efforts of five newcomers, *Los Cinco Pintores* (The Five Painters), and their efforts to create studio homes on the Camino. The five—Fremont Ellis, Willard Nash, Wladyslaw (Walter) Mruk, Jozef Bakos, and William Howard Shuster—came to Santa Fe after hearing of the colony's camaraderie and spirit from their mentors Robert Henri, Randall Davey, and John Sloan. Each of the five was less than thirty years of age when they arrived, and all of them became essential members of the art community.

With little money or construction experience, but plenty of energy, time, and determination, each of Los Cinco Pintores set out to build a home of his own in the foothills near town. Frequent construction mishaps—toppling of wobbly and unanchored adobe walls, dubious design and infrastructure decisions (the five installed their own electrical and plumbing systems)—were chronicled by their neighbors, who affectionately referred to them as those "five little nuts in five adobe huts." Even the *New Mexican* frequently commented on the progress of the five's "interesting studio homes" that gave the Camino "the appearance of an enormous anthill."

Los Cinco Pintores persevered, and each managed to complete a habitable studio-home. During the summers, the five moved into tents and rented out their handmade abodes to tourists who paid good money to stay in the charmingly rustic casitas. Ellis, Nash, Mruk, Bakos, and Shuster all became nationally respected painters. Nearly a century later, the handmade adobe dwellings built by Los Cinco Pintores remain standing and habitable—and worth a great deal of money—on the Camino del Monte Sol.[17]

Santa Fe and New Mexico in the 1920s also became the destination for educated and emancipated women of means from New York City, Boston, Philadelphia, and Chicago. Natalie Curtis Burlin, Mary Austin, Alice Henderson, Mabel Dodge Luhan (Mabel married Taos native Tony Luhan in 1923), and others discovered New Mexico before 1920, and their high-profile lives attracted scores more women who, like them, were seeking a place where they could work and live free of the gender-based restrictions and expectations endemic to their class and culture back home.

The modern women who made homes in Santa Fe and its environs became a force to be reckoned with when they joined together and championed cultural and political causes, before and after they won the right to vote. Their influence and sway over Indian land protection issues and the preservation of indigenous arts and crafts, and the ease with which they assumed and maintained power in Santa Fe in the 1920s, gave the City Different the additional designation of the City of Ladies.[18]

Elizabeth "Elsie" Shepley Sergeant, with whom Carol Pfäffle and Alice Corbin planned Natalie's Santa Fe memorial service, had come to see New Mexico after hearing about the charms of the Great Southwest from her good friend Willa Cather. Sergeant was close in age to Carol—thirty-nine when she came to Santa Fe in 1920—and was also born near Boston, in Brookline, Massachusetts. Like Carol and Natalie, Elsie Sergeant had little family income, and in spite of her connections to a well-known and respected New England family (her sister, Katherine, married E. B. White and was the fiction editor for the *New Yorker* from 1925 until 1960), had to support herself to maintain an independent life. Educated at Bryn Mawr, Sergeant was an early proponent of the social reform and settlement house movement, and worked as a journalist in New York City, where she wrote exposés about the sweatshops, slum tenements, and exploitation of the city's immigrant population.

Sergeant was a confidant and close friend of Willa Cather, whom she met in 1910 at *McClure's* magazine. Cather told Sergeant details about her adventures in the Southwest and in 1914 took her to the Museum of Natural History to see the exhibition of artifacts and ceramics that Dr. Edgar Hewett and friends had excavated in canyons in a faraway place called New Mexico. Sergeant was enchanted by

Cather's descriptions of the Southwest and wanted to see Hewett's field camps for herself, but she would not get to New Mexico until after the war.

In 1917 Sergeant was sent to France to write about the Great War for the *New Republic*. She was seriously wounded in the leg by a land mine and had a long recovery in Paris before returning to New York City. Cather was even more insistent that Sergeant needed to go to the Southwest, and in 1920 a wounded and weary Sergeant took Cather's advice and set out to see the landscape of the American West. Sergeant's physical and psychological recovery began on the train journey with a fellow Bryn Mawrter, Gertrude Ely. "The luminous light that burns on the Arizona desert, out of long miles of untouched sage and sand. . . . Yes, that's where I want to be, on an observation car traveling swiftly into the Southwest. Losing myself in a shimmer of fine dust."[19]

Sergeant and Ely made their way to Santa Fe and stayed in Tesuque at Bishop's Ranch, now called Bishop's Lodge. The Pfäffles continued to organize the expeditions and pack trips for guests at Bishop's Lodge, and "lazy old yellow Buck," Natalie's horse, remained in the Tesuque stable after the Pfäffles moved out to Alcalde. Sergeant was introduced to Carol and perhaps met Natalie, too, in the summer of 1920.

Sergeant and Ely rented Natalie's gelding and other horses for overnight trips, and Sergeant finally saw with her own eyes Hewett's excavations on the Pajarito Plateau and toured the Tewa pueblos of the Rio Grande she had read about in the Museum of Natural History back in New York. The freedom Willa Cather, Natalie, Carol, and other women had found in the Southwest was indeed a reality, even for a middle-aged, wounded spinster from New York. "But the moral of the tale is that the real way to see New Mexico is simply to go off on a horse, and then on and on, rejoicing that nobody knows or cares whether you ever come back, taking adventure and beauty and night's lodging as they come."[20]

During their first summer in Tesuque, Sergeant and Ely decided to become at least seasonal residents and together purchased an adobe ruin down the road from Bishop's Lodge. With building plans drawn up by Alice Corbin's husband, Will, and a crew of local workers, they commenced renovation of the crumbling mud house. By July 1921

Sergeant returned and moved into the partially renovated adobe. Although the dwelling was still barely habitable—she shared the house with a gopher snake that moved freely through the rooms— Sergeant loved the rustic life in the Tesuque hills, and joined the creative community she found a few miles up the road in Santa Fe at the homes of Randall Davey and Alice Corbin.

Willa Cather had told Sergeant that she would find a new identity in the American West. And so she did. "The truth is, it is enough to *live* in this country. Just to live. Work isn't necessary for the salvation of the soul."[21]

But Sergeant did work, as she needed to generate income to sustain even a frugal life, and she wrote about her experiences on the exotic frontier of New Mexico in a series of articles for *Harper's Magazine* titled "The Journal of a Mud House." She also joined in the civic and cultural activities championed by Santa Fe's growing league of vigorously active women. With Alice Corbin, Mary Austin, Carol Pfäffle, and the newly arrived (and fellow Bryn Mawr graduates) sisters Elizabeth (Amelia) and Martha White, Sergeant joined the simmering political battle surrounding Indian land rights that erupted with the Bursum Bill.

In 1921 New Mexico senator Holm O. Bursum introduced legislation that would allow non-Indian settlers living on Indian lands to take legal title to those lands if they could prove ten years of continuous possession. Hewett and the American archaeological community, joined by the Santa Fe art and literary colony, launched a loud and forceful protest to stop the bill. The national campaign against the Bursum Bill was organized by John Collier, the research and publicity agent for the Indian welfare department of the National Federation of Women's Clubs. With the publicity and press brought to the issue by such internationally known writers as D. H. Lawrence and Carl Sandburg, and with the tireless and continuous efforts by numerous regional and local women's organizations, the bill was defeated in 1923.

With the defeat of the Bursum Bill, New Mexico's artists, writers, archaeologists, and activists realized how their united voices could mobilize and influence public opinion on a national scale. Soon after the Bursum Bill fight, Collier and company formed the American Indian Defense Fund, and in 1925 the Santa Fe art and archaeology community, focusing their energy on the preservation of Indian art, created the Indian Arts Fund.

The Indian Arts Fund was actually the result of an accident that had occurred in 1922 during a dinner party at Elsie Sergeant's pink-walled adobe hut on the Tesuque River. Sunmount cofounder Dr. Harry Mera (who was serving as the Santa Fe County health officer) and his wife, Reba, Amelia and Martha White, and at least one other guest were seated about Sergeant's rustic supper table when Sergeant's maid dropped an old Zuni *olla* (jar). The apologetic maid told Sergeant she would clean up the mess and throw the broken jar into the Tesuque River. Harry Mera, a respected amateur archaeologist whose specialty was dating and classifying ceramics, took the pieces of the Zuni jar from the maid and said he would take them to Ken Chapman for reconstruction. The evening's conversation at Sergeant's dinner table became a discussion about the need to protect historic Indian ceramics, and within a few weeks Sergeant, Mera, and friends started the Pueblo Pottery Fund.[22]

The preservation effort initiated by the Pueblo Pottery Fund was expanded to include the collection and protection of all Indian arts and crafts and was incorporated as the Indian Arts Fund in 1925. The founding members included Chapman and Mera; artists Frank Applegate, Andrew Dasburg, and J. O. Nordfeldt; writers Alice Corbin, Mary Austin, and Elsie Sergeant; archaeologists Samuel J. Guernsey, Frederick Webb Hodge, Alfred V. Kidder, Sylvanus Morley, and Jesse Nusbaum; and Santa Fe attorney Francis Wilson, land manager Nate Stern, Amelia White, Carol Pfäffle, and Carol's new Alcalde neighbor, Mary Cabot Wheelwright.[23]

17

NEW WOMEN OF THE RIO GRANDE

The *new woman* means the woman not yet classified, perhaps not
classifiable, the woman *new* not only to men, but to herself.
—*Elsie Clews Parsons*

THE PFÄFFLES' SUCCESSFUL and popular San Gabriel Ranch brought
a steady influx of tourists and dudes to the small village of Alcalde
from late March until late October. The region from Española north
along the Rio Grande to Alcalde also became a desirable location for
seasonal and permanent homes for Carol's friends. In 1923, after a
brief marriage that produced a son, newly divorced Dorothy Kent
came for a stay at San Gabriel. Kent loved what Carol had created,
and deciding it was time for her, too, to have a home of her own in
New Mexico, she purchased a property adjacent to San Juan Pueblo
on the Rio Grande a few miles southwest of the Alcalde village plaza.
With help from Carol and a crew of local workers, Kent renovated a
primitive two-room adobe into a peaceful ranchito with a painting
studio, barns for horses, rambling flower and vegetable gardens, and
several shaded courtyards. Kent would live out her life at the ranch
she named Chinguague (Tewa for "the wild place") and would die
here in her own bed in 1981.

Mary Cabot Wheelwright returned to New Mexico for an extended
stay at San Gabriel Ranch in 1920. Mary and Carol, although friends
who had met at Boston's South End Music School, which Mary founded

and funded, were from very different worlds. Mary was the definitive blue-blood Brahmin. Her mother was a fifth-generation Cabot, and she was raised in the heart and soul of good old Boston, where "the Lowells talk to the Cabots, and the Cabots talk only to God." Mary's and Natalie's relatives sipped tea in the same New England drawing rooms, and Mary's parents' home on Mt. Vernon Street was frequented by many of the same contemporary luminaries found at Natalie's Uncle George Curtis's home, notably Ralph Waldo Emerson.

In New Mexico, however, the class boundaries that defined the society of old Boston blurred and even dissolved. Mary still had the financial resources and freedom from economic concerns that Carol could only dream about, but Carol had the experience, contacts, and equipment that Mary needed to negotiate the frontier of the Southwest.

Mary's new life in New Mexico began when she was forty, precipitated by the death of her widowed mother, Sarah Perkins Cabot. Born a year before Carol, in 1878, Mary did not attend college but in keeping with the custom of New England's upper classes was educated at home by tutors and governesses. As a young woman, tall, angular, aristocratic Mary was awkward and opinionated, intelligent, curious, and a nonconformist. The decidedly unfeminine Mary, for all her wealth and position, never attracted suitors or married. By middle age and her journey to the Southwest, she was a sheltered but powerful spinster. "She was an entity," one of her relatives remembered. "You knew when you were talking with Mary that she was somebody."[1]

By the time of her mother's death in 1917, Mary was ready to experience life beyond her parents' Beacon Hill palace. Once released from her life sentence as the dutiful, unmarried daughter who cared for her parents, Mary "woke up" and began to travel the world in search of intellectual stimulation, spiritual inspiration, and personal renewal. She was blessed with an abundance of family money, but she also inherited the Cabot's practical, fiercely independent character, and a "strong interest in nature and a need to get away from civilization."[2]

By 1920 middle-aged Mary was increasingly preoccupied with a personal study of the myths and symbols of the world's great religions. After exploring the mystical and spiritual traditions of Europe, Greece, and Egypt, she turned her attention to the world of Native America found in Arizona and New Mexico.

Figure 52. Mary Cabot Wheelwright.

Mary and a traveling companion, Katie Scott, had come to New Mexico just after Mary's mother died in 1918, and stayed on the Pajarito with Carol at the Rancho Ramon Vigil. Returning after her travels overseas, she immersed herself in the emancipated society of women and men gathering in and around Santa Fe. Mary especially appreciated the bohemian culture of Santa Fe where material wealth was not the measure of a person's worth. "It was exciting to come to a region where individuals counted so much, coming as I had from a community where family customs and possessions made a great deal of difference."

At San Gabriel Ranch, Mary unpacked her trunks and set up her headquarters from which to explore the Southwest. San Gabriel and its owners gave Mary "a wonderful introduction to the country," with Roy giving the guests "an atmosphere of casual adventure" and his "Choate from Massachusetts" wife, the "musical, imaginative and adventuresome" Carol "bringing the appreciation of a cultivated woman to the imaginative quality of the Indian and Spanish life" of the region.[3]

The village of Alcalde was, in Mary's opinion, a "very primitive place" where the Spanish-speaking residents still adhered to the traditions, customs, and superstitions of their forefathers, and where daily conversations frequently included stories of *brujas* (witches) and supernatural goings-on. The villagers were devout Catholics, and the Penitente morada on the village plaza, literally over the wall from San Gabriel Ranch's main office, was close enough that guests could hear and observe the clandestine activities of the hermanos. The Pfäffles had a good relationship with their Spanish neighbors, and in exchange for the Pfäffles' silence about the activities of the Alcalde hermanos, the villagers allowed Carol, Roy, and their wide-eyed San Gabriel guests, including Mary, to huddle in the shadows and observe the procession at Lent of the primitive Penitente death cart.

Mary was fascinated by the traditions and Old World culture of Spanish New Mexico, but it was the world of the American Indians that especially captured her imagination. The mysticism and ceremonies of the Navajo were of particular personal interest to Mary and her quest to understand her place in the world. In Indian rituals, Mary, like one of her favorite writers, D. H. Lawrence, hoped to find "freedom from two of the curses of civilization: loneliness and boredom."

In the symbols and myths of the American Indians, Mary saw commonalities with other world religions she had studied in her travels, especially those found in the East Indies. "I remember quite well when this idea came to me—of religion as a great tide which moved men all around the world. It gave me a feeling of peace and took away much of the feeling of loneliness from my life."[4]

During her stay at San Gabriel in 1920, Mary heard the details of Carol's arrival in the Southwest five years before and of her several months' stay with the Wetherills at Kayenta, "at that time one of the wildest and most lawless parts of the West." Carol's stories of her expeditions through Indian Country stirred Mary's desire to experience for herself "the untouched wilderness, where [Carol] had met untamed Indians" and witnessed private Ute, Hopi, and Navajo ceremonies.

"I began to hear from Mrs. Pfaffle and others about the Navajo religion, the ceremonies they had," Mary wrote, ". . . finally Mrs. Pfaffle and Miss [Evelyn] Sears and I went on a trip to try and get in touch with some of this life."[5]

With San Gabriel's premier auto wrangler and guide, Orville Cox, Mary went to Gallup for the annual Navajo Ceremonial. During this event, where hundreds of Navajos came to dance and trade, and hundreds of tourists came to buy Navajo rugs and jewelry, Mary purchased a remarkable, one-of-a-kind ceremonial tapestry woven by the legendary Navajo medicine man Hostiin (Hosteen) Klah. Klah was perhaps the most influential cacique on the Navajo Reservation, the first Navajo man to become a master weaver, and the very first Navajo, male or female, to weave sacred Yeibichai sandpainting designs into a tapestry.

Following the devastation brought to the Navajos by the flu epidemic of 1919–20, the fifty-three-year-old Klah worried about the preservation of Diné ceremonials and chants. Among the Navajo, nothing was ever recorded or written down, and the details of all songs, chants, and ceremonies were orally passed from medicine man to apprentice. Although he had a young apprentice, Beaal Beyal, Klah realized that recording his sacred sandpaintings—traditionally destroyed after use—in woven tapestries would tangibly preserve valuable knowledge of the Navajo Way for future generations.

Even though Klah's intention was to save the spiritual traditions of his people, his first Yeibichai weaving, the Whirling Log painting, caused so much distress among the Navajos (who feared the rendition of a sacred sandpainting in permanent form would bring disaster to the tribe) that Klah's gigantic twelve-by-twelve-foot outdoor loom had to be guarded at night.[6]

The Hail Chant tapestry that Mary bought in late summer of 1920 and its medicine man creator were Mary's gateway into the world of Navajo symbolism and mysticism. Mary returned from Gallup to San Gabriel and asked Carol to arrange an excursion into the outback so that she could witness authentic Navajo ceremonials and, perhaps, locate and talk with Hostiin Klah.

Figure 53. Hostiin Klah.

Carol had met Klah during her travels through Navajoland with Louisa Wetherill, and she knew the best way to locate the famous cacique and the ceremonies taking place on the reservation was to contact Arthur and Franc Newcomb, traders at Nava south of Shiprock. After making arrangements to stay in one of the Newcombs' guest cottages, and with confirmation of at least one Navajo ceremony being held near Canyon de Chelly, Carol and her driver, Orville Cox, went into Indian Country with Mary and her friend, Evelyn Sears.

Like Carol, Mary was raised near the sea in a family of sailors, and the immense, unpeopled expanses of the desert were strangely similar to those found on the open ocean. Mary was an experienced sailor, and Indian Country's nearly featureless landscape edged by the wavering line of an unreachable horizon was an environment in which she was comfortable. "My particular release and joy in the East was sailing and cruising on the sea in the summer, and when I came to the desert I found it gave me a similar feeling of vastness and escape, and I came to love that, too."[7]

The auto route from Alcalde to Chinle and Canyon de Chelly eventually became nothing more than rutted tracks. Carol had made arrangements for them to stay overnight at Cozy McSparron's trading post, but when they arrived at Canyon de Chelly they learned there was a *Tlegi* or Night Chant ceremony taking place that very night at another location in the desert. Although they had traveled all day and it was already dark, Orville gassed up the Lincoln and with the three women headed out into the night to find the Navajo camp.[8]

Carol and Orville managed to find the ceremony as much by the chanting and singing, which Mary thought sounded very much like coyotes, as by the fires and smoke of the Indian camp. Mary, Carol, Evelyn Sears, and Orville stood and watched the dancers through "a pall of smoke so thick it was like a tent." With their eyes smarting from acrid smoke and tears running down their cheeks, they climbed back into the Lincoln and drove over the Chuska Mountains. It began to snow, and by dawn when they reached the trading post at Crystal, New Mexico, they were negotiating a blizzard. The guest quarters at the post were filled with storm-stranded travelers, and the three women slept on the floor of the unheated lumber room.

From Crystal they drove twenty miles northeast on a road that was "nothing but a track going up and down and across all the arroyos" to Nava and the Newcombs' trading post. The weather had turned bitter cold and it continued to snow. While the car bumped and slipped across the rough terrain at the foot of the Chuska Mountains, Mary "saw a thing I have never understood to this day, a solitary man on horseback, pursued by an eagle." Like the Hopis, the Navajos captured eagles and used their feathers in sacred ceremonies. The man Mary observed had likely just raided the eagle's nest.

At Nava, the Newcombs told the San Gabriel travelers that Hostiin Klah was performing a Night Chant ceremony at a trading post seventy miles to the east. After a fitful night of sleep in rooms that had formerly housed chickens, the women climbed into Orville's trusty auto and headed back into the desert. Their destination was Kimpeto (Kimbeto), and their mostly roadless route took them east again and skirted the northern end of Chaco Canyon.[9]

The four rooms of the Kimpeto trading post were packed with people sleeping wherever they could find a space. Mary slept under a bed already occupied by a nurse. At dawn, everyone trekked through heavy snow to find the ceremony. It was everything Mary had hoped for: "We managed to reach the ceremony nearby where the dancers were to be seen through the whirling snow, while the fires blew out sideways. Out of this turmoil appeared Klah, calm and benign. He had been conducting the ceremony in the Hogan. He joined us for a while and I got a very strong impression of power from him."

The next morning, the weather cleared, and while Mary and her San Gabriel compatriots were making their breakfast over a cook stove shared with several dozen other campers, Klah walked into the trading post. He sought out Mary and asked her if she was the one who had bought his sandpainting blanket at Gallup. During their first conversation, Mary asked Klah the meaning of the dance she had just seen. When he asked her why she wanted to know, she told him that she was interested in religion. Klah studied Mary for a moment and then asked, "How deep is the sea?"

Klah's question startled Mary, since her primary fear and fascination since childhood had been the ocean. In the trading post, Klah began to tell Mary children's stories and Navajo morality tales that gave no significant insight into Navajo ceremonies and religious beliefs. Mary, known for her impatience and lack of social graces, stopped Klah mid-tale and told him she wanted to hear "the great stories."[10]

Thus began the relationship between the Yankee spinster Mary Cabot Wheelwright and the Navajo medicine man Hostiin Klah. Mary returned to San Gabriel Ranch but stayed only long enough to confirm the location of Klah's next ceremony, organize and pack up her gear, and, with Orville as her driver, head back into Indian Country. Mary would repeat this journey deep into the land of the Navajos by automobile and eventually on horseback dozens of times in the next few years.

Hostiin Klah's role in the social, religious, and daily life of the Diné was hardly summed up by his title of medicine man. As a Navajo shaman, Klah was priest, physician, historian, artist, and teacher, virtually a "centralized source of Indian culture, a human library of primitive lore." Recognized as one of the preeminent ceremonial practitioners of his time, Klah's esoteric knowledge of complex Navajo rituals was acquired through decades of study with an elder cacique. In his fifties when he met Mary, Klah had memorized and mastered four complete ceremonies (Nightway, Hailway, Chiricahua Windway,

Mountainway), each of which incorporated complex chants, sand-paintings, prayers, and rituals that took days to perform. Klah also carried in his head the tribe's oral histories, myths, and symbols used in many more ceremonies.[11]

There was no elder held in higher esteem by the Diné than Hostiin Klah. His mother, Slim Woman, had survived the Long Walk to Bosque Redondo, and her father was the great Navajo chief Narbona. In his lifetime Klah had witnessed the escalation of U.S. government intervention in the life and culture of the Navajos, and seen the incursions of meddling missionaries who sought to eradicate his people's "heathen" religious practices. Klah feared the Navajo Way was facing extinction.

By 1920 and his first meeting with the wealthy Bostonian Mary Wheelwright, Klah had been told by the Great Spirit to document and preserve Navajo stories, rituals, and religious objects. Klah continued to pass along his knowledge to his understudy, but he also employed his remarkable skills as a weaver to permanently document the sacred sandpaintings and designs carried in his head.[12]

Klah was a *nadle*, a transformed "man-woman" deserving of special status and prestige among the Navajos. There is disagreement among his biographers as to whether Klah was born a hermaphrodite or emasculated as a child by the Utes. Whatever his biological and sexual orientation, Klah's career as a venerated medicine man and a master weaver enabled the preservation of valuable and sacred Navajo religious customs.[13]

There was a remarkable and nearly instantaneous connection between Klah and Mary, and their friendship seemed preordained in both their lives. Klah recognized that Mary's quest to understand Navajo religion was sincere, personal, and without ulterior motives. He also understood that she had the resources and the sensitivity to gather and preserve his people's stories and ceremonies. And not unlike Natalie's self-appointed task to record the music of Native America begun twenty years before, Mary's collaboration with Klah to preserve the stories and rituals of the Diné became a consuming vocation that directed and engaged her intellect and passion for the rest of her life.

Mary followed Klah to the farthest camps and gatherings in Navajoland. Because note taking was forbidden in a ceremonial hogan,

Mary's recording of Klah's rites and chants were done from memory after the ceremony. Franc Newcomb often accompanied Mary and would memorize the actual sandpainting associated with a ritual while Mary would memorize the myth (translated by Klah's apprentice, Beyal) told in a ceremony.

Over the next decade, using a recording machine when she and Klah worked privately and relying on her memory when she attended a ceremony, Mary amassed a comprehensive collection of Navajo chants, myths, and ceremonies. Klah, Beyal, and Mary met at the homes of traders, at schools, even in the underground sample room of the Gallup Harvey House. Klah and Beyal also came to San Gabriel Ranch to work with Mary. In nonceremonial recording sessions, Klah and Mary worked two three-hour sessions a day, or until Klah became weary. Mary always wrote her notes in longhand because a typewriter interrupted Klah's flow, and she never asked questions during a session because Klah's stories were "told in a kind of rhythm which should not be broken any more than necessary."[14]

In the 1920s the only published materials about Navajo religion and ceremonies were by an army surgeon, Washington Matthews, who had lived at Fort Wingate in the 1890s. Matthews had gained the confidence of the Navajos under his care and had been invited to observe sacred dances and ceremonies. The surgeon kept diaries and records and published his experiences in articles and academic monographs about Navajo myths, legends, rituals, silverwork, sandpaintings, and weavings before his death in 1905. Matthews's published studies became Mary's "Bible on the subject" of Navajo religion.[15]

San Gabriel Ranch was comfortable and private and provided Mary with everything she needed for long stays in New Mexico, including the wranglers and guides necessary for travel into the outback. Mary liked the San Gabriel cowboys and was stimulated by their "relationship to my kind of woman" even as she "found that being from Boston was a distinct handicap, and I was determined that one of my missions was to convince cowboys that it was possible for a person to be a good sport and also drink tea."

In the Southwestern outback, women were expected to shed the prissy helplessness acceptable back east and pull their own weight, whether on top of a horse or alongside it, through dust storms, thunder, lightning, pouring rain, pounding hail, burning heat, or howling snowstorms at high noon or in the dead dark of night. Mary enjoyed being treated "as a person who would be brave in an emergency" and the cowboy notion that she, like all women on the trail, was able "to live up to a difficult situation."[16]

Just as she had overcome her fear of the sea and become a proficient sailor and navigator, Mary became a capable horsewoman and competent traveler of the high desert of Indian Country. As Carol, Alice, and Natalie before her, Mary had to learn to ride astride a western saddle. By her third season in Alcalde, she was ready for a grand expedition through the outback. With her friend Evelyn Sears, and with Jack Lambert—a father now, his daughter, Louise, a little more than a year old—as their guide, Mary departed Alcalde in late April 1923 for a pack trip that would cover 550 miles in twenty-nine days, and take her across the magnificent and brutal Rainbow Trail.

Lambert had a natural, friendly way with city slickers like Mary, but he never pampered a dude or a dudette, no matter their age or experience. Even for someone used to a western saddle, the route called for long days on the trail with stops few and far between. With Lambert's encouragement, dudes came to be secure on a horse and proficient around camp. Lambert taught his charges how to make biscuits in the Dutch oven, create a bed on the ground, and pass an evening staring contentedly into the fire or up at the stars.[17]

Figure 54. Mary Cabot Wheelwright and Jack Lambert, ca. 1925.

Kayenta was still the gateway to the last real frontier in the continental United States. In 1923 the half dozen stone, wood, and mud buildings of John and Louisa Wetherill's trading post and home remained a virtually inaccessible outpost on the vast red and orange desert. There were still no roads north and west from Kayenta, and the trail from the Wetherills' to Nonnezoshe was no easier when Mary attempted it in 1923 than it had been for the expeditions of Roosevelt and Zane Grey a decade before.

A journey to Rainbow Bridge was a lesson in improvisation and endurance. Whatever was useless or frivolous was left at the Wetherills'. If Mary had read the harrowing accounts of previous travelers across the raw, scalded desert near Navajo Mountain and the harsh landscape of the Rainbow Trail, she did not let it sway her resolve to see the legendary stone bridge.

"No one who has not seen it can imagine the difficulties of the trail," Mary wrote, "where it was necessary for the horses to climb up the slick rocks, or petrified sand dunes and where we went afoot and the horses follow Ben Wetherill's horse as best they could. At times I felt I could not possibly get through. At one point the trail was so steep that I could only get up by holding onto the tail of my horse."[18]

The better-bred horses, Mary observed, like the better-blooded humans, were the ones that balked and lost their nerve in the most difficult stretches of the trail. Mary, however, defied her breeding and with her guides Jack Lambert, Everett Cheetham, and Ben Wetherill, and with every one of their horses and pack mules, crossed the Rainbow Trail and reached Nonnezoshe. She slept on the sand under the great stone arch in full moonlight, and like pilgrims before her, woke in the night and gazed into the canyon. "The other sleepers lay calm and white in the starlight," Zane Grey wrote from his desert bedroll, "There was something nameless in that canyon, and whether or not it was what the Indian embodied in the great Nonnezoshe . . . the truth was that there was a spirit."[19]

On the morning of May 8, 1923, Mary, Evelyn Sears, Jack Lambert, and their companions signed their names in the registry kept in a metal box under the bridge. Mary was pilgrim number 168.[20]

Mary did manage to convince the San Gabriel horse wranglers and auto guides that a person who drank tea could also be a good sport. Jack Lambert was perhaps Mary's first convert, and he, like all the

San Gabriel staff, learned that although Mary may have looked the pampered maiden, she was in fact from a line of women who had traveled to the rough edges of the world and "none of them minded much being uncomfortable."[21]

Dorothy Kent went with Roy, Lambert, and Carol to Rainbow Bridge in the mid-1920s and insisted on taking along her violin. It was an awkward and certainly nonessential item, but Lambert secured Kent's instrument case to a horse, and the violin went with their expedition over the ridiculously difficult Rainbow Trail. If Carol and Kent recorded their names in the bridge log, the pages from their visit were lost. But Kent's was likely the first violin to reach the sacred arch, and she was surely the first graduate of the Juilliard School of Music to play classical music in the light of the full moon at Rainbow Bridge.[22]

In the autumn of 1923, while out riding with Carol through the golden-leafed cottonwoods of the Rio Grande bosque, Mary saw the abandoned, two-story adobe mansion with sagging wraparound porches called Los Luceros. Carol and Roy had purchased the dilapidated house and the surrounding 138 acres of fields, orchards, and outbuildings on the east banks of the Rio Grande in January of that year. The Pfäffles were using the property to grow alfalfa and to pasture San Gabriel's horses, but they had no plans to rehabilitate the old hacienda.

Mary wanted to see the interior and toured the house with Carol. Cattle had broken into the first floor and had wreaked havoc on doorways and floors, and portions of the forty-two-inch-thick adobe walls had been damaged by Rio Grande floodwaters. The once-manicured vegetable and flower gardens and the massive apple orchard were unrecognizable and overgrown. The property was in ruins, but Mary fell in love with Los Luceros on sight.

Soon after that autumn ride, Carol and Roy sold Mary the circa 1840 two-story adobe dwelling and six acres of land along the banks of the Great River. Before Mary left New Mexico for the East, she placed Carol in charge of the renovation of the once-elegant Luceros mansion. A local builder, Ted Peabody of Española, who had worked with the Pfäffles in the renovation of San Gabriel, became Carol's foreman and head carpenter for Los Luceros.

Los Luceros was a classic Territorial-style adobe (although two-story dwellings of any kind were rare in northern New Mexico), but

Figure 55. Los Luceros, 1923.

most of the renovations done in 1923–24 reflected the popular Santa
Fe style and used Spanish-Pueblo Revival design elements. Mary told
Carol she wanted New England touches like bay windows, built-in
cabinets, bookshelves, and closets. Outside, Mary wanted flagstone
walkways (unheard of in rural New Mexico), a duck pond, and a lawn
of bluegrass and clover. The hacienda's exterior walls were white-
washed instead of stuccoed, and the window trim and doors were all
painted a dark Yankee green.

    After more than a year of renovation, Los Luceros was a ranch
worthy of a Boston Brahmin, and Mary called New Mexico home
for at least part of each year. She was not the only woman creating a
place of her own along the Rio Grande in the early 1920s. The Pfäffles
sold off more of their property to the millionaire writer Marie Tudor
Garland, who built the H & M Ranch with her husband, Henwar
Rodakiewicz (renamed the White Swan Ranch after they divorced)
alongside the Alcalde plaza. By the mid-1920s the dirt road that

went north from Española past San Juan Pueblo into the Rio Grande Gorge and up to Taos and Mabel's turf wound past the ranches of four New Women—Dorothy Kent, Marie Garland, Carol Pfäffle, and Mary Wheelwright.

In the fall of 1923 Elsie Clews Parsons joined the neighborhood of New Women along the Rio Grande when she moved into one of Carol's guest cottages for the first of many prolonged stays at San Gabriel. Parsons was a notable addition to the valley community, since she was among the world's most unconventional, prolific, and outspoken sociologists, anthropologists, and feminists. She was born in Grosvenor House at 10 Fifth Avenue in 1874, one year before her Greenwich Village neighbor Natalie Curtis. Her father, Henry Clews, founded the New York banking firm that bore his name, and her mother, Lucy Madison Worthington, was a descendent of President James Madison. As a teenager, Elsie Clews rebelliously opted out of the debutante social life expected of the daughters of the very wealthy and instead pursued an undergraduate degree at Barnard College, and eventually a masters and PhD in sociology at Columbia.

Even after marrying Herbert Parsons, a New York lawyer and Republican congressman who was a close friend and political ally of Theodore Roosevelt, and after giving birth to six children, four of whom lived, the restless, inquisitive, and brilliant Mrs. Parsons insisted on pursuing a life and career "characterized by a strenuous revolt against convention." In the first decade of the twentieth century, she focused her independent research on the problems of the modern family, and on how, in her opinion, those problems were the result of the subordinate status of women. Parsons's book *The Family*, published in 1906, scandalously recommended the concept of "trial marriage" and proposed the popular feminist manifesto that women would only become fit wives and mothers when they were given the same opportunities for personal and professional development as men. *The Family* raised aristocratic eyebrows and ruffled the feathers of conformists and conservatives, and following its publication Mrs. Parsons was dropped from the New York Social Register.[23]

Parsons's personal and professional life was shaped by her passionate feminism, her dazzling intellect, and her fearless temperament. "Women try hard to live down to what is expected of them," she declared in 1913. In New York City, Parsons, like her neighbor Mabel

Figure 56. Elsie Clews Parsons at San Gabriel Ranch.

Dodge, was a member of the Greenwich Village feminist discussion group Heterodoxy, begun in 1912. She was also an erudite and vociferous participant in the lively discussions about sex, marriage, and the emancipation of women held weekly at Mabel Dodge's apartment near Washington Square.[24]

Before she came to the Southwest and began her studies of the cultures and people of Native America, Parsons published more than seventy-five academic papers and magazine articles and four books that boldly challenged traditional American ideals regarding women's reproductive rights, the rights of children and adults in marriage, the burdens placed on women who married, and the domination of women by men. Discouraged by the slow progress of American cultural reform movements, especially the feminist movement, in 1916 Parsons turned her full attention to the Indian cultures of the American Southwest.

It was a turning point in her life and in her career. In the fall of 1913 Parsons visited the New Mexico pueblos of Acoma and Laguna, but it was her journey to Zuni Pueblo in 1915 that initiated her extended ethnological study of the pueblo people. After the death of an infant, and the discovery that her husband, Herbert, was having an extramarital affair, Parsons sought solace in New Mexico. The solitude of the land and the satisfaction she found in fieldwork gave the forty-one-year-old Parsons a personal and professional remedy for a midlife crisis.

Between 1915 and 1917 Parsons escaped the social and physical confines of upper-class New York City in the wide-open spaces of New Mexico and Arizona and conducted her research while living in a tent near a pueblo, or in a cave if she was working on the Pajarito Plateau. "This cave room faced south," Parsons wrote of her cliff-hugging quarters at Puye, the same pueblo ruin where Alice camped with Hewett in 1916, "and that night I looked out from its frame on the moonlit talus below and the pines beyond and thought that whether Indian or White one was fortunate indeed to live for a time in a world of such beauty."[25]

Elsie Clews Parsons's father died in 1923, and with a hefty inheritance, the already liberated Parsons became an independently wealthy woman who could travel and live precisely as she liked. When she moved into the adobe casita at San Gabriel Ranch in November 1923, she had lived at Laguna (where she worked alongside Natalie's friend Franz Boas), Acoma, Zuni, and Jemez Pueblos. She had stayed with Mabel Dodge in Taos, and had also lived at Hopi First Mesa and was an honorary member of one of the native families.

Often the sole woman on anthropological research trips into the outback, Parsons was breaking down the taboo that had long prevented academic camaraderie between men and women and pushing back the social barrier that kept women barred from all fieldwork. She herself underwrote the research trips of her male and female colleagues, and in 1918 was instrumental in the formation of the Southwest Society, an organization that raised money and funded anthropological fieldwork.[26]

When she moved into San Gabriel, Parsons was forty-nine and a new grandmother. And although she was still the wife of Herbert Parsons, Elsie Clews came to San Gabriel Ranch with her lover of five years, the novelist Robert Herrick.[27]

From her home base in Alcalde, Parsons intended to study the culture and collect the folk stories of the Tewa people living along the Rio Grande at San Juan, Santa Clara, and San Ildefonso Pueblos. Parsons may have met Carol and Roy Pfäffle during previous visits to New Mexico, since their ranch was a popular lunch stop for automobile travelers on the road between Santa Fe and Taos. At San Gabriel Ranch, Parsons had access to the neighboring Tewa pueblos, but she also had access to the Pfäffles, who by the 1920s had developed an extensive network of friends and confidants in the Tewa pueblos and Hispanic villages of the Rio Grande and Chama River valleys. Although the Tewa pueblos allowed formal visits by tourist groups and permitted limited access to their ceremonial dances, they were guarded and tight-lipped about their myths, social structure, and kinship patterns. Parsons needed Carol and Roy to personally open doors to their friends in northern New Mexico. "Imitating the secretiveness observed in all the Rio Grande pueblos, I settled in Alcalde, the Mexican town two or three miles north of San Juan," Parsons wrote in the opening pages of her book about the Tewa, "and here, thanks to my helpful and understanding hosts of San Gabriel ranch, I secured informants from San Juan, Santa Clara, and San Ildefonso."[28]

November weather in New Mexico is pleasant and moderate, and Carol was pleased to have their ranch filled with guests almost until Christmas of 1923. Parsons and Herrick stayed from mid-November until mid-December. In letters to her husband, Parsons wrote of San Gabriel's proximity to "the seven mountains & blue sky, mostly." Although the food was delicious and her room was warm and quiet, Parsons pined for the utter solitude she had known in cliff-hugging caves and mesa-top campsites and complained about having to share the ranch with other guests. Nonetheless, San Gabriel suited her. "A dude ranch indeed, and I stick to it. My informants are brought out from the pueblo." Parsons would return to the adobe casita at San Gabriel until 1926 when she bought her own ranch several miles downriver near the pueblo of Santa Clara.[29]

The residents of Santa Fe and the villagers of northern New Mexico were becoming accustomed to unconventional and unescorted white women moving through and often into their communities. But even among the expats, the tall, thin Parsons, with her chiseled face and intense, confident gaze, was remarkable. Like Natalie and Alice, once she set foot on New Mexico's soil, Parsons happily shed all semblance of her fashionable high society upbringing and donned the standard outback uniform of leather boots, wide-brimmed hat, and khaki. At a time when women were forbidden to smoke in public, Parsons defiantly wore her cigarette holder and lighter on a chain around her neck, and declared that her greatest enjoyment was to have "*at the same time* a cigarette, a cup of coffee, and an open fire. . . . It is very hard to get all three together. It is easier among Indians than among ourselves."[30]

Parsons's reentry to life in New York City was reminiscent of Natalie's, and was disconcerting for her and for her family. Parsons's mother found her just-back-from-the-desert-daughter's appearance to be "perfectly dreadful," even "scandalous," in that she "wore khaki clothes" and "an old felt hat and she was touching up her hair and of course it hadn't been touched up while she'd been away, so she wore a bandanna tied around it, and then these saddle bags full of manuscripts."[31]

In New Mexico, Parsons and her dusty skirts, saddlebags stuffed with stenographer notebooks, and unkempt hair blended into the emerging community of like-minded women who embodied in greater and lesser proportions the evolving characteristics of twentieth-century feminism. In Santa Fe and in the Spanish villages along the Rio Grande, Parsons joined Carol Stanley, Mary Wheelwright, Dorothy Kent, Marie Garland, Mabel Dodge Luhan, Alice Corbin, Elsie Shepley Sergeant, Margretta Dietrich and her sister Dorothy Stewart, and the sisters Amelia and Martha White in the first wave of what would become a historic groundswell of single and married women who re-created their lives in northern New Mexico.

In December 1925, following the accidental death of her husband (killed while demonstrating a motor-drive bicycle just given to his son Mac), Elsie Clews came to San Gabriel with her two youngest children, Mac, fourteen, and Herbert Jr., sixteen. Elsie was still involved with Herrick, with whom she would journey to Egypt and the Sudan in April, but he did not accompany Elsie Clews and her grieving children to New Mexico in 1925.

The Christmas vacation gave Elsie a rare long, uninterrupted holiday with her two sons. Although she did some fieldwork at the nearby pueblos, her primary focus was the simple joys found in New Mexico during the holiday season and reconnecting with her own sense of purpose. "I ride horseback daily, and it has done me good," she wrote her daughter Lissa, who was married with a newborn baby. "Most of all though the interest in my old job has been restorative. . . . The beauty of the country I have never succeeded in getting across to you or anyone who has not seen it for himself."[32]

Gaga Pfäffle's diary records the comings and goings of "Dr. Parsons and her boys" throughout the month they lived in the casita at San Gabriel. Mary Wheelwright was at Los Luceros for Christmas that year and came almost daily to San Gabriel to dine or play cards (seven-up was a favorite), ride horses, or go for walks with the Pfäffles' guests and extended family. "Mother Lambert" was at the ranch visiting her son Jack, his wife, Lois, and their three-year-old daughter, Louise. Roy and Lois's sister, Marie Wolfe, and her husband also came for Christmas that year. Marie Garland, George King, Alice and Bill Henderson, Mabel Dodge and Tony "her colored friend" (as Gaga referenced Mabel's husband, Tony Luhan) came with Spud Johnson (now living with Witter Bynner in Natalie's former home in Santa Fe) for lunch and leisurely conversation around the San Gabriel dining room table just before New Year's.

Figure 57. Margaret "Gaga" Pfäffle at her San Gabriel Ranch casita, ca. 1924.

Roy and Orville Cox drove the Parsons family to Frijoles Canyon for day hikes, up the road above the Rio Grande to Taos, and northwest along the Chama River to Abiquiú. On Christmas Eve, Mary Wheelwright went with the Parsons family, Gaga, Roy, Mother Lambert, and the extended Lambert-Pfäffle family to watch the all-night dances at the nearby pueblos.[33]

Only Carol was missing from the holiday festivities. From early December until mid-January, she was at the Mayo Clinic in Minnesota. She spent her forty-sixth, and Roy's fortieth, birthday in a bed in the Rochester clinic, and underwent surgery on December 22 for a condition that Gaga did not specify or elaborate upon in her diary.

18

"ROUGHNECK AND LOW-BROW"

Irony drives every good story about women's lives in the West.
The best stories run like the braided streams of the region's great
river system, liberally strewn with ironies and ambiguities.

—*Virginia Scharff*

SAN GABRIEL WAS RIDING THE economic high brought to the
Southwest in the mid-1920s by the surge in American train and automobile travel. Dude ranches in northern New Mexico were suddenly
the rage among savvy easterners, and dudes reserved rooms at San
Gabriel and other guest ranches in the West months before the season began in late March.

After six years of hard work, the Pfäffles' guest ranch and outfitting business was operating at capacity and making real money. San
Gabriel Ranch was the featured centerpiece of the Santa Fe Railway's
promotion "America's Most Famous Fifty Mile Square." The ranch
was expensive and exclusive, and before a potential guest was granted
a reservation Carol's assistant, Minnesotan Margaret Phillips (who
would marry a San Gabriel wrangler, Sandy MacLean), looked up
their credit report in Dun & Bradstreet. If someone was not favor-
ably listed, they were not given a reservation at San Gabriel.[1]

Carol's guest roster included members of America's most influential families. Jack Lambert guided the family of the Santa Fe Railway executive J. Sanford Otis into the Four Corners, and Nicholas

Roosevelt, now a seasoned writer with the *New York Times*, stayed at San Gabriel and went on at least one extended expedition into the outback with Carol's wranglers and equipment. Winfred Douglas stayed at San Gabriel every summer, and if one of his visits happened to coincide with Nick Roosevelt's, perhaps age and maturity had mellowed Roosevelt's adolescent dislike of the Episcopalian canon he had met at Walpi.

From early May until late October, Roy, Jack, and the San Gabriel cowboys, Sandy MacLean, brothers Jack and Lester McKinley, and Pete Coleman, packed up and guided groups of between two and twelve individuals, male and female, adults and children, to Chaco Canyon, Canyon de Chelly, Mesa Verde, Hopiland, the Grand Canyon, Monument Valley, Bryce and Zion Canyons, and the Natural Bridges of Utah. Orville Cox offered guests excursions through Indian Country in one of the ranch's touring cars. And at least once each season, Roy or Jack led a few intrepid guests to Kayenta and, with John Wetherill or Albert Smith, crossed the legendary trail to Rainbow Bridge.

In late June 1925, Willa Cather and her companion, Edith Lewis, left the comforts of the Hotel La Fonda and the pleasant camaraderie of artists and writers found in old Santa Fe for the rural village experience of San Gabriel Ranch. Cather wrote Elsie Sergeant, who was not in New Mexico that summer, how Alcalde was "awfully hot." In spite of the June heat, Cather found the Pfäffles' ranch on the banks of the Great River to be exactly what she needed. Since her first journey to the Southwest more than a decade before, Cather had loved hiking and riding in the desert and mountain outback, and sleeping in rustic, close-to-the-earth quarters. "I have a regular Zane Grey mind," Cather wrote, "roughneck and low-brow is [the] name for me."[2]

Cather was reading the proofs of her new novel, *The Professor's House*, and within the San Gabriel Ranch community, she was in the company of individuals—Carol and Roy, Mary Wheelwright, Dorothy Kent, Jack Lambert, Orville Cox—who had personal experience with the place (the canyon and cliff country of Mesa Verde) and the story (based in part on the Wetherills' discovery and excavation of the Mesa Verde) central to *The Professor's House*. In Carol and her Alcalde crowd were individuals whose lives had parallels to that of

Cather's character, Tom Outland: Carol, Dorothy Kent, and Mary Wheelwright, among many others, had rejected the disillusionment, rigid structure, and materialism of modern life for the psychological space, spiritual freedom, and unconventional society of New Mexico.

In late June, Tony and Mabel Dodge Luhan drove the forty miles from Taos to Alcalde to retrieve Cather and Lewis, who spent the next two weeks at Los Gallos with Mabel and her other illustrious houseguests, including D. H. and Frieda Lawrence. Cather returned to Santa Fe in late July, and during that stay in the old capital found and read the book, *The Life of the Right Reverend Joseph P. Machebeuf*, that launched her research and writing of *Death Comes for the Archbishop*. The Bishop's Ranch (Bishop's Lodge) in Tesuque where Carol, Roy, and family had lived in 1918 and 1919 was the home of the first archbishop of Santa Fe, Jean-Baptiste Lamy, who had attended seminary in France with Machebeuf and built Santa Fe's Cathedral Basilica of St. Francis of Assisi. Cather based her character Jean Marie Latour on Archbishop Lamy.

The prosperity the Pfäffles had worked and hoped for had become a reality. In 1925 San Gabriel Ranch expanded to include a mountain retreat, El Rito Canyon Ranch, a homestead located in the high mountains between the villages of El Rito and Canjilon, New Mexico. By 1926 the renamed Canjilon Camp was a well-appointed haven with a grand main lodge and headquarters, half a dozen private log cabins, corrals of saddle and pack horses, a resident kitchen and housekeeping staff, and wranglers. Guests seeking the cool air and silence found at eight thousand feet above sea level could stay comfortably on the mountain for weeks at a time.[3]

San Gabriel's success enabled the Pfäffles to maintain the four-room apartment in Santa Fe on Canyon Road, and Carol and Roy enjoyed overnights in town. Carol also continued to come in alone for Indian Arts Fund board meetings, and for solitary retreats from the guests, staff, and family of San Gabriel Ranch. On July 19, Carol and Roy were among the guests at the gala bathing party that celebrated the opening of the White sisters'—and Santa Fe's first—swimming pool. Martha and Amelia Elizabeth White's home, El Delirio (The Madness), at 660 Garcia Street had been transformed from a humble adobe casita surrounded by sage and cactus hills in 1923 into a sprawling estate designed by Alice Corbin's husband, William P.

Figure 58. Jack, Lois, and Louise Lambert at Canjilon Camp, 1923.

Henderson. Amelia White was a founding member of the Indian Arts Fund, for which Carol served a six-year term as a trustee and executive committee member. Amelia, like her Bryn Mawr classmates Elsie Sergeant and Margretta Dietrich, had been an active participant in the defeat of the Bursum Bill in 1922, and also joined Mary Austin and the Santa Fe art colony's vehement opposition to and defeat of the Southwest Federation of Women's Clubs' attempt (supported by Hewett) to build a Chautauqua retreat in Santa Fe.[4]

The swimming party in July 1926 included nearly every member in good standing (Hewett was not invited) of Santa Fe's famous, forceful, and illustrious art, literary, and anthropology colony. As with most of the White sisters' parties at El Delirio, there was a theme to the bathing party, and Carol and Roy, like all the guests, were expected to show up in costume. The theme for the July bash around the new swimming pool was a Mayan ceremony, and guests dressed in beaded and fringed skirts, moccasins, stick and feather headdresses, sandals, silver belts, bathing suits, and very little else.

The poet Witter Bynner wrote the script for the evening's main event, the "Ceremonial Sacrifice at the Sacred Pool," and Alice Corbin directed the final act, the sacrificial pool dunking of the virgins, the title roles played by the two White sisters.

It was a time of gaiety, exuberance, and innocence, and Santa Feans enjoyed "the ferment of the times without the lost feeling of the Paris group of American expatriates."[5]

The Roaring Twenties brought years of prosperity and happiness to the Pfäffles and their friends in northern New Mexico. But there was a shadow side to Carol's life that the San Gabriel staff and her closest friends were acutely aware of: Roy's gambling and drinking. By the late 1920s, the tension and discord created by Roy's addictions began to affect the people around him, and Carol's life and the community of San Gabriel Ranch began to unravel.

The New Year of 1927 began ominously with an automobile accident. Roy was driving Carol down the steep, snow-packed mountain road from Canjilon Camp when the Lincoln overturned, injuring Carol's leg and sending her to the hospital. In the first week of July, Mother Gaga, out on a picnic with Carol's secretary and a guest, nearly drowned in the swollen waters of the Rio Grande when the road gave way and their Chevrolet plunged sixty feet into the river. Gaga and her friends were "saved almost by a miracle" when two men from San Ildefonso Pueblo heard their cries and, after a herculean effort, pulled each of the three from the rising waters with ropes and a team of horses. The car was sucked into quicksand and never seen again. A traumatized and hypothermic Gaga was taken to the hospital in Santa Fe where she was treated for a broken nose and numerous bruises.[6]

Carol was not sleeping well and suffered migraine headaches throughout the summer. By late fall Roy's gambling debts had dug so deeply into San Gabriel's funds that the Pfäffles were forced to enter into mortgage agreements with family and friends. Mary Wheelwright alone loaned San Gabriel twenty thousand dollars.[7]

Even with a wife and small child at the ranch, Jack Lambert preferred to spend the dude season on horse expeditions of four to six weeks in Indian Country. But by 1927 he could no longer ignore his brother-in-law's alcoholism. After a particularly challenging horse and auto journey to the Grand Canyon with a doctor whose wife became violently ill after eating poisonous mushrooms, Lambert returned to Alcalde, found Roy "was drinking," and decided it was time to severe his ties with San Gabriel Ranch.[8]

By season's end, Jack asked the Pfäffles for a letter of recommendation. Three days before Carol and Roy's birthday in December, Roy reluctantly penned a statement To Whom It May Concern recommending Jack as a pack and motor trip manager, adding that he regretted Mr. Lambert was leaving his employ.[9]

The end of their ten-year partnership was a bitter and painful ordeal for both Roy Pfäffle and Jack Lambert. For Lambert, who considered the ranch and the community on the Rio Grande his home, moving his wife and daughter out of the adobe Jack himself had built at San Gabriel was among the lowest moments of his life. "How I loved that place!" Lambert said years later. "Losing it almost broke my heart."[10]

With wife, Lois, and daughter, Louise, Jack moved into Santa Fe, where the Lamberts managed a little restaurant opened by the White sisters in Sena Plaza. But the Lambert marriage was in trouble, and by 1929 Jack and Lois were divorced. Jack went looking for ranch work in Arizona. Lois and seven-year-old Louise went east and lived in Tarrytown near or with Dorothy Kent and Canon Douglas and his wife, Dr. Jo, while Louise attended the junior St. Mary's School in Peekskill.

Jack Lambert returned to New Mexico and worked as the manager of the White sisters' El Delirio. Although he was married five times, Lambert had only one child, Louise. His fifth and final wife was Margery Ferguson, a Hewett-trained archaeologist and the curator at the Museum of New Mexico for over thirty years. Lambert and Ferguson married in 1950, and they lived the next forty-one years on Garcia Street in Santa Fe until Lambert's death in 1991.[11]

The winds of unrest swirled like dust devils through the once-peaceful gardens and grounds of San Gabriel Ranch. During an autumn visit in the late 1920s, Hostiin Klah pulled ranch wrangler Sandy MacLean aside and said, "Tell my friend [Carol] that her man is hurt." Around San Gabriel and Alcalde, Klah's psychic abilities were widely respected, and Gaga, Carol, and the ranch staff waited nervously for Roy to return from Santa Fe. Within a few hours of Klah's ominous statement, Roy had not returned, and Carol learned that his horse had lost its footing in the rodeo parade and fallen, injuring Roy.[12]

Carol kept meticulous account books for San Gabriel and knew there was absolutely no disposable income. But Roy continued to gamble, and his nights at the poker tables of northern New Mexico fueled Carol's migraines and escalating sense of doom. However, in 1928 Roy participated in a card game that would change Carol's life and offer her, paradoxically, one last chance to make a permanent home in the Southwest.

The actual where and when of the poker game is the stuff of myth and legend. Somewhere in Rio Arriba County, perhaps in a village bar, a ranch barn, or at a kitchen table, or maybe out under the stars by a campfire at some cow camp, Roy Pfäffle and at least one member of the Alfredo Salazar family played a high stakes game of cards. What Roy Pfäffle wagered in that game can only be speculated upon: as of late December 1927, San Gabriel Ranch was incorporated with shareholders and was heavily mortgaged. The Pfäffles still owned Canjilon Camp and approximately six hundred acres in the mountains above El Rito, but it is unlikely Roy could have staked the land without Carol's consent and cosignature. Roy may have held title to one or more of the San Gabriel Lincolns, and to its horses, saddles, and expedition equipment. But in the winter of 1928, Roy Pfäffle had little to nothing to lose in a poker game.

The Salazars were sheep ranchers who had lived for generations on the high desert of the Piedra Lumbre (Shining Stone) basin below Cerro Pedernal ten miles north of Abiquiú. The family had extensive landholdings in Rio Arriba County that included an abandoned and reputedly haunted homestead at the mouth of Yeso (Gypsum) Canyon under the spectacular cliffs on the northern edge of the Piedra Lumbre basin. Called El Rancho de los Brujos (Ranch of the Witches) by the locals, the Rito del Yeso homestead consisted of one dilapidated *jacal* (cedar post and mud) dwelling, a few corrals and sheds, and the homestead's most valuable asset, a perennial source of water.

Roy had visited the haunted homestead under the great cliffs north of Abiquiú many times. He watered horses at the stream and used the corrals for San Gabriel expeditions en route to Navajoland to the northwest and Mesa Verde to the north. There was also access to the mountains and to Canjilon Camp via a narrow, rocky, horse and mule trail that climbed up and out of a box canyon where the waters of the Yeso stream literally oozed from sheer rock walls.

By 1928 no one had lived in the spirit-infested landscape of the Rito del Yeso homestead for nearly thirty years. The Salazar family may have been looking to rid themselves of the place and purposefully lost the deed to the gringo Roy Pfäffle in the fabled poker game. Ghosts and witches were not taken lightly in northern New Mexico, and local residents had kept clear of the Ranch of the Witches since the late 1800s when the homestead had been the hideout for a mean bunch of cattle rustlers led by the notorious Archuleta brothers. From the 1880s until the mid-1890s, cattle stolen by the Archuleta gang was held in Yeso Canyon. Any rancher unlucky enough to stumble upon the Archuleta's operation was never seen again. An undetermined number of bodies were believed buried in the red and gold sands under the cliffs, but the saddles, firearms, and horses of the murdered could be counted among the possessions of the Archuletas.

The Archuletas' reign of terror ended in the 1890s when one brother murdered the other during an argument concerning a gold payment. The remaining Archuleta was either hung by a sheriff's posse or run out of town by the local ranchers. By 1900 the ghosts of those murdered by the cattle rustlers created such an incessant racket in the canyons and sand hills of the northern edge of the Piedra Lumbre that not even seasoned shepherds and cowboys from the nearby communities of Abiquiú, Coyote, Cañones, or Youngsville would stay a night at the place. Only a gringo outsider would be foolish enough to want El Rancho de los Brujos.

Roy won the deed to HES 127, the 157-acre homestead at the Ranch of the Witches, in the early spring of 1928. In her account ledger, Carol recorded that the place she called Ghost Ranch, valued at six thousand dollars, was *acquired* that year. It took the Salazar family ten or twelve months to legally sign over the deed, but in February 1929 the place of Ghost Ranch was recorded in the Rio Arriba County records to be the property of one Caroline S. Pfäffle. Roy was not mentioned on the deed.

Even before the stock market crash in October 1929, San Gabriel Ranch was in a death spiral. Mary Wheelwright, Marie Garland, and Florence Dibell Bartlett had loaned the Pfäffles substantial amounts of money, hoping to keep the ranch, and the local economy it supported, afloat. The walls of the guest ranch flanked the Alcalde village church and plaza, and San Gabriel generated jobs and brought cash into the rural community. Because it was on the main road to Taos from Santa Fe and all points south, San Gabriel's dining room had become a popular meal stop for auto travelers. San Gabriel Ranch had essentially put Alcalde on the map.

But after Lambert departed as manager, and Roy's addictions became impossible to ignore, the ranch's neighborhood support faltered. Bartlett purchased the land that her house El Mirador was built on (she had leased the property throughout the 1920s), and Mary Wheelwright told her lawyer, Francis Wilson (also the Pfäffles' attorney), that there would be no more loans to bail out the Pfäffles.

The crash of 1929 brought the New Mexico tourism industry to an abrupt end. For Carol, the last months of 1929 marked the collapse of San Gabriel Ranch and her partnership with Roy. Divorce was surely on Carol's mind, but she waited another eighteen months before formalizing the end of her marriage.

Ironically, it was the haunted, decrepit homestead at Ghost Ranch that offered Carol her last best chance for redemption. The three-room mud and wood ruin was little more than a leaky flat roof and crooked walls, but it boasted a spectacular view of red and gold badlands, carved buttes, faraway mountains, and the distinctive flat-topped mountain called Pedernal. The Piedra Lumbre basin, 6,500 feet above sea level, was located on the easternmost lip of the Colorado Plateau and geologically and spatially resembled the high desert country Carol had first known at Kayenta. The Chama River cut from north to south across the basin, but excepting the narrow verdant canyon through which flowed the Rito del Yeso, this was a parched and uninhabitable landscape.

The Ghost Ranch homestead Roy won in the poker game bordered the historic Piedra Lumbre land grant, a fifty-thousand-acre parcel of community grazing land granted to a prominent military family, the Martín Serranos, by the king of Spain in 1766. By the 1920s the grant was no longer community grazing land, but had become the possession of A. B. Renehan, one of the lawyers of the notorious Santa Fe Ring that bought or "legally" seized land held by native New Mexicans. After Roy won the deed to the Rito del Yeso, the Pfäffles evidently asked Francis Wilson to make inquiries into the ownership of the Piedra Lumbre lands adjacent to the homestead, because in late 1928 Carol and Roy were negotiating with the owners to buy the northern third of the land grant.

For the last sixteen years, Carol had rented out her house on Nahant island. The home built by J. Bishop Johnson was all that was left of her inheritance and represented her only physical connection to her past life. If Carol had any sentimental feelings for the home of her grandparents, she set them aside when her life with Roy began to unravel. If the Nahant house were sold, Carol would have the money to underwrite a new beginning on the Piedra Lumbre.

During Christmas of 1928 Carol and Roy traveled east to initiate the sale of the Johnson home on Dorothy Cove to the man who had leased the house for the last decade. The building that was once the Johnson fish market had burned to the ground several years before, so the sale was for the plot of land near the beach and the three-story house that had been struck by lightning the same June night that Carol's mother had died in her bed.

It took a year for the sale to become final, a small miracle considering that the year included the collapse of the American banking system and the economic ruination of most businesses and individuals. In March 1930 Francis Wilson, Esq., of Santa Fe and Healey & Healey, attorneys at law, Lynn, Massachusetts, exchanged the final papers, and Carol relinquished all legal ties to the island of Nahant.[13]

The sum was undisclosed, but letters suggest Carol received thirty thousand dollars for the Johnson house. The sale enabled the Pfäffles—specifically Carol—to buy the northern third of the Piedra Lumbre land grant (16,582 acres) and also an adjacent section of land called the Arroyo Seco, from the widow of A. B. Renehan in June 1930. In August, Roy signed the jointly held deed for the Piedra Lumbre land over to Carol. Two months later, Carol initiated divorce proceedings, and all business correspondence was placed on the letterhead of Caroline B. Stanley, president of San Gabriel Ranch, Canjilon Camp, and a place called Ghost Ranch.[14]

Carol's decision to divorce Roy, with whom she remained friends, and go it alone at fifty years of age may have found reinforcement within the circle of independent, educated, "roughneck and lowbrow" women who came and went at San Gabriel Ranch throughout the 1920s: Elsie Clews Parsons, Mary Wheelwright, Willa Cather and Edith Lewis, Dorothy Kent, Mabel Dodge. All of these women lived lives that subtly or overtly sanctioned the code of the New Woman. Marriage was a choice, not a dictum, and in New Mexico even middle-aged divorced women were given a place in society.

The shareholders, who included Mary Wheelwright and several members of Roy Pfäffle's immediate family, foreclosed on San Gabriel Ranch in July 1931. Mary took possession of 132 acres of Los Luceros land still held by the Pfäffles. Bartlett claimed 75 acres of the San Gabriel land that surrounded her two-story home, El Mirador. Orville Cox and San Gabriel's fleet of touring cars—a 1928 and a 1930 Lincoln seven passenger, and one 1929 five passenger (the enormous twelve-passenger Lincoln remained Carol's property)—joined Hunter Clarkson's "Couriercars" associated with the Fred Harvey Company's tour business. Gaga gave up the only home she had ever owned (Roy and Carol had given her one of San Gabriel's casitas) and moved in with her daughter Marie and her husband and family in Santa Fe.[15]

In mid-June 1931, before Carol walked away from her home on the Rio Grande, she drove her former husband to a sanatorium in Pueblo, Colorado. Roy was left in the care of professionals (likely recommended by the Pfäffles' good friend Canon Douglas) in a residency program where, with time and treatment, it was hoped that Roy's alcohol- and tobacco-ravaged body would find the trail back to healthy and productive living. Carol returned alone to New Mexico to begin a new life on the high desert beyond Abiquiú.[16]

In a letter to Elsie Sergeant, Willa Cather remarked how trekking about the Southwest outback had taught her the meaning of Balzac's statement "In the desert there is everything and nothing—God without mankind." If Carol had not come to an understanding of Balzac's words before the summer of 1931, she surely appreciated their meaning when she moved all that she owned into the everything and nothing that was the faraway place called Ghost Ranch.[17]

19

EVERYTHING AND NOTHING

> I want to go right back into that canyon and be mauled about
> by its big brutality, though all my bruises are not gone yet. It's
> a country that drives you crazy with delight, and that's all
> there is to it. I can't say anything more intelligible about it.
> —*Willa Cather*

FEW OF CAROL'S FRIENDS would have been surprised if, after losing San Gabriel Ranch and divorcing Roy, she had left New Mexico and returned to live out her life on the East Coast. But in the years since 1915 and her first expedition into Indian Country with Louisa Wetherill, Caroline Bishop Stanley had become an adopted daughter of the desert, for better and for worse. Carol knew, too, that New England would hardly welcome her back as one of its own. Not only was she a divorcee, her ex-husband was a cowboy and a gambler drying out in a hospital in Pueblo, Colorado. And following the bankruptcy of her ranch, Carol had chosen to sell off her ancestral home on Nahant to finance yet another venture in the middle of Nowhere, New Mexico. At fifty-two, she had secured the black sheep status in the Johnson-Stanley clan of Massachusetts.

By late summer of 1931, Carol moved all that she could lay claim to—clothing and personal items, the piano Roy had given her as an anniversary present in 1918, a few good horses, tack and saddles, some furniture, several Indian rugs, and dishes and cookware—twenty miles up the Chama River to the haunted homestead on the northern edge of the wide bright Piedra Lumbre basin. Alice Pring, Carol's English maid and friend, and several of her tried and true San Gabriel cowboys went with her to help her build a new ranch.

To reach the homestead, now called Ghost Ranch, at the base of the red and gold cliffs, Carol departed the main road along the Chama River and followed a rutted horse and wagon track due east into the badlands. A cow, ox, or horse skull (customarily removed and replaced with whatever animal's skull was readily available) was kept propped on the entrance gate over a primitive wooden sign that said "Ghost Ranch" with an arrow pointing into the sandlands beneath the stone cliffs.

The Painted Desert landscape of Ghost Ranch bore no resemblance to the lush riverside setting of San Gabriel Ranch. San Gabriel was situated in a village on one of the main roads through northern New Mexico. Ghost Ranch was an isolated outpost with a watering hole, fifteen miles away from the tiny village of Abiquiú and the nearest telephone and post office. Santa Fe could be reached by automobile in a half day in good weather, but all journeys south meant navigating the narrow, precipitous road through the five-hundred-foot deep Chama River canyon. Carol was comfortable driving dangerous roads that clung to narrow ledges, but most of her city slicker clients were not.

This region of northern New Mexico was still considered the frontier in the 1930s, even by New Mexicans. Spanish was the first language, and the traditional Old World Roman Catholic ranchers, farmers, and villagers of Rio Arriba County maintained a lifestyle independent of modern Anglo America. The community of Abiquiú was a unique blend of Indian and Spanish Americans. The historic village began as a pueblo built around a Franciscan mission given to *genízaros* (detribalized Native Americans) by the Spanish in the 1700s. Abiquiú, the Piedra Lumbre basin, and the lands of Ghost Ranch were the homelands of the prehistoric Tewa used in historic times by the Navajos, Utes, and Apaches. The Spanish called the Piedra Lumbre *la Tierra de Guerra*, the Land of War, and considered the region to the north and west too dangerous to settle; the basin remained an unpeopled frontier used only by a handful of intrepid ranchers until well after U.S. occupation in the mid-1800s.

Figure 59. The old homestead at Ghost Ranch that became Carol Stanley's home in 1931.

In 1931, when Carol moved into the *jacal* dwelling built by the infamous Archuleta brothers, she became the first Anglo woman ever to live at the Ranch of the Witches. She was also the first full-time resident, male or female, to move into the homestead in thirty years. Carol's only neighbor on the northern side of the hundred-square-mile basin was an elderly Navajo, Juan de Dios Gallegos, who had a house on the main road beside the Chama River at the bridge called Vadito de Chicos (Crossing of the Willows).

Ghost Ranch and the Piedra Lumbre basin were nearly as remote as the Wetherills' home on the edge of Monument Valley. The landscape was nearly as dramatic too, although on a smaller scale. Red and gold stone mesas rose like islands from the multicolored sands of a painted desert, and narrow spires and pinnacles carved by wind and weather stood out against the skyline. The vertical wall of shining stone rose seven hundred feet from the badlands and was banded in dusty orange, red, yellow, lavender, grey, white, and buff that shimmered and gleamed at sundown.

To the southwest the horizon followed the lift and fall of the Jemez Mountains defined by the peaks of Tschicoma and Polvadera. The volcanic country of Frijoles Canyon and the Pajarito Plateau was just thirty miles as the crow flies south across the sierras. And standing like a blue sentinel 9,800 feet into the sky above the basin was the knife-like mountain, Cerro Pedernal. Known as Tsiping (Flint-topped Mountain) to Carol's friends at San Juan and the other Tewa-speaking pueblos of the Rio Grande, the *cerro* was sacred to the Navajo and Apache. Carol had used Pedernal's distinctive, angular profile to orient horse expeditions into Indian Country for nearly two decades. Now the *cerro* was the dominant feature on her western horizon and marked her home country.

To Carol, Ghost Ranch and the Piedra Lumbre were a familiar and soothing landscape of magnificent light and infinite space. Where others had seen only an evil, haunted hideout, she recognized one of the great, good-spirited places where the human heart beats up against the soul of the earth. And so in spite of the place having no modern conveniences, no rail connection, terrible roads, and virtually no infrastructure, Carol envisioned a home and guest ranch under the cliffs.

With the moneys left from the sale of her Nahant house, Carol began construction of ranch headquarters, a dining room, several guest casitas, and a bunkhouse and machine shed. Ted Peabody, Carol's principal foreman for the Los Luceros renovation and several building projects at San Gabriel, was able to sketch out her ideas and make rough plans from which to build the first casitas and facilities for the new guest ranch. A labor crew was assembled from local villages and moved into a camp on the ranch. With thousands of adobes made in the field before La Patrona's (the Spanish workmen's

Figure 60. Pedernal Mountain seen from Carol Stanley's home at Ghost Ranch.

Figure 61. Ghost Ranch headquarters, ca. 1935.

name for Carol) three-room casita under the cottonwoods, the first guest cottages were built.

The cowboys from San Gabriel lived in tents pitched in the sage field near headquarters, and had meals over the campfire or on Carol's patio when Alice Pring cooked supper in the small kitchen in the old homestead. In the evenings, the workers sat out under the stars and listened to Carol playing her piano by candlelight—there would be no electricity for at least the next year—and classical pieces long ago rehearsed and performed at the New England Conservatory of Music echoed out into the thin, cool air of the high desert canyon. By 1933 the Ranch of the Witches had begun its transformation to the Faraway Nearby, to the Good Country, the magic place known as Ghost Ranch.

Nearly all of the Ghost Ranch staff was made up of the cowboys and wranglers who had worked with Carol and Roy in Alcalde, and even earlier at Bishop's Ranch: Pete Coleman, Alfred "Slim" Jarmon, shy Archie McKellor, and the McKinley brothers Jack, Marvin, and Lester. A friend of Roy's, Pete Dozier, a half-French, half-Indian guide from Santa Clara Pueblo, left a position at Bishop's Lodge and came to live and work for Carol at Ghost Ranch. And San Gabriel's widely respected and experienced driver and auto mechanic Orville Cox rejoined Carol and her new outfit at Ghost Ranch by 1933.

Without Roy Pfäffle or Jack Lambert as partners, Carol had no manager or foreman. She made herself the Ghost Ranch manager and named Lloyd Miller, a Texas cowboy who had lived and worked at San Gabriel for several years, ranch foreman. Miller was a compact man with an easygoing nature who had made his living in the saddle as a cowboy and a horse jockey since he was a teenager in the Texas Panhandle. Miller had moved into the community at San Gabriel in the mid-1920s, and by 1930 was a valuable member of the ranch staff. A year before the Pfäffles divorced, there was talk around Alcalde and in Santa Fe that even though Lloyd Miller was ten years Carol's junior, and she was married, he was sweet on her. And Carol was doing nothing to discourage Miller's attention.[1]

The guest ranch under the cliffs at the mouth of Yeso Canyon was becoming a comfortable oasis on the high desert. It was surrounded, however, by country where bandits and ruffians still roamed. The most notorious bandits of the modern era, the Night Riders of Rio

Figure 62. Lloyd Miller, Ghost Ranch foreman and Carol Stanley's second husband.

Arriba, had been apprehended by 1931, but residents in remote villages and ranches from Española to Tierra Amarilla were still nervous, and most everyone carried a gun. Carol carried a pistol at all times, and told her visitors to explore and enjoy the beautiful country of her new home but always in the company of one of the Ghost Ranch cowboys.[2]

Carol went into Santa Fe infrequently after moving out to Ghost Ranch. It was a hard day's journey by car, and Carol could no longer lease the apartment on Canyon Road for leisurely overnights in the capital. Orville Cox went into Española and Santa Fe to retrieve guests and to run errands for the ranch. Once or twice a month, Carol dined at La Fonda with friends and had her hair done at the De Vargas Beauty Shop. But the days of shopping sprees to Denver and Chicago for dresses, boots, and jewelry were over. Carol paid her ten-dollar annual dues and remained an active member in the Archaeological Institute of America. But as the 1930s progressed,

Carol Stanley's name disappeared from the Santa Fe society pages and from the member rosters of art and cultural boards.[3]

By 1933 Ghost Ranch could comfortably accommodate twenty-five guests in four adobe casitas. There was a bunkhouse for the cowboys, and a ranch headquarters with an office, lounge, and dining room. The corral held a string of good saddle horses and expedition equipment filled the sheds. Carol had at least two touring cars: an indestructible Lincoln named the Clay Car because it survived a dunking in the Chama River, and an older touring car that Orville dubbed Bad News.[4]

Every cottage had a fine view to the west of Pedernal and the Piedra Lumbre sandlands and basin. Interiors were furnished with sturdy wood tables, chairs, and *trasteros* (cupboards) made by Ted Peabody and Pete Dozier. Carol's Navajo rugs—many of which had been purchased during her first trips to Canyon de Chelly and Ganado—were hung on the walls, and her collection of Indian baskets and pottery decorated shelves and window ledges. Like the Wetherills' trading post home at Kayenta, Carol's Ghost Ranch was an oasis of shade and comfort on the hot, bright desert. The ranch headquarters and casitas were shaded by young trees planted by Carol's gardener, and the water of the Ycso stream fed an orchard, a large vegetable garden, and flower beds of hollyhocks and Carol's favorite flower, blue morning glories.

Ghost Ranch had the potential of becoming a fine guest ranch. But the ranch would survive only if Carol could immediately fill its rooms with paying guests. And in the 1930s in New Mexico, paying guests were as scarce as rain.

The paralysis brought to the American tourist industry by the Great Depression was intensified in the Southwest by the suffocating heat and drought of the Dust Bowl. Only the ultrawealthy continued to come to the Southwest for vacation and retreat. Ghost Ranch might have folded a year after it opened had it not been for the timely and seemingly destined arrival of three very wealthy men and their families. The first was Arthur Newton Pack, cofounder and editor of *Nature Magazine*, who had come with his staff and stayed at San Gabriel in the late 1920s. Pack's father, Charles Lathrop Pack, after making his fortune in the lumber industry, realized the need to conserve and protect forests. Pack helped found the American Forestry Association and raised his son to appreciate nature. After Arthur graduated from Harvard, he funneled his family's money into conservation causes. By the time Pack came to see Carol at her new ranch under the cliffs north of Abiquiú, he was one of America's most important writers about and crusaders for environmental protection and education.

The Packs made their home in Princeton. In 1933 Arthur and his wife, Eleanor (Brownie), were told by a doctor that they had to move their ailing daughter, Peggy, to a drier climate. Pack learned that Carol and Roy Pfäffle had divorced and that Carol had begun a new ranch on a homestead north of Abiquiú. Pack had ridden across the Piedra Lumbre and well remembered the "gorgeous cliffs there in Navajo country. They had been like a magnet drawing me back . . . and now all at once here was a legitimate excuse. . . . We made our plans to go."[5]

The Packs wrote Carol and asked if they and their three children could come to Ghost Ranch in early spring and stay the entire summer. Ghost Ranch was not yet open for business, but Carol could hardly turn the Pack family away, since they promised to bring her new dude ranch its first guests and income. Pack wrote about his family's arrival to Ghost Ranch in 1933: "The main road of poorly graded clay had been rough enough, but after a dozen miles we turned off on a mere track marked only by a cow's skull propped against a rock, slid down an incredibly steep hill, crossed a creek on a narrow log bridge and wound up on the other side beneath a spectacular array of cliffs seen years before."[6]

For their first night at Ghost Ranch, Arthur, Brownie, and their children placed bedrolls out under the sky bright with the moon and listened to Carol play the Steinway piano in the tiny, candlelit dwelling that was now her home. The very next day, Pack asked Carol to sell him land on which to build a house. Carol took Pack and Brownie out to the Painted Desert under the cliffs where they chose a building site with a grand and glorious view of Pedernal. With Carol's help, Pack and his wife designed a simple U-shaped adobe dwelling. Ted Peabody supervised construction, and by Christmas the Pack family moved out of Princeton and into the house on the Piedra Lumbre they called Rancho de los Burros, Ranch of the Burros.

Pack brought Carol's new venture the economic stability it desperately needed. He became Carol's partner in the Piedra Lumbre Cattle Company, and within the first year after his family's move to Ghost

Ranch, he also held the mortgage for most of Carol's property. But Pack did more than just inject a sizable cash flow into Ghost Ranch: he brought his wealthy friends to the ranch.

The Pack home in Princeton shared a garden wall with the Robert Wood Johnson family. Bob Johnson and his brother, Seward, of the Johnson & Johnson medical empire, were good friends with Arthur and Brownie Pack, and Bob Johnson traveled with Arthur on several expeditions into the Canadian outback. After the Packs secured their piece of paradise on the Piedra Lumbre and moved into Rancho de los Burros, they began to share their love of Ghost Ranch with close friends. In 1934 Bob and Maggie Johnson came to see for themselves the place that had so enchanted their former neighbors. The Johnsons liked what they found at Ghost Ranch, and leased land near the ranch headquarters from Carol; soon they built a two-story adobe summerhouse for their extended family.[7]

In spite of the distance from Taos and Santa Fe, and the rigorous and demanding road from Española to Abiquiú and north to the Piedra Lumbre, Ghost Ranch became a destination for the rich and famous living in or visiting New Mexico in the 1930s. Mabel and Tony Luhan brought carloads from Taos to Carol's new ranch, and Mary Wheelwright came out from Alcalde with nieces, cousins, and friends. Members of the Fred Harvey family stopped in for lunch with Carol, and the conductor Leopold Stokowski came several times each summer for overnights with his wife, Evangeline Johnson, the sister of Seward and Robert Wood.[8]

In July 1933 Carol was visited by the retired Chicago architect Edward H. Bennett and his son, Ted. The Bennetts had grown bored with the "polo-playing crowd" found in Tesuque near Bishop's Lodge, and had come out to Abiquiú to see if Ghost Ranch was indeed a different sort of dude ranch. Carol had met Bennett before (he may have been a Chicago friend of Winfred Douglas). Bennett and his circle in the upper-class Chicago suburbs of Winnetka, Highland Park, and Oak Park—including Archibald MacLeish, the family of George Hemingway (uncle of Ernest), and the Santa Fe Railway executives J. Sanford and Stuart Otis—were already in Carol's client book in the 1920s.

Bennett, one of the primary architects of the Chicago Plan and the designer of Buckingham Fountain, the centerpiece of the city's

Grant Park, had recently retired and was looking for a summer retreat far from the tourist scene in Santa Fe. Carol showed father and son one of the newly completed and available guest cottages near ranch headquarters. The Bennetts liked what they saw, and they returned the next day with the whole family, who spent the entire summer at Ghost Ranch. Before they left in the fall, Carol sold Edward Bennett 212 acres of land directly under the Puerto del Cielo, Gate of Heaven, a chimney-like formation in the cliffs west of Arthur Pack's home site. Within the year, the Bennetts' Casa Monte Rojo, Red Hill House, was completed.

By the summer of 1934, the Pack and the Bennett families were living under the cliffs, and the adobe cottages clustered around the old homestead were filled with paying guests—rich folks who were, in the words of Ted Bennett Jr., "waiting out the depression." Robert Wood Johnson's house was under construction and would be completed by winter, and at the mouth of the canyon east of headquarters there was a new swimming pool filled with the cold water of the Yeso stream. Auto and horse expeditions departed weekly for the Four Corners and Indian Country, a homesteader named Dave Burnham called squares at the weekly square dance in the ranch headquarters, and every Friday night Carol's cowboys held a rodeo and invited local riders, bronco busters, and ropers to show off their skills for the ranch dudes. Carol loved to throw a good party for friends and visitors up at headquarters or on her front patio, but after witnessing the havoc wreaked by Roy's alcoholism, Carol enforced a no-liquor law at Ghost Ranch for both staff and guests.[9]

The dude ranch under the gleaming cliffs beyond old Abiquiú had become a topic of conversation in social circles back east. Pack, delighted with Ghost Ranch, raved about his new home in New Mexico to friends in Princeton and New York City. One of these friends was David McAlpin, the grandnephew of John D. Rockefeller (whose family had stayed at Carol's Canjilon Camp for a month in 1930). After hearing Pack's descriptions of the magical high desert place called Ghost Ranch, McAlpin decided to go to New Mexico and see Pack's home for himself.

Soon afterward, at a party in New York City in the winter of 1934, McAlpin told a friend, the painter Georgia O'Keeffe, about Arthur Pack's adobe home on the high desert of New Mexico at a ranch that was possibly "the best place in the world." O'Keeffe had spent time in New Mexico, including a four-month stay at Mabel's in Taos in 1929, and several weeks in Alcalde in a cottage at Marie Garland and Henwar Rodakiewicz's ranch. The H & M (Henwar and Marie) Ranch was built on land sold to Garland by the Pfäffles, and the property, like San Gabriel, flanked the Alcalde plaza. Following Jack and Lois Lambert's departure from San Gabriel in 1928, Garland had purchased their adobe home and additional San Gabriel acreage.[10]

O'Keeffe returned to Alcalde and the H & M ranch in the summer of 1934. She had learned to drive and went on solo painting excursions up the Chama River valley toward Abiquiú and the country she called the Faraway. O'Keeffe loved the little hills and landscape near the old village, and she also liked the space, light, and the utter lack of people. O'Keeffe had become weary of Taos and Santa Fe's frenetic social scenes. Even Marie Garland's little ranch in rural Alcalde hosted all-night parties attended by large mobs of artists and writers from Santa Fe and Taos. Now that O'Keeffe knew there was a guest ranch out on the high, bright desert of the Piedra Lumbre, she set out to find "someplace where the people do not run me crazy—," the place called Ghost Ranch.[11]

In midsummer, in the company of young Charles Collier, son of John Collier, who was now the commissioner of Indian affairs, O'Keeffe headed out to find the most beautiful landscape in the world. It was a frustrating day: although they successfully navigated the road up through the Chama canyon and reached the Painted Desert below the Cliffs of Shining Stone, Collier and O'Keeffe could not find the road across the badlands to Ghost Ranch. Several days later at San Juan Pueblo, O'Keeffe saw a pickup truck with "GR" painted on its door parked out front of the Kramer Mercantile. She waited by the truck, and when the driver returned, she asked him for *very* specific instructions about the location of the road to Ghost Ranch. The driver explained that there was no sign marking the ranch gate, only a skull. With the directions firmly in hand, O'Keeffe drove her Model A back out onto the Piedra Lumbre and alone found the road to Ghost Ranch.

It was August and high summer, and the sky over Pedernal was intensely blue. The road led O'Keeffe across the hot, dry landscape of red-gold sandlands and deeply carved arroyos to a cluster of adobe buildings beneath the sheer walls of the luminous cliffs. "Perfectly mad looking country—hills and cliffs and washes too crazy to imagine all thrown up into the air by god and let tumble where they would. It was certainly as spectacular as anything I've ever seen—and that was pretty good."[12]

From the front steps of the Ghost Ranch headquarters, the world that O'Keeffe was looking to find, to paint, to immerse herself in, unfolded to the horizon. "It was a new world," O'Keeffe said years later. "And I thought it was my world."[13]

Thus began the half-century love affair between the painter Georgia O'Keeffe and the place of Ghost Ranch. O'Keeffe would eventually claim ten acres of the ranch as her own, but in August 1934 the Faraway was owned by Carol Bishop Stanley. And it was to Carol's crooked little house under the cottonwood trees that O'Keeffe went to inquire about a renting a room.

O'Keeffe had been introduced to Carol when she stayed at Marie Garland's in 1929, but in O'Keeffe's accounts of her first years at Ghost Ranch she never acknowledges Carol Stanley by name. Perhaps Carol's ownership of Ghost Ranch, and her remarkable, even accidental role as the creator of modern Ghost Ranch, were not easily conceded by O'Keeffe. From the moment O'Keeffe connected with Ghost Ranch, she claimed it as her own. Legal ownership was of little interest to her. Whatever O'Keeffe formed an affection for—the Faraway Nearby, Ghost Ranch—belonged to her. She was especially fond of Pedernal. "It's my private mountain," she declared decades after she first came to the ranch. "It belongs to me. God told me if I painted it enough, I could have it."[14]

When O'Keeffe arrived at Carol's doorstep that August day in 1934, the ranch's guest cottages were all spoken for. Carol did, however, have one room unoccupied for just one night. One night at Ghost Ranch was better than nothing, and O'Keeffe drove all the way back to Alcalde—forty miles over very poor roads—packed up a few necessities, and returned to the ranch by evening. During the night, the child of one of the families staying at the ranch became very ill with appendicitis. By morning, the family had departed for the hospital in Santa Fe, and their casita was available for the remainder of the summer. O'Keeffe gleefully claimed the cottage. "I went immediately to Ghost Ranch, and I never left."[15]

Figure 63. Georgia O'Keeffe at Ghost Ranch, ca. 1935.

BY THE LATE 1920S, Mary Wheelwright's collaboration with Klah had amassed a significant and rare collection of tapestries, rugs, and recordings of Navajo ceremonies and chants. After the Night Riders' robbery at Los Luceros of Navajo rugs and jewelry (the items were recovered in late summer of 1931), Mary knew she had to find a secure and permanent home for the collection. In 1927 she offered the recordings, sacred items, rugs, and transcriptions of chants and stories—and the money necessary to build a museum devoted to Navajo ceremonialism and religion—to the new Laboratory of Anthropology in Santa Fe.

The Laboratory of Anthropology, recently funded by John D. Rockefeller, was to be built on fifty acres of land donated by the White sisters in the hills southeast of the Santa Fe plaza. The architect John Gaw Meem had been selected to design a Pueblo Revival–style complex for the new facility that would house, among other things, the substantial and valuable collection amassed by the Indian Arts Fund begun by Harry Mera and friends at Elsie Sergeant's Tesuque dinner party in 1922.

When Mary approached the lab's new board of directors—a virtual who's who in American anthropology, including Hewett, Kenneth Chapman, Jesse Nusbaum (who was the lab's first director), Natalie's friends and colleagues Franz Boas and F. W. Hodge, Alfred "Ted" Kidder (the young archaeologist at the Wetherills' the month Carol arrived in 1915), and Elsie Clews Parsons, among others—they were in the early phases of planning the institution's future. The directors, although delighted to consider the acquisition of Mary and Klah's collection, were immediately averse to Mary's one condition: that the museum to be built (with her money) for her collection be an octagonal structure patterned after a traditional Navajo hogan (hooghan).

Several members of the new board claimed the hogan design was incompatible with Meem's Santa Fe–style structure that would house the laboratory. But it was not just Mary's architectural preference that the conservative men on the board found objectionable. Several members argued that Mary and Klah's collaboration had no place in the collections of a scientific organization. Mary's plans "represent an artistic interpretation and are not the real thing at all," Francis I. Proctor, a Boston eye doctor, reasoned, because "in a scientific institution everything should be founded on the truth."[16]

Mary's vision of a museum celebrating Navajo ceremonialism and her institutionally unsanctioned and amateur research partnership with Hostiin Klah had run into the stone wall of the academic patriarchy. Mary did not hold an advanced degree, or any other degree for that matter. She was also a wealthy, entitled, determined, progressive, unmarried woman, and the accomplished men of the Laboratory of Anthropology were not about to let an independent female dictate policy or suggest aesthetic directives.

Alice Corbin understood what Mary was up against and told Amelia Elizabeth White what she thought of the lab's board of directors: "The Committee is, I think, frankly *scared*, because the Hogan is unique and different. Though this is just what would make it an asset. But they have no architectural imagination and no courage."[17]

True to form, Mary was not intimidated by the esteemed members of the board, nor was she in awe of the academic community. She was thick-skinned to criticism about her supposed lack of scientific rigor, and she shrugged off comments by conservative scholars about her eccentric and unconventional relationship with Navajo cacique Hostiin Klah.

Undaunted by the board's initial opposition to her proposal, Mary persevered with her intention to build a museum linked to the

Laboratory of Anthropology that was devoted to Navajo religion. For the next five years, she wrote letters, made calls, submitted and resubmitted ideas and designs, negotiated, cajoled, socialized, and haggled about the project with the Laboratory of Anthropology board members.

And then she gave up.

Mary sensed that time was running out for Hostiin Klah. In 1935 she withdrew her offer to the lab of her collection and went forward with her museum with help from her friend Amelia Elizabeth White. In a move that surely incensed several of those staunchly scientific board members, White donated the land adjacent to their Laboratory of Anthropology to Mary and Klah's museum of Navajo religion.

If the boys of the Santa Fe art and anthropology colony had forgotten, they were quickly reminded: in the City of Ladies, the ladies were a mighty—and often resolutely united—force to be reckoned with.

With her remarkable and straightforward gift, Amelia White empowered Mary Wheelwright to build the Museum of Navajo Ceremonial Art. Mary chose Alice Corbin's husband, William Henderson, as the architect for the project. With Klah as his consultant, Henderson designed a larger-than-life hogan complete with interlocking cribbed-log ceiling and an east-facing door that opened directly onto the piñon-studded foothills of the Sangre de Cristos. The museum's primary directive was to provide a sanctuary for Klah's recordings and sacred paraphernalia. Klah wanted the collection to assist future generations of Navajo singers, and he gave Mary explicit instructions that his ceremonial items be available for study in perpetuity.

Klah conducted the traditional House Blessing ceremony at the groundbreaking, but he did not live to see the museum completed. In the early winter of 1937 influenza raged across the Navajo Reservation, and Klah, after caring for dozens of sick neighbors, succumbed to pneumonia. He died in the Rehoboth Hospital near Gallup in late February. Per Klah's instructions, his body was placed in a "white" casket and buried in the cemetery in Tohatchi, New Mexico, where his male relatives kept vigil for four days and nights and chanted the traditional Navajo prayers that accompanied his departing spirit along the Rainbow Trail.

With the passing of Hostiin Klah "went many a precious secret of the tribe's religious life." Mary was in Florida when Klah died, and when she returned to New Mexico, she called upon Arthur and Franc Newcomb to help her get permission from Klah's relatives to disinter his casket and bring his body to Santa Fe for burial near the new museum. After assuring Klah's family that the removal of the casket would be discreet and that the exact time would be known only by the funeral director and his workers (the family did not want to know when his body was above ground), Mary sent a hearse from Santa Fe to retrieve Klah's body. He was reburied on the hill beside the nearly completed museum. Mary had wild plants and herbs important to Klah's ceremonies—desert goldenrod, water grass, grass daisy, and dwarf sage—brought from Navajoland planted in the earth surrounding his grave.[18]

Nine months after Klah's death, the House of Navajo Religion opened in Santa Fe in November 1937. Klah's nephew, Big Man's Son, oversaw the House Blessing ceremony. Twenty-one Navajos, including fifteen of Klah's nieces and nephews, came to Santa Fe in a private bus arranged by Mary. Attendance at the museum dedication was by invitation only and was conducted in the Navajo way, with Klah's Navajo family seated on the south side of the massive hogan, and the few white people—Mary, Alice Corbin (named the museum's first curator) and William Henderson, the Newcombs, and the workers who built the museum—seated on the north side of the octagon. Before they departed for their homes in Navajoland, Klah's family sang the "Traveler's Song," a prayer for safe passage for Mary, who was about to embark on a trip to China.

The museum's hogan design that had garnered such vociferous disapproval from the Laboratory of Anthropology architectural team received national attention and was awarded Honorable Mention for "Works of Major Importance in Architecture" from the Architectural League of New York in 1938.

In the next decades Mary and Klah's renamed Museum of Navajo Ceremonial Art (later called the Wheelwright Museum of the American Indian) became a repository for sound recordings, paintings, manuscripts, sandpainting tapestries, and valuable Navajo ceremonial materials. Washington Matthews's papers that had been Mary's "bible" in the first years of her work with Klah were transferred to the Santa Fe museum from the University of California, Berkeley, and dozens of valuable ethnographic films, an archive of reproductions of more than five hundred sandpaintings, Navajo song texts and recordings by Mary and others working in the field, and manuscripts from other major studies of Navajo religion were placed in the museum's permanent collection.

CAROL LOVED GHOST RANCH as much as any home she had ever known. But love didn't pay the massive bills associated with the startup of a guest ranch. Even with the Packs, Bennetts, Johnsons, and O'Keeffe in residence, and with every bed taken by dudes throughout the summers of 1933 and '34, Carol could not bring in enough income to cover Ghost Ranch's operating expenses. Her personal funds from the sale of the Nahant house had been exhausted by the construction of the ranch headquarters, guest cottages, bunkhouse, animal sheds, corrals, and auto garage. The historic drought had dried up the meager grasslands of the Piedra Lumbre, and by early 1935 Carol and Arthur Pack's Piedra Lumbre Cattle Company was defunct.

Ghost Ranch operated in the red during its first years, and no one but a millionaire could absorb those sorts of losses. Pack was a millionaire who loved the country and the ranch life, and he offered to buy out Carol in March 1935. "It became evident that Carol couldn't keep the place," Ted Bennett Jr. recalled years later. "For all her charm, there wasn't enough money coming in. Arthur Pack wanted to buy it from her, and this turned out to be a blessing in disguise. For a naturalist, he was very wealthy, and the considerable cost of the Piedra Lumbre grant was no burden to him."[19]

Pack bought Ghost Ranch from Carol for seventy-five thousand dollars. Fifty thousand dollars were deposited into Carol's Santa Fe bank account; the remaining twenty-five thousand paid off her mortgage to Pack. The deal included sixteen thousand acres of land; the ranch's buildings, sheds, and barns, wagons, generators; all of the furniture in all of the casitas, headquarters, and bunkhouse; and Carol's fleet of pickup trucks and her four twelve-passenger Lincoln touring cars. Pack became the owner of the ranch's saddle horses, pack burros, herd of cows, one bull and one sow, and Carol's 150 chickens, 25 ducks, and 86 turkeys. Pack also took possession of some but not all of Carol's Indian art collection—Carol kept several of the rugs purchased years ago at Canyon de Chelly and Ganado. The Steinway piano remained with Carol.[20]

Pack asked Carol to stay in residence on the ranch until late fall and the end of the 1935 guest season. All of the cowboys, guides, and drivers employed by Carol were kept on, and Lloyd Miller was retained as the head wrangler, although Pack knew Miller would remain at Ghost Ranch only as long as Carol was living there. Carol had fallen in love with Miller, and he with her. By 1935 the relationship that had begun quietly during the last tumultuous years of Carol and Roy's marriage was now a widely accepted liaison. In September, Carol journeyed with Harriet Ropes Cabot (Mary Wheelwright's relative), O'Keeffe, and Mabel and Tony Luhan to the Jicarilla Apache fiesta at Stone Lake. In spite of losing yet another home and ranch, and having just said good-bye to her maid, Alice Pring, who returned to England after working in Carol's household for fifteen years, Carol was optimistic and happy, and told her companions that she would marry Lloyd before Christmas.[21]

Carol's friends were nervous about her decision to marry again. Lloyd Miller, although respected as one of the nicest, kindest, most dependable cowboys in northern New Mexico, had spent his whole life around the racetracks of Texas and New Mexico. Lloyd loved to train racehorses, and he loved to bet on racehorses. And although Lloyd did not drink, he had won and lost more money at the track than anyone cared to remember or to mention to Carol.

In October, after most of the guests had departed Ghost Ranch, Carol went to Kayenta to visit Louisa and John Wetherill. Exactly twenty years had come and gone since Carol had learned to ride astride a horse and journeyed through Indian Country with Louisa. Carol was fifty-five years old. She had built, managed, and lost two remarkable and significant ranches, had married and divorced, and with Lloyd Miller, was about to embark on what would likely be the last chapter of her life.

Carol took a Boston friend, Helen Appleton, with her to the Wetherills'. Mid-October was a grand time of year to see Monument Valley, and Carol and Helen moved into agreeable but crowded quarters in the Wetherill home. A Mr. and Mrs. C. B. Green of Williamstown, Massachusetts, Pamela Parsons and Jack Stacy of Santa Fe, and Bill Brimhall of Gallup were also staying at the Wetherills'. The guesthouse near the trading post was being used by a group from Flagstaff that included the painter Mary-Russell F. Colton and her husband, Harold S. Colton. On October 14, Carol signed Louisa's guest book as Caroline B. Stanley of Los Luceros, New Mexico, and gave as her mailing address the post office in Chamita, New Mexico.[22]

The friendly advice and counsel Louisa Wetherill may have given Carol during her October visit was never recorded. In her Louisa, Carol surely found support for her decision to sell her home in Nahant and remain in New Mexico following the loss of San Gabriel. But Louisa's opinion of her decision to remarry must remain unknown.

One month later, on November 14, Caroline Bishop Stanley of Nahant, Massachusetts, married Lloyd Miller of Content, Texas, at the United Brethren Church in Española, New Mexico. The marriage certificate revealed the curious fact that Lloyd Miller, like Roy, shared Carol's birthday of December 16. Born in 1890, the groom, eleven years younger than the bride, may not have known the precise difference in their ages, since the marriage license erroneously claimed Carol was born in 1886. Lloyd also may not have known that he was the second man Carol had married who shared her and her deceased twin brother's birthday.

With the fifty grand left from the sale of Ghost Ranch, the Millers bought a small ranch on the Rio Grande near Los Luceros. Cottonwood Ranch was developed to accommodate Lloyd's quarter horse breeding and training business. It was an expensive operation to get up and running, and the Depression had yet to loosen its grip on the economy. There was no money coming in, and Lloyd, who was hanging out around the local racetracks, lost a lot of money gambling. By 1940 Carol's bank account was drained and the Millers faced foreclosure.

"We all saw it coming," Dorthy Fredericks remembered. "Carol turned her money over to Lloyd just like she had to Pfäffle before him. Carol began to avoid her old friends—never went to lunches at La Fonda or any social event where she might meet people who knew what had happened. Carol couldn't take the humiliation of being broke twice by men."

Cottonwood Ranch was sold and with it everything Carol owned, including her Steinway piano. Carol and Lloyd departed New Mexico with one good quarter horse stallion and a borrowed saddle and moved to Arboles, Colorado, a small town just over the New Mexico border at equal distance from Durango and Pagosa Springs.

Surrounded by the Navajo and Southern Ute Reservations at the northernmost end of the geologic formation that reached south to Chaco Canyon, Carol was still in the country where her affair with the American Southwest had begun. She had ridden through this landscape dozens of times, and camped alongside the streams and in the mountain meadows en route to Mesa Verde. Carol Stanley Miller had lost everything she owned except the country she loved.

The Millers moved into a two-room adobe outside the small town. After the war began in 1942, Lloyd opened a feed store in Arboles, and Carol served as the town postmistress. There was no money for Carol's annual trip to Boston, and she would never again visit the Douglases in Denver or any of her friends in Chicago. Carol never returned to Ghost Ranch, or to Santa Fe or Alcalde. She simply slipped out of sight.

A few of Carol's friends, mostly the cowboys, stayed in touch with her after she left New Mexico. In 1946 Dave Burnham and Ghost Ranch cowboy Slim Jarmon went to Arboles and dropped in on Carol and Lloyd. Carol, now in her mid-sixties, wore patched jeans and a wrinkled plaid shirt, her former wardrobe of stylish dresses and fashionable riding clothes a distant memory. To Burnham and Jarmon's surprise, Carol cooked supper (neither man had ever seen Carol prepare a meal except over a campfire in the outback), and with Lloyd, they spent a pleasant evening around the kitchen table talking about old times. Lloyd took Burnham and Jarmon out to the corral to see his two quarter horses and spoke optimistically about their chances at the track. But Carol's health was not good, and it was obvious to their old friends that the Millers had hit rock bottom.

Caroline Bishop Stanley Miller died in that two-room adobe house outside Arboles on the afternoon of December 4, 1948. The cause of death was thrombosis of the coronary artery. She was sixty-eight years of age, and her death certificate, signed by Lloyd, correctly gave her birthdate as December 16, 1879. Carol was buried in the small cemetery near Pagosa Springs on December 7, Pearl Harbor Day.

There was no announcement of Carol's death in the *Santa Fe New Mexican*, nor in any newspaper in Boston or Nahant. The cowboys who had worked with Carol at the Ramon Vigil, Bishop's Ranch, San Gabriel, and Ghost Ranch learned of her passing the old-fashioned way, person to person, and according to Dave Burnham's daughter, Dorthy, "all of the cowboys showed up for her funeral. *All* of them."

Lloyd Miller left Colorado after Carol's death, and died several years later back in New Mexico. Carol's first husband, Roy Pfäffle, outlived her by seven years. After treatment in the hospital in Pueblo, Roy returned to New Mexico in the mid-1930s and took jobs wrangling horses and dudes where he could find them. Roy eventually married a teacher named Helen Fowler Nolan, who taught school in the coal-mining town of Gramerco on the Navajo Reservation a few miles north of Gallup. They shared a good and simple life, and Roy remained employed and sober until Helen died after World War II.

Roy moved into Gallup in the 1950s, and tried to make a living as a cattle wrangler at the rail yards. But the work he did so effortlessly as a younger man was too much for his aged body. In his last letter, dated November 7, 1955, Roy confessed to his sister Lois and her husband, Tom, that he had almost not survived the last two weeks of thirteen-hour shifts as a night watchman in the cattle yards. After being knocked down by a steer, and spending several weeks laid up in bed in a poorly heated Gallup boarding house, Roy decided that "the old boy isn't what he used to be." Roy was hoping to get enough money to leave Gallup and join his sisters and their families in Santa Fe. "Things are pretty rough here now," he told Lois at the close of his letter.

Richard Leroy Pfäffle died in Gallup six weeks later, on December 21, 1955. He was buried on Christmas Eve in the Fairview Cemetery in Santa Fe. Roy's mother, Margaret "Gaga" Pfäffle, had been laid to rest in Santa Fe just eleven months before.[23]

AFTERWORD

Something of the Spirit

Here is the desert of silence,
Blinking and blind in the sun—
An old, old woman who mumbles her beads
And crumbles to stone.
—*Alice Corbin*

MARY WHEELWRIGHT AND ALICE KLAUBER both lived to see their eightieth birthday. Mary's primary residence remained in the Northeast among the Brahmins, but even as she aged, she continued to make an annual pilgrimage to Los Luceros on the Rio Grande. Her last visit was in May 1958, just two months before she died.

Alice, however, did not go back to New Mexico again after Natalie's death in Paris in October 1921. Following three years of a self-imposed European exile, she returned to San Diego in late 1924. She was in her mid-fifties, and after years of living out of steamer trunks in hotels and rented rooms in foreign places, Alice was ready to settle down in the ocean-side community that had been her home since birth.

Before she embarked for Paris and the meeting of the International Congress of Art History at the Sorbonne, Alice and a small group of San Diego artists had founded Friends of Art, a society of like-minded creative people who shared the idea that "the real status of the community is measured not alone by its commercial achievements, laudable as they may be, but by the things which make for culture."[1] By the time of Alice's return to California from Europe in the mid-1920s, discussions about the building of an art museum in

San Diego had become formalized, and Friends of Art had merged with the Art Guild of San Diego. Alice and other members of the renamed Fine Arts Society became the directors of San Diego's first fine art museum. While the new museum was under construction, the directors' meetings were held in the New Mexico Building at Balboa Park, a place whose rooms held the echoes and memories of a dozen of Alice's closest friends, including Natalie.

Alice was not just a founding member of the Fine Arts Gallery of San Diego (later renamed the Museum of Art), she was a major donor, and also served as the museum's first curator. Her personal art collection given to the museum over several decades reflected her remarkable life among some of the most influential and important artists of her time. After visiting Japan in the 1930s, Alice also became an avid collector of and authority on Asian art. In 1935, with her friend Elsie Kimberley, she created San Diego's Asian Arts Committee, and in the ensuing years her collection of Japanese woodblock prints, Persian miniature paintings, and rare Chinese porcelains became the nucleus of the San Diego Museum's Oriental art collection.[2]

In her sixties Alice was teaching art to children and adults, and comfortably assumed the role of San Diego's first lady of the arts. But beneath the civic dynamo and celebrated matron of the local arts, the skilled and serious painter persisted and continued to seek the nourishment found in her private studio among her paints and canvases. Alice's paintings appeared regularly in exhibitions at the San Diego Museum of Art and were exhibited at the California Pacific International Exposition in 1935.

By the time of her death in her bed in Lemon Grove, California, in early July 1951, Alice was an important and respected member of the Southern California fine art community. But she was unknown in the American art world. Although her teachers and advocates included many of the most prestigious artists of her time, Alice never sought fame or expected recognition as a painter. Hardly surprising, as she was often apologetic about her passion to paint, and rarely if ever used the term "artist" to describe herself. Indeed, the time and society into which Alice was born hardly encouraged a woman to make such a bold and self-affirming declaration, or to entertain the pursuit of such an identity. "Locally her social activities seemed more newsworthy than her achievements as an artist," one art historian wrote of Alice, "if a paucity of newspaper accounts is considered any criteria."[3]

In spite of the prevailing climate of expectation that urged women to stay home and concern themselves with domestic matters, Alice traveled to exotic and often challenging destinations in pursuit of her muse. However, her travel journals, diaries, and surviving letters offer only cryptic and abbreviated references to her own work and rarely shed light on her private thoughts or opinions about her irrepressibly independent spirit. Natalie was the rare friend with whom Alice discussed the challenges and conflicts endured by women artists, and Natalie's death left her with few women friends who personally understood the dilemmas of the creative modern woman.

Like Natalie, Carol, Mary, and their spirited female contemporaries in the early twentieth century, Alice was a New Woman not so much by sociopolitical choice as by disposition and circumstance. Alice's poems leave a few veiled clues to her feelings about life as a single woman and an artist. The poem aptly titled "Untitled" perhaps sums up her acceptance of her place in the world.

> The least of His reporters I
> Who take some small note from His sky
> and let the Universe pass by.[4]

Mary Wheelwright died in her own bed in her summerhouse, the White Hen, on Sutton Island, near Mount Desert, Maine, in July 1958. She was eighty years of age and, like Alice, was vigorous and sharp-minded until the end of her life. Mary knew her death was near—she'd been told by her doctor that she had serious heart trouble. On her last day of life, she spent the morning in her garden. The White Hen faced west and had a fine view of the sea. After a good lunch, Mary retired to her room to read. With her book in her hand, she dozed off into a sleep from which she never awoke.[5]

Two of Mary's cousins, sisters Aimee and Rosamond Lamb of Boston, were visiting Sutton Island that day, and they watched in silence as the undertaker carried Mary's body on a stretcher out of the summerhouse and down to a small rowboat tied to the dock. The sisters placed flowers on the canvas-wrapped body and said their farewells by the water.

Sutton Island was famous for its fog, and that afternoon the Lamb sisters stood with Mary's bereft house staff and watched as the little boat carrying her body was rowed out into the mist. "It was really just what she would have liked," Rosamond said years later. "Could anything be more appropriate for Mary than just to go out into the void like that, into the deep fog, just by herself in a boat."[6]

Mary's body was buried among the Brahmins in the family cemetery in Boston, but if her Indian friends and their beliefs held sway over her spirit, Mary's soul was far away on the Rainbow Trail.

A memorial service was held for Mary Cabot Wheelwright in Santa Fe at the Museum of Navajo Ceremonial Art. Oliver La Farge, whose novel about the Navajo people, *Laughing Boy*, won the Pulitzer Prize in 1930, recalled the obstacles that Mary and Klah had overcome to make the museum a reality. Mary's unscientific methods, La Farge told the audience, were ultimately responsible for the preservation of extraordinary and irreplaceable materials. La Farge praised Mary and her ability to study and respond to "a very remarkable primitive religion as a whole instead of approaching it only from the rather timid point of view of the anthropologist seeking his purely so called objective data."

The memorial concluded with a written statement from the Navajo tribal chairman, Paul Jones. "It is certainly most unusual and difficult for a museum to achieve the purpose of keeping alive something of the spirit of the religion of the people who never had a written language. . . . The Navajo people will be forever grateful to [Mary] for . . . building the thing of the spirit into visible and physical form in the Museum of Navajo Ceremonial Art."[7]

THE MUSEUM OF NAVAJO CEREMONIAL ART (Wheelwright Museum of the American Indian) gave visible and physical form to the remarkable, unconventional life and work of Mary Cabot Wheelwright. It is more difficult to find tangible reminders or memorials for the other women whose journeys to their individual destinies are recounted in this book. Their lives and their contributions to the story of their times most often remain nebulous, something of the spirit.

Natalie Curtis Burlin's work among the Hopis and dozens of other Native American tribes, and her articles, books, recordings, and transcriptions are valued and recognized by specialists in the field of ethnomusicology. Alice Klauber is revered among those who work at and frequent the museum in San Diego she helped to build, but Alice's name, like her own paintings and her friendships with Henri, the Steins, and Pach, garner little public interest. Carol Bishop Stanley's intrepid and risky move onto the faraway desert beyond Abiquiú resulted in the creation of one of the most iconic places in American art history, yet her story remains only tenuously tethered to Ghost Ranch and the world-famous relationship, between O'Keeffe and the ranch, that her movements and choices inadvertently precipitated.

Of course, a life is not necessarily more valuable because it is broadly remembered or publicly applauded. Even celebrated worldly success may ultimately amount to a handful of sand scattered in the winds of time, and stupendous failure may spark a fire that burns brightly for decades. When all is said and done, a life well lived leaves only silence and beauty behind on the trail, and footprints and dreams merge seamlessly into the landscape.

The last words spoken at Mary Wheelwright's memorial service in Santa Fe were from an ancient Navajo song-prayer. We can imagine the prayer intended for Mary resonated among her kindred spirits Carol, Natalie, and Alice and all their fellow travelers across the wide, bright sky of their beloved Indian Country.

> Before her it is beautiful.
> It shows the way
> Behind her it is beautiful
> It shows the way
> This that is beautiful
> It shows the way
> May she ever walk in beauty.

ACKNOWLEDGMENTS

IT MAY TAKE A VILLAGE TO raise a child, but it takes a continent of friends and colleagues to write a book. I was able to undertake the grand journey to find the ladies of the canyons because I was supported every step of the way by family, friends, scholars, and editors. Kristen Buckles at the University of Arizona Press was enthusiastic about the project from the get-go and agreed to administer a research fund that afforded me the luxury of two years devoted almost entirely to this book. This fund was initiated by major gifts from Dona Bolding and Roger Hamilton, and from Diane and Tom Arenberg and family. I am humbled by their generosity and sense of adventure. The project received additional funding from Mary Ann Bumgarner, Joyce and Rex Davidson, Rebecca DeLair, Isabel and Sam Jewell, Carol and William Padden, Willie Picaro, Ann Sherman, and Suzanne and Robert Snow. You are all patrons of the arts in the truest sense. I am blessed as a writer to have such a splendid circle of history-loving friends and benefactors.

The stories told in *Ladies of the Canyons* were waiting to be discovered in archives, libraries, and private collections located in the Southwest, Midwest, and on both coasts. My search was facilitated by the expertise and energy of professional librarians and researchers, by relatives of the women themselves, and by professional and amateur historians who shared precious clues and valuable keys to these women's lives and the world they were part of.

Lea Armstrong of the Wheelwright Museum of the American Indian gave advice and expert counsel as I sought to understand the connections between Mary Cabot Wheelwright and Carol Bishop Stanley. Cheri Falkenstien-Doyle, also of the Wheelwright Museum, guided me through the photo and manuscript collections held in the Wheelwright archives.

Alfred Bredenberg's articles and publications about Natalie Curtis Burlin brought important attention to Natalie's life and work, and his Natalie Curtis Burlin Archive is an invaluable source of information and context for Natalie's life and work. Michelle W. Patterson, author of *Natalie Curtis: A Life in Native and African American Music*, kindly shared her extensive research and professional insights and gave coherence to Natalie's professional life.

Author historians Carolyn Brucken, Chief Curator, Autry National Center, and Virginia Scharff, Professor of History and Director of the Center for the Southwest at the University of New Mexico, offered valuable and thoughtful insights and suggestions during the first months of research. Historian and author Don D. Fowler was a source of expert and friendly advice about Southwest archaeology.

James Grebl, Manager, Library & Archives, The San Diego Museum of Art, graciously assisted and guided me through the Klauber archive. Nada Borsa was an invaluable source of information about the Klauber family and San Diego's cultural history.

Laura Holt, Librarian, School for Advanced Research, Santa Fe, facilitated my many research visits to the SAR library and cheerfully endured my many requests to view files, books, and papers held in the archives.

Patricia Hibbard, Jack Lambert's granddaughter and Roy Pfäffle's grandniece, graciously copied and identified family photos, sent me the diaries of Margaret "Gaga" and Lois Pfäffle, and helped me comprehend her family's story. Peggy Terrell shared scrapbooks, diaries, and newspaper clippings, and her own memories of the Pfäffle family saga.

Harvey Leake, grandson of Louisa Wade and John Wetherill, brought to my attention Louisa Wade Wetherill's diary and its astonishing revelations about Carol Stanley, provided me with historic photographs, and identified people and locations. Waldo M. Wedel alerted me to the extraordinary anecdotes about Natalie, Douglas, and Theodore Roosevelt at Walpi in the 1913 diary of Nicholas Roosevelt.

Beverley Spears, FAIA, architect in charge of the historic Los Luceros restoration, shared her substantial knowledge of Los Luceros's past and present and gave me an insider's tour of the magnificent property she helped to preserve. Robert Archuleta of El Mirador opened the grounds and historic buildings of the Pfäffles' San Gabriel Ranch on the Rio Grande. Isabel Ziegler shared memories of

Dorothy Kent, Carol Stanley Pfäffle, and Mary Cabot Wheelwright. Philip Blood graciously showed me Dorothy Kent's former home in Alcalde, New Mexico. John Steinle, Administrator, Hiwan Homestead Museum, Evergreen, Colorado, assisted my research into the life and family of Canon C. Winfred Douglas.

Calantha Sears, Nahant Historical Society volunteer curator extraordinaire, shared her over ninety-year knowledge of Nahant during a five-star tour of her magical home island. Dona Bolding was my savvy guide through the streets of old Boston and the cliff-hugging roads of Nahant island. Joyce and Rex Davidson explored with me many a road less traveled, and with Jim helped me locate Carol Stanley's high mountain treasure, Canjilon Camp. Christine Mather showed me Santa Fe's back roads and historic alleys and answered all my questions about Santa Fe style. My cousin Reid Meloy, with his wife MJ and daughter Olivia, gave me a room with a view to the La Jolla world that Alice Klauber loved and painted. Cristina McCandless was my companion during two days of intense excavation in the archives of the San Diego History Center and the San Diego Museum of Art in Balboa Park. The University of Arizona Press loaned me the services of two student interns, Sarah Parker and Corrine Ng, for which I am most grateful. Thank you all!

My partner and husband, Jim Kempes, explored the desert outback near Kayenta and Chinle, Arizona, with me, and was my scout through astonishing Hopiland. My son, Chris Kempes, was my navigator through greater Los Angeles and shepherded me through the research collections at the UCLA, Huntington, and Braun libraries. My daughter, Mari, and my daughter-in-law, Suzanne, provided unwavering encouragement and optimism, especially during the homestretch, and my parents, Ann Reid and David Poling, were, as always, tireless cheerleaders throughout the journey to write this book.

I am also indebted to the following individuals and institutions: Joan Bacharach, Lisa Riedel, and Rosemary Sucec of the National Park Service, Rainbow Bridge Registry; Brandon E. Barton, Duplication Services Coordinator, UCLA Library Special Collections; Eric Berkemeyer, Curatorial Assistant, Native Arts, Denver Art Museum; Marjorie Bixler; Ed Chamberlin, Museum Curator, Hubbell Trading Post National Historic Site; Heather Cole, Assistant Curator of Modern Books & Manuscripts and Curator of the Theodore Roosevelt

Collection, Houghton Library, Harvard University; Sarah Dana, Research Archivist, The Archives of the Episcopal Church; Lesley Daniel, Library Assistant, Royal Academy of Music, London; Amanda Donohue, Alumnae Information Services, and Patricia J. Albright, Archivist, Mount Holyoke College; Bonnie Ayers D'Orlando, Assistant Curator, and all of the volunteers and staff at the Nahant Historical Society; Cecilia Esposito, Director, and Charline Gannon, Plattsburgh State Art Museum; Arcadia Falcone, Public Services Intern, Harry Ransom Center; Scott Ferris; Mary French, Curator of Archives, The Explorers Club; Claudia Gallardo de Campbell, New Mexico State Monuments, Department of Cultural Affairs; Gina Giang, Department of Manuscripts, Sue Hodson, Curator of Literary Manuscripts, and Natalie Russell, Library Assistant, Literary Manuscripts, The Huntington Library; Tomas Jaehn, DCA, The Fray Angélico Chávez History Library; Jane Kenealy, Archivist, and the staff of the San Diego History Center, Balboa Park; George and Mary Jeanette Kennedy, and Judith and Harold W. Lavender; Daniel Kosharek, Photo Curator, Palace of the Governors; Lisa Kulyk-Bourque, Reference Librarian, Lynn Public Library; Frederick Lewis; Mike Martin; Robin Martin; Mary Morganti, Director of Library and Archives, California Historical Society; Liza Posas, Head Librarian, Braun Research Library, Archivist, Autry National Center; Maryalice Perrin-Mohr, the New England Conservatory of Music; Earle E. Spamer, Ann Reinhardt, Valerie-Anne Lutz, and Michael Miller of the American Philosophical Society; Hope Shannon, Executive Director, The South End Historical Society, Boston; Amy S. Wong, Library Special Collections, Charles E. Young Research Library, UCLA; Martha Yates, Ghost Ranch Education and Retreat Center.

ABBREVIATIONS

ACH/HRC	Alice Corbin Henderson papers, Harry Ransom Center, University of Texas Austin
CWD/DMA	Charles Winfred Douglas papers, Denver Museum of Art
GRA	Ghost Ranch Archives, Abiquiú, New Mexico
KS/NYPL	Kurt Schindler papers, New York Public Library
LAHM/PPC	Los Alamos Historical Museum, Peggy Pond Church collection
LC/BRL	Charles Lummis Collection, Braun Research Library, Southwest Museum, Los Angeles
LOC	Library of Congress, Washington, DC
MCW/WM	Mary Cabot Wheelwright papers, Wheelwright Museum of the American Indian
NCBA	Natalie Curtis Burlin Archive, Raleigh, North Carolina
NHS	Nahant Historical Society
RK/AAA	Rockwell Kent papers, Archives of American Art, Smithsonian Institution
SDHC	San Diego History Center
SDMA	San Diego Museum of Art Library and Archives
SRA	New Mexico State Records and Archives
UCLA	Special Collections, UCLA
WACC/NPS	Western Archeological and Conservation Center, National Park Service, Tucson, Arizona

NOTES

Epigraph

Isak Dinesen, "The Monkey," *Seven Gothic Tales*, 109.

Prologue

1. Pack, *We Called It Ghost Ranch*, 23.
2. Scharff, *Twenty Thousand Roads*, 12.
3. Corbin, "From the Stone Age," in *Red Earth*, 37.

Chapter 1

Virginia Scharff, "Introduction: Women Envision the West," 1.
1. Bridgham Curtis, "Memorial."
2. George DeClyver Curtis, "In Memory of Natalie."
3. Natalie Curtis to Bessie Day, November 30, 1891, NCBA.
4. Patterson, *Natalie Curtis Burlin*, 42.
5. Ibid., 47.
6. Natalie Curtis to Bessie Day, June 29, 1890, NCBA.
7. Natalie Curtis to Bessie Day, May 1893, NCBA.
8. Bridgham Curtis, "Memorial."
9. Frank Shaw to Lincoln Stone, in Foote, *Seeking the One Great Remedy*, 120. Robert Gould Shaw and the Massachusetts 54th Infantry are the subject of the 1989 film *Glory*. A memorial to Shaw and his men is on Beacon Street in Boston, across from the Massachusetts State House.
10. Walt Whitman quoted in Milne, *George William Curtis*, 232.
11. Bridgham Curtis, "Memorial."
12. George DeClyver Curtis, "Natalie Curtis Burlin," unpublished biography; Bridgham Curtis, "Memorial."
13. George DeClyver Curtis, "Natalie Curtis Burlin."
14. Clements, *Native American Verbal Art*, 47.
15. Lummis, *The Land of Poco Tiempo*, x.
16. Ibid., ix.

17. Ibid., 2–3.

18. Starr, *Inventing the Dream*, 84.

19. Edwin R. Bingham, *Charles F. Lummis, Editor of the Southwest*, quoted in Fowler, *Laboratory for Anthropology*, 251.

20. Diary of George DeClyver Curtis, January 11, 1908.

21. Lummis, *The Land of Poco Tiempo*, 140.

22. Natalie Curtis, "The Words of Hiparopai."

Chapter 2

Willa Cather, "The Bohemian Girl," 440.

1. Natalie Curtis, *The Indians' Book*, xxviii.

2. All quotations from Chiparopai from Natalie Curtis, "The Words of Hiparopai," 294, 297.

3. Natalie Curtis, "A Western Reverie," 591.

4. Natalie Curtis, "An American Indian Composer," 626. In 1849 the BIA was transferred to the newly created U.S. Department of the Interior. For years thereafter, the bureau was known variously as the Indian office, the Indian bureau, the Indian department, and the Indian Service. The Interior Department formally adopted the name Bureau of Indian Affairs for the agency in September 1947.

5. Clements, *Native American Verbal Art*, 157.

6. Talayesva, *Sun Chief*, ix.

7. See Hagan, *Theodore Roosevelt & Six Friends of the Indian*, 125.

8. James, *Pages from Hopi History*, 123–24.

9. Natalie Curtis, "An American Indian Composer," 627–28.

10. Natalie Curtis, "Indian Song on a Desert Path," 344.

11. Natalie Curtis, *The Indians' Book*, 474–78.

Chapter 3

Elizabeth Shepley Sergeant, *Willa Cather: A Memoir*, 71.

1. Bridgham Curtis, "Memorial."

2. Hagan, *Theodore Roosevelt & Six Friends of the Indian*, 5–6.

3. Natalie Curtis, "Mr. Roosevelt and Indian Music," 399–400.

4. Hagan, *Theodore Roosevelt & Six Friends of the Indian*, 5–6.

5. Natalie Curtis, "Mr. Roosevelt and Indian Music," 399–400.

6. Theodore Roosevelt to Indian Agents, July 22, 1903, quoted in Hagan, *Theodore Roosevelt & Six Friends of the Indian*, 149.

7. Theodore Roosevelt to Ethan Allen Hitchcock, July 22, 1903, quoted in Hagan, *Theodore Roosevelt & Six Friends of the Indian*, 150.

8. See Hagan, *Theodore Roosevelt & Six Friends of the Indian*, 149–50.

9. Natalie Curtis to Theodore Roosevelt, July 29, 1903, NCBA.

10. Natalie Curtis, "The Winning of an Indian Reservation," 327.

11. Natalie Curtis to Charles Lummis, June 5, 1903, LC/BRL. Mead and Lummis did connect, and Mead would found the East Coast chapter of the Sequoyah League. But even the defiantly unconventional Lummis considered Mead unusual and questioned his "mental ballast." When Roosevelt asked Lummis about Mead, Lummis told him that Mead was "a good deal saner than he looks, and I am inclined to trust him; but still would hardly *vouch* for his balance." Lummis quoted in Hagan, *Theodore Roosevelt & Six Friends of the Indian*, 151.

12. Natalie Curtis, "The Plight of the Mojave-Apache Indians," 30.

13. Natalie Curtis to Theodore Roosevelt from Wave Crest, August 31, 1903, LOC.

14. Natalie Curtis, "The Winning of an Indian Reservation," 329–30.

15. Natalie Curtis, "Mr. Roosevelt and Indian Music," 399.

16. George DeClyver Curtis, "Biography of Natalie Curtis Burlin."

17. Natalie Curtis, *The Indians' Book*, 475.

18. Ibid., 477–78. Natalie's mood reflected the prevalent attitude among Anglo America that the language, traditions, village life, identity, and sovereignty of Native America would not endure another half century. Natalie's recording and collecting of Indian music, chants, and stories was considered "salvage" ethnology. Although she vigorously defended the innate value and intrinsic importance of the art and culture of native people, in the twenty years that Natalie would work and live among the Indians of North America, she did not personally or professionally challenge the popular contemporary notion among whites that Native America was in its twilight years.

19. Ibid., 474. A former Mennonite minister and one of the first missionaries to work among the Hopis, Rev. H. R. Voth translated Lololomai's song and explained its content and nuances for Natalie. Natalie called upon Voth, then at the Field Columbian Museum, Chicago, for assistance with all her Hopi recordings. See ibid., 478.

20. Bridgham Curtis, "Memorial."

21. Natalie Curtis, *The Indians' Book*, 490.

22. Ibid., 347.

23. Natalie Curtis, "Mr. Roosevelt and Indian Music," 400.

24. Ibid.

Chapter 4

Ansel Adams and Mary Austin, *Taos Pueblo.*

1. George DeClyver Curtis, diary from St. Louis World's Fair, 1904.
2. Natalie Curtis, *The Indians' Book*, 323–24.
3. Natalie Curtis, "The Winning of an Indian Reservation," 330.
4. Natalie Curtis to Charles Lummis, April 4, 1905, LC/BRL.
5. Hagan, *Theodore Roosevelt & Six Friends of the Indian*, 123, 159.
6. Charles Lummis to Natalie Curtis, December 14, 1905, LC/BRL.
7. Theodore Roosevelt to Natalie Curtis, May 7, 1906, *The Indians' Book*, xx.
8. Angel De Cora was born in a wigwam on the Winnebago Reservation in Dakota (Thurston) County, Nebraska, on May 3, 1871. At the age of twelve, she went to study at the Hampton Institute. She began her career as an artist when she entered the art department of Smith College, from which she graduated in 1896. After studying at the Drexel Institute in Philadelphia, De Cora became a professional illustrator.
9. Natalie Curtis, *The Indians' Book*, xii.
10. George DeClyver Curtis, diary, January 6, 1908.
11. The Sherman Institute, opened in 1902 as a grammar and junior high school, boarded Indian students from all over the West. The school was modeled on Commissioner Francis Leupp's Indian policy that concentrated on preparing Indian youth for farm and ranch work. At Sherman, Native Americans from a dozen tribes learned English, math, American history; attended classes on Christianity; and received instruction in agricultural and industrial arts. By 1908, 550 students were enrolled.
12. See James, *Pages From Hopi History*, 132–39.
13. Theodore Roosevelt to Leonard Wood, June 16, 1903, quoted in Hagan, *Theodore Roosevelt & Six Friends of the Indian*, 159. Natalie was acquainted with Leupp, who was the former chief of the *New York Evening Post*'s Washington bureau. Although she did not leave a written record of her reaction to the 1906 events at Oraibi, it is not difficult to imagine her disappointment with Leupp's decision to exile Tawakwaptiwa and his people.
14. Natalie Curtis, *The Indians' Book*, 480.
15. Talayesva, *Sun Chief*, 134.

Chapter 5

Gregory Marwood (George DeClyver Curtis), *The Wooing of a Recluse*, 110.

1. Heyneman, *Arthur Putnam Sculptor*, iii.

2. Although he would always struggle financially, Putnam did become a celebrated sculptor in his lifetime. Rodin, upon seeing Putnam's bronze sculptures of wild cats on exhibit in Paris in 1907, remarked, "This is the work of a master." See Carol M. Osborne, "Arthur Putnam, Animal Sculptor," *American Art Review* 3 (September–October 1976).

3. Laura wed a bridge engineer named Julius Wangenheim, who joined the family business and was soon chairman of the board of the renamed Klauber-Wangenheim business. By 1900 Wangenheim was among San Diego's most influential visionaries and community builders, and the already prestigious Klauber family now had members and in-laws at the forefront of virtually every important civic undertaking. Wangenheim established banks and title companies, helped found the Scripps Institution of Oceanography, built the San Diego Library, and would serve on numerous boards including the first board of trustees of Scripps College.

4. See Scharff, "Introduction: Women Envision the West."

5. Details of Alice's trip from Diary "My Vacation," SDMA; and "Italian Trip, Chase Notes," SDHC.

6. Robinson, *Georgia O'Keeffe*, 57, 59.

7. Klauber, "My Vacation," June 9, 1907.

8. Klauber, Diary, July 25, 1907.

9. Gertrude Stein in Perlman, *Robert Henri*, 3.

10. Walter Pach to Alice Klauber, December 24, 1924, SDMA.

11. Alice Klauber, Diary, September 1, 1907.

12. Ibid., October 26, 1907.

13. Walter Pach to Alice Klauber, November 16, 1907, SDMA.

14. Ibid., August 19, 1908. See Walter Pach letters to Alice Klauber, November 1907–November 1909, SDMA.

15. Walter Pach to Alice Klauber, November 2, 1908, SDMA.

16. Bridgham Curtis, "Memorial."

17. Natalie Curtis to Aleš Hrdlička, March 30, 1916, in Patterson, *Natalie Curtis Burlin*, 193.

18. The Chicago Kindergarten Institute, considered a pioneer in social settlement education, partnered with local churches and universities, including the University of Chicago and Northwestern University. See Johnston, "The Chicago Kindergarten Institute," 573–74. For Mary Walton Free Kindergarten for Colored Children, see Patterson, *Natalie Curtis Burlin*, 218.

19. Frank and Walter Damrosch were the German-born sons of Leopold Damrosch, the former general manager and chief conductor of the Metropolitan Opera. Walter Damrosch, the "youthful Adonis" conductor over whom Natalie swooned as a teenager, was in 1911 director of both the

Oratorio Society and the New York Symphony Society (which merged with the New York Philharmonic in 1928). During a trans-Atlantic voyage in 1877, Walter began a conversation with a young newlywed named Andrew Carnegie. By the end of the crossing, Walter had inspired Carnegie to build New York's Carnegie Hall. His older brother, Frank, founded the New York Institute of Musical Art in 1905, which merged with the Juilliard Graduate School to become the Juilliard School. Walter still holds the record for Carnegie Hall appearances. From opening night in 1891, when he shared conducting duties with Tchaikovsky, until his final performance conducting the New York Philharmonic on March 27, 1942, the maestro played a stamina-busting 850 performances at Carnegie Hall.

20. The story goes that Douglas's recovery made a dramatic turn when a fellow priest, Father Irving P. Johnson, came to the hospital to give him his last rites. Douglas managed to a make a feeble joke about his own demise that caused Pastor Johnson and a very weak Douglas such hysterics that the deepest abscess in Douglas's lung punctured, thus saving his life. See Ellinwood and Douglas, *To Praise God*, 14.

21. Gertrude House, a settlement house named for Pestalozzi's ideal woman, opened its doors in 1904. It was the headquarters for the Chicago Kindergarten Institute, and by 1910 it was also a boarding house for over sixty women training for social settlement work. Plainsong refers to a style of liturgical vocal music developed in Europe early in the first millennium.

22. Ellinwood and Douglas, *To Praise God*, 20.

23. Bridgham Curtis, "Memorial," 9.

24. Marwood, *The Wooing of a Recluse*, 110.

25. Natalie Curtis, "A New Type of Architecture in the Southwest," 334.

26. Guest book of Wheeler Bailey, April 28, 1913, collection of David N. Reynolds.

27. The Palomar incorporated the exotic North African architectural elements Mead loved—arches and balconies, inlaid tile, and plants and fountains in an oasis-like atrium enclosed and private from the street. Future residents of the Palomar Apartments included Wallis Warfield Simpson and Charles Lindbergh.

28. George DeClyver Curtis, Diary, July 18, 1913.

29. Ibid., various entries, July 1913. Natalie Curtis to Charles Lummis, December 1913, LC/BRL.

Chapter 6

Virginia Scharff, "Introduction: Women Envision the West," 5.

1. In 1870 the Nahant town officers—the town clerk, selectmen, assessors, and the town treasurer—were *all* Johnsons, and twenty-five of

eighty-seven households on the island were headed by someone named Johnson. See *Essex-Country History*.

2. In author interviews and correspondence with Caroline Bishop Stanley's living relatives and with individuals who knew her, there was no evidence that she ever mentioned to anyone that she was born a twin.

3. Programme, Graduating Exercises, Town of Nahant School Report, 1893–94, 16–17, NHS.

4. Offord, "The Foremost American School of Music."

5. New England Conservatory of Music's 1905 yearbook; author correspondence with Vicky R. Harrison, archivist, Alpha Chi Omega.

6. "Italian Count Elopes with Miss M. F. Johnson," *Lynn (MA) Daily Item*, January 7, 1907.

7. "Cardinal in Frederick," *Baltimore Sun*, November 18, 1906.

8. "Hannah More Academy Opens," *Baltimore Sun*, October 6, 1907.

9. *Lynn (MA) Daily Evening Item*, June 9, 1913.

10. See Natalie Curtis, "Value of Music School Settlements in Cities." Details of Carol Stanley in Boston ca. 1913 from interview with Harriet Cabot Ropes, MCW/MW.

Chapter 7

Willa Cather, *The Selected Letters*, 262.

1. See Heller and Rudnick, *1915*, 169.

2. Hutchins Hapgood quoted in Heller and Rudnick, *1915*, 69.

3. Rudnick, *Mabel Dodge Luhan*, 170.

4. Martin Green, "The New Art," in Heller and Rudnick, *1915*, 159. The name "Ashcan" referred to the "mildly squalid scenes" their art portrayed. See Robinson, *Georgia O'Keeffe*, 96.

5. The Eight were Henri, William Glackens, John Sloan, George Luks, and Everett Shinn, who had all been pupils of Henri's, plus Arthur B. Davies, Ernest Lawson, and Maurice Prendergast.

6. See Notebooks of Alice Klauber, "Bits of the Summer 1912," and "Robert Henri, Class in Spain."

7. Klauber, "Bits of the Summer 1912," June 22–26.

8. Henri, *The Art Spirit*, 15.

9. Klauber, "Robert Henri lectures," 22.

10. Henri, *The Art Spirit*, 16, 111.

11. Margery Ryerson's book written with Henri, the classic *The Art Spirit*, appeared in 1923 while Henri was still alive. Alice's transcriptions of Henri's lectures and notes, known among art history scholars as the Klauber

Manuscript, were published in their entirety in Bennard B. Perlman's *Robert Henri: His Life and Art.*

12. See Fowler, *A Laboratory for Anthropology*, 272; and Chapman and Barrie, *Kenneth Milton Chapman*, 87. "San Diego Exposition News," October 1912, quoted in Chauvenet, *Hewett and Friends*, 102.

13. Fowler, *A Laboratory for Anthropology*, 274.

14. Natalie Curtis to Alice Klauber, March 11, 1915, SDMA.

15. "New Mexico's Exhibit at San Diego in 1915," *El Palacio*, November 1913, 5.

16. Robert Henri to Alice Klauber, March 11, 1914, SDMA.

17. In the collection of SDMA.

18. Robert Henri to Edgar Hewett, October 25, 1914, SDMA.

19. Petersen, *San Diego's First Lady of the Arts*, 21, 32. Henri's California visit has been the subject of several articles. See Henri, "My People," *Craftsmen* 27 (February 1915), 459–69; Martin Petersen, "Henri's California Visit," *FASM Newsletter* 1 (February 1971); Petersen, "Modern Art Goes to California," *Southwest Art* 2 (September 1972); Jean Stern, "Robert Henri and the 1915 San Diego Exposition," *American Art Review* 2 (September–October 1975).

20. Trenton, *Independent Spirits*, 75.

Chapter 8

John Wetherill, quoted in Gillmor and Wetherill, *Traders to the Navajos*, 256.

1. Charles Winfred Douglas to Kurt Schindler, March 8, 1913. Details of the Douglas-Schindler relationship from correspondence, Charles Winfred Douglas to Kurt Schindler, 1913, KS/NYPL.

2. Diary of George DeClyver Curtis, September 21, 1913.

3. Charles Winfred Douglas to Kurt Schindler, March 8, July 22, and August 2, 1913, KS/NYPL.

4. Natalie Curtis Burlin, "Theodore Roosevelt in Hopi-land," 87. Natalie and Roosevelt must have corresponded about their Arizona itineraries because their individual accounts make reference to their rendezvous at Walpi as an anticipated and orchestrated event, including rooms reserved for their meeting at the government agency below Third Mesa.

5. The assassin's bullet was thwarted when it became lodged in the steel spectacle case Roosevelt carried in his right breast pocket. Following his near miss with death, Roosevelt roared the famous line "It takes more than that to kill a Bull Moose!"

6. Morris, *Colonel Roosevelt*, 267. In April 1913 Roosevelt's daughter Ethel was married at Christ Church in Oyster Bay. The ceremony was attended by Nahant resident Henry Cabot Lodge and by Roosevelt's old friend, and Carol Stanley's grandmother's cousin, the former ambassador to Great Britain Joseph Choate.

7. Mellow, *Charmed Circle*, 171; Morris, *Colonel Roosevelt*, 268.

8. Theodore Roosevelt, "Across the Navajo Desert," 309.

9. Charles Winfred Douglas to Kurt Schindler, July 22, and August 2, 1913, KS/NYPL.

10. Diary of Alice Klauber, August 10, 1913, SDMA.

11. Diary of Alice Klauber, August 13, 1913, SDMA.

12. Natalie Curtis Burlin, "Theodore Roosevelt in Hopi-land," 87.

13. Diary of Alice Klauber, August 12, 1913, SDMA.

14. See Froeschauer-Nelson, *Cultural Landscape Report*.

15. Ellinwood and Douglas, *To Praise God*, 20.

16. Diary of Alice Klauber, August 13 and August 18, 1913, SDMA.

17. Kirk owned two stores near the canyon. He would be bought out by George Kennedy in 1916. Kennedy's business would be bought in 1919 by "Cozy" McSparron and partners and become the trading post and dude ranch known as the Thunderbird Lodge.

18. Diary of Alice Klauber, August 14, 1913, SDMA.

19. Mummy Cave, named for the dozens of mummified skeletons found here by archaeologists, was the site of a massacre of the Navajos by the Spanish in 1804.

20. Natalie Curtis Burlin, "Theodore Roosevelt in Hopi-land," 87.

Chapter 9

Zane Grey, foreword, *The Rainbow Trail*.

1. James, *Pages from Hopi History*, 165, 169.

2. Diary of Alice Klauber, "Arizona Trip Summer 1913," August 18–19, 1913.

3. This quotation and the following quotations in the next several paragraphs are from Natalie Curtis Burlin, "Theodore Roosevelt in Hopi-land," 87–88.

4. Morris, *Colonel Roosevelt*, 199.

5. N. C. Burlin, "Theodore Roosevelt in Hopi-land," 88.

6. Theodore Roosevelt, "Across the Navajo Desert," 316.

7. N. C. Burlin, "Theodore Roosevelt in Hopi-land," 87–88.

8. Nicholas Roosevelt Diary, August 22, 1913, AC 194-p, Fray Angélico Chávez History Library, New Mexico History Museum, Santa Fe, New Mexico.

9. N. C. Burlin, "Theodore Roosevelt in Hopi-land," 88.

10. T. Roosevelt, "The Hopi Snake Dance," 366.

11. Ibid., 367. Douglas was referring to his extended time among the Hopi in the first years of the century when he had spent six months in the Southwest outback.

12. All excerpts from Diary of Nicholas Roosevelt, August 22, 1913.

13. T. Roosevelt, "The Hopi Snake Dance," 368–69.

14. Diary of Nicholas Roosevelt, August 22, 1913.

15. N. C. Burlin, "Theodore Roosevelt in Hopi-land," 88.

16. Ibid., 88–89. Roosevelt wrote three articles for *Outlook* about his six weeks in Arizona. "Across the Navajo Desert" was the second of the series.

17. Diary of Nicholas Roosevelt, August 22, 1913.

18. Petersen, *San Diego's First Lady of the Arts*, 13.

19. Diary of Nicholas Roosevelt, August 22, 1913.

20. N. C. Burlin, "Theodore Roosevelt in Hopi-land," 89.

21. Diary of Nicholas Roosevelt, August 22, 1913.

22. Natalie wrote that the brief introduction to Hopi culture helped prepare the crowd for the astonishing ceremony they witnessed that day. Nicholas Roosevelt, however, was appalled by her suggestion that Roosevelt be involved and blamed what he saw as Natalie's poor judgment on Douglas's influence. See Natalie's "Theodore Roosevelt in Hopi-land," and Diary of Nicholas Roosevelt, August 22, 1913.

23. The Snake Dance is the grand finale of Hopi ceremonies that pray for rain. The Hopis believe their ancestors originated in an underworld, and that their gods and the spirits of their ancestors live there. Snakes are their brothers, and the Hopis believe that snakes will carry their prayers for rain to the Rainmakers beneath the earth. Thus the dancers carry snakes in their mouths to impart prayers to them.

24. Petersen, *San Diego's First Lady of the Arts*, 13.

25. Alice did not record her Hopi name or its translation. Natalie referenced the name and addressed Alice's Christmas cards in 1913 and 1914 to "My dear friend Koiyahoinim" or Koyahoynim. Alice Klauber archive, SDMA.

26. Alice Klauber, "Arizona Trip Summer 1913," August 26, 1913; Ellinwood and Douglas, *To Praise God*, 21.

27. Douglas's obituary in *The Explorers Journal*, Spring 1945, stated, "He located the ancient trail leading up the Enchanted Mesa near the pueblo of Acoma and he was the first to describe the flute altar at Shimgopavi."

28. Alice Klauber, "Arizona Trip Summer 1913," September 4, 1913.

29. Diary of George DeClyver Curtis, September 16 and 23, 1913.

30. T. Roosevelt, "The Hopi Snake Dance," 365, 367–68.

Chapter 10

Willa Cather, *The Song of the Lark*, 278.

1. Milne, *George William Curtis & the Genteel Tradition*, 188.

2. See Pack, *We Called It Ghost Ranch*, 23; Poling-Kempes, *Ghost Ranch*, 19.

3. Bernheimer, *Rainbow Bridge*, 44; T. Roosevelt, "Across the Navajo Desert," 314.

4. T. Roosevelt, "Across the Navajo Desert," 316.

5. Bernheimer, *Rainbow Bridge*, 29.

6. Hegemann, *Navaho Trading Days*, 228, 239.

7. Roosevelt, "Across the Navajo Desert," 311.

8. Hegemann, *Navaho Trading Days*, 224.

9. Gillmor and Wetherill, *Traders to the Navajos*, 34. Details about Kidder's early career are from Chapman and Barrie, *Kenneth Milton Chapman*, 62–64.

10. Gillmor and Wetherill, *Traders to the Navajos*, 219.

11. Diary of Louisa Wetherill, June 26–July 8, 1915.

12. Several years after his acquittal and return to his father's tribe, young Tse-ne-gat died of tuberculosis. See Frank Pyle, "The Uprising of Polk and Posey in 1915," in Berkholz, *Old Trading Posts of the Four Corners*, 21–22; and Gillmor and Wetherill, *Traders to the Navajos*, 211–16.

Chapter 11

Alice Corbin, "Pedro Montoya of Arroyo Hondo," *Red Earth*, 43.

1. *Santa Fe New Mexican*, January 17, 1916, in La Farge, *Santa Fe*, 222.

2. *Santa Fe New Mexican*, July 8, 1916.

3. Ibid., April 11, 1916.

4. *Chicago Daily Tribune*, October 31 and November 1, 1915.

5. Bridgham Curtis, "Memorial," 9.

6. Patterson, *Natalie Curtis Burlin*, 269.

7. Natalie Curtis, "Busoni's Indian Fantasy," 538. See also Bredenberg, "Natalie Curtis Burlin," 7.

8. Weigle and Fiore, *Santa Fe and Taos*, 5–10.

9. Tobias and Woodhouse, *Santa Fe*, 53.

10. Weigle and Fiore, *Sante Fe and Taos*, 10.

11. Henderson, "Early Impressions of Santa Fe, 1916–1934," ACH/HRC.

12. Alice Corbin quoted in Hildegard Hawthorne, "The Literary Digest International Book Review, 1916," ACH/HRC.

13. E. Lewis, *Willa Cather Living*, 95–96.

14. Ina Sizer Cassidy quoted by Robertson and Nestor, *Artists of the Canyons and Caminos*, 31.

15. Ibid., 48.

16. Rothman, *On Rims and Ridges*, 138.

17. Richard Leroy Pfäffle was called by various names in his lifetime, including Richard, Dick, and Roy. Except where the name is quoted otherwise, he is Roy throughout this text.

18. Jack Lambert to Peggy Pond Church, January 3, 1980, LAHM/PPC.

19. Diary of George DeClyver Curtis, April 19, 1916.

20. Ibid., May 20–23, 1916.

21. Ibid., May 27, 1916.

22. Ibid., May 29, May 30, 1916.

23. Natalie Curtis to Roy D. Chapin, July 14, 1916, LAHM/PPC.

24. Long, *Roy D. Chapin*, xix; Roy D. Chapin to Natalie Curtis, July 7, 1916, LAHM/PPC.

25. Natalie Curtis to Roy Chapin, July 5, 1916, LAHM/PPC.

26. Carol Stanley to Roy D. Chapin, August 7, 1916, LAHM/PPC.

27. Natalie Curtis to Roy D. Chapin, September 1916; Roy D. Chapin to Ashley Pond, August 23, 1916, LAHM/PPC.

28. Natalie Curtis to Roy Chapin, July 14, 1916; Roy D. Chapin to Natalie Curtis, July 20, 1916, LAHM/PPC.

29. Roy D. Chapin to partners, August 22, 1916, LAHM/PPC.

30. Ashley Pond's daughter, Peggy Pond Church, became a highly respected poet and writer who researched the relationship between her father and the Detroit partners. See Peggy Pond Church to Francesca, May 7, 1979, LAHM/PPC. With the exception of Roy Chapin, who visited the Ramon Vigil Ranch and later sent his son, Roy Jr., to Ashley Pond's Los Alamos Ranch School in 1929, the Detroit partners were woefully ignorant about their ranch's natural resources, climate, cultural context, and remote location, and thus about how these factors were as responsible for the failure of the Pajarito Club as Pond's business ineptitude. Peggy Pond Church believed the "scheme of those two women [Carol Stanley and Natalie Curtis] to form a cultural Indian art center was even more hair-brained" than any of her father's ideas (ibid.). During World War II the Pajarito Club was seized by the U.S. government for the Manhattan Project. The headquarters area became a fenced and guarded "radioactivity site" and later a facility for remotely controlled critical assemblies. The main lodge was torn down, but the log house built by Pond in 1915 was still standing in 1979. See Peggy Pond Church to Francesca, May 7 and 21, 1979, LAHM/PPC. For the complete story of Peggy Pond Church and her family at Los Alamos, see Sharon Snyder, *At Home on the Slopes of Mountains*.

Chapter 12

Marjorie Lambert quoted in Chapman and Barrie, *Kenneth Milton Chapman*, 69.

1. See Traugott, *The Art of New Mexico*.
2. Alice visited Santa Fe in March 1915, but her diary did not record the details of this trip. Diary of Alice Klauber, August 12, 1916, SDMA.
3. Carol Stanley to Roy Chapin, August 7, 1916, LAHM/PPC.
4. McCarthy, *Walter Pach (1883–1958)*, 80, 81.
5. Diary of Alice Klauber, August 14, 1916, SDMA.
6. Crescensio and his brother Julian Martinez would exhibit their paintings in New York and, with artists Fred Kabotie, Awa Tsireh, and others, set style precedents that would dominate Indian painting for fifty years. See Chapman and Barrie, *Kenneth Milton Chapman*, 177.
7. Diary of Alice Klauber, August 16, 1916, SDMA.
8. Marjorie Lambert quoted in Chapman and Barrie, *Kenneth Milton Chapman*, 69.
9. Ibid.
10. Diary of Alice Klauber, August 23–26, 1916, SDMA.
11. Rainbow Bridge Registry, 1916, WACC/NPS.
12. *Santa Fe New Mexican*, October 5, 1916; Journals of C. W. Douglas, July, 1921, 10, CWD/DMA.
13. Carol Stanley to Roy D. Chapin, August 22, 1916, LAHM/PPC.
14. Peterson, *Alice Klauber*, 27.
15. Udall, *Modernist Painting in New Mexico*, 20.
16. Diary of Alice Klauber, September 4, 1916, SDMA.
17. Natalie Curtis to Roy Chapin, September 19, 1916, LAHM/PPC; *Santa Fe New Mexican*, "Personals," Tuesday, September 26, 1916.
18. Natalie Curtis to Roy Chapin, September 19, 1916, LAHM/PPC.
19. *Santa Fe New Mexican*, "Personals," September 13, 1916.
20. *Santa Fe New Mexican*, October 23, 1916.
21. Details of the Pfäffles' trip to Kayenta and Rainbow Bridge in ibid.

Chapter 13

Alice Corbin, "A Litany in the Desert," in Powell, *The Spirit of Democracy*, 27.

1. Annual Report of the School of American Research, 1918, quoted in Lewis and Hagan, *A Peculiar Alchemy*, 24.
2. Udall, *Modernist Painters in New Mexico*, 28.

3. *Santa Fe New Mexican*, January 13, 1917.

4. *Avoca News*, September 29, 1907.

5. Udall, *Modernist Painters in New Mexico*, 26; Patterson, *Natalie Curtis Burlin*, 282.

6. Augusta Curtis to George DeClyver Curtis, August 18, 1917, NCBA.

7. Diary of George DeClyver Curtis, March 2, 1917, UCLA.

8. Natalie Curtis to Aunt Natalie, May 27, 1917, NCBA; "after first youth" is from Sergeant, *Willa Cather*, 150.

9. Natalie Curtis to Aunt Natalie, May 27, 1917, NCBA.

10. Robert Henri to Alice Klauber, June 18, 1917, SDMA.

11. Ibid., August 2, 1917, SDMA.

12. Ibid., June 18, 1917, SDMA.

13. Ibid., August 2, 1917, SDMA.

14. Simmons, *Charles. F. Lummis, Author and Adventurer*, 34; Charles Lummis to Natalie Curtis Burlin, August 2, 1917, LC/BRL.

15. Augusta Curtis to George DeClyver Curtis, August 18, 1917, NCBA.

16. Faunce, *Desert Wife*, 242, 278.

17. Carol Pfäffle to Roy Chapin, December 13, 1917, LAHM/PPC.

18. Carol Pfäffle to Roy Chapin, November 30, 1917, LAHM/PPC.

19. *Santa Fe New Mexican*, November 26, 1917.

20. Robertson and Nestor, *Artists of the Canyons and Caminos*, 55.

21. Chauvenet, *Hewett and Friends*, 128.

22. Diary of George DeClyver Curtis, September 8, 1917, UCLA.

23. Robert Henri to Alice Klauber, September 22, 1917, and October 9, 1917, SDMA.

24. Robert Henri quoted in Robertson and Nestor, *Artists of the Canyons and Caminos*, 53.

25. *Santa Fe New Mexican*, November 26, 1917.

26. LC/BRL.

Chapter 14

Mabel Dodge Luhan, *Edge of Taos Desert*, 17.

1. Luhan, *Edge of Taos Desert*, 19–20.

2. Ibid., 22.

3. Ibid., 22–23.

4. Ibid., 3.

5. Udall, *Modernist Painters in New Mexico*, 34, 41.

6. Hartley, "Aesthetic Sincerity," 333.

7. Weigle and Fiore, *Santa Fe and Taos*, 13. Mary Austin's Santa Fe Little Theater, founded in 1922 (today the Santa Fe Playhouse), incorporated

the same open-door policy for amateurs and professional adopted by the Museum of Art a few blocks away on the plaza.

8. Cronyn, *The Path on the Rainbow*, xiii, xxii.

9. Peggy Pond Church, "Early Days," 2, LAHM/PPC.

10. Carol Pfäffle to Roy Chapin, March 6, 1918, LAHM/PPC; Diary of Margaret Pfäffle, December 15, 16, 17, 1917.

11. Diary of Margaret Pfäffle, January 24–31, February 12, 22, March 28, April 23, May 4, 1918. Frederic "Eric" H. Douglas (born October 29, 1897) received a BA degree from the University of Colorado in 1921 and then did five years of graduate work in fine arts at the University of Michigan and the Pennsylvania Academy of Fine Arts. In 1929 he joined the Denver Art Museum as curator of Indian art and was director of the museum from 1940 to 1942. In 1947 Douglas became curator of the Department of Native Art, a position he held until his death in 1956. Douglas brought a new approach to the art of Native American peoples and was credited with single-handedly creating a new benchmark for Indian art in the contemporary art world. See "Frederic Douglas, His Story," Douglas Society newsletter, Denver Art Museum, October 2006.

12. Carol Pfäffle to Roy Chapin, February 26, 1918, LAHM/PPC.

13. See Jenkins and Thorpe, *From Retreat to Resort.*

14. Carol Pfaffle to Roy Chapin, February 26 and March 6, 1918, LAHM/PPC.

15. Jack Lambert biography from Peggy Pond Church Collection, undated notes, "Lambert & Pfäffle," LAHM/PPC; Love, "A Cowboy Recollects," *Santa Fean* magazine, December 1981; King, "Jack Lambert"; author interviews with Henry McKinley and Peggy Pack McKinley.

16. Diary of Margaret Pfäffle, July 26, October 2 and 3, December 16, 1918. Roy Chapin would serve as Hoover's secretary of commerce in 1932–33. In 1933 Chapin helped draft Franklin D. Roosevelt's automobile industry code for the National Industrial Recovery Act. Chapin's son Roy Jr., born in 1915, was the first of Chapin's six children and grew up to become the chairman and CEO of American Motors. See Long, *Roy D. Chapin.*

17. *Santa Fe New Mexican*, November 11, 1918; Diary of Margaret Pfäffle, November 11, 1918.

18. Sze, "The Witter Bynner House," 8.

19. Natalie Curtis Burlin to George Curtis, March 9, 1921, NCBA.

20. Robertson and Nestor, *Artists of the Canyons and Caminos*, 74.

21. Pach, "John Sloan," 3.

22. Robertson and Nestor, *Artists of the Canyons and Caminos*, 76.

23. Ibid., 78. The Davey's home on Upper Canyon Road became the Randall Davey Audubon Center in 1983.

24. Patterson, *Natalie Curtis Burlin*, 307.

25. Lois Pfäffle to Margaret Pfäffle, September 23, 1919.

26. Dairy of Lois Pfäffle, January 3, 20, 21, February 8, 20, March 5, 1920; Dorothy Kent to Rockwell Kent, January 13, 1919, RK/AAA.

27. Details of Pfäffle purchase from Pfäffle papers, Francis O. Wilson files, SRA. At least one of the ranch underwriters, Florence Dibell Bartlett of Chicago, began construction on her own summer house in 1922, on property leased from the Pfäffles. Pfäffle papers, Wilson files, SRA.

Chapter 15

Alice Corbin, "Sunlight," *Red Earth*, 40.

1. Natalie Curtis to Augusta Curtis, June 18, 20, 1921, NCBA.

2. Natalie Curtis Burlin to George Peabody, July 1, 1921, NCBA.

3. Natalie Curtis Burlin to friends, July 27, 1921, Peabody Papers, LOC.

4. Natalie Curtis Burlin to Augusta Curtis, July 4, 1921, NCBA.

5. Natalie Curtis Burlin, "A Futurist Experiment."

6. Natalie Curtis Burlin to friends, July 13, 1921, Peabody papers, LOC.

7. Leo Stein quoted in Rudnick, *Mabel Dodge Luhan*, 168.

8. Stein told Hemingway, "You are all a '*génération perdue*.'. . . That is what you are. That's what you all are . . . all of you young people who served in the war. You are a lost generation." See Hemingway, *A Moveable Feast*, 61.

9. Diary of Alice Klauber, September 11, 1921; Walter Pach to Alice Klauber, December 24, 1924, May 6, 1925, February 15, 1944, SDMA.

10. Diary of Alice Klauber, October 11, 1921, SDMA.

11. Natalie Curtis Burlin to friends, October 16, 1921, NCBA.

12. Tappert, *Out of the Background*.

13. Natalie Curtis Burlin to Peabody and friends, October 16, 1921, NCBA.

14. Ibid.

15. Diary of Alice Klauber, October 3, 1921, SDMA.

16. Hemingway, *A Moveable Feast*, 15.

17. Diary of Alice Klauber, October 24, 1921, SDMA.

18. Diary of George DeClyver Curtis, October 26, 1921.

19. Diary of Alice Klauber, October 24, 1921, SDMA.

20. Alice Klauber to Augusta Curtis, October 24, 1921, NCBA.

21. Details of the memorial service and procession from Diary of Alice Klauber, October 29, 31, 1921, SDMA; Paul Burlin to Augusta Curtis, November 2, 1921, NCBA.

22. George DeClyver Curtis to Bridgham Curtis, October 29, 30, 1921, NCBA; Diary of George DeClyver Curtis, October 30, 1921.

23. Augusta Curtis to George Curtis, October 27, 1921, NCBA.
24. Paul Burlin to Augusta Curtis, November 2, 1921, NCBA.
25. Diary of Alice Klauber, November 17, 1921, SDMA.
26. George DeClyver Curtis, "Natalie Curtis Burlin."
27. Natalie Curtis Burlin, "Theodore Roosevelt in Hopi-land," 87.

Chapter 16

Mabel Dodge Luhan, "Taos and Individualism."
  1. Douglas, Journals, July–August 1921, 33, 36. Richard Leroy Pfäffle reached Rainbow Bridge at least four times between 1916 and 1923, including twice in 1918 (May and August). Because the registry at the bridge was lost or stolen several times after it was started in 1909, and many years are missing, it is impossible to say how many trips Roy, or Carol, made to the bridge. On July 10, 1921, John Wetherill wrote in the registry, "Every trip I see new beauties. It improves on acquaintance." Roy, Winfred and Eric Douglas, and Albert Smith's signatures follow Wetherill's on July 29, 1921. It was Smith's second trek to the bridge in two weeks. Rainbow Bridge Registry transcribed by Harvey Leake.
  2. Carol Pfäffle to Elbridge Adams, December 16, 1921, NCBA.
  3. Paul Burlin to Augusta Curtis, November 2, 1921, NCBA.
  4. Bynner, "Alice and I," 36; Rudnick, *Mabel Dodge Luhan*, 243; Bynner, "A City of Change," 45–46.
  5. Witter Bynner to Alice Long, in Sze, "The Witter Bynner House," 8, 14.
  6. Dietrich, *New Mexico Recollections*. Dietrich's properties in Santa Fe included several historic homes on Canyon Road including El Zaguan (the Johnson house), the Borrego House, and the Juan Jose Prada House, where Dietrich made her home.
  7. Witter Bynner quoted in Museum of New Mexico, *Window on the West*, 191.
  8. Sze, "The Witter Bynner House," 4–5.
  9. D. H. Lawrence, *New Mexico*, quoted in Hillerman, *The Spell of New Mexico*, 30–31.
  10. *Santa Fe New Mexican*, May 3, 1922.
  11. Klauber, "In Hospital," *Poems*.
  12. Inside back cover, Diary of Alice Klauber, 1923, SDHC.
  13. Alice Klauber, untitled, *Poems*.
  14. Carol Pfäffle to Elbridge Adams, December 16, 1921; copied by Augusta Curtis for George D. Curtis, December 13, 1922, NCBA.
  15. Parsons, *Social Organization of the Tewa*, 32.

16. Pfäffle lease agreements, April and September 1926, Francis Wilson papers, SRA. The address is given as both 537 #2 and 547 Canyon Road.

17. Robertson and Nestor, *Artists of the Canyons and Caminos*, vii, 106; Ina Sizer Cassidy, *Santa Fe New Mexican*, October 29, 1921. In 1924 Will Shuster created the giant puppet effigy Zozobra, Old Man Gloom, burned each year at the Santa Fe Fiesta.

18. See Mullin, *Culture in the Marketplace*, 61.

19. Sergeant, *Shadow-Shapes*, 205.

20. Sergeant, "Journal of a Mud House, IV," 61.

21. Sergeant, "Journal of a Mud House, III," 778.

22. In 1922 Harry P. Mera's simple Zia sun symbol, based on the historic design motif found on local ceramics, won the competition for the New Mexico state flag.

23. Chapman and Barrie, *Kenneth Milton Chapman*, 333.

Chapter 17

Elsie Clews Parsons, *Social Rule*, 55.

1. Maud Cabot Morgan, July 22, 1985, tape transcription, 1, MCW/WM. Mary's mother, Sarah Perkins Cabot Wheelwright, was related to Thomas Handyside Perkins, the prominent Boston businessman who built the first resort hotel on Nahant island in 1823.

2. Ibid.; Wheelwright, "Journey Towards Understanding," 2.

3. Wheelwright, "Journey Towards Understanding," 8.

4. Wheelwright, tape transcription, July 2003, reel 1, 12, 13, MCW/WM.

5. Ibid., 13.

6. Newcomb, *Hosteen Klah*, 157–58.

7. Wheelwright, "Journey Towards Understanding," 7.

8. Wheelwright, tape transcription, July 2003, reel 1, 7–8, MCW/WM.

9. Wheelwright, "Journey Towards Understanding," 17; Wheelwright, tape transcription, July 2003, reel 1, 8, MCW/WM. Franc Newcomb recounts Mary Wheelwright's first visit to Nava differently and wrote that the San Gabriel group, guided by Cox, arrived on horseback. Cox never went on horse expeditions, and only went into the outback as an automobile driver and guide. Wheelwright's version was given in a taped interview and repeated in her unpublished memoir, "Journey Towards Understanding." See Newcomb, *Hosteen Klah*, 159–60.

10. Wheelwright, "Journey Towards Understanding," 18, 19. Family historians claim that when Mary was a very young child her father had tied her to the mast of his boat to force her to overcome her fear of water. She

did and she became a confident sailor and competent navigator—unusual for a woman of her time—and was known to urge captains into rough water. See interview with Mrs. W. Rodman "Gertrude" Fay (daughter of the founder of the Schirmer Music Co.), Northeast Harbor, Maine, August 1, 1985, MCW/WM.

11. Newcomb, "Symbols in Sand," 2.

12. Klah's apprentice, his nephew Beyal (or Beaal) Begay, died in 1931. Klah knew that he did not have enough time and energy to begin the training with another apprentice. See McGreevy, "Why Navajo Studies?"

13. In her memoir, Mary dismissed references to Klah being a transvestite. See "Journey Towards Understanding," 23; Newcomb, *Hosteen Klah*, 97.

14. Wheelwright, "Journey Towards Understanding," 31, 53, 68.

15. Ibid., 14. Matthews's notebooks of medicinal plants, diaries of ceremonies attended, and files were moved from the University of California, Berkeley, to the Wheelwright Museum in 1951.

16. Wheelwright, "Journey Towards Understanding," 9.

17. King, "Jack Lambert."

18. Wheelwright, "Journcy Towards Understanding," 42.

19. Grey, *Tales of Lonely Trails*, 16–17.

20. Rainbow Bridge Registry, May 8, 1923, NPS.

21. Wheelwright, "Journey Towards Understanding," 5.

22. Phillip Blood, interview with author, April 2012; Church, "notes," LAHM/PPC. Several years between 1909 and 1925 are missing from the Rainbow Bridge Registry held in the National Park Service collection. Not everyone who visited the bridge signed in, and John Wetherill often later recorded names based on his recollections. Harvey Leake to author.

23. Boas, "Elsie Clews Parsons," 480; Lavender, *Scientists and Storytellers*, 51.

24. Parsons, *The Old-Fashioned Woman*, 50.

25. Parsons, *Tewa Tales*, ix.

26. Lavender, *Scientists and Storytellers*, 55. Parsons donated thousands of dollars to the society and aided the work of Ruth Benedict, Franz Boas, Ruth Bunzel, Esther Goldfrank, Morris Opler, Gladys Reichard, Ruth Underhill, and many others.

27. Robert Herrick wrote two novels, *Chimes* (1926) and *The End of Desire* (1932), based on his relationship with Elsie Clews Parsons. See Deacon, *Elsie Clews Parsons*, 279.

28. Parsons, *Social Organization of the Tewa*, 7.

29. Elsie Clews Parsons to Herbert Parsons, November 17, December 4, 1923, quoted in Deacon, *Elsie Clews Parsons*, 286.

30. Elsie Clews Parsons, quoted by Gladys Reichard, in Lavender, *Scientists and Storytellers*, 68.

31. Elsie (Lissa) Parsons Kennedy, in Lavender, *Scientists and Storytellers*, 67.

32. Elsie Clews Parsons to Lissa, November 25, 1925, in Deacon, *Elsie Clews Parsons*, 300.

33. Diary of Margaret Pfäffle, December 7, 1925–January 10, 1926.

Chapter 18

Virginia Scharff, "Introduction: Women Envision the West," 1.

1. *Grand Canyon MacLeans*, 8.

2. Willa Cather to Elizabeth Shepley Sergeant, June 23, 1925, and Willa Cather to Harriet Fox Whicher, October 16, 1925, in Cather, *Selected Letters*, 370–71, 374.

3. John D. Rockefeller III and his family rented Canjilon Camp for an entire month in the summer of 1930. See *Grand Canyon MacLeans*, 10.

4. Diary of Margaret Pfäffle, July 19, 1926.

5. Pen LaFarge, in Stark and Rayne, *El Delirio*, 106.

6. *Santa Fe New Mexican*, July 6, 1927.

7. Francis Wilson papers.

8. Love, "A Cowboy Recollects."

9. Richard Leroy Pfäffle, December 13, 1927, Lambert papers, Fray Angelico Chavez History Library.

10. King, "Jack Lambert."

11. Lois Lambert returned to New Mexico by 1930 or 1931 and managed the dining room run by the Fred Harvey Company at the Puye Cliff Dwellings at Santa Clara Pueblo. While working at Puye, Lois met a forest ranger named Tom Buchanan, whom she married and lived with near Santa Fe the rest of her life.

12. *Grand Canyon MacLeans*, 8.

13. The American Southwest, especially the Spanish-speaking region of New Mexico, was still an untamed frontier to the folks around Nahant. In the minds of the attorneys in Lynn, Mass., who were assembling the legal documents for sale of the Johnson property on Nahant, they were managing an international real estate deal because Carol Bishop Stanley had moved to a foreign country. In a letter to Francis Wilson, Esq., Joseph D. A. Healey, Esq., suggested that Carol Pfäffle needed to travel to the nearest American consul to sign papers before a notary public. Wilson responded to Healey via Healey's real estate partner Fred A. Wilson (no relation) that Mrs. Pfäffle

wanted it known that the nearest American consul was in Juarez, Old Mexico, a distance greater than from Lynn to New York City. Wilson went on to explain to Mr. Healey that New Mexico had been admitted to the Union in 1912, and that Santa Fe had been settled by Europeans "about twelve years before the Pilgrims set foot on Plymouth Rock." Before closing, Wilson mentioned that he himself had been born and raised in Massachusetts, and had "spent four years in the shade of the old elms in the Harvard yard." Francis C. Wilson to Fred A. Wilson, December 23, 1919, SRA.

14. Francis Wilson papers, Pfäffle files, various correspondence from 1929 to 1930.

15. Francis Wilson papers, Mary Cabot Wheelwright files, Pfäffle files, SRA; Dorthy Fredericks to author.

16. Mary Cabot Wheelwright to Francis Wilson, June 19, 1931, MCW/WM.

17. Willa Cather to Elizabeth Shepley Sergeant, August 14, 1912, *Selected Letters*, 166.

Chapter 19

Willa Cather, *Selected Letters*, 209.

1. Harriet Ropes Cabot interview, MCW/WM.

2. The Night Riders terrorized Rio Arriba County in the 1920s, stealing cattle, burning barns, and robbing private homes, including Mary Wheelwright's. One of gang's leaders, Big Bill McKinley, was the older brother of the three McKinleys who worked for Carol at San Gabriel and Ghost Ranch. Big Bill, convicted as the leader of the notorious gang, was pursued and finally apprehended by a private detective, Bill Martin, after the Night Riders' sensational burglary of Wheelwright's valuable Navajo rugs collection kept at Los Luceros. See Poling-Kempes, *Ghost Ranch*, 45.

3. Carol Stanley Accounts Ledger, 1928–1935, Peabody family collection.

4. Bennett, "Reminiscences from the Thirties"; Joe Fitzgibbon and Dorthy Fredericks to author.

5. Pack, *We Called it Ghost Ranch*, 21.

6. Ibid., 23.

7. Pack was a childhood friend of John D. Rockefeller, and took John D.'s college-aged son, Laurence, on at least one Canadian expedition. Pack may have introduced the Rockefellers to the Pfäffles and their Canjilon Camp, where the Rockefellers spent a month in 1930.

8. The John Bartol family included Charlotte Cabot Bartol, Lucy Cabot, and Harriet Ropes Cabot. Harriet Ropes Cabot interview, MCW/WM. On Fred Harvey family at Ghost Ranch, Ed Groesbeck to author.

9. Edward H. Bennett Jr. and Dorthy Fredericks to author.

10. O'Keeffe, quoted in Tryk, "O'Keeffe," 20; Francis C. Wilson correspondence to Mrs. Garland, March 4, 1931, regarding land transactions 1927–28, Francis C. Wilson papers.

11. Georgia O'Keeffe to Rebecca Strand [James], April 26, 1934, in Cowart, Hamilton, and Greenough, *Georgia O'Keeffe*, 221.

12. Georgia O'Keeffe to Alfred Stieglitz, September 20, 1937, in O'Keeffe, *Catalogue of the 14th Annual Exhibition*, 10.

13. Georgia O'Keeffe quoted in Tryk, "O'Keeffe," 25.

14. Georgia O'Keeffe quoted in Wallach, "Georgia O'Keeffe."

15. Georgia O'Keeffe quoted in Tryk, "O'Keeffe," 20. In 1940 O'Keeffe purchased Rancho de los Burros from Arthur Pack.

16. Francis I. Proctor quoted in Stark and Rayne, *El Delirio*, 99.

17. Alice Corbin to Amelia White, November 1930, quoted in ibid., 99.

18. AP story, March 3, 1937, quoted in Newcomb, *Hosteen Klah*, 211, 214.

19. Bennett, "Reminiscences from the Thirties."

20. Dorthy Fredericks to author; Carol Stanley Account Book, Peabody family collection.

21. Harriet Ropes Cabot interview, MCW/WM.

22. Wetherill Guest Registry, October 14 and 19, 1935, Harvey Leake collection. The Coltons founded the Museum of Northern Arizona, and were in Kayenta with the museum's curator, Katharine Bartlett.

23. Dick (Roy) Pfäffle to Lois and Tom Buchanan, November 7, 1955, Peg Terrell and Patricia Hibbard collection.

Afterword

Alice Corbin, "Untitled," *Red Earth*, 3.

1. From *The Sun Dial*, quoted in Petersen, *San Diego's First Lady of the Arts*, 44.

2. Among Alice's donations to the Museum of Art were the cowboy sketches and drawings given to her long ago by a young, handsome, and unknown artist named Arthur Putnam. See Petersen, *San Diego's First Lady of the Arts*, 23. Surgery to remove a brain tumor in 1911 had left Putnam partially paralyzed and unable to sculpt. He died in 1930 at the age of forty-seven, but he enjoyed success as an animal sculptor in the first decade of the twentieth century. The face of one of Putnam's sculptures, *The Mermaid*, bore an uncanny resemblance to Alice, or so his wife, Grace, told Alice in a letter. In 1903 a commission of five large bronze sculptures for the San Diego estate of E. W. Scrips introduced Putnam to the writer Jack London, who

became a close friend. Among Putnam's best-known pieces is the Jack London Writing Tablet carved from California Redwood. When London died in 1916, he owned the tablet, which features Old Buck from *Call of the Wild*. The tablet was lost from 1917 until 2003 and is today considered a California treasure. See tablet owner Christian Chaffee's website, jacklondontablet .com, and *National Geographic*'s *America's Lost Treasures* series website.

3. Petersen, *San Diego's First Lady of the Arts*, 25.

4. Klauber, "Untitled," *Poems*.

5. Marjorie Lambert interview, March 3, 1985, MCW/WM.

6. Aimee and Rosamond Lamb interview, July 21, 1985, MCW/WM.

7. Comments from Memorial Service, MCW/WM.

SELECTED BIBLIOGRAPHY

Adams, Ansel, and Mary Austin. *Taos Pueblo*. Grabhorn Press, 1930.

Babcock, Barbara A., and Nancy J. Parezo. *Daughters of the Desert: Women Anthropologists and the Native American Southwest, 1880–1980*. University of New Mexico Press, 1988.

Bennett, Edward H., Jr. "Reminiscences from the Thirties." GRA.

Berkholz, Richard C. *Old Trading Posts of the Four Corners*. Western Reflections Publishing Company, 2007.

Bernheimer, Charles L. *Rainbow Bridge: Circling Navajo Mountain and Explorations in the "Badlands" of Southern Utah and Northern Arizona*. Center for Anthropological Studies, 1999.

Boas, Franz. "Elsie Clews Parsons, Late President of the American Anthropological Association." *Scientific Monthly* 54, May 1942.

Bredenberg, Alfred R. "Natalie Curtis Burlin: A Pioneer in the Study of American Minority Cultures." *Connecticut Review*, Spring 1991.

Burlin, Natalie Curtis [see also Natalie Curtis]. "A Futurist Experiment." *Freeman* 5, July 5, 1922.

———. "Letter to friends." July 13, 1921. George Foster Peabody papers, Library of Congress.

———. "Theodore Roosevelt in Hopi-land: Another Personal Reminiscence." *Outlook* 105, September 17, 1919.

Burlin, Paul. Letter to Augusta Curtis, November 2, 1921. NCBA.

Bynner, Witter. "Alice and I." *New Mexico Quarterly Review* 19, Spring 1949.

———. "A City of Change." *Laughing Horse* 11, September 1914.

Cather, Willa. "The Bohemian Girl." *McClure's Magazine* 39, 1912.

———. *The Selected Letters of Willa Cather*. Edited by Andrew Jewell and Janis Stout. Knopf, 2013.

———. *The Song of the Lark*. Signet Classic, 1991.

Chapman, Janet, and Karen Barrie. *Kenneth Milton Chapman: A Life Dedicated to the Indian Arts and Artists*. University of New Mexico Press, 2008.

Chauvenet, Beatrice. *Hewett and Friends: A Biography of Santa Fe's Vibrant Era*. Museum of New Mexico Press, 1982.

Church, Peggy Pond. "Early Days." LAHM/PPC.

———. "Lambert & Pfäffle." LAHM/PPC.

———. Various papers and letters. LAHM/PPC.

Clements, William M. *Native American Verbal Art: Text and Context*. University of Arizona Press, 1996.

Corbin, Alice. "Early Impressions of Santa Fe, 1916–1934." ACH/HRC.

———. "A Litany in the Desert." *Yale Review* 7, no. 3 (April 1918): 612.

———. *Red Earth: Poems of New Mexico*. Ralph Fletcher Seymour, 1920.

Cowart, Jack, Juan Hamilton, and Sarah Greenough. *Georgia O'Keeffe: Art and Letters*. National Gallery of Art, 1987.

Cronyn, G. W., ed. *The Path on the Rainbow: An Anthology of Songs and Chants from the Indians of North America*. Boni and Liveright, 1918.

Curtis, Augusta. Letter to George Curtis, October 27, 1921. NCBA.

Curtis, Bridgham. "Memorial." n.d. ACH/HRC.

Curtis, George DeClyver [Gregory Marwood, pseud.]. Diaries of George DeClyver Curtis. UCLA.

———. "In Memory of Natalie." n.d. NCBA.

———. Letter to Bridgham Curtis, October 29, 30, 1921. NCBA.

———. "Biography of Natalie Curtis Burlin." 1957. NCBA.

Curtis, Natalie [see also Natalie Curtis Burlin]. "An American Indian Composer." *Harper's Magazine* 107, September 1903.

———. "Busoni's Indian Fantasy." *Southern Workman* 44, 1915.

———. *The Indians' Book*. Dover Publications, 1968.

———. "Indian Song on a Desert Path." *Southern Workman* 33, June 1904.

———. "Mr. Roosevelt and Indian Music: A Personal Reminiscence." *Outlook* 121, March 5, 1919.

———. "A New Type of Architecture in the Southwest." *Craftsman* 25, January 1914.

———. "The Plight of the Mojave-Apache Indians." *Outlook* 129, September 7, 1921.

———. "Value of Music School Settlements in Cities." *Craftsman* 21, December 1911.

———. "A Western Reverie." *The Nation*, November 24, 1920.

———. "The Winning of an Indian Reservation." *Outlook* 122, June 25, 1919.

———. "The Words of Hiparopai: A Leaf from a Traveler's Diary." *Craftsman* 13, December 1907.

Deacon, Deasley. *Elsie Clews Parsons: Inventing Modern Life*. University of Chicago Press, 1999.

Dietrich, Margretta Stewart. *New Mexico Recollections*. Vergara Print Company, 1961.

Dinesen, Isak. *Seven Gothic Tales*. Vintage Books, 1972.

Douglas, Charles Winfred. Journals of C. W. Douglas. CWD/DMA.

Ellinwood, Leonard, and Anne Woodward Douglas. *To Praise God: The Life and Work of Charles Winfred Douglas*. Hymn Society of America, 1958.

Essex-Country History. Boston: C. A. & J. F. Wood, 1870.

Faunce, Hilda. *Desert Wife*. Bison Books, 1981.

Foote, Lorien. *Seeking the One Great Remedy: Francis George Shaw and Nineteenth-Century Reform*. Ohio University Press, 2003.

Fowler, Don D. *A Laboratory for Anthropology: Science and Romanticism in the American Southwest, 1846–1930*. University of New Mexico Press, 2000.

Froeschauer-Nelson, Peggy. *Cultural Landscape Report: Hubbell Trading Post National Historic Site, Ganado, Arizona*. U.S. Department of the Interior, 1998.

Gillmor, Frances, and Louisa Wade Wetherill. *Traders to the Navajos: The Wetherills of Kayenta*. University of New Mexico Press, 1979.

Grand Canyon MacLeans. No. 3, July 1996. Leonard and Millan, 1996.

Grey, Zane. *The Rainbow Trail*. Harper & Brothers, 1915.

———. *Tales of Lonely Trails*. Wildside Press, 2004

Hagan, William T. *Theodore Roosevelt & Six Friends of the Indian*. University of Oklahoma Press, 2002.

Hartley, Marsden. "Aesthetic Sincerity." *El Palacio*, December 2, 1918.

"Hawthorne, Hildegard. "The Literary Digest International Book Review, 1916." ACH/HRC.

Hegemann, Elizabeth Compton. *Navaho Trading Days*. University of New Mexico Press, 1987.

Heilbrun, Carolyn G. *Writing a Woman's Life*. W. W. Norton, 1988.

Heller, Adele, and Lois Rudnick, eds. *1915: The Cultural Moment, The New Politics, the New Woman, the New Psychology, the New Art, and the New Theater in America*. Rutgers University Press, 1991.

Hemingway, Ernest. *A Moveable Feast: The Restored Edition*. Scribner, 2010.

Henri, Robert. *The Art Spirit*. Compiled by Margery Ryerson. Westview Press, 1984.

Heyneman, Julie Helen. *Arthur Putnam, Sculptor*. Johnck and Seeger, 1932.

Hillerman, Tony. *The Spell of New Mexico*. University of New Mexico Press, 1984.

Hoard, Dorothy. *Historic Roads of Los Alamos*. Los Alamos Historical Society, 2009.

James, Harry C. *Pages from Hopi History.* University of Arizona Press, 1974.

Jenkins, Myra Ellen, and James R. Thorpe. *From Retreat to Resort: A History of Bishop's Lodge.* Bishop's Lodge Ranch and Resort, 2008.

Johnston, Bertha. "The Chicago Kindergarten Institute." *Kindergarten Magazine* 12, September 1899–June 1900.

Kelley, Klara Bonsack, and Harris Francis. *Navajo Sacred Places.* Indiana University Press. 1994.

Kent, Dorothy. Letter to Rockwell Kent, January 13, 1919. RK/AAA.

King, Mary Scott. "Jack Lambert: The Last of His Kind." *Santa Fe New Mexican.* February 17, 1974.

Klauber, Alice. "Arizona Trip Summer 1913." SDMA.

———. "Bits of the Summer 1912." SDMA.

———. Diaries, 1907–1924. SDMA.

———. *Poems.* Denrich Press, 1928.

———. "Robert Henri, Class in Spain." June 25, 1912. SDMA.

———. "Robert Henri lectures." SDMA.

La Farge, Oliver. *Santa Fe: The Autobiography of a Southwestern Town.* University of Oklahoma Press, 1959.

Laird, Carobeth. *Encounter with an Angry God: Recollections of My Life with John Peabody Harrington.* University of New Mexico Press, 1975.

Lavender, Catherine J. *Scientists and Storytellers: Feminist Anthropologists and the Construction of the American Southwest.* University of New Mexico Press, 2006.

Lewis, Edith. *Willa Cather Living: A Personal Record.* University of Nebraska Press, 2000.

Lewis, Nancy Owen, and Kay Leigh Hagan. *A Peculiar Alchemy: A Centennial History of SAR 1907–2007.* SAR Press, 2007.

Long, J. C., and Charles K. Hyde. *Roy D. Chapin: The Man Behind the Hudson Motor Company.* Wayne State University Press, 2004.

Love, Marian F. "A Cowboy Recollects." *Santa Fean,* December 1981.

Luhan, Mabel Dodge. *Edge of Taos Desert: An Escape to Reality.* University of New Mexico Press, 1993.

———. "Taos and Individualism, a Brief Résumé of an Environment." *New Mexico Quarterly* 21 (Summer 1951): 135–80.

Lummis, Charles F. *The Land of Poco Tiempo.* University of New Mexico Press, 1973.

Marwood, Gregory [George DeClyver Curtis]. *The Wooing of a Recluse.* Devin-Adair, 1914.

McCarthy, Laurette E. *Walter Pach (1883–1958): The Armory Show and the Untold Story of Modern Art in America.* Penn State University Press, 2012.

McGreevy, Susan. "Why Navajo Studies? The Example of Hastiin Klah and Mary Cabot Wheelwright." MCW/WM.

McPherson, Bruce. *Measure by Measure: A History of the New England Conservatory of Music since 1867*. The Trustees of the New England Conservatory of Music, 1995.

Mellow, James R. *Charmed Circle: Gertrude Stein & Company*. Praeger, 1974.

Milne, Gordon. *George William Curtis & the Genteel Tradition*. Indiana University Press, 1956.

Morris, Edmund. *Colonel Roosevelt*. Random House, 2010.

Mullin, Molly H. *Culture in the Marketplace: Gender, Art, and Value in the American Southwest*. Duke University Press, 2001.

Museum of New Mexico. *Window on the West: The Collector's El Palacio*. Museum of New Mexico Foundation, 1989.

Newcomb, Franc Johnson. *Hosteen Klah, Navajo Medicine Man and Sand Painter*. University of Oklahoma Press, 2012.

———. "Symbols in Sand." New Mexico Association on Indian Affairs, 1936.

Norwood, Vera, and Janice Monk, eds. *The Desert Is No Lady: Southwestern Landscapes in Women's Writing and Art*. Yale University Press, 1987.

Offord, John A. "The Foremost American School of Music—the New England Conservatory." *New York Observer*, August 2, 1906.

O'Keeffe, Georgia. *Catalogue of the 14th Annual Exhibition of Paintings, with some Recent O'Keeffe Letters: December 27–February 11, 1938*. An American Place, 1937.

Pach, Walter. Letters to Alice Klauber, December 24, 1924, May 6, 1925, February 15, 1944. Alice Klauber Collection, SDMA.

———. "John Sloan." *New Mexico Artists*. New Mexico Artists Series, no. 3. University of New Mexico Press, 1952.

Pack, Arthur Newton. *We Called It Ghost Ranch*. Ghost Ranch Conference Center, 1979.

Parsons, Elsie Worthington Clews. *The Old-Fashioned Woman: Primitive Fancies about the Sex*. G. P. Putnam's Sons, 1913.

———. *Social Organization of the Tewa*. American Anthropological Association, 1929.

———. *Social Rule: A Study of the Will to Power*. G. P. Putnam's Sons, 1916.

Patterson, Michelle Wick. *Natalie Curtis Burlin: A Life in Native and African American Music*. University of Nebraska Press, 2010.

Perlman, Bennard B. *Robert Henri: His Life and Art*. Dover Publications, 1991.

Petersen, Martin E. *San Diego's First Lady of the Arts: Alice Ellen Klauber & Friends*. SDMA.

Pfäffle, Carol Stanley. Correspondence with Augusta Curtis; Elbridge Adams. NCBA.

———. Correspondence with Roy Chapin. LAHM/PCC.

Pfäffle, Lois. Diaries and letters. Collection of Patricia Hibbard.

Pfäffle, Margaret. Diaries. Collection of Patricia Hibbard.

Pfäffle, Richard Leroy. Correspondence with Lois and Tom Buchanan, November 7, 1955. Collection of Patricia Hibbard.

Poling-Kempes, Lesley. *Ghost Ranch.* University of Arizona Press, 2005.

Powell, Gertrude Wilson. *The Spirit of Democracy.* Rand, McNally, 1918.

Rainbow Bridge Registry. Various years 1909–1926. National Park Service, and Collection of Harvey Leake/Wetherill family.

Robertson, Edna, and Sarah Nestor. *Artists of the Canyons and Caminos: Santa Fe, the Early Years.* Ancient City Press, 1996.

Robinson, Roxana. *Georgia O'Keeffe: A Life.* Harper Collins, 1989.

Roosevelt, Nicholas. Diary, July–August 1913. Nicholas Roosevelt Collection, Fray Angélico Chávez Historical Library, New Mexico History Museum, Santa Fe, New Mexico.

Roosevelt, Theodore. "Across the Navajo Desert: Prayer to the Dawn." *Outlook* 105, October 11, 1913.

———. "A Cougar Hunt on the Rim of the Grand Canyon." *Outlook* 105, October 4, 1913.

———. "The Hopi Snake Dance." *Outlook* 105, October 18, 1913.

Rothman, Hal K. *On Rims and Ridges: The Los Alamos Area since 1880.* University of Nebraska Press, 1997.

Rudnick, Lois Palken. *Mabel Dodge Luhan: New Woman, New Worlds.* University of New Mexico Press, 1987.

Scharff, Virginia. "Introduction: Women Envision the West: 1890–1945." In *Independent Spirits: Women Painters of the American West, 1890–1945,* edited by Patricia Trenton, 1–7. University of California Press, 1995.

———. *Twenty Thousand Roads: Women, Movement, and the West.* University of California Press, 2002.

Schindler, Kurt. Correspondence. KS/NYPL.

Sergeant, Elizabeth Shepley. "Earth Horizon." *The Nation,* June 29, 1927.

———. "The Journal of a Mud House." *Harper's Magazine,* March, April, May, June 1922.

———. *Shadow-Shapes: The Journal of a Wounded Woman, October 1918–May 1919.* Houghton Mifflin, 1920.

———. *Willa Cather: A Memoir.* Ohio University Press, 1992.

Simmons, Marc. *Charles. F. Lummis, Author and Adventurer.* Sunstone Press, 2008.

Snyder, Sharon. *At Home on the Slopes of Mountains: The Story of Peggy Pond Church*. Los Alamos Historical Society Publications, 2011.

Stark, Gregor, and E. Catherine Rayne. *El Delirio: The Santa Fe World of Elizabeth White*. SAR Press, 1998.

Starr, Kevin. *Inventing the Dream: California through the Progressive Era*. Oxford University Press, 1986.

Sze, Corinne P. "The Witter Bynner House." *Bulletin of the Historic Santa Fe Foundation* 20, no. 2 (September 1992).

Talayesva, Don C. *Sun Chief: The Autobiography of a Hopi Indian*. Edited by Leo W. Simmons. Yale University Press, 1963.

Tappert, Tara Leigh. *Out of the Background: Cecilia Beaux and the Art of Portraiture*. Traditional Fine Arts Organization, Inc., 2009.

Tobias, Henry J., and Charles E. Woodhouse. *Santa Fe: A Modern History, 1880–1990*. University of New Mexico Press, 2001.

Traugott, Joseph. *The Art of New Mexico: How the West Was One*. University of New Mexico Press, 2001.

Tryk, Sheila. "O'Keeffe." *New Mexico Magazine*, January–February 1973.

Udall, Sharyn Rohlfsen. *Modernist Painting in New Mexico, 1913–1935*. University of New Mexico Press, 1984.

Wallach, Amei. "Georgia O'Keeffe." *Newsday*, October 30, 1977.

Weigle, Marta, and Kyle Fiore. *Santa Fe and Taos: The Writer's Era, 1916–1941*. Ancient City Press, 1982.

Wetherill, Louisa Wade. Diary of Louisa Wetherill. Collection of Harvey Leake.

Wetherill Guest Registry. Collection of Harvey Leake.

Wheelwright, Mary Cabot. "Journey Towards Understanding." Unpublished manuscript, Wheelwright Museum of the American Indian.

Wilson, Francis O., Esq. Papers and correspondence. SRA.

Wineapple, Brenda. *Sister Brother: Gertrude and Leo Stein*. Putnam Adult, 1996.

ILLUSTRATION CREDITS

Figure 1.   Photograph by Charles C. Pierce. California Historical Society Collection at the University of Southern California. Title Insurance and Trust/C.C. Pierce Photography Collection, CHS-1426.

Figure 2.   Courtesy Natalie Curtis Burlin Archive.

Figure 3.   Photograph by John K. Hillers. Collection of the Smithsonian Institution, NARA record: 3028457.

Figure 4.   Courtesy Natalie Curtis Burlin Archive.

Figure 5.   San Diego Museum of Art Archives, Alice Klauber Collection.

Figure 6.   Archives of American Art, #4903.

Figure 7.   Gertrude Stein and Alice B. Toklas Papers, Yale Collection of American Literature. Beinecke Rare Book and Manuscript Library, Yale University.

Figure 8.   Rotograph Co.

Figure 9.   Nahant Historical Society.

Figure 10. *The Bay State Monthly*, vol. 2, December 1884.

Figure 11. *The Neume Yearbook*, 1905, New England Conservatory of Music.

Figure 12. Carol Stanley Collection.

Figure 13. San Diego Museum of Art Archives, Alice Klauber Collection.

Figure 14. San Diego Museum of Art Archives, Alice Klauber Collection.

Figure 15. Carleton Monroe Winslow, *The Architecture and Gardens of the San Diego Exposition* (San Francisco: Paul Elder and Company, 1916).

Figure 16. San Diego Museum of Art Archives, Alice Klauber Collection.

Figure 17. San Diego Museum of Art Archives, Alice Klauber Collection.

Figure 18. Photograph by Ben Wittick. NPS photo, HUTR Neg. RP-312.

Figure 19. Photograph by Timothy H. O'Sullivan. Library of Congress digital ID ppmsca.10057.

Figure 20. Photograph by John K. Hillers, National Archives and Records Administration, NARA record: 3028457.

Figure 21. Courtesy John and Louisa Wetherill Collection.

Figure 22. Theodore Roosevelt Collection, #560.8, Houghton Library, Harvard University.

Figure 23. San Diego Museum of Art Archives, Alice Klauber Collection.

Figure 24. Photograph by Emery Clifford Kolb. Northern Arizona University, Cline Library Emery Kolb Collection, NAU 98183 Kolb.

Figure 25. Still from the motion picture "Hopi Indians dance for TR at [Walpi, Ariz.] 1913." Library of Congress.

Figure 26. San Diego Museum of Art Archives, Alice Klauber Collection.

Figure 27. Photograph by George Wharton James. California Historical Society Collection, CHS-4624.

Figure 28. Courtesy John and Louisa Wetherill Collection.

Figure 29. Arizona State Museum, University of Arizona, Wetherill Collection.

Figure 30. Courtesy John and Louisa Wetherill Collection.

Figure 31. Carol Stanley Collection.

Figure 32. Photograph by T. Harmon Parkhurst. Courtesy Palace of the Governors Photo Archives (NMHM/DCA), #10786.

Figure 33. Courtesy Palace of the Governors Photo Archives (NMHM/DCA), #059757.

Figure 34. Jesse Nusbaum Collection, Courtesy Palace of the Governors Photo Archives (NMHM/DCA), #046554.

Figure 35. San Diego Museum of Art Archives, Alice Klauber Collection.

Figure 36. Courtesy Natalie Curtis Burlin Archive.

Figure 37. Carol Stanley Collection.

Figure 38. Carol Stanley Collection.

Figure 39. Carol Stanley Collection.

Figure 40. Courtesy Palace of the Governors Photo Archives
(NMHM/DCA), #006713.

Figure 41. Courtesy Natalie Curtis Burlin Archive.

Figure 42. Courtesy Palace of the Governors Photo Archives
(NMHM/DCA), #016755.

Figure 43. Courtesy Palace of the Governors Photo Archives
(NMHM/DCA), #014232.

Figure 44. Carol Stanley Collection.

Figure 45. Carol Stanley Collection.

Figure 46. Carol Stanley Collection.

Figure 47. Project Canterbury.

Figure 48. Carol Stanley Collection.

Figure 49. Courtesy Natalie Curtis Burlin Archive.

Figure 50. Carol Stanley Collection.

Figure 51. Collection of Patricia Hibbard.

Figure 52. Collection of the Wheelwright Museum of the American
Indian.

Figure 53. Courtesy Palace of the Governors Photo Archives
(NMHM/DCA), #132146.

Figure 54. Collection of the Wheelwright Museum of the American
Indian.

Figure 55. Photograph by Edward Kemp. Courtesy Palace of the
Governors Photo Archives (NMHM/DCA), #151372.

Figure 56. Collection of the American Philosophical Society.

Figure 57. Collection of Patricia Hibbard.

Figure 58. Collection of Patricia Hibbard.

Figure 59. Betty Bartlett Seals Collection, Ghost Ranch Archive.

Figure 60. Courtesy Palace of the Governors Photo Archives
(NMHM/DCA), #089626.

Figure 61. Courtesy Palace of the Governors Photo Archives
(NMHM/DCA), #89665.

Figure 62. Betty Bartlett Seals Collection, Ghost Ranch Archive.

Figure 63. John Candelario Collection, Courtesy Palace of the Governors Photo Archives (NMHM/DCA), #165666.

INDEX

Page numbers in *italics* represent illustrations.

ABOUT THE AUTHOR

Lesley Poling-Kempes is the award-winning author of six books about the American Southwest. Her novel *Bone Horses* won both the Tony Hillerman Award for Best Fiction and the WILLA Award for Contemporary Fiction. Her books of nonfiction include *The Harvey Girls: Women Who Opened the West* (Zia Award for Excellence), and *Ghost Ranch* (Southwest Books of the Year "Top Choice" award), and she co-authored *Georgia O'Keeffe & New Mexico: A Sense of Place*. Poling-Kempes's first novel, *Canyon of Remembering*, was a Western Writers of America Spur Award finalist for Best First Novel. *Valley of Shining Stone* is the history of her adopted home, Abiquiú and the Chama River Valley in northern New Mexico, where she has lived with her husband and family for several decades.